Gender, Sex, and Sexualities

Gender, Sex, and Sexualities

Psychological Perspectives

EDITED BY

NANCY K. DESS

JEANNE MARECEK

LESLIE C. BELL

OXFORD
UNIVERSITY PRESS

OXFORD
UNIVERSITY PRESS

Oxford University Press is a department of the University of Oxford. It furthers
the University's objective of excellence in research, scholarship, and education
by publishing worldwide. Oxford is a registered trade mark of Oxford University
Press in the UK and certain other countries.

Published in the United States of America by Oxford University Press
198 Madison Avenue, New York, NY 10016, United States of America.

© Oxford University Press 2018

Library of Congress Cataloging-in-Publication Data
Names: Dess, Nancy Kimberly, editor. | Marecek, Jeanne, 1946– editor. |
Bell, Leslie C., 1970– editor.
Title: Gender, sex, and sexualities : psychological perspectives / edited by
Nancy K. Dess, Jeanne Marecek, Leslie C. Bell.
Description: New York, NY : Oxford University Press, [2018] |
Includes bibliographical references and index.
Identifiers: LCCN 2017023279 | ISBN 9780190658540 (hardcover : alk. paper)
Subjects: LCSH: Sex differences (Psychology) | Sex role—Psychological aspects. | Sex (Psychology)
Classification: LCC BF692.2 .G46735 2018 | DDC 155.3—dc23
LC record available at https://lccn.loc.gov/2017023279

CONTENTS

CONTRIBUTORS

Glenn Adams
Department of Psychology
The University of Kansas
Lawrence, Kansas, USA

Y. Gavriel Ansara
Sydney, Australia

Meg-John Barker
School of Psychology
The Open University
Milton Keynes, England, UK

Leslie C. Bell
Berkeley, California, USA

Monica Biernat
Department of Psychology
The University of Kansas
Lawrence, Kansas, USA

Nancy K. Dess
Department of Psychology
Occidental College
Los Angeles, California, USA

Lisa M. Diamond
Department of Psychology
University of Utah
Salt Lake City, Utah, USA

Ngaire Donaghue
School of Humanities
University of Tasmania
Tasmania, Australia

Justin R. Garcia
Kinsey Institute
Indiana University
Bloomington, Indiana, USA

Patricia Adair Gowaty
Department of Ecology and
    Evolutionary Biology
University of California,
    Los Angeles
Los Angeles, California, USA

Peter Hegarty
Department of Psychology
University of Surrey
Guildford, England, UK

Leslie L. Heywood
Department of English
Binghamton University
Binghamton, New York, USA

Melissa Hines
Department of Psychology
University of Cambridge
Cambridge, England, UK

Tuğçe Kurtiş
Department of Psychology
University of West Georgia
Carrollton, Georgia, USA

Campbell Leaper
Department of Psychology
University of California,
   Santa Cruz
Santa Cruz, California, USA

I-Ching Lee
Department of Psychology
National Chengchi University
Taipei, Taiwan

Eva Magnusson
Department of Psychology
Umeå University
Umeå, Sweden

Jeanne Marecek
Department of Psychology
Swarthmore College
Swarthmore, Pennsylvania, USA

Patricia H. Miller
Department of Psychology
San Francisco State University
San Francisco, California, USA

Felicia Pratto
Department of Psychological
   Sciences
University of Connecticut
Storrs, Connecticut, USA

Ellin K. Scholnick
Department of Psychology
University of Maryland
College Park, Maryland, USA

Amanda K. Sesko
Department of Psychology
University of Alaska Southeast
Juneau, Alaska, USA

Stephanie A. Shields
Department of Psychology
Pennsylvania State University
State College, Pennsylvania, USA

Leah R. Warner
School of Social Science and
   Human Services
Ramapo College of New Jersey
Mahwah, New Jersey, USA

Since its inception, inquiry into gender, sex, and sexualities has produced knowledge that has changed psychologists' ways of understanding human behavior. Much of this knowledge has had practical import, influencing law and public policy, schools, clinical and counseling psychology practice, and, in the general public, norms, attitudes, and practices related to gender and sexualities. For example, psychologists' research has played a role in Supreme Court decisions protecting women's reproductive rights, addressing workplace discrimination and harassment, and upholding the civil rights of lesbians and gay men. It has shaped public policies regarding sexual assault, domestic violence, pay equity, and educational access. Feminists in psychology have designed and evaluated educational practices aimed at closing the gender and ethnic gaps in science, technology, engineering, and mathematics (STEM) participation. Indeed, many of the psychologists who study topics pertaining to sex, gender, and sexualities came to the field because they had a commitment to social change and activism.

The broad scope of psychology is one of its signature strengths. Psychologists attend to scales of organization ranging from cells to societies and to time scales from evolutionary to momentary. Accordingly, as the field has developed since the late 1800s, psychologists have organized themselves into specialties—such as perception and psychophysics, clinical, developmental, cognitive, social, comparative, cultural, evolutionary, personality, and physiological psychology. In each specialty, psychologists generated theoretical frameworks and research methods—*tools for thinking*—appropriate to the scales of organization and time with which they concerned themselves. Questions concerning gender and sexuality have been taken up in all of these specialty areas.

During the last quarter of the 20th century, new questions about gender, sex, and sexualities were raised in Western high-income societies, and many of these became important topics of investigation for psychologists. New questions and topics often demanded new approaches to research, and scholars embraced innovations in theory, research methods, and epistemology. They generated critical reinterpretations of existing concepts and bodies of knowledge, and they raised new considerations of the ethical dimensions of research and clinical practice. Critical theory, discursive psychology, and feminist psychology have been established as vibrant scholarly endeavors. Over the same period, technological innovations enabled research that radically altered ideas about events at low scales of organization. Genes, hormones, and neurons are now regarded in a new light by researchers interested in sex and gender; paradigm shifts related to epigenetics and neural plasticity are two examples. Some scholars began to develop and use theories that mirror how life unfolds in complex, recursive ways across scales of organization and time. Dynamical systems theory and cultural neuroscience are examples of multilevel integrative approaches that are being used to study gender and sexualities. Feminist psychologists are increasingly reaching across disciplinary, international, and cultural borders, working with biologists, sociologists, anthropologists, economists, philosophers, and others across the globe.

WHY THIS BOOK NOW?

The literature on gender, sex, and sexualities today looks very different than it did even ten years ago. The contemporary landscape includes new synergies, persistent tensions, and entirely new ideas and methods. We designed this book to welcome students—the next generation of scholars—into this dynamic landscape. The collected chapters reflect current movements, developments, and potential future directions. The book encompasses key topics—such as prejudice and discrimination, sexual desires and erotic practices, the development of gendered identities, and the emergence of nonbinary genders. Equally important, however, is its focus on *tools for thinking*. That is, the chapters provide conceptual tools to understand where psychological scholarship on gender, sex, and sexualities has been and the directions it is now taking. The chapters are written by experts who are able to provide first-hand accounts of the contemporary state of the discipline.

The goal, then, is to facilitate students' development as thinkers—enhancing their intellectual flexibility, fostering their appreciation for complexity, and preparing them to engage critically with policy debates, popular culture representations, and public discourse on gender, sex, and sexualities.

ORGANIZATION

The book begins with a section entitled *Part I: Emerging Frameworks: Beyond Binaries*. The chapters in this section present current perspectives that challenge dualisms such as male/female, nature/nurture, individual/society, and heterosexual/homosexual and offer more complex formulations. The second section is entitled *Part II: Contemporary Avenues of Inquiry*. This section presents a broad range of scholarly perspectives on gender, sex, and sexualities. These chapters illustrate how conceptualizations of gender, sex, and sexualities shape the research that gets done and also point to directions for future theory and research.

The usual convention of ordering chapters from "biology" to "culture" is not followed in this book. Such an order conveys the mistaken premise that "biology" serves as the immutable bedrock upon which developmental learning, social relations, cultural worldviews, and societal structures are overlaid. As you will see, several chapters in the book present more multiplex models. Readers can devise their own pathways through the book. Instructors and students might together imagine alternate pathways and what such pathways would represent. Such imaginings can bring forward new ways of grappling with complex questions.

APPRECIATIONS

The co-editors gratefully acknowledge the assistance of colleagues Deborah Best (Wake Forest University, USA), Nicola Gavey (University of Auckland, New Zealand), Eva Magnusson (Umeå University, Sweden), Stephanie Shields (Pennsylvania State University, USA), and Ingrid Waldron (University of Pennsylvania, USA), as well as Abby Gross and Courtney McCarroll at Oxford University Press, USA. We are especially grateful to the authors who contributed chapters to the book. Finally, thanks are due for the inspiring efforts of colleagues, friends, students, and courageous activists around the globe.

PART I

Emerging Frameworks

Beyond Binaries

The chapters in this section set the stage for those you will read in Part II. They take up four focal points in current scholarship on gender, sex, and sexualities. In particular, they examine and challenge a number of binaries upon which early scholarship on sex and gender was built—male/female, nature/nurture, gay/straight, and individual/society. In place of such dualisms, the authors put forward more complex formulations. The ideas that these authors put forward draw upon scholarly work that is in development. The chapters are intended to spark debate and discussion. You are invited to join the conversation.

Setting the Stage

Gender, Sex, and Sexualities in Psychology

EVA MAGNUSSON AND JEANNE MARECEK

Psychologists' interest in sex and gender was forged in the crucible of societal upheavals. By the end of the 19th century, feminists' demands for suffrage, bodily autonomy, and legal and property rights were vigorously debated across Western Europe and the United States. Members of the fledgling discipline of psychology joined in those debates, offering a wide range of conjectures about women's nature, differences between the sexes, and proper relations between men and women. In the latter decades of the 20th century, feminist movements emerged once again in much of Western Europe and North America. Feminists challenged discriminatory practices enshrined in law, custom, and religion that barred women from public life and subordinated them to men. Feminists in psychology were vigorous supporters of campaigns to end the pathologizing and criminalizing of nonheterosexual people. Feminists also called attention to the gender-based violence, rape, and sexual abuse that were part of the fabric of women's lives. During this era of activism, vibrant intellectual communities of feminist psychologists took form in many countries (cf. Rutherford, Marecek, & Sheese, 2013). Some of these psychologists sought to understand the social processes and structures that sustained social inequalities; others wanted to understand how best to help women and girls from diverse communities, backgrounds, and classes flourish. Yet others turned their sight on men and boys and the strictures that conventional masculinities imposed on them.

In the decades since feminist psychology took form, there have been dramatic changes in women's legal status, bodily and personal autonomy, freedom of movement, and access to education. In many parts of the world, there have been dramatic—albeit uneven and sometimes unstable—changes in women's participation in the public sphere. Intimate relations have changed as well, including norms and practices regarding patterns of cohabitation, marriage, childcare, and sexual encounters. In some parts of the world (especially in the global North), nonheterosexual sexualities and same-sex relationships are now accorded both social acceptance and legal legitimacy. There is a growing acknowledgment that the gender binary (that is, the two-sex model) does not capture the variety of ways that people experience and express their gender. In many countries, political movements in support of transgender people and people with nonbinary gender identities have gained considerable momentum in assuring full recognition of these identities, as well as equitable treatment of such individuals in the public sphere and in personal life. The contributors to this book take stock of these changes in the social, political, and cultural landscape.

Turning back to the discipline of psychology and its neighboring disciplines, we can trace noteworthy advances in knowledge about human behavior. For example, new technologies in neuroimaging and genetic analysis have yielded substantial evidence for the plasticity of physical systems, as well as an emerging consensus that human brains are not sextyped (cf.; Joel et al., 2015; Rippon, Jordan-Young, Kaiser, & Fine, 2014; Schmitz & Höppner, 2014). Several of the chapters in this book describe these developments and what they portend for future theorizing about gender, sex, and sexualities. At the same time, new concepts and approaches have made possible new understandings of sex, gender, and sexualities. As you will read in Chapter 2, intersectionality theory has drawn attention to the multiplicity of social identities people hold, and their implications for the way power is distributed in society. Cultural psychologies—which examine the mutual constitution of culture and persons—have given psychologists new means of understanding subjectivity and social life. New research technologies have been devised. The Implicit Association Test (IAT), for example, which promises to tap implicit attitudes, has been harnessed to study prejudice (cf. Chapter 8). There have been advances in statistical procedures for modeling complex social processes, as well as efforts to improve the veracity and replicability of results of experiments. At the same time, an array of qualitative methods has come into use (Levitt, Motulsky, Wertz, Morrow, & Pontoretto, 2017; Magnusson & Marecek, 2017). Some of these methods have been of special interest to feminists. Participatory methods, for example, forge direct links between activism and research. Critical discursive methods, discussed in Chapter 6, give researchers tools for observing cultural resources.

In this chapter, we lay the groundwork to help you navigate the scholarship on gender, sex, and sexualities. We present some central concepts in these fields, as well as tools for thinking about and asking questions about these concepts and their uses. As you will see, researchers have often given different meanings to these concepts, reflecting their different disciplinary backgrounds and different epistemological stances. We present the concepts separately, casting their meanings in stark relief. We adopt this strategy for clarity's sake. In actual practice, you may find that authors splice together various meanings or shift from one usage to another.

We begin with a discussion of *social categories* and *categorization*, and then move to a focus on *sex categories*. Such a discussion is especially relevant now because the customary sex categorizations, in particular, the two-sex model or gender binary, have been called into question by transgender activists, queer theorists, and others who are gender nonconforming. (Chapter 3 takes up nonbinary and transgender identities in detail.) Next we take up three concepts that psychologists employ with great frequency, but with varying and sometimes ambiguous meanings: *gender, difference,* and *"the social."* We examine the various meanings given to these concepts with the goal of helping you become a more discerning reader of the literature on gender, sex, and sexuality. We end this chapter with a set of questions to guide your reading of books and articles on the psychology of gender, sex, or sexualities.

SOCIAL CATEGORIES AND CATEGORIZATION

The term *social category* refers to a group of people who have a certain characteristic in common. People, of course, are members of several such groups. For example, a woman is a member of the category "women" and she is also a member of a certain social class, a certain ethnic group, a certain age group, and so on. Many such categorizations have cultural, social, and political significance. In many cases, membership in a social category also functions as a marker of social status; that is, membership in that category confers a particular location and ranking in the larger social structure. Social categories play an important part both in social life and in personal identity. We therefore discuss categories and categorizations in some detail.

People use categories to know about the world. They use their knowledge about the characteristics of categories to decide which things are similar and which things are not. In everyday life such *categorization* is usually easy and uncontroversial. Note, however, that even when category membership seems uncontroversial and easy to decide (as, for example, membership in the categories "plants" and "animals"), the origin of the categories themselves may be controversial. This is especially true of categories that societies use to group and rank people (like "women," "men," "gay," or "straight"). Debates about the origins of categories have a lengthy history in philosophy (Hacking, 1994); these debates have also influenced psychologists' studies of gender, sex, and sexuality. (Chapter 14 discusses additional aspects of categories and categorizations.)

Of interest here are two starkly different positions on the origin and nature of categories. One position holds that category systems are based in the world as it is in itself. Plato's phrase "carving nature at its joints" nicely captures this point of view. It would follow from this position that human categories represent universal divisions that exist independently of culture and society, analogous to the division between the category "plants" and the category "animals." On this view, the categories precede, and are discovered by, the knower. This is the commonsense view of many human categories—for example, the category "men" and the category "women" seem to capture a universal, enduring distinction among humans. Some may also regard racial categories (such as White, Asian, or Black) to be universal, enduring, and natural divisions of the human species, although the historical record does not support such beliefs. For those who regard certain human categories as universal, an important task is to identify, describe, and catalogue the distinctive properties of these categories. Often this involves comparing members of different categories in order to ascertain which properties are distinctive, as well as to ascertain which properties do not distinguish between the categories.

The second position regarding the origin and nature of social categories holds that many or even most human categories are human-made. Human-made categories are contingent; that is, they are products of people's efforts to understand the world. On this view, the categories are created by knowers. Such creations are inevitably laced with presuppositions that are part of the time and place in which a person lives. One should not expect such categories to be universally held or to be unchanging. Nor should one assume that distinctions between such categories would be universally upheld. In this view of categories, the meanings given to categories are a matter of social negotiation.

Consider, for example, the category attention-deficit/hyperactivity disorder (ADHD). Most of us would agree that ADHD is a human-made category. It is of recent vintage, its definition (i.e., the "official" diagnostic criteria specified in diagnostic manuals) continually shifts, and it continues to spark a good deal of public controversy. Note that when we say that the *category* ADHD is human-made and contingent, we are not concerned with whether there are people who regulate attention and activity in a way that makes it difficult to function in some environments. Nor are we

concerned with whether such difficulties might originate in brain function. Those concerns are different matters. We are instead referring to the
set of meanings conferred on those difficulties by invoking the *category*
ADHD. These meanings include, for instance, labeling the difficulties as a
form of psychiatric illness and viewing the difficulties as requiring special
educational accommodations and practices.

If a category is seen as human-made, it makes little sense to try to dis-
cover its fundamental or inherent properties. It should come as no surprise
to find that many human-made categories have changed their meanings
throughout history, and that some have disappeared entirely. Consider,
for example, the categories "hysteria," "latch-key children," and "frigid
women," all of which were in common use in the United States until about
40 years ago. Furthermore, if human categories are produced and upheld
through social negotiations, then questions arise about which members
of society have the power to define categories and to set the boundaries
between them. By and large, people in positions of power and high status
have been most successful in this boundary setting.

Sex Categories

What kind of categories are human sex categories? Are sex categories
(such as "men," "women," "transgender," and "intersex") universal categories that preexist people's efforts to make sense of the world? Or are
they human-made categories that are contingent on time and place and
wrought in the crucible of social interactions? The everyday view is that
the sex categories "women" and "men" are natural and preexisting categories. In recent times, however, reports from non-Western societies, as well
as the growing visibility of other sex categories in Western high-income
societies, have challenged that view.

In many societies, sex category is one of the prime social categories
used for describing people; sorting and ranking people according to their
sex category has long been a linchpin of social organization. This is true
in society at large, as well as in intimate relations such as marriages and

families. Most Western high-income countries have firmly held in place a two-sex model based on the categories "men" and "women" (i.e., the gender binary). This model has been institutionalized in law and religion, and sex categorization has formed one of the major axes of privilege and hierarchy in formal social structures as well as in everyday interactions.

Even though the gender binary may seem natural and universal to some people, anthropologists and historians have amply documented that such a two-sex model is not a universal way of categorizing humans. Furthermore, many societies do not assign members to sex categories on the basis of genital anatomy or reproductive function. (Chapter 3 describes several such instances.) In addition, societies throughout South and Southeast Asia have long recognized more than two sex categories (Blackwood, 2005; Morris, 1995). Against this background, and in the light of existing chromosomal variations, the biologist Anne Fausto-Sterling (2000) has suggested that a five-sex model more adequately captures human variation than a two-sex (or binary) model.

At present in Western European and North American societies, the two-sex model is being challenged on various fronts. As you will read in Chapter 3, the two-sex model does not capture current social realities in these societies. In addition, some neuroscientists have argued that although human reproductive anatomy and genitalia typically fit the two-sex model, the human brain does not (Joel et al., 2015).

Considering the varied ways in which human sex categories have been defined, given meaning, and even enumerated across societies, it is difficult to hold that sex categories are strictly natural categories that "carve nature at its joints." A view of sex categories as human-made categories opens the way to a number of questions for psychological investigation. If the number and meanings of human sex categories are matters of social negotiation, what do those negotiations consist of? How do children and adults in a particular society make gender attributions? How do parents of gender-nonconforming children (for example, a child whose preferred self-presentation is as a member of a sex category other than the one assigned at birth) help their children move through a social world that is still largely organized according to a two-sex model? And, if the sex category system were expanded to encompass more than two sexes, would this change the existing patterns of inequality between women and men?

Gender

The word *gender* has become commonplace in everyday talk as well as in academic and professional psychology. Given how often and how casually people use the word, you might think that its meaning was unambiguous. However, this is far from the case. For instance, you will hear the word *gender* used as a synonym for "sex category" (as in "a person's gender" or "male gender"). Alternately, you might hear it used as an adjective that means "specific to a sex category" (as in "gender differences," "gendered behavior"). Some scholars use the word *gender* to refer to a social status that is an integral part of the social order. And "gender" is sometimes used as a stand-in for "women" (as in "gendercide" or "Gender Center" [to mean "Women's Center"]).

Looking at the psychological literature on gender and sexuality, we find that even among experts, there is no consensus about how to define gender. Think about the following statements, all taken from recent textbooks on the psychology of gender:

"... gender [refers to] behaviors and attitudes that relate to (but are not entirely congruent with) biological sex."

"... gender is a classification system that influences access to power and resources."

"... gender is the backcloth against which our daily lives are played out."

"... gender refers to being a boy/man or a girl/woman in a cultural context."

"... gender refers to the traits and behaviors considered characteristic of and appropriate to members of each [sex] category."

"... gender affects people's social lives."

Does it matter that experts in the field put forward so many incompatible meanings of the term *gender*? Yes, it does. Different ways of defining gender turn researchers' attention toward different topics and questions. Just as important, any definition deflects researchers' attention away from some questions and topics. Furthermore, differing ways of thinking about gender have different practical implications. For example, different meanings of gender are conducive to different mental health interventions and to different social change programs. The experts' statements that you have just read raise several questions:

- What are the implications of thinking of gender as something that resides "inside" the person (e.g., as traits, dispositions, behaviors, hormones, or brain structures)?
- Does it make sense to think of gender as if it were a force that has the power to exert "effects" on people?
- What are the implications of thinking of gender as "outside" a person (e.g., as a societal "classification system" or "an integral part of the social order")?
- Should "gender" be used as a catch-all term for every aspect of human psychology that is related to sex category?

We do not propose to tell you what the correct meaning of gender ought to be. Instead, we focus on two meanings of gender. The first takes gender to refer to traits and characteristics that reside "inside" an individual. The second shifts the locus of gender to the social context, effectively placing it "outside" the individual.

Let us begin to clarify these two meanings with an illustration: For the past several decades, epidemiological studies in Western Europe and North America have shown that, by and large, women experience clinical depression and subclinical depressive symptoms at a rate that is roughly two and half times higher than men's. (There are, of course, within-group variations for both sex categories.) Women's elevated risk of depression has been a matter of great interest to mental health professionals for many years, and several explanations have been proposed.

Some of the explanations rest on a conception of gender as characteristics "inside" individuals. They have attributed women's elevated risk of depression to enduring characteristics or dispositions that are sex specific. Sigmund Freud, for example, argued that women's depression was an inevitable part of female nature—namely, a disguised manifestation of women's despair over lacking a phallus. Other theories have attributed women's depression to dysfunctional habits of thought, such as self-blaming attributional style or rumination, or to dysfunctional patterns of interacting with others, such as self-silencing. Yet other explanations have tied the increase in girls' depression during adolescence to poor body image and acceptance of traditional stereotypes of feminine behavior. All of these explanations have in common a focus on "the inside," that is, on dispositions or characteristics that are thought to be prevalent among women.

Other explanations for women's elevated risk of depression rest on a conception of gender as a principle by which society is organized and by which power and privilege are distributed to its members. Some explanations of this type have linked depression to the heavy burdens of caring for others that women often shoulder and the limited care and support that women often receive from others. Other explanations have linked women's depression to stressors connected to gendered power relations. These include various forms of sexual and relationship violence; workplace harassment and discrimination; the paucity of social and economic supports for single mothers; and the social isolation often experienced by mothers of newborns. Other explanations have related elevated rates of depression and suicidal thoughts reported by lesbian and bisexual women to experiences such as taunting, bullying, teasing, ostracism from one's family, and homophobic physical violence. These explanations all focus attention on the "outside," that is, the social and cultural context. The lenses afforded by both these types of explanations are useful, but they point in different directions. Consider, for example, the kinds of prevention programs or therapeutic interventions that follow from each.

Let us look more closely at these two ways of thinking about gender. We begin with a brief detour into etymology in order to examine the history of the word *gender*. "Gender" originates from the Latin word *genus*, which means "kind, sort, or class"; the word has been and still is used for this purpose by grammarians. In its grammatical meaning, gender does not refer to sex categories, but to the patterns for declining nouns that are found in many languages. The English language stopped declining nouns many hundred years ago, and, as you know, grammatical gender is not a feature of modern English. In recent times, English speakers have instead come to use the word *gender* as a synonym for "sex category" (as in "Indicate your gender: male or female").

In the 1970s, feminist theorists in the English-speaking world expanded upon the English-language use of the word *gender*. They kept the reference to sex category, but they gave the word an additional meaning. This additional meaning is what is of interest here. Terms such as the *sex/gender system* (Rubin, 1975) and the *gender order* indexed institutionalized relations of power and privilege that are organized around distinctions between sex categories. These definitions served to make gender a feature of the sociopolitical structure and of societal hierarchies in which sex categories serve as the markers of status and position. More recently, intersectionality theorists (Collins, 1990; Crenshaw, 1991) have pointed out that social categories are intertwined, such that systems of stratification and privilege cannot meaningfully be analyzed one by one. (Chapter 2 discusses intersectionality theory in detail.)

In psychology, the term *gender* and its meaning have a somewhat different history. When gender entered the vocabulary of psychology at the end of the 1970s, the urgent agenda for feminists in psychology was to challenge beliefs regarding women's nature. These beliefs—often enshrined by the psychological theories of the time—held women to be intellectually inferior to men; destined by nature for marriage and motherhood; incapable of leadership; naturally passive; and so on. Feminists strove to insert the term *gender* into psychology's vocabulary in order to disrupt such assertions about women's nature (Crawford & Fox, 2007). They defined gender as the "nonphysiological components of sex" (Unger, 1979, p. 1086). This definition indicated a sharp demarcation between socially based characteristics and physiologically based ones. Unger's definition further specified that gender referred to "traits and behaviors" characteristic of the members of each sex category (p. 1093). This formulation—unlike those of Rubin and Crenshaw—had a distinctly individualist cast; that is, by defining gender as "traits," "dispositions," and "characteristics," it placed gender firmly "inside" the individual.

Placing gender on the "inside" of the individual is still quite common in psychology. However, over the past 30 years, many feminist psychologists have moved toward thinking of gender as "outside" the individual (Magnusson & Marecek, 2012). That is, their work addresses aspects of the gender order and the fundamentally social quality of the distinctions that are drawn between the sexes. Several chapters that you will read take this approach, especially Chapters 2, 3, 5, and 6. At the same time, current research in developmental psychobiology, neuroscience, and behavioral genetics has cast serious doubt on the idea of a dichotomy between "physiological" and "nonphysiological" that was the original rationale for introducing the term *gender* in psychology.

REFLECTIONS ON THE MEANINGS OF *GENDER*

What should a student make of the multiple meanings and complicated history of the term *gender*? Perhaps the most important lesson is that when you read psychological literature that uses the word *gender*, you must ask yourself what the writer means by the word. Meanings of the word have shifted since it was taken into use by psychologists nearly 40 years ago. Writers may not signal to readers which meaning of gender they are invoking in a particular argument. Also, it is not unusual that writers invoke several different meanings in a single article (or even perhaps in a single paragraph) without alerting their readers. There are also lessons for your own writing. You would do well to steer clear of misuses of the word *gender*, such as "gendercide" or referring to the "gender" of animals. We also recommend that you avoid using "gender" as a euphemism for "women" and vague poetic expressions, such as "gender is a backcloth." In any case, whenever you use the word *gender*, you must specify what you mean by it. In many instances, the term *sex category* might be a more appropriate choice because it does not carry implications regarding the origins of the differences between the categories.

Differences

Differences between sex categories are common topics of conversation. Think about the times you heard someone exclaim, "Men are all alike!" or "That's just like a woman!" Such claims about the way that men and women "just are" imply that all men or all women are the same and at the same time that all the members of one sex category are different from all the members of another. Such talk is sometimes followed by an assertion that a purported difference is grounds for treating the sex categories unequally.

Let us look at a historical example, namely, the prolonged struggles during the 19th century in Western Europe and North America over whether women should be allowed to vote in political elections. In the debates, assertions about women's difference from men loomed large as reasons for denying women the vote. For example, women were said to be too emotional or too ignorant. In the same period, similar assertions of differences between social categories were advanced to argue against granting the vote to working-class people and, in the United States, to African Americans. The comparisons that were drawn in these suffrage debates were loaded, taking certain characteristics of the dominant group (usually White, middle- or upper-class men) as the norm. This automatically ranked those in social categories that deviated in any way (whether relevant or not) from the dominant group as being of lower worth.

Traces of this pattern of reasoning appear when people in a less valued social category (such as "women") are compared to people in a more highly valued social category (such as "men"). It is still not uncommon to regard certain characteristics of the members of the more highly valued category as the norm, again regardless of whether those characteristics are relevant for the issue at hand. Members of the less valued category must demonstrate those characteristics when, for instance, competing for a job. Furthermore, assertions can still be heard that virtually any difference from the valued social category constitutes a valid reason to oppose the equal treatment of members of the less-valued category. Such arguments, if drawn to their logical conclusion, would mean that in order to deserve equal treatment, people in the disfavored category would have to become identical in practically all respects to people in the highly valued category.

Against this background, it is not surprising that the debates about the sameness or differentness (and implicitly thereby the value) of the categories "men" and "women" have roiled the discipline of psychology since its very beginning in the late 19th century. In the debates about female suffrage, psychologists were sometimes called upon to pronounce authoritatively on "woman's nature" and what "woman's difference from man" implied for women's proper place in society and public life. For the most part, psychologists in that era shared the beliefs about women's inferiority that permeated Western European and North American societies (Richards, 2010).

Researchers who study differences between the two sex categories typically compare two groups that are each composed of members of one sex category. Finding a statistically significant difference between the two groups, however, is not the end of the study. The crucial step is to interpret such differences. Since the inception of psychology, there has been continual debate about how to interpret observed differences. In what follows, we describe three ways of interpreting observed differences between sex categories. In debates, these ways, in the stark form that we describe them, are often set against one another, although in actual practice, researchers sometimes combine them to yield more complex understandings. We end this section by taking up some of the logical and methodological complexities of carrying out studies comparing men and women and interpreting the results.

SEEING OBSERVED PSYCHOLOGICAL SEX DIFFERENCES AS CAUSED BY INHERENT PHYSIOLOGICALLY BASED DIFFERENCES BETWEEN THE SEX CATEGORIES

In one view of "difference," an *observed* difference (in some aspect of behavior) between a group of men and a group of women is interpreted as caused by some inherent—that is, inborn and permanent—physiological difference. Suppose a researcher compares how a group of men and a group of women perform on a cognitive task, and the data indicate a difference in performance between the two groups. A researcher taking this view will assume that the cause of the observed difference is some inherent physiologically based characteristic shared by members of one category but not the other. Throughout the history of psychology, researchers have posited such possible causal characteristics in many sites, such as men's and women's sexual organs; their levels of certain hormones; sex-specific genetic make-up; and the development of certain brain structures.

SEEING OBSERVED PSYCHOLOGICAL SEX DIFFERENCES AS CAUSED BY INHERENT, PSYCHOLOGICALLY BASED DIFFERENCES BETWEEN THE SEX CATEGORIES

Another view of the causes of observed sex differences postulates that observed differences between women and men are caused by differences between the sex categories in some *inherent psychological* characteristic that is the enduring effect of sex-specific childhood socialization. Let us again say that a researcher compares a group of men and a group of women on a cognitive task and that the data indicate a difference between the two groups. A researcher taking this view will interpret this difference to be caused by sex-specific childhood experiences that have shaped girls and boys psychologically. One example of such theorizing is found in psychoanalytic theories, which hold that early childhood experiences inevitably differ for boys and girls and lead to different inherent personality patterns in adult men and women. Another example of such theorizing is found in social learning theories that argue that sex differences in adults are caused by the long-term effects of early experiences in which boys and girls were reinforced for different behaviors.

SEEING OBSERVED SEX DIFFERENCES AS CAUSED BY DIFFERENTIAL OR UNEQUAL TREATMENT

Feminists in psychology have repeatedly challenged assertions that observed differences between men and women should be seen as based in inherent differences between those two sex categories. Instead, they have argued that many observed sex differences are in fact the consequences of ongoing differential treatment of boys and girls, or men and women. An earlier case in point was that in most Western high-income countries, boys scored consistently higher than girls on mathematics tests. Feminist psychologists argued that these findings could well be the result of unequal access to schooling in mathematics, rather than genetic or brain differences between the two sexes. Changes in mathematics performance in recent decades would seem to have vindicated the feminists' view. Today, with math training for boys and girls roughly comparable, the earlier average differences between boys' and girls' scores on standardized math tests and in mathematics performance in school have dramatically diminished, sometimes to the point of vanishing. In some countries, they have even been reversed (Hyde, Lindberg, Linn, Ellis, & Williams, 2008).

Feminists in psychology have also studied settings in which individuals in a certain social category (for example, a certain sex category) are evaluated like or treated as the stereotype of that category, not as individuals. Recent attention has focused on the experiences of women in science, technology, engineering, mathematics, and medicine (STEMM) professions and female students who aspire to enter such professions. A number of studies have suggested that some members of the scientific community still regard women's scientific capabilities as inferior to those of men; this is especially true for women of color (Muhs, Niemann, González, & Harris, 2012; Racusin, Dovidio, Brescoli, Graham, & Handelsman, 2012).

REFLECTIONS ON STUDYING DIFFERENCES

Methodologists have pointed out several cautions that researchers must exercise when carrying out and interpreting comparisons of different social categories. The first caution applies to any study that explores observed differences between groups, regardless of the specific groups or the probable cause of the difference. This caution is based on the fact that studies that find statistically significant differences between the means of two groups (such as a group of men and a group of women) typically also find substantial overlap between the two groups. Take, for example, a study of performance on a cognitive task (such as a mathematics test). Suppose that a researcher finds a mean difference between the boys and girls in the study. Along with the mean difference, there will also be a good deal of variation among the girls and among the boys, such that the size of the mean difference between the two groups is only a small fraction of the variation in performance that the boys and girls share. This is a common pattern of findings in sex difference studies. Such findings refute the view that the categories *girls* and *boys* are homogeneous.

A second caution is that if researchers intend to make group comparisons, they must take care to assure that the groups they study are comparable in all respects other than their group membership. Otherwise, a researcher cannot attribute an observed difference between the groups to their category membership.

In sex difference studies, researchers must therefore ensure that the group of men and the group of women are comparable on relevant characteristics. This means that the groups must be selected so that they are equivalent as regards relevant prior experience, as well as educational background, age, social class, and racial or ethnic category. Depending on what is being studied, composing comparable groups of men and women can be very difficult, and sometimes impossible.

A third caution in designing studies of group comparisons is that the indices and tasks to be studied must be equivalent for the groups. For example, the test materials or tasks must be equally familiar to and equally suitable for both groups. The same holds for the content and wording of scale items. For example, response biases such as the social desirability of the scale items must be comparable for the groups under study. With regard to comparing men and women, the more the two sex categories are segregated in daily life and the more they are channeled by society into different roles, the less likely it is that these requirements will be met.

A fourth caution concerns the logic of sex difference studies. To use technical language, sex category is not an independent variable that researchers can manipulate, nor is it an experimental condition to which research participants can be assigned. These limitations mean that sex difference studies are correlational studies, not causal studies. In correlational studies, an association between two variables (in this case, sex category and a pattern of behavior) tells the researcher nothing about causality. This fact presents a knotty problem for researchers who seek to determine whether psychological differences between men and women are the result of inherent differences. Associations between observed sex differences in behavior and sex differences in a biological structure or function can tell nothing about causation. Put differently: finding a sex difference in behavior and an associated sex difference in a physiological structure or function does not indicate that the latter caused the former.

As a final reflection, given the formidable difficulties in carrying out adequate and interpretable studies of sex differences, it is remarkable that the search for psychological sex differences has continued for over 100 years, whereas similarities between the two sex categories are rarely a topic of interest (Hyde, 2005).

THE "SOCIAL"

Like many other terms that feminist scholars use, the word *social* has several different meanings in social science research. This should not be surprising. Different disciplines in the social sciences, as well as different theoretical traditions in psychology, have focused on different aspects of social life.

Many social psychologists who study gender—especially social psychologists in the United States—have limited their scope of interest in "the social" to how each individual experiences others, for example, the judgments they render about one another and the personal consequences of such judgments. "The social" as a collective force usually is beyond the scope of investigations. This has led to a focus on individual attitudes, beliefs, prejudice, and attributions of causality, rather than on larger societal forces or structures. Psychologists who are interested in gender have, for example, studied prejudicial beliefs and invidious attitudes about members of disfavored social categories (women, LGB individuals, members of non-White ethnic/racial groups, and, more recently, transgendered or gender-nonconforming individuals). Psychology researchers have also asked how research participants regard (and interact with) others who do not conform to societal norms (e.g., scientifically inclined women or "sissy" boys). They also have examined the psychological consequences of being the object of such invidious distinctions—for example, diminished self-esteem or self-confidence, heightened depressive affect, or diminished well-being. Psychologists have also studied how individuals allocate blame and responsibility for sexual harassment, abuse, and rape. (Chapter 3 discusses research regarding the consequences of prejudicial treatment for LGB, transgendered, and gender-nonconforming individuals, and Chapter 8 describes research about implicit and explicit biases and prejudicial beliefs about women and about members of other disfavored social categories.) As you can see, all these studies focus on individuals—their reactions, judgments, or attributions, beliefs about stereotypes, and so on; there is little attention paid to social structures or to the gender order.

A second aspect of "the social" is society, that is, large-scale and highly organized social groups. Societies are stratified into status groups, with differing amounts of power and privilege available to members of these status groups. Societies are governed by formal institutions but also by shared, often informal, norms. In most societies, sex categorizations form a prominent axis along which people are ordered and social status is assigned, as do racial or ethnic categorizations.

Although few psychologists have studied societal hierarchies and social stratification, some feminist psychologists have addressed questions about how the gender order intersects with class stratification. In Britain, Walkerdine, Lucey, and Melody (2001) have examined how class position shapes the life trajectories and developmental imperatives of working-class girls. Other British feminist psychologists have also studied class and motherhood (Rickett, 2016). Psychologists interested in intersectionality theory are seeking ways to incorporate axes of social organization such as sex categorization, racial/ethnic categorization, and social class into psychological research.

A third aspect of "the social" has also garnered a good deal of interest among feminist psychologists. This aspect concerns the ways in which day-to-day living is shaped by the cultural context of people's lives. Examples of the topics that have been investigated include the negotiations about sharing housework and childcare (Magnusson, 2008) and the "cultural scaffolding" that maintains (hetero)sexual coercion and rape (Gavey, 2005). Feminist psychologists have also investigated real-time practices and interactions in societal institutions. Some examples are analyses of courtroom dialogue during rape trials; observations of psychologists' discussions as they certify or deny patients' requests for gender reassignment surgery; and conversations between doctors and their female patients about prescriptions for antidepressant medication. In such studies, researchers have sought insight into the everyday practices and institutional forces that maintain the status quo and hold power differences in place. Many of these researchers have found that the theories and methods of *discursive psychology* offer a useful framework for situating individuals within cultural life and societal structures. We therefore take a moment to introduce feminist discursive psychology.

Feminist Discursive Psychology: From "the Social" to the Sociocultural

Feminist discursive psychologists have taken inspiration from such theoretical frameworks as sociocultural psychology, cultural psychology, and discursive psychology. They share with many feminist psychologists an interest in socially shared views of gender and other social categories. Feminist discursive psychologists diverge, however, from other feminist psychologists in that they do not regard people's views about gender as enduring individual attitudes or opinions. Instead, feminist discursive psychologists conceive of such views as the ways of understanding that are available in a certain social setting and that serve as resources for making sense of the world and oneself. An example would be the notion that there are immutable psychological differences between women and men. In a cultural setting where this is a shared understanding, people will be more prone to take note of differences between men and women and to overlook similarities, and to use it to account for their own behavior and that of others. Feminist discursive psychologists view these shared ways of understanding as tools that people use in interactions in order to accomplish such goals as portraying themselves in a positive light (Edley, 2001; Magnusson & Marecek, 2012, 2015, 2018). Chapter 6 describes feminist discursive psychology in more detail.

BEING A DISCERNING READER OF RESEARCH ON GENDER, SEX, AND SEXUALITY

We end this chapter by suggesting some strategies for reading that will help you master the literature on gender, sex, and sexuality. This scholarship is complex and growing; few questions can be considered settled, even including what are the best methods of investigation. Moreover, many issues evoke debate not only in the scholarly community but also in the political arena and in popular culture. This state of affairs calls for careful and critical readings of the literature.

Critical reading as a scholar goes beyond reading for the "bare facts"; it requires discernment and engagement with the works that you are reading. If you are reading a research report, you need to think carefully about the methods by which the findings were produced, as well as the logic of the interpretations that the authors make. This is necessary because data rarely, if ever, "speak for themselves." If you are reading a theoretical argument, you need to situate that argument in the context of the author's orienting assumptions and point of view, in order to appraise the evidence that is offered in support of the argument. Also you need to consider what the author regards as alternative or competing arguments. For instance, if the theory is advanced as an improvement over previous theories, what are those previous theories, and are they fairly presented?

In what follows, we suggest some questions that pertain specifically to the psychological literature on gender, sex, and sexuality. We drew up these questions to help our own students become adept readers of the psychological literature. They have found them helpful and we hope you will, too. We encourage you to use these questions both in your own reading and when reading and discussing with others.

Interpreting Group Differences

If a research study reports an observed difference between social categories (for example, sex categories or categories pertaining to sexualities),
how does the author interpret this difference? Does the author discuss
how differences in past experiences or in current conditions might have
influenced the results? Or does the author attribute the observed differences to some inherent difference between the categories? On what basis
does the author rule out alternate interpretations?

Homogeneity or Heterogeneity of Social Categories

Does the researcher portray sex categories and other social categories
as if they were homogeneous groups? Does the researcher examine (or
at least discuss) possible differences among members of each category?
(Chapter 14 discusses this matter in more detail.) Given the nature of the
study, which of these approaches seems appropriate?

Familiar or Unfamiliar Research Situations

Have the researchers ascertained that the research situation is equally
familiar and comfortable for participants regardless of their sex category
or other social categorizations? Or are there grounds for concern that the
conditions of the research could disfavor members of some social groups?
What might this imply for the trustworthiness of the results?

Measurement Equivalence

If a researcher has used concepts, scales, or behavioral measures that
were designed for one cultural setting or one social group in a different

setting or with a different social group, what evidence is offered that the meanings in the new setting are equivalent to those in the original setting?

Generalizations

Consider carefully which groups of people researchers have studied, and which groups of people they draw conclusions about. For example, does an author exercise appropriate caution about generalizing from the specific participants who were studied (e.g., female college students) to an entire category (e.g., "women" or "lesbians")? Under what conditions are such broad conclusions warranted?

Universalizing Versus Specifying

Do the researchers use their study of specific situations and specific participants to draw conclusions about universal abilities or characteristics? Do the researchers discuss why such generalizations are warranted? Alternately, do the researchers keep their focus on socially anchored meanings in different social categories or different social and cultural settings?

Locus of Explanation: Inside the Individual or in the Context?

Does the author offer explanations or interpretations of behavior that focus exclusively on causes "inside" the individual? Or do the explanations or interpretations also consider the "outside," that is, the surrounding conditions, especially structural inequalities? Do authors endeavor to show how these might be connected?

Authors' Biases

Can you discern indications of biased or prejudiced views or prereflective understandings on the part of the author? This could include biases against women or against men, biases against nonheterosexual people, or biases against children or adults who do not conform to the gender binary. If you believe that you have detected biased points of view, consider whether those views might have influenced aspects of the research method, the interpretation of the findings, or the practical implications or policy recommendations that the author suggests.

Reflexivity About the Social Context of Research

Do the researchers acknowledge that every research project is carried out in a social, political, historical, and geopolitical context? Do the researchers discuss how the context might have influenced the research questions, the research design, and the research process?

Silences and Exclusions

If you are reading a book or article that does not deal specifically with gender, sex, or sexualities, can you discern instances where the author might have (or even *should* have) brought in such issues? When a book or article ignores these issues, what might be the consequences for the quality of the information or arguments it puts forward?

REFERENCES

Blackwood, E. (2005). Gender transgression in colonial and postcolonial Indonesia. *The Journal of Asian Studies, 64,* 849–879.
Crawford, M., & Fox, A. (2007). From sex to gender and back again: Co-optation of a feminist language reform. *Feminism & Psychology, 17,* 481–486.

Collins, P. H. (1990). *Black feminist thought: Knowledge, consciousness, and the politics of empowerment.* New York, NY: Routledge.

Crenshaw, K. W. (1991). Mapping the margins: Intersectionality, identity politics, and violence against women of color. *Stanford Law Review, 43,* 1241–1279.

Edley, N. (2001). Analysing masculinity: Interpretative repertoires, ideological dilemmas, and subject positions. In M. Wetherell, S. Taylor, & S. Yates (Eds.), *Discourse as data: A guide for analysis* (pp. 189–228). London, UK: Sage.

Fausto-Sterling, A. (2000). *Sexing the body: Gender politics and the construction of sexuality.* New York, NY: Basic Books.

Gavey, N. (2005). *Just sex? The cultural scaffolding of rape.* London, UK: Routledge.

Hacking, I. (1994). The looping effects of human kinds. In D. Sperber, D. Premack, & A. J. Premack (Eds.), *Causal cognition: A multidisciplinary approach* (pp. 351–394). Oxford, UK: Clarendon Press.

Hyde, J. S. (2005). The gender similarities hypothesis. *American Psychologist, 60,* 581–592.

Hyde, J., Lindberg, S., Linn, M., Ellis, A., & Williams, C. (2008). Gender similarities characterize math performance. Standardized tests in the US indicate that girls now score just as well as boys in math. *Science, 321,* 494–495.

Joel, D., Berman, Z., Tavor, I., Wexler, N., Gaber, O. & Stein, Y., . . . Assaf, Y. (2015). Sex beyond the genitalia: The human brain mosaic. *Proceedings of the National Academy of Sciences of United States of America, 112,* 15468–15473.

Levitt, H. M., Motulsky, S. L., Wertz, F. J., Morrow, S. L., & Ponteretto, J. (2017). Recommendations for designing and reviewing qualitative research in psychology: Promoting methodological integrity. *Qualitative Psychology, 4,* 2–22.

Magnusson, E. (2008). The rhetoric of inequality: Nordic men and women argue against gender equality. *NORA: Nordic Journal of Feminist and Gender Research, 16,* 79–95.

Magnusson. E., & Marecek, J. (2012). *Gender and culture in psychology: Theories and practices.* Cambridge, UK: Cambridge University Press.

Magnusson, E., & Marecek, J. (2015). *Doing interview-based qualitative research: A learner's guide.* Cambridge, UK: Cambridge University Press.

Magnusson, E., & Marecek, J. (2018). Qualitative inquiry. In C. B. Travis and J. W. White (Eds.), *Handbook of the psychology of women* (pp. 109–126). Washington, DC: American Psychological Association.

Morris, R. (1995). All made up: Performance theory and the new anthropology of sex and gender. *Annual Review of Anthropology, 24,* 567–592.

Muhs, G. G., Harris, A. P., Flores Niemann, Y., & González, C. G. (2012). *Presumed incompetent: The intersections of race and class for women in academia.* Boulder: University Press of Colorado.

Racusin, C. A., Dovidio, J. F., Brescoli, V. L., Graham, M. J., & Handelsman, J. (2012). Science faculty's subtle gender biases favor male students. *Proceedings of the National Academy of Sciences of the United States of America, 109* (41), 16474–16479.

Richards, G. (2010). *Putting psychology in its place. A critical historical perspective* (3rd ed.). London, UK: Routledge.

Rickett, B. (2016). Feminist psychology—poststructuralism, class, and maternal subjectivities: Where are we and where should we go next? *Feminism & Psychology, 26,* 320–326.

Rippon, G., Jordan-Young, R., Kaiser, A., & Fine, C. (2014). Recommendations for sex/gender neuroimaging research: Key principles and implications for research design, analysis, and interpretation. *Frontiers in Human Neuroscience, 8,* 1–13.

Rubin, G. S. (1975). The traffic in women: Notes on the "political economy" of sex. In R. Reiter (Ed.), *Toward an anthropology of women* (pp. 157–210). New York, NY: Monthly Review Press.

Rutherford, A., Marecek, J., & Sheese, K. (2013). Psychology of women and gender. In D. K. Freedheim & I. B. Weiner (Eds.), *Handbook of psychology, vol. 1: History of psychology* (pp. 279–310). Hoboken, NJ: John Wiley & Sons.

Schmitz, S., & Höppner, G. (Eds.) (2014). *Gendered neurocultures: Feminist and queer perspectives on current brain discourses.* Vienna, Austria: Zaglossus.

Unger, R. (1979). Toward a redefinition of sex and gender. *American Psychologist, 34,* 1085–1094.

Walkerdine, V., Lucey, H., & Melody, J. (2001). *Growing up girl: Psycho-social explorations of class and gender.* New York, NY: NYU Press.

2

Intersectionality as a Framework for Theory and Research in Feminist Psychology

LEAH R. WARNER AND STEPHANIE A. SHIELDS

We write this chapter for a very specific audience at a very specific time. As the next generation of researchers and practitioners, your interpretations and applications of intersectionality will shape psychology. This chapter offers a pragmatic approach to intersectionality that engages with issues that you, as advanced undergraduate and graduate students, will confront as you plan to incorporate an intersectional perspective into your work now and in the future. Furthermore, we write as two US-based academic feminist psychologists navigating disciplinary standards; we integrate both international and US contexts, although our expertise lies most in the United States. The debates and methodologically focused struggles that we describe in the United States may differ substantially or not be as marked elsewhere.

Intersectionality theory in the United States originated in Black feminist thought as early as the mid-19th century (May, 2015), in the sense of using identity categories to understand and challenge societal systems of power and privilege (Collins, 2015). Intersectionality theory has shaped much of contemporary women's, gender, and sexuality studies (Cho, Crenshaw, & McCall, 2013). The development of intersectionality perspectives in psychology has been described by Cole (2009) and Shields (2008). In this chapter, we focus on current pressing issues as you strive to incorporate an intersectional perspective into your work; specifically, we look toward the future of the developing relationship between intersectionality and feminist psychology. By feminist psychology, we mean psychological research and practice that is informed by feminist theory, that is concerned with issues relevant to women, gender, or sexualities with the goal of examining gender inequity, and that uses the results of research to promote positive social change.

We are writing at a moment in the development of intersectionality theory in psychology when there is openness to the idea, especially among social justice researchers. At the same time, however, in the growing number of publications that invoke intersectionality, it can be hard to find outstanding models of how to go forward with research. It is also discouraging to see "intersectionality" interpreted as no more than the inclusion of underrepresented populations in research, more of an "add and stir" approach than one that takes full advantage of intersectionality as a theory, interpretive perspective, or framework for designing research. (By "add and stir," we mean the acknowledgment of underrepresented groups without actually using the perspectives of those groups to inform and transform theory and research.) As May (2015, p. 6) observed, "intersectionality exposes how conventional analyses or approaches to addressing inequality" are limited because they tend to "rely on single-axis modes of analysis and redress; deny or obscure multiplicity or compoundedness; and depend upon the very systems of privilege they seek to address in order to operate." Using an intersectional perspective requires moving from the single-axis mode (i.e., treating one dimension of social identity as if it could be isolated from others) to "matrix" thinking—an analytic approach that "acknowledges the complexity and the diversity within an intersectional position as well as commonalities that connect across these positions" (Collins, 1998).

Three trends emerging within US psychology give us hope that this is a good moment for intersectionality. First, as a field, there has been growing interest in the use of social applications of psychology, whether through specific interventions or more generally a move to "give psychology away" by showing its relevance to real-world problems. Second, psychological science, both within and outside the United States, is in a period of transition as it deals with questions concerning what has been dubbed "the replication crisis" (Sharpe & Whelton, 2016). Psychologists are rethinking approaches to support integrity in the research process, for example whether preregistration of studies and the involvement of multiple labs should become standard practice. As in any time of change or transition, there is opportunity for innovation; thus, there is an opportunity for an intersectional perspective to take root through promotion of collaborative research and methodological innovations. Third, feminist psychology remains a thriving specialization within psychology, cutting across many subfields (e.g., social, developmental, clinical/counseling, and neuroscience) and concerned with issues that can benefit substantially from employing an intersectional framework. Thus, the advances that are made regarding intersectionality today have promise for continuing and growing in sophistication and impact.

In this chapter we first provide a brief overview of the history of intersectionality theory and then address how intersectionality challenges psychology, both in terms of the methods psychologists employ and the way psychology conceives of the person who is studied. In a concluding section we speculate on the future of intersectionality in psychological science and practice.

DEFINING INTERSECTIONALITY

Up to this point we have avoided offering a specific definition of intersectionality and, instead, have referred to an intersectionality perspective in a variety of ways: as a theory, as framework for research, as a set of research practices, and as a field of research. So which is it? Our currently evolving position is that fundamentally "intersectionality is the embodiment in theory of the real-world fact that systems of inequality, from the experiential to the structural, are interdependent" and that the implication for psychology is that "social identities cannot be studied independently of one another, nor separately from the processes that maintain inequality" (Warner & Shields, 2013, p. 804). We encourage you to consult one or more of the useful and accessible overviews of intersectionality that provide deeper background, development of the perspective to the present point, and issues that remain to be addressed (e.g., Collins, 2015; Grzanka, 2014; May, 2015).

Among scholars in women's studies, gender and sexuality studies, and critical race studies, there is debate as to whether there is a definitive set of assumptions that characterize intersectionality theory (e.g., Collins, 2015). As we have suggested elsewhere, two assumptions are particularly relevant to an intersectional perspective in psychological research (Else-Quest & Hyde, 2016; Warner, Settles, & Shields, 2018).

First, social identities, that is, the social groups to which individuals belong, such as gender, social class, and race, are defined in relation to one another. In other words, identities are not isolated like beads on a string (Spelman, 1988), but they create qualitatively different experiences because of their interrelation (e.g., Anthias & Yuval-Davis, 1983; Bowleg, 2008; Collins, 1990). Social identities—which are culturally specific and historically contingent—mutually constitute, reinforce, and naturalize one another. *Mutually constitute* means that the meaning of one category of identity is evident in relation to another social identity category, and those categories cannot be "decomposed"; that is, for example, the category woman is always already viewed as comprised of inseparable features (e.g., race, age, ethnicity) that define other identity categories. Body shaming, for example, takes different forms and has different consequences depending on which women are targeted. *Reinforce* means that individuals are not passive recipients of an identity position, but practice each aspect of identity as informed by other identities they claim (Collins, 2015). When a person presents herself as a woman, that identity and the reception of that identity by others is inseparable from her racial ethnicity, social class, and sexual orientation, and other social identity markers. *Naturalize* means that identities in one category become simplified and are taken for granted when viewed through the lens of another category. For example, in the contemporary United States, social identity categories, such as race, are construed as containing two gender categories, female and male, rendering these two categories as the only "natural" gender categories that exist. This excludes other possibilities for gender, such as genderqueer or a temporary gender standing. In other words, a focus on one identity, in this case race, implicitly ascribes meanings to other social categories (e.g., "gender" denotes a gender binary). In fact, naming one category of identity but ignoring another assumes the normative category of the identity not mentioned. For example, discussions of "race" typically do not recognize that experiences of race differ by gender or sexual orientation and thus promote an analysis of race that presumes heterosexual male as the prototype.

Second, aspects of identity such as gender, race, or social class may be experienced as features of individual selves, and these social identity categories reflect the operation of power relations among groups. Or put another way, experienced identity both reflects and embodies the operation of societal position and privilege (Warner et al., 2018). Persons are at intersectional positions; persons are not intersectional. A person (consciously or not) occupies (or is placed in) an intersectional position vis-à-vis others, and these positions differ in status and power. Intersections create both oppression and advantage and, importantly, advantage offers more than simple avoidance of disadvantage in that it opens up access to rewards, status, and opportunities unavailable to other intersectional positions. For example, an Asian American woman may be privileged by her heterosexuality compared to lesbians but experience disadvantage as an Asian American woman who, because of her appearance, is forever treated as "foreign" in the United States where European/Caucasian is presumed "native." (See Ridgeway & Kricheli-Katz, 2013, for additional examples.) And, furthermore, this is a dynamic system, where different categories (and therefore intersections) become more relevant in some settings, times, and places than others.

This broad framework of intersectionality grew out of critiques by feminist and womanist activists and scholars of color in late 19th century, such as Sojourner Truth and Anna Julia Cooper. May (2015) argues that it is important to understand the 19th-century roots of intersectionality because tracing those roots enables us see that even though intersectionality's meaning is dynamic and changing, there have been continuities across time and cultural and political contexts. (See also Shields, 2016.) By capturing those continuities within the term "intersectionality," the "name provides a concrete means to identify and expand upon longstanding intellectual and political projects which have examined the workings of power, underscored the importance of location, thought through the complex nature of privilege, and sought to refashion notions of personhood at work in the body politic" (p. 3).

As the feminist movement gained momentum in the 1970s, it was clear that "women" did not constitute a monolithic group within the United States and that, to be successful, the movement had to take into account other significant social identities, especially race and social class (e.g., Hull, Scott, & Smith, 1982; Lorde, 1980). Crenshaw (1989) is credited with coining the term "intersectionality" in her analysis of violence against women of color, which revealed the ways that structural inequalities lead to marginalization of some groups' legal status or social needs.

HOW INTERSECTIONALITY CHANGES
AND CHALLENGES PSYCHOLOGY

Intersectionality has made tremendous inroads into psychology over the past 15 years, not only in the psychological study of women, gender, and sexualities, but even in US psychology, which, in its most conventional form, does not appear to be particularly open to the possibilities of intersectionality. Within a span of a few years, intersectionality has become a "buzzword" (Bilge, 2013). For example, the number of journal articles and books that include "intersectionality" in the title or article abstract in PsycInfo has increased dramatically in recent years: More were published in the past 3 years ($n = 399$) than in *all* years prior to 2013 ($n = 324$). Intersectionality is even the topic of a planned special issue of a "mainstream" social psychology journal (Remedios & Sanchez, in preparation). Teaching about intersectionality is a success story, too, with excellent resources that represent the full complexity and implications of intersectionality (e.g., Case, 2016; Grzanka, 2014).

Despite the enthusiastic uptake and the prevalence of intersectionality in titles, the use of the term is no guarantee that an intersectionality framework is actually used (see, for example, critiques by Grzanka, 2014, and Warner & Shields, 2013). Collins (2015) pointed out that the differing ways that scholars use the term intersectionality is to some degree driven by variability in how much they emphasize particular guiding assumptions, with some assumptions more likely to be taken up than others.

Broadly speaking, the assumption that individual identity is irreducibly complex should be easily accepted in psychology. The sticking point for psychology in the United States in particular, however, is that identities reflect social structures of inequality, and US psychology historically has been preoccupied with universals rather than strata, although several subdisciplines in the field of psychology, such as social, industrial-organizational, and developmental, are concerned with the study of the individual in groups and society. In a way, it is not surprising that psychology tends to gravitate toward concerns about the relational nature of identity, while being less attentive to the matrix of social inequality out of which these identities emerge (and which social identities maintain and promote).

The oversimplified representation of intersectionality in psychology can be traced to two concerns. First is the relatively pedestrian question of methods: Can an intersectionality framework be grafted onto the "gold standards" of US psychological science: (1) laboratory experimentation, which requires limiting the number and levels of variables, and (2) constructs and standardized measures that are assumed to be generalizable across people. The researcher may have all intentions to employ an intersectional perspective, but not appreciate the radical transformation of thinking about research processes needed for intersectional analyses

(Bowleg, 2008). Second, and more challenging to the core definition of the discipline, is how intersectionality transforms psychology's concern with the individual by shifting the focus to sociostructural frameworks and their social and political underpinnings. We consider each of these concerns in more detail because they help us visualize the transitional, liminal space that psychology, specifically feminist psychology, is presently in with respect to fully adopting/incorporating an intersectionality approach to research.

Issue 1: Experimental Methods and Their Fit With an Intersectional Perspective/Framework

Methodological issues (e.g., Bowleg, 2008; Else-Quest & Hyde, 2016; Warner, 2008) have probably gained the most attention in discussions of intersectionality in psychology. These discussions have been generative in at least demonstrating that experimental research business-as-usual is inadequate to fully employ an intersectional analytic framework (e.g., Else-Quest & Hyde, 2016). In terms of innovative methods, little substantive work has emerged, despite the fact that many have identified this as a need (e.g., Shields & Dicicco, 2011). As we detail later, researchers' choices affect whose knowledge is privileged and whose experiences are made visible, and this, in turn, affects the generalizations made from research results. In even more concrete terms, choice of research methods is often influenced by concerns about getting a job and advancing professionally, not the situation any of us would choose, but a pragmatic consideration, nevertheless.

In our conversations with other feminist psychologists about the methodological challenges of doing intersectional research, three themes typically arise.

1. *Deal with the apparent poor fit between conventional quantitative methods and their capacity to address psychological questions within an intersectional framework.* In many academic contexts, especially in the United States, in order to get a job and keep a job, one needs to

demonstrate facility with quantitative, especially experimental, methods. Thus, researchers, especially early in their careers, are faced with the problem of how to marry conventional methods with an intersectional framework.

Most quantitative methods are based on assumptions that the researchers have a priori identified all relevant questions to ask, and they are based on additive statistical techniques (e.g., analysis of variance; multiple regression). Analysis of variance (ANOVA) and other such parametric statistics share an assumption that the different variables captured in the analytic model have additive effects. Total variance is partitioned into main effects, interactions, and error terms, each independent sources of variance. Their interaction is the portion of the analysis that treats the variables as intersectional. However, main effects are additive, in that "race" and "gender" are treated separately from each other in general linear modeling. This assumption is at cross-purposes with an intersectional analytic framework that assumes co-influences of social identity status are inseparable, rather than additive in their impact (Bowleg, 2008; Warner, 2016).

One challenge for feminist psychologists and others who want to do genuinely intersectionally informed quantitative research is to find a way to adapt conventional experimental strategies where possible and continue to find or create novel quantitative techniques that have a better fit with intersectionality-inspired research questions. At the present time, progress toward this end seems to be limited to baby steps.

For example, experimental strategies that have been proposed partially represent an intersectional perspective. They provide a pragmatic approach, given current disciplinary standards, but their drawbacks show that further innovation is needed. One way to adapt existing additive ANOVA is an incremental approach that employs a series of 2 x 2 designs across different studies with each study incorporating a subset of identities (e.g., gender x race in one study, followed by race x class in another study), the idea being to assess the entire set of studies rather than individual studies (Warner, 2008). Alternatively, a 2 x 2 could be reconceived as a single factor with four levels, which would preserve intersectional locations (e.g., Muslim woman, Muslim man, Jewish woman, Jewish man) and interrupt the convention of discussing main effects as if features of identity could be reduced to independent dimensions of identity (e.g., 2 [Race: Muslim vs. Jewish] x 2 [Gender: man vs. woman]) that act as independent causal agents on behavior. Of course, the rationale for why specific intersectional locations were chosen for study should clearly be spelled out.

These designs, however, do not resolve other limitations; for example, the additive assumptions involved in separating identities in 2 x 2 main effects is at odds with Crenshaw's (1991) depiction of intersectionality, in which she envisioned that it is a political act of resistance to portray intersecting identities as a nonseparable, cohesive whole rather than pitting an additive versus intersectional view as simply a hypothesis to be tested (Warner et al., 2018, Warner, 2016).

2. *Promote qualitative research as a core research method, not simply as preliminary or ancillary evidence* (Marecek, 2016). At present, in the US, qualitative data, no matter which of the many qualitative analytic techniques are employed, are often treated as providing preliminary findings that can then serve as the basis for designing experimental studies. This means that qualitative methods are underutilized tools for implementing an intersectional approach to psychological research.

Among the qualitative research methods compatible with an intersectional perspective, discursive psychology and critical discourse analysis (of which there are several variants), stand out as useful because they closely examine people's talk in order to observe the subject positions that are available to a person in a particular cultural setting, as well as the cultural repertoires people use to make sense of themselves and others. Discursive psychology sees language as *constitutive*, meaning that language is a form of creative action. In other words, identity is not simply reflected in language but *created* through its use in interaction with others. Using this lens, discursive psychologists investigate how social categories are constructed through the use of language, with no preset number of meanings attached to identities (e.g., gender is not a priori considered just "women" and "men"). (Chapter 6 describes discursive psychology in more detail.)

Hussain, Johnson, and Alam (2017), for example, use narratives to investigate the complexity of self-identity of British migrant Pakistani women in higher education. Critiquing binary identity distinctions of South Asian women as "traditional" versus "modern," Hussain et al. take a narrated subject approach, which exposes a more complex notion of identity compatible with intersectionality. In the narrated subject approach, participants make sense of their own experiences through time and events. This making sense of experiences is itself the social construction of identity, essentially "build a sense of self" (Hussain et al., 2017, p. 5) with available cultural discourses. Through that, they "emphasize a more psychological focus, foregrounding processes of acceptance, resistance, silencing, contradiction and negotiation, and thus the steering of a path between the personal and the social" (p. 15). In other words, via the participants' narrations, researchers determined how participants negotiated their own agency as they interacted with institutions, such as higher education, and navigated gender expectations within both migrant Muslim and dominant British cultural contexts.

At the same time, focusing only on qualitative approaches allows us to not do the hard work of thinking through ways in which conventional quantitative methods themselves may be adapted to new forms of research questions or used to complement (not replace) qualitative methods. For example, qualitative methods' approach of relying on self-report provides participants' perspectives on their intersectional positions (Oswald & Lindstedt, 2006), but it does not provide evidence about implicit cognitive processes unrelated to human talk patterns, nor does it provide data on other overt nonverbal behavior (Shields & Steinke, 2003), for which observational or experimental behavioral research may be more informative. For example, Goff, Thomas, and Jackson's (2008) study of facial perception revealed that research participants made more errors in determining the gender of Black female faces than Black male or White female faces.

3. *Conceptually and operationally defining identity in terms of social categories while acknowledging both the fluidity of identity and social constructedness of the identity categories.* In US social psychology, intersectionality is often described in terms a list of social categories that combine

to create a particular set of experiences, yet the foundation for forming these categories is not interrogated (Choo & Ferree, 2010; Robertson & Sgoutas, 2012). The fluidity of categories needs to be acknowledged in two ways. First, individuals may not permanently identify with a single category. Second, the categories themselves are historically and culturally situated and change over time. So we can contrast negotiated/temporary/historically contextualized categories imposed on individuals (e.g., What is Black? What is heterosexual?) with the experience of persons, for example, being a person who can experientially slip between established and provisional categories (e.g., claiming multiracial identity or bisexuality).

Sexuality is a good example of both types of fluidity. Sexual identity can change based on the ease and social acceptability of pursuing same-sex relationships, awareness of one's own sexual responsiveness, and individual differences in variability of sexual desires, to name just a few influences (Diamond, 2008). And in broader society, the meaning of a specific sexual identity category can change. For example, male homosexual behavior was famously illegal in late 19th-century Britain, but the law ignored lesbian sexuality as if it did not exist (Kent, 1999); therefore, the meaning of homosexuality solely concerned sexual behaviors between males.

If researchers fail to acknowledge the fluidity of social categories used in research, they lose the complexity of experience that is a core tenet of intersectionality theory (McCall, 2005). In addition, intersectionality must also acknowledge how categories are socially constructed within cultural contexts and by dominant members of society (Robertson & Sgoutas, 2012). The criteria used to place people in different identities, such as "disabled" or "middle class," are often politically motivated to meet a variety of different objectives, such as to artificially increase or decrease the numbers in the group to justify fund allocation for program initiatives. And the use of such categories without acknowledging their social construction can reinforce stereotypic beliefs about those groups (Robertson & Sgoutas, 2012).

One way to address the problems of using categories is to use them provisionally to expose how the categories reinforce structures of inequality (McCall, 2005). For example, Riggs (2012) problematizes the use of "White" versus "Asian" categories in his study of Australian White gay men's use of the term "Asian" in social media sites. He explains that the term "Asian" falsely assumes that those housed in this category have uniform experiences rather than distinct cultural backgrounds that inform experience. Although Riggs still uses the term "Asian," he explains the problems behind the term, and he also shows in his study how the term reinforces inequality. In this way, the meanings given to the category identify the category itself as an object of study.

Another way to address provisional categories is for publication standards to require justification for the categories used in research. Journal editors and APA publication guidelines ask for justification of measures and analyses; surprisingly, there is no corresponding requirement for justification of research participant profile. Authors could include a paragraph in the Methods section that explains why this particular intersectional position or set of positions was chosen for study. Likewise, the Discussion section could include a paragraph or two that directly addresses the implications (or not) for other intersectional positions. Bowleg's (2008) reassessment of her own project serves as a model for examining one's own research and for identifying where unfounded generalizations lurk and where additive thinking may have found its way into a research report.

Issue 2: Who Is the "Individual" That Psychologists Study?

The second issue goes close to the heart of psychology as a discipline concerned with "the individual." Engaging with intersectionality theory first requires shifting the focus from atomized individual experience to the systems of power and privilege that frame and constrain individual psychological experience.

From its foundation, experimental psychology has had as its main goal description and explanation of perception, cognition, emotion, and so on in the individual. When differences among individuals are acknowledged, it is on a categorical basis: gender, racial ethnicity, age, culture. Intersectionality leads us to question: Who is the "subject" in psychology?

What is the relation between psychology as science and efforts toward social justice? Who is the individual that concerns psychology? These intersectionality-inspired questions reveal a limitation in psychology's conventional treatment of the individual as a social actor.

One way to unpack these questions is to approach them from a slightly different angle: How is intersectionality-informed research different from what psychologists are already doing? Exhortations to do intersectional work are not as helpful as concrete examples. We first take an example from social psychology and then one from clinical and counseling psychology to show how work that might superficially resemble work having an intersectional perspective differs from work that actually does. These are useful contrasts because social psychologists for decades have been concerned with race, gender, and sexual orientation as social identities and more recently with religion, socioeconomic status, and ability status. Both clinical and counseling psychology are also apt examples because over the past three decades these fields have become increasingly concerned with the distinctive problems and needs of clients from different sociocultural backgrounds. Social, clinical, and counseling psychology all acknowledge diversity, but without necessarily being intersectional.

As an example from US social psychology, consider factors that affect how we perceive others, that is, person construal. Freeman and Ambady (2011) propose a person construal model that aims to examine the role of lower level perceptual mechanisms and determinants of categorization (e.g., stereotypes) that are activated from simple communicative cues, such as voice and body movements. In reviewing the extensive and complex research literature on person construal, the authors consider social identity as if it had only gender or race or another identity feature as the driving force in judgments. For example, in one section of the paper, the authors consider how facial expression of emotion shapes gender categorization. In this paper (as in others) gender is treated as if there were no influence of other identity categories, such as racial ethnicity, perceived sexual orientation, or perceived social class. Although they acknowledge "initial evidence for sex-race interactive effects" (Freeman & Ambady, 2011, p. 16), they stop short of grappling with the idea that gender categories and racial categories are not separable, that categories operate as power structures, or that one must be mindful of the specific historical and contextual features that define individual identity categories.

Another example relates to counseling and psychotherapeutic practices that emphasize the importance of positively acknowledging diversity, whether in ethnic background, sexual orientation, or other aspects of identity. Instead of addressing axes of oppression, the clinical and counseling psychology version of intersectionality is often a type of multiculturalism, which, like intersectionality, is a perspective that acknowledges the multiple social constituents of individual selves, but one that focuses on identity per se and not axes of privilege and oppression. Multiculturalism as an approach in therapy, furthermore, tends to treat dimensions of social identities (race, gender, etc.) as distinct and somewhat independent elements that together comprise a community mosaic (Warner et al., 2018), a kind of identity politics that does not directly confront structural inequities. Grzanka and Miles (2016) investigated this multiculturalist approach in therapy through their evaluation of training videos for mental health providers working with LGBT clients. They found that the videos, although affirming of sexual identity and encouraging providers to think of sexual orientation in terms of other aspects of identity, specifically race and ethnicity, ignored structural inequalities. They term this approach "intersectionality-*lite*" as it can have "the effect of simplifying or depoliticizing [intersectionality's] most potent analytical and political ambitions" and, in the case of multiculturally based forms of psychotherapy, may "unintentionally reflect a neoliberal logic of inclusion that obscures the structural dimensions of social inequality" (Grzanka & Miles, 2016, p. 14; emphasis in original). In other words, the multicultural approach redirects the discussion in such a way that disadvantage and privilege are absent and identities are presented as if they all operate on a level playing field. Furthermore, a multicultural approach tends to erase one or more dimensions of social identity that should not be decoupled from cultural/racial ethnic identity. Burman (2005), for example, shows how prevailing research approaches to cultural psychology, such as multiculturality, each in their own way marginalizes or erases gender.

Intersectionality, unlike multiculturalism, problematizes rather than ignores the relation between identity positions. This focus encourages researchers "to re-orient attention away from identity in and of itself and toward identities in structural context—identities in relationship to the systems of power that engender them" (Grzanka & Miles, 2016, p. 14).

Bowleg's work offers a useful example of how to apply intersectionality theory to psychological questions. In a study on US Black gay and bisexual men's experiences, Bowleg (2013) investigated the participants' awareness of how their identities intersected to inform a unique experience. She found that participants both ranked their identities in terms of importance (an additive view) and considered all aspects of their social identities to be inextricably fused together. She stated that participants did "identity work," in that they chose to identify by saying "I'm Black first" or "I can't just be Black and then just be gay," as they reacted to power dynamics in particular social situations. The participants emphasized that racial microaggressions and discrimination in their specific US contexts made race particularly salient; however, in the same interviews they emphasized that all of their identities "comes as one package" (p. 764). Bowleg concluded from these findings that both the ranking and inseparability of the identities coexist, with ranking being particularly sensitive to the contextual salience of the identity. Bowleg emphasizes that her results do not challenge intersectionality theory's proposition that intersectional identities are inseparable, but rather that situational and cultural context can make individual identities more or less salient at any given moment.

FUTURE DIRECTIONS

In this last section we identify two future directions for intersectionality theory, in particular, how psychological research on intersectionality can facilitate social activism, and current developments in intersectionality theory.

Psychological Research on Intersectionality Can Facilitate Social Activism

One critical area of growth involves integrating social activism into appli-cations of intersectionality to psychology. As Crenshaw (2015) argues, the creation of the term "intersectionality" was not simply an exer-cise in abstraction. Rather, it was created to stimulate systemic changes to improve the lives of women of color, and it has since been expanded to address structures of inequality at other intersections. However, this central aspect of the theory has largely been underdeveloped in research (Alexander-Floyd, 2012; Collins, 2015; May, 2015; Rosenthal, 2016).

Rosenthal (2016) reminds us that challenging restrictive social struc-tures and promoting social justice fit squarely with psychologists' focus on human behavior. Evidence is mounting that structural oppression, from laws restricting rights to residential segregation, affects a wide range of human experiences. Structural oppression is linked to outcomes such as poorer cognitive functioning, health behaviors, and a variety of other mental and physical outcomes; on the flip side, counteracting structural oppression can improve well-being (see Rosenthal, 2016). Furthermore, interpersonal-level stereotyping, prejudice, and discrimination are fun-damentally linked to structural oppression (e.g., Fuller-Rowell, Evans, & Ong, 2012). Although there are many ways that a social activist approach might incorporate intersectionality (e.g., Collins, 2015; Rosenthal, 2016), three central approaches are coalition building, policy implications of research, and community engagement.

COALITION BUILDING

Intersectionality is particularly amenable to coalition building that involves "temporary, means-oriented alliances among individuals or groups which differ in goals" (Gamson, 1961, p. 374, as cited in Cole, 2008). A central challenge to coalition building is that individuals who are divided based on identity politics must forge a connection with one another in a way that addresses the social inequalities that produce and reinforce this divide. So, for example, by working together, LGBTQ+ and Black communities might strengthen their efforts to increase state funding for an AIDS advocacy program, but they would need to address both the racism within LGBTQ+ communities and heterosexism in Black communities to do so. Research on the psychology of coalition building has found that intersectionality is constructive in revealing the interconnections both within and across social groups (Cole, 2008; Rosenthal, 2016).

POLICY IMPLICATIONS OF RESEARCH

Taking a social activism approach to psychological research on intersectionality requires integration of theory with praxis (Warner et al., 2018; Warner, Shields, & Settles, 2016). Researchers must address the impact of their research on individuals' lives by taking into consideration the policy implications of their research, engaging in communicating findings to those who influence public policy, and using public policy to stimulate research ideas. Crenshaw's (1989) development of intersectionality theory brought attention to how legal status, resources, and social needs advantage or marginalize individuals, specifically due to the convergence of identity statuses. Attention to policy implications suggests an activist science. To some, this might conjure images of inquiry that is aimed at gathering evidence to support a particular point of view. As Shields (2008) observes, however, "The goal of activist science itself is not to create policy, but inform [its creation]" (p. 309). An activist scientist is not like a lawyer seeking supportive evidence for her client's defense. Rather, activist science is an investigation of factors that can potentially result in bettering people's lives or identifying factors that potentially harm them. In both cases, the concern is particularly for groups who have been systemically marginalized.

COMMUNITY ENGAGEMENT

Applying research to social justice requires engagement with communities (Rosenthal, 2016). Researchers need to learn research methods that facilitate collaboration between researchers and relevant communities. Rosenthal's (2016) *American Psychologist* article on using intersectionality theory to integrate a social justice approach to psychology provides a roadmap for community engagement. Intersectionality demands that researchers orient themselves to structural inequality and to understanding the experiences of multiply marginalized individuals, and Rosenthal argues that engagement and collaboration with communities links these two demands. In particular, she focuses on community-based participatory research (CBPR), which is an approach that is based on an equal partnership between researchers and communities being studied and that focuses on social change. Via CBPR, communities contribute to all parts of the research process, including determining research questions and hypotheses. This inclusion ensures that research is centered on the issues most relevant to those communities and that communities are empowered to be leaders in creating the scientific knowledge that is used to solve social problems within their communities. CBPR is not inherently intersectional, but it facilitates the types of questions that intersectionality theorists ask, specifically in terms of ensuring that all stakeholder groups are represented and that issues of power within and across those groups are acknowledged.

Future Directions in Intersectionality Theory

Psychological approaches to intersectionality must keep current with cutting-edge revisions and critiques of the theory. Davis (2008) argues that for intersectionality to thrive, scholars need to be willing to consider multiple interpretations and extensions, so as to avoid a dominant, static perspective that could limit conversation about what intersectionality can do. Although versions of intersectionality theory in addition to Crenshaw's exist (e.g., Lorde, 1980), Crenshaw's intersectionality theory has become a dominant paradigm for understanding the mutually constitutive relations among social identities and social structures (Bilge, 2013; Puar, 2007). Revisions and critiques of Crenshaw's intersectionality help us question our epistemological assumptions, inspire us to grapple with methodological issues, and identify new questions for us to ask, all exercises necessary in order to move intersectionality theory forward.

As one example that is potentially useful, Puar (2007, 2011) introduced assemblage theory as re-envisioning intersectionality. Assemblage theory asserts that it is through the connections with other concepts that concepts receive meaning (Puar, 2011). In other words, categories such as race or gender are not seen as attributes of individuals, but rather as actions or events between bodies. Assemblage offers a framework for understanding how heterogeneous physical bodies (bodies that vary from one another in many different ways) become connected to one another. For example, how does it come to be that a "woman of color" could both mean a Black transwoman living in the Bronx and a Pakistani woman living in Islamabad? Using textual analysis, assemblage examines the changing, fluid process organizing and arranging these bodies via a multitude of factors, including moment in time, historical context, geographic location, and social context.

Puar argues that assemblage theory addresses limitations of Crenshaw's intersectionality. Citing postcolonial and transnational scholars' observations (e.g., Brah & Phoenix, 2004), Puar argues that Crenshaw's intersectionality ironically centers White women's experiences by constructing women of color as the resistant, subversive "Other." Puar offers assemblage theory as destabilizing women of color "as a prosthetic capacity to white women" (p. 57). The focus of assemblage theory is that "categories—race, gender, sexuality—are considered events, actions, and encounters, between bodies, rather than simply entities and attributes of subjects" (Puar, 2011, p. 61). In other words, bodies are unstable assemblages that cannot be reduced to static, intersecting identity categories. Puar does not advocate for abandoning intersectionality as a result of these limitations, but rather by re-reading intersectionality as assemblage (Puar, 2011).

For those who are versed in both psychology and interdisciplinary fields, a critical next step is to introduce assemblage and other theories to a psychological audience. This means that the theories need to be applied to psychological research, which will include acknowledging how the theories might critique psychology as a discipline. For example, by employing assemblage theory, researchers may challenge dominant theories of identity.

CONCLUSION

Feminist psychology has gone through developmental stages since the era of Leta Stetter Hollingworth (e.g., Hollingworth, 1916) in the early 1900s and its phenomenal growth since the early 1970s. At each stage of the way, new insights have caused us to rethink what research we do and how we do it. In the early 1970s it seemed reasonable to distinguish between sex and gender and to define psychology of gender as the study of sex-related differences. Today, we know that the sex/gender dichotomy is contrived and misleading (e.g., Joel, 2016) and that psychology of gender entails far more than enumeration of similarities and differences (e.g., Jordan-Young & Rumiati, 2012; Shields, 2013; Yoder & Kahn, 2003). Holding onto the single-axis manner of studying social identity, disconnecting personal identity from the sociopolitical power structures in which identity is embedded, and worrying overly about how to "do" intersectionality in an ANOVA might someday, too, seem quaint. That said, there is much to do before these issues are considered the concern of a previous generation. Theoretical and empirical work up to this point provides something of a roadmap, but truly innovative work is needed to integrate intersectionality theory more fully into psychology. As the next generation of researchers and practitioners, you have the challenge of seizing this opportunity.

REFERENCES

Alexander-Floyd, N. (2012). Disappearing acts: Reclaiming intersectionality in the social sciences in a post-black feminist era. *Feminist Formations, 24*, 1–25.

Anthias, F., & Yuval-Davis, N. (1983). Contextualising feminism: Gender, ethnic and class divisions. *Feminist Review, 15*, 62–75.

Bilge, S. (2013). Intersectionality undone: Saving intersectionality from feminist intersectionality studies. *Du Bois Review, 10*, 405–424.

Brah, A., & Phoenix, A. (2004). Ain't I a woman: Revisiting intersectionality. *Journal of International Women's Studies, 3,*75–86.

Bowleg, L. (2008). When Black + Lesbian + Woman ≠ Black Lesbian Woman: The methodological challenges of qualitative and quantitative intersectionality research. *Sex Roles, 59*, 312–325.

Bowleg, L. (2013). "Once you've blended the cake, you can't take the parts back to the main ingredients": Black gay and bisexual men's descriptions and experiences of intersectionality. *Sex Roles, 68*, 754–767.

Burman, E. (2005). Engendering culture in psychology. *Theory & Psychology, 15*, 527–548.

Case, K. A. (2016). *Intersectional pedagogy: Complicating identity and social justice.* New York, NY: Routledge.

Cho, S., Crenshaw, K. W., & McCall, L. (2013). Toward a field of intersectionality studies: Theory, applications, and praxis. *Signs, 38*, 785–810.

Choo, H. Y., & Ferree, M.M. (2010). Practicing intersectionality in sociological research: A critical analysis of inclusions, interactions, and institutions in the study of inequalities. *Sociological Theory, 28*, 129–149.

Cole, E. R. (2008). Coalitions as a model for intersectionality: From practice to theory, *Sex Roles, 59*, 443–453.

Cole, E. R. (2009). Intersectionality and research in psychology. *American Psychologist, 64*, 170–180.

Collins, P. H. (1990). *Black feminist thought: Knowledge, consciousness, and the politics of empowerment.* New York, NY: Routledge.

Collins, P. H. (1998). *Fighting words: Black women and the search for justice.* Minneapolis: University of Minnesota Press.

Collins, P.H. (2015). Intersectionality's definitional dilemmas. *Annual Review of Sociology, 41*, 1–20.

Crenshaw, K. W. (1989). Demarginalizing the intersection of race and sex: A Black feminist critique of antidiscrimination doctrine, feminist theory and antiracist politics. *University of Chicago Legal Forum, 140*, 139–167.

Crenshaw, K. (1991). Mapping the margins: Intersectionality, identity politics, and violence against women of color. *Stanford Law Review, 43*, 1241–1299.

Crenshaw, K.W. (2015). Why intersectionality can't wait. Retrieved from *The Washington Post*, https://www.washingtonpost.com/news/in-theory/wp/2015/09/24/why-intersectionality-cant-wait/?utm_term=.ab0773a39ec5

Davis, K. (2008). Intersectionality as a buzzword: A sociology of science perspective on what makes a feminist theory successful. *Feminist Theory, 9*, 67–85.

Diamond, L. M. (2008). *Sexual fluidity: Understanding women's love and desire.* Cambridge, MA: Harvard University Press.

Else-Quest, N. M., & Hyde, J. S. (2016). Intersectionality in quantitative psychological research: II. Methods and techniques. *Psychology of Women Quarterly, 40*, 319–336.

Freeman, J. B., & Ambady, N. (2011). A dynamic interactive theory of person construal. *Psychological Review, 118*, 247–279.

Fuller-Rowell, T. E., Evans, G. W., & Ong, A. D. (2012). Poverty and health: The mediating role of perceived discrimination. *Psychological Science, 23*, 734–739.

Gamson, W. A. (1961). A theory of coalition formation. *American Sociological Review, 26*, 373–382.

Goff, P. A., Thomas, M. A., & Jackson, M. C. (2008). "Ain't I a woman?": Towards an intersectional approach to person perception and group-based harms. *Sex Roles, 59*(5-6), 392–403.

Grzanka, P. R. (Ed.) (2014). *Intersectionality: A foundations and frontiers reader.* Boulder, CO: Westview Press.

Grzanka, P. R., & Miles, J. R. (2016). The problem with the phrase "Intersecting Identities": LGBT affirmative therapy, intersectionality, and neoliberalism. *Sexuality Research and Social Policy, 13,* 371–389.

Hollingworth, L. S. (1916). Sex differences in mental tests. *Psychological Bulletin, 13,* 377–383.

Hull, G. T., Scott, P. B., & Smith, B. (Eds.). (1982). *All the women are white, all the blacks are men, but some of us are brave: Black women's studies.* Old Westbury, NY: Feminist Press.

Hussain, I., Johnson, S., & Alam, Y. (2017). Young British Pakistani Muslim women's involvement in higher education. *Feminism & Psychology.* First published online, February 1, 2017. doi:https://doi.org/10.1177/0959353516686123

Joel, D. (2016). Captured in terminology: Sex, sex categories, and sex differences. *Feminism & Psychology, 26,* 335–345.

Jordan-Young, R. M., & Rumiati, R. I. (2011). Hardwired for sexism? Approaches to sex/gender in neuroscience. *Neuroethics, 5,* 305–315.

Kent, S. K. (1999). *Gender and power in Britain, 1640–1990.* New York, NY: Routledge.

Lorde, A. (1980). Age, race, class, and sex: Women redefining difference. Paper delivered at the Copeland Colloquium, Amherst College, April 1980. In A. Kesselman, L. D. McNair, and N. Schniedewind (Eds.), *Women: Images and realities, a multicultural anthology* (pp. 361–366). Mountain View, CA: Mayfield, 1999.

Marecek, J. (2016). Intersectionality theory and feminist psychology: Reflecting on Else-Quest and Hyde. *Psychology of Women Quarterly, 40,* 177–181.

May, V. M. (2015). *Pursuing intersectionality: Unsettling dominant imaginaries.* New York, NY: Routledge.

McCall, L. (2005). The complexity of intersectionality. *Signs, 30,* 1771–1800.

Oswald, D. L., & Lindstedt, K. (2006). The content and function of gender self-stereotypes: An exploratory investigation. *Sex Roles, 54,* 447–458.

Puar, J. K. (2007). *Terrorist assemblages: Homonationalism in queer times.* Durham, NC: Duke University Press.

Puar, J. K. (2011). "I would rather be a cyborg than a goddess:" Becoming-intersectional in assemblage theory. *philoSOPHIA, 2,* 49–66.

Remedios, J., & Sanchez, D. (in preparation). Intersectional and dynamic social categories in social cognition. *Social Cognition.*

Ridgeway, C. L., & Kricheli-Katz, T. (2013). Intersecting cultural beliefs in social relations: Gender, race, and class binds and freedoms. *Gender & Society, 27,* 294–318.

Riggs, D. W. (2012). Anti-Asian sentiment amongst a sample of white Australian men on gaydar. *Sex Roles, 68,* 768–778.

Robertson, M. A., & Sgoutas, A. (2012). Thinking beyond the category of sexual identity: At the intersection of sexuality and human-trafficking policy. *Politics & Gender, 8,* 421–429.

Rosenthal, L. (2016). Incorporating intersectionality into psychology: An opportunity to promote social justice and equity. *American Psychologist, 71,* 474–485.

Sharpe, D., & Whelton, W. J. (2016). Frightened by an old scarecrow: The remarkable resilience of demand characteristics. *Review of General Psychology*, [online first publication, Nov 7, 2016].

Shields, S. A. (2008). Gender: An intersectionality perspective. *Sex Roles*, *59*, 301–311.

Shields, S. A. (2013). Gender and emotion: What we think we know, what we need to know, and why it matters. *Psychology of Women Quarterly*, *37*, 423–435.

Shields, S. A. (2016). Functionalism, Darwinism, and intersectionality: How an intersectional perspective reveals issues of power, inequality, and legitimacy in psychological science. *Feminism & Psychology*, *26*, 353–365.

Shields, S. A., & Dicicco, E. C. (2011). The social psychology of sex and gender: From gender differences to doing gender. *Psychology of Women Quarterly*, *35*, 491–499.

Shields, S. A., & Steinke, P. (2003). Does self-report make sense as an investigative method in evolutionary psychology? In C. B. Travis (Ed.), *Evolution, violence, and gender* (pp. 87–104). Cambridge, MA: MIT Press.

Spelman, E. (1988). *Inessential woman*. Boston, MA: Beacon Press.

Warner, L. R. (2008). A best practices guide to intersectional approaches in psychological research. *Sex Roles*, *59*, 454–463.

Warner, L. R. (2016). Invited reflection: Contested interpretations and methodological choices in quantitative research. *Psychology of Women Quarterly*, *40*, 342–346.

Warner, L. R., Settles, I. R., & Shields, S. A. (2018). Intersectionality theory in the psychology of women (pp. 521–539). In C. B. Travis, & J. W. White (Eds.), *The handbook of the psychology of women*. Washington, DC: American Psychological Association.

Warner, L. R., & Shields, S. A. (2013). The intersections of sexuality, gender, and race: Identity research at the crossroads. *Sex Roles*, *68*(11-12), 803–810.

Warner, L. R., Shields, S.A., & Settles, I. R. (2016). Invited reflection: Intersectionality as an epistemological challenge to psychology. *Psychology of Women Quarterly*, *40*, 171–176.

Yoder, J. D., & Kahn, A. S. (2003). Making gender comparisons more meaningful: A call for more attention to social context. *Psychology of Women Quarterly*, *27*, 281–290.

3

Nonbinary Gender Identities

PETER HEGARTY, Y. GAVRIEL ANSARA,
AND MEG-JOHN BARKER

This chapter examines "nonbinary gender," a term used to refer to genders that are viewed as somewhere between or beyond the gender "binary" of *man and woman*, as well as genders that incorporate elements of both *man* and *woman*. Nonbinary genders can be *identities* that reflect how individual people describe and position themselves and/or they can be *social roles*: normative categories through which societies are organized. In our own time, as in previous decades, the claim that such genders exist at all can appear like a radical idea within the "Minority World" in which the field, discipline, and profession of psychology are well populated. We use the terms "Minority World" and "Majority World" here, borrowing from Alam (2008), who used them to challenge implicit assumptions about priorities in terms such as "developing" and "developed world" or "first world" and "third world." In the majority of the societies in which the world's people now live, many other different gender systems are practiced. As we hope to show here, nonbinary genders are relevant to several core topics in psychology, including identity, mental health, culture, language, and cognition, and even the way we code our variables.

Here, we first introduce research on nonbinary gender-identified people as a social group in the Minority World. Next, we turn our attention to gender binaries, examine what kinds of concepts they are, and discuss how they have been entrenched in the thinking of Minority World psychologists. Third, we examine forms of culturally specific knowledge about gender that are relatively free of the influence of Western psychology, leading to our assertion that a psychology of nonbinary gender must also be a cultural and intersectional one. Each section of this chapter might make the unfamiliar world of nonbinary gender more familiar to you. But just as important, if not more so, we aim to defamiliarize gender binaries, to render explicit that they are culturally particular systems, not just "how the world works." This chapter should raise questions about things that you may have assumed about gender until now. By so doing, we hope it will lead you to novel work in an area of psychology that demands your passion and gives your critical stance a leading edge.

WHOM ARE WE TALKING ABOUT?

In the Minority World context, *identifying* as having a nonbinary gender is typically viewed as a pretty new thing. One recent review of the UK literature defined nonbinary as "an umbrella term for any gender (or lack of gender) that would not be adequately represented by an either/or choice between man or woman" (Titman, 2014). This review found that at least 0.4% of the UK population defines as nonbinary when given a three-way choice between defining themselves as female, as male, or as another description. About one quarter to one third of people who identify as trans also identify in some way outside binary gender. Broadly speaking, the umbrella term "nonbinary gender" includes the following experiences of gender and related identities:

- Having no gender (e.g., gender neutral, nongendered, agender, neutrois)
- Incorporating aspects of both man and woman or being somewhere between those (e.g., mixed gender, androgynous)
- Being to some extent, but not completely, one gender (e.g., demi man/boy, demi woman/girl, femme man)
- Being of a specific additional gender (e.g., third gender, other gender, pangender)
- Moving between genders (e.g., bigender, trigender, gender fluid)
- Disrupting the gender binary of women and men (e.g., genderqueer, genderfuck) (see Barker & Richards, 2015)

The term *genderqueer* is also sometimes used as an umbrella term to capture all nonbinary people.

As most major surveys and censuses do not offer gender options beyond *man* and *woman*, or *male* and *female*, they don't allow estimates of the proportion of people who might identify beyond the binary if given the choice to do so (Ansara, 2016a). However, survey practices are changing in response to activists' and activist/scholars' concerns. For example, the 2016 Australian Census offered a third gender category, but still required anyone who did not select "M" or "F" to call to request a special census form on which they might be recognized. One UK study that did offer alternatives found that around 5% of young LGBT people identified with a gender category other than male or female (METRO Youth Chances, 2014). The "Injustice at Every Turn" study gathered responses from over 6,000 trans people in the United States and found that over 13% of respondents chose the open-ended option "a gender not listed here," writing in their own gender identity terms (Harrison, Grant, & Herman, 2012). A recent Canadian study found that 41% of young trans people identified as nonbinary (Frohard-Dourlent, Dobson, Clark, Doull, & Saewyc, 2016). Thus, when dealing with some populations, such as those labeled LGB or trans, it seems particularly important for researchers to allow participants to identify beyond the gender binary. Nonbinary gender identification also appears to be rising in some countries; more people, particularly young adults, are identifying and making sense of their experience in nonbinary ways. Understandings of gender are more readily available than before through online resources and communities (Barker, 2014) and through articles and celebrities in mainstream media (e.g., Brisbane, 2015; Ford, 2015).

Much of the existing research that includes nonbinary people as a distinct demographic group has focused on mental health. McNeil, Bailey, Ellis, Morton, and Regan (2012) found that those who identify as nonbinary and/or express themselves in ways that explicitly challenge binary gender both face similarly high levels of mental health difficulties than do people classified as trans. Harrison, Grant, and Herman (2012) found that over 40% of nonbinary people in their US survey had attempted suicide at some point. One third had experienced physical assault, and one sixth had experienced sexual assault based on their gender—experiences that are strongly related to psychological distress. These rates were even higher than for those reported by women and men classified as trans (see also Richards et al., 2016).

There are clearly new avenues for psychological research here. We conjecture about the causes of these mental health findings by drawing analogies from related literatures. Research on people with transgender experience links high levels of distress to the common experience of explicit and implicit discrimination (Riggs, Ansara, & Treharne, 2015) and to living in a cisgenderist world (Ansara, 2010). People of trans experience and/or identity often face familial and societal pressure to conform to cisgenderist views of gender in order to "fit in" and be seen as "legitimate" (Blumer, Ansara, & Watson, 2013; Iantaffi & Bockting, 2011). Nonbinary people may well share such experiences.

Cisgendered bisexual people share with nonbinary people the experience of falling outside of binary understandings of sexuality and gender (i.e., that a person is either a man or a woman, and either attracted to the "same" or "opposite" sex, but only one of them). They also experience worse mental health than either heterosexual or lesbian/gay people (Barker, Richards, Jones, Bowes-Catton, & Plowman, 2012; Barker, 2015).

As is the case among bisexual people, being positioned outside a social binary can lead both to erasure and invisibility (as when people rarely recognize or validate a person's gender or sexuality), and to discrimination on the basis of not fitting either side of the binary (particularly for those who are identifiably nonbinary in some regard).

Of course, as in other areas, *intersectional* thinking is vital here (see Chapter 2 and also Cole, 2009). Nonbinary experiences differ markedly depending upon a person's class, ethnicity, age, cultural background, geographical location, and so on. Additionally, it is important to remember that some nonbinary people are trans and some are not, some nonbinary people are bisexual and some are not. Nonbinary people may encounter very specific forms of exclusion as well as those forms of exclusion more familiar to LGB, trans, queer, and intersex populations and other groups targeted for marginalization (Ansara, 2016a, 2016b). Future research should innovate by addressing the potential for positive mental health aspects of nonbinary and androgynous gender identities and expressions, rather than focusing on problems and difficulties (Belgrave et al., 2004).

Intersectional analysis is also demanded in psychology because social identities are complex and vary more in their salience than demographic items on surveys can capture (Tajfel & Turner, 1986). Few people may *identify* as nonbinary to the point of refusing to tick either the "male" or "female" box on a form, but many more people *experience* themselves in nonbinary ways. For example, Joel, Tarrash, Berman, Mukamel, and Ziv (2013) found that over a third of people in the general population in Israel felt to some extent that they were the "other" gender, "both" genders, and/or "neither" gender.

As we wrote this chapter in 2016–2017, the relative lack of research on nonbinary gender was beginning to change. The year 2016 saw the first academic conference on nonbinary gender (Vincent & Erikainen, 2016), the first PhD on nonbinary experience (Vincent, 2016), and a call for the first journal special issue on nonbinary gender (*Nursing Inquiry*, 2016; Frohard-Dourlent et al., 2016) of which we are aware. As has often happened with both feminist and LGBT research, psychological research questions are emerging from bottom-up research that is initially being conducted outside of academia (Ansara, 2016a; Bergman & Barker, 2017; Hegarty, 2017). Following the claim by the UK Ministry of Justice in 2015 that nonbinary people suffer no "specific detriment" due to their genders, the #specificdetriment twitter hashtag was created to collate such experiences, and the Beyond the Binary website and ScottishTrans.org then both conducted surveys with the nonbinary people to which they had access (Beyond the Binary, 2015; ScottishTrans.org, 2016). This grassroots research found that, for example, over three quarters of UK nonbinary people avoid situations for fear of being *misgendered* (assumed to be a gender other than the one that they are), "outed" by others as nonbinary, or harassed. Two thirds of respondents felt that they were never included in services, such as those relating to health, legislation, education, or media. Very few felt able to be openly nonbinary at work (Barker & Lester, 2015; Valentine, 2016).

Vincent's (2016) research builds on such community-based survey data with an in-depth qualitative study of nonbinary people's experience over time, focusing particularly on their interactions with LGBT communities and medical professionals. Vincent found that nonbinary people keenly experienced "a hierarchy of transness" which left them feeling "not trans enough" within trans communities, and fearful that this might also play a part if they endeavoured to access medical services such as hormones or surgeries. Participants particularly reported exclusion and discrimination from many gay men and lesbians, denial of hormones and surgeries, and erasure of their genders and misgendering in everyday interactions with medical professionals (see also Ansara, 2012). Several participants also felt that Gender Identity Clinics, where the anatomical and physiological aspects of gender affirmation processes are managed, would regard nonbinary gender as "too difficult" to work with and that it might be necessary to feign a binary gender identity and expression in order to access gender-affirming treatments. However, several nonbinary participants had had positive experiences with specific clinics and clinicians.

The 2016 academic conference on nonbinary gender in the United Kingdom (Vincent & Erikainen, 2016) gives a flavor of the further research that is currently being conducted in this area. Most presenters were PhD students and early-career researchers who were nonbinary themselves, and much of the research was in its early stages at the time of presentation. The conference included auto-ethnographic research on the experience of teaching in higher education as a nonbinary person, qualitative research on nonbinary gender experience and expression within Chinese and Vietnamese cultures, phenomenological research on what an understanding of gender dysphoria might look like which was "bottom up" (grounded in everyday trans experience) rather than imposed "top down" by medical professions, media research on the representation and reception of nonbinary gender in comics, an analysis of the overlaps and distinctions between intersex and nonbinary experience and activism, and historical studies of nonbinary gender expression in the 18th century and early modern periods. We hope that by the time you are reading this, more of this research will be available in publication to enrich your sense of the historical and cultural particularity of the gender binary with which some people do not identify.

WHAT IS "THE GENDER BINARY" ANYWAY?

When people tick a demographic box to say that they do or don't identify with the categories "male" and "female," with what kinds of categories are they *not* identifying? We turn to the meaning of this binarizing system next. The assumption that people can be simply and uncritically divided into such discrete, nonoverlapping, mutually exclusive and exhaustive categories as "male" and "female" is often reproduced in everyday language and practice in ways that go without saying. When it is made up in everyday fashion, such a gender binary relies on and cites cultural defaults that are not consciously intended. This category system is culturally and historical specific, internally contradictory, and amenable to change. In his early sociological studies, the influential and innovative American sociologist Harold Garfinkel (1967) argued that a system of beliefs about gender was made up through everyday interactions. Garfinkel's system was reformulated by Bornstein (1994) as follows:

1. There are two and only two genders.
2. One's gender is invariant.
3. Genitals are the essential sign of gender.
4. Any exceptions to two genders are not to be taken seriously.
5. There are only *ceremonial* transfers from one gender to another.
6. Everyone must be classified as a member of one gender or another.
7. The dichotomy is a natural one.
8. Membership in one gender category or another is something "natural."

Garfinkel (1967) described this system as a *natural attitude to gender*. In so doing, he was not claiming that these beliefs follow from human nature. Quite the opposite. He insisted that our everyday practices usually ground, and sometimes challenge, the assumption that binary gender categories are *natural* and bodily. If it seems difficult to understand how social interaction can make this category system seem natural, then consider how referring to an audience as "Ladies and Gentlemen," encountering bathrooms in public that recognize two and only two genders, or asking expectant parents if they are hoping to have a son or a daughter reifies these assumptions.

Garfinkel formulated these rules through extensive interviews with a young woman identified as "Agnes," who was navigating the gate keeping in the UCLA gender identity clinic in the 1960s. Social psychologists Kessler and McKenna (1978) adapted Garfinkel's last rule to emphasize that the rules linking genitals to gender—in their own time and place at least—were asymmetric (for example, the absence of a penis was more important than the presence of a vagina in locating a person in the female category). Tee and Hegarty (2006) used Garfinkel's scale to create a measure of gender-related beliefs that among UK students was correlated with measures of authoritarianism, homophobia, and opposition to trans people's civil rights (see also Hill & Willoughby, 2005). Norton and Herek (2013) completed a larger replication of these findings in the United States, and Winter, Webster, and Cheung (2008) carried out related work in Hong Kong.

The persistence of a natural attitude to gender relies upon *essentialist* assumptions that some hidden "essence" defines and explains all of the things that can signify a person's social identity (Prentice & Miller, 2007). For Garfinkel, the natural attitude was particularly anchored in *cultural genitals*—assumptions about the genitals that others are *assumed* to have, whilst physical genitals are rarely made visible in public. Psychologists display the natural attitude when they use terms like "woman" and "female," or "sex" and "gender," interchangeably, as if social identities and physical bodies were interchangeable. Teachers of statistics do so when they use "sex" unreflexively to exemplify a binary nominal variable. Researchers do so when they design empirical studies that allow people only to identify as one of two genders, or when they then assume that people who identified within the binary on that occasion *are* men or women in all other contexts (see also Ansara, 2016b). Publishers' style guides do so when they insist *both* that participants be asked to self-report their gender *and* that the number of "men and women" be reported, as if there were two and only two genders. Publishers also do so when they prescribe that people whose inclusion would trouble the gender boundary be described in degendered terms only as "persons" (see Ansara & Hegarty, 2014).

Garfinkel's research is but one snapshot of how a binary gender system operated in California in the 1960s. Psychologists operating within this binary gender system have produced intriguing results about social cognition that trouble the gender binary itself. Consider the following findings:

- The order of words in *binomial phrases* like "men and women" and "Bill and Mary" can be saturated with semantic meaning about social relationships. In 16th-century English, binomial phrases referencing men first were prescribed by grammarians to reflect beliefs about gender hierarchy. Such phrases remain preferred in more recent centuries, particularly (1) when referencing strangers, (2) when spoken by male speakers, (3) when addressing male listeners, and (4) prior to feminist critiques of language in the 1970s (see Hegarty, Mollin, & Foels, 2016). Word order has a gender.

- A *spatial agency bias* in mental imagery leads men to be imagined as appearing "first (e.g., left in English, right in Arabic) and women "second" (e.g., right in English, left in Arabic) (Suitner & Maass, 2016). Physical space can have gender.
- Numbers can have gender. Wilkie and Bodenhausen (2012) presented images of babies along with random digits and asked participants to guess each baby's gender. Babies were more commonly guessed to be girls when images were accompanied by odd numbers and as boys when accompanied by even numbers. These findings are less odd when it is remembered that Pythagoras (570–495 BCE) gendered odd numbers female and even numbers as male early on in Western thought (Wertheim, 1997).

These intriguing studies were not conducted to challenge the gender binary; their methods participated in the natural attitude to gender as much as any others. Nonetheless, they inform a nonbinary psychology because they demonstrate how far-ranging *gender polarization* (Bem, 1995) can be. Clearly, gender systems are capable of grounding new associations even with very abstract categories (e.g., female = second, right, and odd, whereas male = first, left, and even). Such results allow us all to reasonably join Garfinkel (1967) and Kessler and McKenna (1978) in their conviction that the associations male = penis and female = vagina are also, at least somewhat, arbitrary.

If we do not assume that gender is grounded in sex, then we can query some paradigmatic assumptions about gender stereotypes. Gender stereotyping is often described first and foremost as a process of making inferences about people on the basis of their classification as women or men. But, as Garfinkel (1967) insisted, genitals and gender categories are *inferred*, not observed, and often with remarkable force from malleable cues such as hair length (McCrae & Martin, 2007). Similarly, gendered roles do not simply follow from genital differences but genital differences are culturally constructed in gendered ways, whether we look to dictionary definitions or slang terms (Braun & Kitzinger, 2001a, b). Bodies differ from one another, but the interpretations of those differences that matter most are embedded in cultural meaning systems (Butler, 1993).

As with many human category systems, we often classify gender *both* within an Aristotelian system (in which people *are* clearly members of one and only one gender category) and within categories organized by prototypes and ideals, in which some people seem more typical of gender categories than others (Bowker & Star, 1999). How else to understand the metaphor in the deceptively simple statement "Boys will be boys" (Glucksberg & Keysar, 1990)? Indeed, no category system can ever do justice to the complexity and diversity of human experience (Ansara, 2015). For this reason, critiques of *cisgenderism*, the ideology that invalidates people's own understanding of their genders and bodies (Ansara & Hegarty, 2012; Ansara, 2013), have defined both the woman/man distinction and the cisgender/transgender distinction as *binarizing* and *essentializing*. Not all people can be classified as either "cisgender" or "transgender" people, and the assumption that such an Aristotelian binary system covers everyone risks misgendering nonbinary people, and it fails to account for people who live part - but not all - of their lives in the gender typically associated with their assigned sex category.

Gender categorization can seem removed from practical consequences for some people. Kessler (1990) pioneered in demonstrating how gender categorization has social relevance for people born with intersex characteristics - people who are often treated with less ethical concern than other humans (Feder, 2014). As intersex people became subject to increasing medical control in the 19th century, doctors were demanded to reveal the "true sex" of bodies in strictly binary terms, in part because men—but only men—could vote in new liberal nation-states (Laqueur, 1990; Reis, 2009). In the 1980s, Kessler interviewed clinicians in New York City who operated according to the medical policy toward intersex infants that was developed and promoted by psychologist John Money from the mid-20th century onward. Money's system prescribed early surgery on infants' genitals to realign children within the binary gender system, and secrecy about the fact that such procedures had taken place at all. Kessler (1990) described how clinicians tried to calm parents' fears for their intersex

children by transgressing one of the key assumptions of the natural attitude; clinicians emphasized that *only* the child's genitals were abnormal
(and could be fixed) but that the child's *gender* was normal. In so doing,
clinicians contradicted the assumption that gender obviously and always
follows from genitals. Nonetheless, the natural attitude remained in place.
As West African historian Lorelle D. Semley noted, "the social definition of gender is so powerful that it seems 'natural' even as scholars have
shown that the physical definition of sex itself based in appearance and in
scientific testing is not a given" (2011, p. 163).

Money's views had the status of gospel among these clinicians, but they
have been discredited due to challenges from intersex activists, exposure
of unethical treatment, and emerging biomedical theories (Davis, 2015;
Jordan-Young, 2012). When social scientists began to research intersex
people through support and advocacy groups, they found that the medi-
calization of intersex characteristics did little to address, and often wors-
ened, psychological feelings of shame and isolation that followed from
the assumptions of the binary gender system (Alderson, Madill, & Balen,
2004; Preves, 2003). More recent investigations have again demonstrated
that clinical medicine continues to rely upon unstated assumptions about
binary sex in evaluating what is in children's interests and in advising their
parents (Davis, 2015; Karkazis, 2008).

The relevance of this history to understanding the construction of the
gender binary system goes far beyond intersex people and their families.
Some readers will be surprised, or even incredulous, when we say that the
very term *gender* was not used in English to categorize people much prior
to John Money and his colleagues' usage of it in the mid-1950s in their
prescriptions for the management of intersex infants. Prior to this time,
the term "gender" or the idea of "having a gender" was not one that was
applied to women, men, or anyone else. Money's invention of gender is
but one example of how an aspect of human experience was binarized and
polarized, thereby expanding the reach of the discipline of psychology.
Foucault (1977) described such moments as expansions of *disciplinary
power* because the psychological disciplines extended their reach and dis-
ciplined people directly in the process. Consider also the following:

- Sigmund Freud's construction of "masculine" libidinal instincts as those that are drawn toward women, and "feminine" instincts as those that are drawn toward men, to make sense of same-sex desires (see Lewes, 1988; O'Connor & Ryan, 1998)
- The psychologist Lewis Terman's development of personality measures of masculinity-femininity to detect boys who might grow up to be queer (Hegarty, 2013). Masculinity-femininity personality measures were repeatedly used in the following decades to detect and diagnose homosexuality as a mental illness until the 1970s, usually in men (Constantinople, 1973).
- Psychoanalyst Robert Stoller and others' development of the concept of *gender identity*, distinct from *gender*, to make sense of the demands of people in the 1960s—such as Agnes—who wished to have their bodies surgically altered to fit their genders, and to provide some grounds to discriminate between them (Meyerowitz, 2004).

Psychologists have had no small part in the binarizing and polarizing interpretation of human experience as instincts, personalities, identities, roles, hormones, and genitals that appear to *have* a gender. Such psychological systems also create forms of *marking* according to deviations from their norms; *nouns* that describe people who transgress the gender system often preceded nouns for those who do not. "Homosexuality" was around long before "heterosexuality" (Katz, 1996), and "transgender" before "cisgender" (see Ansara, 2010). Traces of disciplinary power are evident in the asymmetric ways that Minority World people interpret data about group differences. For example, gender differences are explained as being about women more than about men, "race" differences as being about non-White people more than about White people, and sexuality differences as being more about lesbians and gay men than heterosexual women and men (Hegarty & Bruckmüller, 2013).

Among the most successful reversals of this process of normalization are the depathologization of homosexuality and the many interventions of feminist psychology from the late 1960s until the present. From our nonbinary perspective, these developments have been uneven and some-times ambivalent. The extraordinarily successful affirmation of lesbian and gay adults and, subsequently, adults identified by themselves or others as bisexual by psychologists did little to address the ongoing pathologi-zation of people who were identified by themselves or others as trans-sexual, as transgender, or as having "gender identity disorder" for some time (Hegarty, 2017). Many influential feminist developments in psychol-ogy focused on gendered behaviors (including occupations, personality traits, and interests) but left the natural attitude to gender untouched. For example, research on usage of masculine terms (such as "he" and "man") as *masculine generics* addressed how those generics misgendered women, but such research was often conducted within a framework that presumed the gender binary (Ansara & Hegarty, 2013). The major shift in gender role theory in the early 1970s toward considering *androgynous* roles bet-ter, more healthy, and more adaptive (Bem, 1974; Spence, Helmreich, & Stapp, 1974) certainly weakened elements of the gender binary system. However, its primary theorist—Sandra Bem—always framed her thought within a logic that assumed that all men and women had a clearly defined "sex" that was determined by reproductive functions, grounding the gen-der binary once again (Bem, 2001; see also Unger, 1979). Rarely did femi-nist psychologists consider "sex" a construction to take on, and those who did—such as Kessler and McKenna (1978)— were largely ignored until the dramatically increased visibility of transgender movements in the 1990s (McKenna & Kessler, 2000).

When transgender activists did assert the case for more nuanced think-ing about sex and gender, many psychologists, including many feminist psychologists, found themselves long committed to incompatible and incommensurate paradigms (Parlee, 1996). Informed by queer and femi-nist thinking, Bem (1995) substantially rethought her assumptions about the gender binary, wondering if a proliferation of diverse genders that "turn the volume up" on gender identity might depolarize gender more than androgynous genders that "turned the volume down." Somewhat more affirmative perspectives on transgender people, which developed within American psychology in the 2000s, did so by expanding the auspices of lesbian, gay, and bisexual structures to "LGBT" structures rather than those oriented around the psychology of women or the psychology of men (American Psychological Association, 2009). Nonetheless, these moves are recent and have limits. Even in the 2000s, most psychologists writing about children who did not identify with the gender to which they were assigned at birth *misgendered* and *pathologized* such children. Moreover, those who did so remained the most highly cited authors of their time (Ansara & Hegarty, 2012).

Gender Binaries Are Culture Specific

Hitherto our discussion has focused on the societies where psychology as a Minority World discipline has been best represented—that is, those in the Minority World. The gender binaries in these societies not only contain contradictions but also are particular. Indeed, a phrase like "*the* gender binary" can suggest that there is only one such binary, and even that this societal binary is free of contradiction. Critical psychologists have long pointed out that such critiques of "society" do not go far enough; they do not take us very far beyond the assumption that conceptual systems cannot change because they are rooted in "nature" (see Henriques, Hollway, Urwin, Venn, & Walkerdine, 1984).

Nonbinary gender is also often characterized dismissively, as a recent or postmodern phenomenon, as part of the "Facebook gender revolution" (Richards, 2014) or the "last identity taboo" (Proctor, 2016). However, nonbinary gender identities and social roles only *appear* new. Globally, many cultures have always recognized more than two gender terms and/ or have regarded gender as a shifting social role or as a primarily functional category (Vincent & Manzano-Santaella, 2017).

For all of recorded human history, every continent has had societies with more than two genders (Morris, 1995). Some societies with only two traditional genders still recognized nonbinary gender in terms of a combination of two traditional genders and/or nongendered forms of being and/or expression. The Yorùbá people are one of the three largest ethnic groups in the contemporary Republic of Nigeria and also live in Benin. Some Yorùbán scholars have highlighted the problems with the ethnocentric assumption that the particular gender binary found in much of the Minority World or even the concept of "gender" at all applies to all African contexts. Such assumptions use the authors' own Minority World culture as a standard against which to conceptualize and evaluate other cultures. Oyèrónké Oyěwùmí (2011) critiqued the colonial ethnocentrism of this gender binary; she drew attention to how gender ideologies vary over time and across regions to promote gender equality. Oyěwùmí emphasized that Western constructions of gender as a timeless fact without regard to its particular historical genesis have erased both Yorùbán history and the value traditionally placed therein on nongendered categories and social relations. Nigerian sociologist Ifi Amadiume similarly critiqued the failure of Eurocentric scholars to identify and document traditional norms for nonbinary gender expression in some African contexts, noting that "the rigidity of the European gender system allows for only male and female" (2009, p. 112). Amadiume suggests an understanding that "in terms of social classification biological sex does not necessarily correspond to ideological gender. Depending on gender systems, men can be reclassified as females and vice versa" (Ibid.). Such gender classification and expression play out beyond the colonial gender binary, both in fluid movement between categories and gender expression beyond its confines. These forms of social organization and relations have been documented by Amadiume (1997, 2009), Semley (2011), Oyěwùmí (1997, 2011), and Nzegwu (2012). Oyěwùmí (1997, 2011) claims that "gender" itself is a European construct that cannot be applied to Yorùbán society. Nzegwu (2012) has provided evidence to suggest that Igbo society was nongendered prior to European colonialism. For this reason, Oyěwùmí (2011) asserts that recognizing nonbinary gender categories and interactions functions as a form of resistance to the ethnocentrism imposed by the colonialist gender binary.

Like binary genders, nonbinary genders may be stable and fixed or they may be fluid, changing over time or varying by context. Amadiume (1998) explored this fluidity of African gender ideologies in research on Igbo social relations. Amadiume explains how "gender" is viewed as fluid in some African societies, based more on the particular social role or function in which an individual is engaged than on any sense of fixed "identity." Thus, the existence of male daughters and female husbands has historically been viewed as traditional and normative. According to Oyěwùmí (2016), the Yorùbán understanding of motherhood is not a counterpart to fatherhood. The Minority World concept of "gender identity" based on binary opposites is radically different from this view of "gender" as based on functional utility in a given moment.

Multiple Majority World societies have viewed nonbinary people as possessing unique spiritual powers and societal roles. For example, in the Bugis society of Southern Sulawesi in Indonesia, the social category of holy people known as Bissu is one of five recognized genders. In the Bugis tradition, Bissu were viewed as having unique powers to protect Bugis royalty, military, and community. Bissu were frequently granted royal status. The elevated social position they occupied stemmed precisely from their nonbinary genders. Bissu were traditionally considered powerful due to their ability to shift between genders, to embody powers associated with multiple genders, and to reflect the nonbinary genders of early Bugis cosmology.

When Minority World scholars describe traditional nonbinary genders from cultures that have historically recognized more genders than women or men, misgendering can ensue. Minority World accounts of the Bissu are a case in point where "etic" schemes can override the value of "emic" constructions. Minority World researchers have described the Bissu as "transvestite priests" or even as "transsexual women," an inaccurate way of classifying people whose social role is predicated on transcendence of such binary expressions of gender. Graham (2007) notes that phrases like "transvestite priest" are inaccurate because Bissu wear distinctive clothing rather than wearing clothing associated with another gender. Instead of moving from an assigned gender into another gender, they combine all genders to constitute what Graham more suitably describes as "meta-gender."

CONCLUSIONS

In this chapter we have discussed social identity, mental health language, cognition, embodiment, history, and culture. Gender is intrinsic to all of these analyses and so too is the question of what nonbinary and binary gender systems do. A *nonbinary psychology* would not fit within one of psychology's subdisciplines but would work across all of them; nonbinary people—being people—exist and can be approached from many levels of analysis, whereas the gender binary system works silently to configure assumptions in all of psychology's subdisciplines. To undo the ethnocentric assumptions that there is *a* (singular) gender binary (that happens to be the Minority World version, of course) and to challenge the disciplinary power that locates difference in people who do not conform to social norms, it is useful to look at the work of anthropologist Mary Douglas (1966), who described five things that cultures do to people who do not fit their category systems, such as children born with "unusual" bodies:

- Reclassify them so they are no longer anomalous
- Eradicate them (as by killing them)
- Avoid contact with them wherever possible
- Categorize them as dangerous to "normal" people
- Incorporate them into myth and story as ways to access other levels of existence

Bem (1995) drew on Douglas (1966) in rethinking her assumptions about what might reduce gender polarization. Theologian Susannah Cornwall (2010) also returned to Douglas to consider how Christian theology does and does not recognize intersex and other forms of sexed embodiment. Not all of these responses are positive—most aren't, but there is widespread evidence for all of them. From the nonbinary people with poorer than average mental health in the United Kingdom and North America to the Bissu of Indonesia, nonbinary people may find their identities and social lives mediated around and by this limited range of options that Douglas (1966) described. No category system can make sense of human experience—least of all a category system that assumes that people *are* always simply one thing or the other, and that it is "natural" to think in such limited terms. Accordingly, a nonbinary psychology requires not a subdisciplinary approach, but a trans-disciplinary one, akin to the brico-lage technique of "moving to the margins" to consistently and persistently refuse the assumptions of this system of thought (Berry & Kincheloe, 2004; see also Frohard-Dourlent et al., 2016). There is scope and need for innovative work to undo the operations of gender binaries in psychology.

REFERENCES

Alam, S. (2008). Majority World: Challenging the West's rhetoric of democracy. *Amerasia Journal, 34*, 87–98.

Alderson, J., Madill, A., & Balen, A. (2004). Fear of devaluation: Understanding the experience of intersexed women with androgen insensitivity syndrome. *British Journal of Health Psychology, 9*, 81–100.

Amadiume, I. (1987). *Male daughters, female husbands: Gender and sex in an African society*. London, UK: Zed Books.

Amadiume, I. (1997). *Re-inventing Africa: Matriarchy, religion and culture*. New York, NY: St Martin's Press.

American Psychological Association (2009). Report of the APA task force on gender identity and gender variance. Washington, DC: American Psychological Association. Retrieved November 15, 2017, at https://www.apa.org/pi/lgbt/resources/policy/gender-identity-report.pdf.

Ansara, Y. G. (2010). Beyond cisgenderism: Counselling people with non-assigned gender identities. In L. Moon (Ed.), *Counselling ideologies: Queer challenges to heteronormativity* (pp. 167–200). Aldershot, UK: Ashgate.

Ansara, Y. G. (2012). Cisgenderism in medical settings: How collaborative partnerships can challenge structural violence. In I. Rivers & R. Ward (Eds.), *Out of the ordinary: Representations of LGBT lives* (pp. 102–122). Newcastle upon Tyne, UK: Cambridge Scholars Publishing.

Ansara, Y. G. (2015). Improving research methodology in adolescent sexual health research. *Journal of Adolescent Health, 56*, 367–369.

Ansara, Y. G. (2016a). Challenging cisgenderism in the ageing and aged care sector: Meeting the needs of older people of trans and/or non-binary experience. *Australasian Journal on Ageing, 34*(S2), 14–18.

Ansara, Y. G. (2016b). Making the count: Addressing data integrity gaps in Australian standards for collecting sex and gender information, March 4, 2016. Newtown, MA: National LGBTI Health Alliance. Retrieved January 16, 2016, at http://apo.org.au/node/64806.

Ansara, Y. G., & Hegarty, P. (2012). Cisgenderism in psychology: Pathologising and misgendering children from 1999 to 2008. *Psychology & Sexuality*, 3, 137–160.

Ansara, Y. G., & Hegarty, P. (2013). Misgendering in English language contexts: Applying non-cisgenderist methods to feminist research. *International Journal of Multiple Research Approaches*, 7, 160–177.

Ansara, Y. G., & Hegarty, P. (2014). Methodologies of misgendering: Recommendations for reducing cisgenderism in psychological research. *Feminism & Psychology*, 24, 259–270.

Barker, M. (2014). 57 genders (and none for me)? Reflections on the new Facebook gender categories. *Rewriting the rules*, February 15, 2014. Retrieved on June 13, 2014, at www.rewritingtherules.wordpress.com/2014/02/15/57-genders-and-none-for-me-reflections-on-the-new-facebook-gender-categories.

Barker, M. J. (2015). Depression and/or oppression? Bisexuality and mental health. *Journal of Bisexuality*, 15, 369–384.

Barker, M-J., & Lester, CN. (2015). *Non-binary gender factsheet*. Retrieved at www.rewriting-the-rules.com/resources-2/non-binary-gender-factsheet.

Barker, M. J., & Richards, C. (2015). Further genders. In C. Richards & M. Barker (Eds.), *Handbook of the psychology of sexuality and gender* (pp. 166–182). Basingstoke, UK: Palgrave Macmillan.

Barker, M., Richards, C., Jones, R., Bowes-Catton, H., & Plowman, T. (2012). *The Bisexuality Report: Bisexual inclusion in LGBT equality and diversity*. Milton Keynes: The Open University, Centre for Citizenship, Identity and Governance.

Belgrave, F., Reed, M., Plybon, L., Butler, D., Allison, K., & Davis, T. (2004, August). An evaluation of sisters of Nia: A cultural program for African American girls. *Journal of Black Psychology*, 30, 329–343.

Bem, S. L. (1974). The measurement of psychological androgyny. *Journal of Consulting and Clinical Psychology*, 42, 155–162.

Bem, S. L. (1995). Dismantling gender polarization and compulsory heterosexuality: Should we turn the volume down or up? *The Journal of Sex Research*, 32(4), 329–334.

Bem, S. L. (2001). *An unconventional family*. New Haven, CT: Yale University Press.

Bergman, S. B., & Barker, M-J. (2017). Activism. In C. Richards, W. Bouman, & M. J. Barker (Eds.), *Genderqueer and non-binary genders*. Basingstoke, UK: Palgrave Macmillan.

Berry, K. S., & Kincheloe, J. L. (2004). *Rigour and complexity in educational research: Conducting educational research*. Columbus, OH: Open University Press.

Beyond the Binary (2015). *#SpecificDetriment: what's your response?* September 15, 2015. Retrieved November 22, 2016, at www.beyondthebinary.co.uk/specificdetriment-whats-your-response.

Blumer, M. L. C., Ansara, Y. G., & Watson, C. M. (2013). Cisgenderism in family therapy: How everyday clinical practices can delegitimize people's gender self-designations. *Journal of Family Psychotherapy*, 24, 267–285.

Bornstein, K. (1994). *Gender outlaw: On women, men and the rest of us*. New York: Routledge.

Bowker, G. C., & Star, S. L. (1999). *Sorting things out: Classification and its consequences.* Cambridge, MA: MIT Press.

Braun, V., & Kitzinger, C. (2001a). Telling it straight? Dictionary definitions of women's genitals. *Journal of Sociolinguistics, 5,* 214–232.

Braun, V., & Kitzinger, C. (2001b). "Snatch," "hole," or "honey-pot?" Semantic categories and the problem of nonspecificity in female genital slang. *Journal of Sex Research, 38,* 146–158.

Brisbane, L. (2015). Why Miley Cyrus and Ruby Rose are embracing "gender fluidity." *The Evening Standard,* June 22, 2015. Retrieved August 10, 2015, at www.standard.co.uk/lifestyle/london-life/why-miley-cyrus-and-ruby-rose-are-embracing-gender-fluidity-10335949.html.

Butler, J. (1993). *Bodies that matter: On the discursive limits of "sex."* New York, NY: Routledge.

Cole, E. R. (2009). Intersectionality and research in psychology. *American Psychologist, 64,* 170–180.

Constantinople, A. (1973). Masculinity-femininity. An exception to a famous dictum? *Psychological Bulletin, 80,* 398–407.

Cornwall, S. (2010). *Sex and uncertainty in the body of Christ: Intersex conditions and Christian theology.* London, UK: Equinox.

Davis, G. (2015). *Contesting intersex: The dubious diagnosis.* New York, NY: NYU Press.

Douglas, M. (1966). *Purity and danger: An analysis of the concepts of pollution and taboo.* London, UK: Routledge & Kegan Paul.

Feder, E. K. (2014). *Making sense of intersex: Changing ethical perspectives in biomedicine.* Bloomington, IN: Indiana University Press.

Ford, T. (2015). My life without gender. *The Guardian,* August 7, 2015. Retrieved August 10, 2015, at www.theguardian.com/world/2015/aug/07/my-life-without-gender-strangers-are-desperate-to-know-what-genitalia-i-have.

Frohard-Dourlent, H., Dobson, S., Clark, B. A., Doull, M., & Saewyc, E. M. (2016). "I would have preferred more options": Accounting for non-binary youth in health research. *Nursing Inquiry, 24,* e12150.

Foucault, M. (1977). *Discipline and punish: The birth of the prison.* New York, NY: Pantheon Books.

Garfinkel, H. (1967). *Studies in ethnomethodology.* Cambridge, UK: Polity Press.

Glucksberg, S., & Keysar, B. (1990). Understanding metaphorical comparisons: Beyond similarity. *Psychological Review, 97,* 3–18.

Graham, S. (2007, July 30). Sulawesi's fifth gender. Retrieved from http://www.insideindonesia.org/sulawesis-fifth-gender-2. Retrieved 26 July, 2017.

Harrison, J., Grant, J., & Herman, J. L. (2012). *A gender not listed here: Genderqueers, gender rebels, and otherwise in the National Transgender Discrimination Survey.* Los Angeles, CA: eScholarship, University of California.

Hegarty, P. (2013). *Gentlemen's disagreement: Alfred Kinsey, Lewis Terman, and the sexual politics of smart men.* Chicago, IL: University of Chicago Press.

Hegarty, P. (2017). *From homophobia to LGBT: A recent history of lesbian and gay psychology.* London, UK: Routledge.

Hegarty, P., & Bruckmüller, S. (2013). Asymmetric explanations of group differences: Experimental evidence of Foucault's disciplinary power. *Social and Personality Psychology Compass*, 7, 176–186.

Hegarty, P., Mollin, S., & Foels, R. (2016). Binomial word order and social status. In A. M. Howard Giles (Ed.), *Advances in intergroup communication* (pp. 119–135). New York, NY: Peter Lang.

Henriques, J., Hollway, W., Urwin, C., Venn, C., & Walkerdine, V. (1984). *Changing the subject. Psychology, social regulation and subjectivity*. London, UK: Methuen.

Hill, D. B., & Willoughby, B. L. B. (2005). The development and validation of the Genderism and Transphobia Scale. *Sex Roles*, 53(7–8), 531–544.

Iantaffi, A., & Bockting, W. O. (2011). Views from both sides of the bridge? Gender, sexual legitimacy and transgender people's experiences of relationships. *Culture, Health & Sexuality*, 13(3), 355–370.

Joel, D., Tarrasch, R., Berman, Z., Mukamel, M., & Ziv, E. (2013). Queering gender: Studying gender identity in "normative" individuals. *Psychology & Sexuality*, 5(4), 291–321.

Jordan-Young, R. M. (2012). Hormones, context, and "Brain gender": A review of evidence from congenital adrenal hyperplasia. *Social Science & Medicine*, 74(11), 1731–1738.

Karkazis, K. (2008). *Fixing sex: Intersex, medical authority and lived experience*. Durham, NC: Duke University Press.

Katz, J. N. (1996). *The invention of heterosexuality*. New York, NY: Plume.

Kessler, S. (1990). The medical construction of gender: Case management of intersexed infants. *Signs*, 16, 3–26.

Kessler, S., & McKenna, W. (1978). *Gender: An ethnomethodological approach*. Chicago, IL: University of Chicago Press.

Laqueur, T. (1990). *Making sex: Body and gender from the Greeks to Freud*. Cambridge, MA: Harvard University Press.

Lewes, K. (1988). *The psychoanalytic theory of male homosexuality*. New York, NY: Simon & Schuster.

McCrae, C. N., & Martin, D. (2007). A boy primed Sue: Feature-based processing and person construal. *European Journal of Social Psychology*, 37, 793–805.

McKenna, W., & Kessler, S. J. (2000). Retrospective response. *Feminism & Psychology*, 10(1), 66–72.

McNeil, J., Bailey, L., Ellis, S., Morton, J., & Regan, M. (2012). *Trans mental health study 2012*. Retrieved June 13, 2014, at http://www.scottishtrans.org.

METRO Youth Chances (2014). *Youth chances summary of first findings: The experiences of LGBTQ young people in England*. London, UK: METRO.

Meyerowitz, J. (2004). *How sex changed: A history of transsexuality in the United States*. Cambridge, MA: Harvard University Press.

Morris, R. C. (1995). All made up: Performance theory and the New Anthropology of sex and gender. *Annual Review of Anthropology*, 24, 567–592.

Norton, A. T., & Herek, G. M. (2013). Heterosexuals' attitudes toward transgender people: Findings from a national probability sample of U.S. adults. *Sex Roles*, 68(11–12), 738–753.

Nursing Inquiry (2016). Beyond gender binaries: Call for manuscripts. Retrieved November 11, 2016, at http://bit.ly/1Dw1SAp.

Nzegwu, N. (2012). *Family matters: Feminist concepts in African philosophy of culture.* Albany, NY: SUNY Press.

O'Connor, N., & Ryan, J. (1998). *Wild desires and mistaken identities.* London, UK: Virago.

Oyěwùmí, O. (1997). *The invention of women: Making an African sense of Western gender discourses.* Minneapolis, MN: University of Minnesota Press.

Oyěwùmí, O. (2011). *Gender epistemologies in Africa: gendering traditions, spaces, social institutions, and identities.* New York, NY: Palgrave Macmillan.

Oyěwùmí, O. (2016). *What gender is motherhood?: Changing* Yorùbá *ideals of power, procreation, and identity in the age of modernity.* New York, NY: Palgrave Macmillan.

Parlee, M. (1996). Situated knowledges of personal embodiment: Transgender activists' and psychological theorists' perspectives on "sex" and "gender." *Theory & Psychology, 6,* 625–645.

Prentice, D. A., & Miller, D. T. (2007). Psychological essentialism of human categories. *Current Directions in Psychological Science, 16,* 202–206.

Preves, S. E. (2003). *Intersex and identity: The contested self.* New Brunswick, NJ: Rutgers University Press.

Proctor, L. (Producer) (2016). *Beyond binary.* Radio 4, May 20, 2016. Retrieved Novemer 22, 2016, at http://www.bbc.co.uk/programmes/b07btlmk.

Reis, E. (2009). *Bodies in doubt: An American history of intersex.* Baltimore, MA: Johns Hopkins University Press.

Richards, S. E. (2014). Facebook's gender labeling revolution. *Time Magazine,* February 19, 2014. Retrieved November 22, 2016, at http://time.com/8856/facebooks-gender-labeling-revolution.

Richards, C., Bouman, W. P., Seal, L., Barker, M. J., Nieder, T. O, & T'Sjoen, G. (2016). Non-binary or genderqueer genders. *International Review of Psychiatry, 28*(1), 95–102.

Riggs, D. W., Ansara, G. Y., & Treharne, G. J. (2015). An evidence-based model for understanding the mental health experiences of transgender Australians. *Australian Psychologist, 50,* 32–39.

ScottishTrans.org (2016). *UK non-binary survey.* Retrieved November 22, 2016, at www.scottishtrans.org/our-work/research/uk-non-binary-survey.

Semley L. D. (2011). *Mother is gold, father is glass: Gender and colonialism in a Yoruba town.* Bloomington, IN: Indiana University Press.

Spence, J. T., Helmreich, R. L., & Stapp, J. (1974). The Personal Attributes Questionnaire: A measure of sex-role stereotypes and masculinity-femininity. *JSAS Catalogue of Selected Documents in Psychology, 4,* 1–44.

Suitner, C., & Maass, A. (2016). Spatial agency bias: Representing people in space. *Advances in Experimental Social Psychology, 53,* 245–301.

Tajfel, H., & Turner, J. C. (1986). The social identity theory of intergroup behavior. In S. Worchel & W. G. Austin (Eds.), *Psychology of intergroup relations* (pp. 7–24). Chicago, IL: Nelson-Hall.

Tee, N., & Hegarty, P. (2006). Predicting opposition to the civil rights of trans persons in the United Kingdom. *Journal of Community & Applied Social Psychology, 16*, 70–80.

Titman, N. (2014). *How many people in the United Kingdom are nonbinary?* Retrieved October 8, 2015, at www.practicalandrogyny.com/2014/12/16/how-many-people-in-the-uk-are-nonbinary.

Unger, R. K. (1979). Toward a redefinition of sex and gender. *American Psychologist, 34*, 1085–1094.

Valentine, V. (2016). Specific detriment: A survey into non-binary people's experiences in the UK. Presentation to the Moving Beyond the Binaries of Sex and Gender conference, University of Leeds, March 22, 2016.

Vincent, B. W. (2016). *Non-binary gender identity negotiations: Interactions with queer communities and medical practice.* Unpublished PhD thesis, University of Leeds.

Vincent, B., & Erikainen, S. (2016). *Moving beyond the binaries of sex and gender: Non-binary identities, bodies, and discourses.* University of Leeds conference, March 22, 2016. Conference booklet accessed from www.gires.org.uk/pdfs/Conference%20Booklet.pdf.

Vincent, B. W., & Manzano-Santaella, A. (2017). History and cultural diversity. In C. Richards, W. Bouman, & M-J. Barker (Eds.), *Genderqueer and non-binary genders.* Basingstoke, UK: Palgrave Macmillan.

Wertheim, M. (1997). *Pythagoras' trousers: God, physics and the gender war.* New York, NY: Norton.

Wilkie, J. E. B., & Bodenhausen, G. V. (2012). Are numbers gendered? *Journal of Experimental Psychology: General, 141*, 206–210.

Winter, S., Webster, B., & Cheung, P. K. E. (2008). Measuring Hong Kong undergraduate students' attitudes towards trans people. *Sex Roles, 59*, 670–683.

4

On Being and Becoming
Female and Male

A Sex-Neutral Evolutionary Perspective

PATRICIA ADAIR GOWATY

This chapter introduces a new way to think about the evolution of behavioral sex differences, one that contrasts with the classical evolutionary view. The classical scenario—sex as destiny—holds that key sex differences in behavior are fixed (invariant) traits of an individual, because innate sex "roles" evolved in concert with morphology and genes are "the blueprints" for expressed behavior. In a recently developed evolutionary theory (mating theory; Gowaty & Hubbell, 2009), such genetically deterministic behavior is very often maladaptive, selecting against individuals with fixed gendered behavior. From this new perspective, "sex is destiny" is a myth. The conclusion from this updated theory is that whenever environments vary, the most evolutionarily successful individuals will be flexible in their behavior. This new way of thinking prioritizes the ecological constraints and opportunities that *individuals* experience throughout their lifetimes. On this view, individuals—regardless of membership in a genetically defined or anatomically defined sex category—are always "becoming," sometimes behaving in ways we consider "female typ-ical" and sometimes in ways we consider "male typical." Thinking this way shifts the study of the evolution of behavioral sex differences, providing a new lens through which to view linkages between research in biology and in psychology.

In this chapter, you will learn about the structure of the classical evo-lutionary argument for fixed sex differences and the structure of the new evolutionary argument for individuals who constantly evaluate and flexibly respond to the circumstances they experience. You will learn some history and vocabulary associated with evolutionary rea-soning. You will learn about the logic of and evidence bearing on the classical and new theories. The chapter is meant to pique your interest and enhance your ability to engage critically with the sweep of evolu-tionary logic and with the science of the evolutionary origins of sex differences in behavior.

ON BECOMING

The title of this chapter announces its conclusion: Being gendered is a lifelong *process of becoming*. Adaptive individuals can be flexible through a lifetime. Being female or male is not necessarily or always or even commonly a static aspect of being, not a binary "trait" fixed at birth. Behaving in ways typical of females or males, or typical of both, or typical of neither, expresses a developmental (ontogenetic) process of continually becoming: Ecological and social contexts continually affect development—from cradle to grave. Accordingly, individuals may be far more flexible in their adaptive behavioral and physiological expression— their gendered behavior and physiology—than many biologists have assumed or predicted.

Few ideas provoke as much ire, frustration, and outright derision as do the classical views of the evolutionary origins of sex differences in behav-ior, but the irritation is not the point of this chapter. Understanding is. To that end, the chapter reviews the following key concepts:

- the nature of selection hypotheses and the relationship of selection to evolution;
- the ways in which information transfers between generations—that is, how heredity can work;
- the classical evolutionary view of sex differences in behavior, and its flaws;
- and a theorem (the switch point theorem) for the origins of sex differences in behavior that is fully evolutionary while being also fully sociological (embedded in social circumstances) and fully psychological (dependent on sensitivities to stimuli and cognition), yielding a view of behavior as environmentally contingent, individually based (rather than determined by morphology or sex), and flexible.

Herein a distinction is made between *proximate* and *ultimate* causes. These terms refer to different kinds of questions that one can ask about the same *phenotypic* traits. When evolutionary biologists talk about *how* a phenomenon develops and expresses, they are referring to *proximate* causes; when they talk about *why* it exists, they are referring to *ultimate* causes.

Some Things About Some Males and Females Are Different

The arguments in this chapter do not take exception to what is commonly observed: The sharing of gametes—sperm and eggs—is an essential element of reproduction in species that only reproduce sexually (as opposed to only reproducing asexually). Humans, up to this time at least, reproduce "sexually" in the sense that to produce offspring to whom they are genetically related, "two must tangle"—that is, share their gametes—to create a zygote, which is the first stage in the developmental process of becoming a human. Human individuals are "diploid," meaning that each of us had an egg-producing parent and a sperm-producing parent. Both parents are necessary because in the particular domain of creating a new human being, there is a great difference in what people can do: Only people bearing XY sex chromosomes ("genetic males") can produce sperm (though some do not), and only people bearing XX sex chromosomes ("genetic females") can produce ova and gestate a baby (though some do not), and internal gestation remains necessary for a human to be born. However, a female *gender identity* (e.g., as a woman, *mujer, nǔrén*, etc.) is not necessary to bear a child: Transgender female-to-male persons have given birth. Constraints on lactation are slightly less dramatic: Lactation is common after parturition among genetic females, and genetic male humans can—with new reproductive technologies—be hormonally induced to lactate. After all, a universal of human morphology is that people have breasts. The *potential* for genetic males to lactate just is not expressed in usual circumstances.

Some other changes are less likely. For instance, a transgender male-to-female person could only give birth with extraordinary medical interventions. Mechanisms of *physiology* that tend to differ between genetic females and males are mutable via hormone injections or pills. *Morphology* is mutable but with even more invasive interventions such as castration or plastic surgery. These kinds of intervention notwithstanding, it is unlikely that a transgender male-to-female person will ever easily produce ova or that a transgender female-to-male person will produce sperm. In any scenario, either will likely remain exceedingly rare.

Despite these impediments to complete flexibility in every aspect of sex, our discussion so far makes the point that even most of what seem to be the most fundamental or "essential" traits of maleness and femaleness coexist within an individual and can change during an individual's lifetime in our species and in many others (Crews, 2012; Fausto-Sterling, 2012; Morris, Jordan, & Breedlove, 2004; Roughgarden, 2013).

There also are aspects of being female and male that are totally, unabashedly flexible, particularly in the domain of *behavior*. Ovulating and ejaculating sperm are hormonally organized and constrained in remarkable ways; they are the exception rather than the rule. Consider a few of the myriad *motor acts* (i.e., behavior) of which humans are capable: walking, talking, playing soccer, teaching, reading, dancing, tending crops, shooting a gun, playing mahjong, speaking multiple languages, negotiating treaties, arguing a case as a barrister, caring for a sick child, or being

Prime Minister of Pakistan. It is difficult to imagine a behavioral skill that cannot be improved with training for any person no matter what her/his/their genetic sex is or what sex was assigned at birth. This sensitivity to opportunity and experience speaks to our abilities to be flexible individuals capable of extreme changes in a single lifetime. Yet many behavioral options are closed for some because of what feminists have identified as a prejudice, a *perception bias*, called "the double standard." Critics rightly have argued that many behavioral sex differences, rather than being rooted in genetically deterministic, fixed limitations, are rooted in the psychology and sociology of gender prejudice (Fausto-Sterling, 2000, 2012).

The next section concerns how evolutionary biologists think about causes and elements in the theory of evolution by natural selection. Then we tackle a classical evolutionary hypothesis that transformed the double standard into a scientific claim of evolved, immutable, sex differences in behavior. Finally, a mathematical equation—the switch point theorem—derived from formal mating theory is described; it says that individual behavioral flexibility is crucial for individuals' evolutionary success and, as such, provides an alternative to the classical theory.

A Primer on Thinking Like an Evolutionary Biologist

THE NATURE OF SELECTION HYPOTHESES

Artificial selection (Darwin, 1859) is a sorting process analogous to the sorting processes that you are familiar with if you are interested, for instance, in the origin of dog breeds. An example is dog breeders who increase the likelihood of producing puppies with certain traits when they control who mates with whom. If the breeders pick parents whose tail is congenitally crooked, the likelihood that their puppies will have a crooked tail increases. This process is known as *selective breeding* (Darwin, 1859), and it is a type of selection that depends on the action of humans. Another example is agriculturalists who use selective breeding to enhance the qualities of crop plants or livestock. Humans have been practicing selective breeding for over 10,000 years. Selective breeding works so well so

often because it is a rule of nature that "offspring resemble their parents."
Darwin used the term "artificial" as a contrast with "natural" selection,
but perhaps "human facilitated selection" is an even better term. Humans,
after all, are part of nature, not separated from it, and all selection is selection, whether people do it to dogs or slave-making ants (e.g. *Polyergus
lucidus*) do it to other species of ants.

In *natural selection*, in contrast, no person acts. Natural selection just
happens, and it has been happening since the dawn of life on Earth.
Charles Darwin's (1859) genius was to realize how the process of natural selection occurs. He figured out that (1) as long as the individuals in
a population (of members of the same species) of any living things varied in heritable traits, and (2) as long as environments—either social or
ecological—impacted (3) the survival or reproductive success of individuals in the population because of their heritable trait variants, then natural
selection will occur. Therefore, whenever we encounter hypotheses of natural selection, we must think about these three important things:

- First, do individuals in a population vary in heritable traits?
- Second, do social or ecological circumstances affect individuals
  because of their traits?
- Third, do individuals with some traits have longer life spans or more
  surviving offspring than other individuals because of their heritable
  trait variants?

If we are able to show these three things, as well as a positive correlation
between the similarities of children to their parents, we can conclude that
natural selection has occurred and that evolution—a change in trait frequencies between generations—has occurred.

To make the above description general and to demonstrate the utility
and flexibility of selection hypotheses, we can characterize the assumptions of selection hypotheses in another, more general, way (Gowaty, 2011,
2014). The first assumption is about the level at which selection operates.
You may: focus on individuals in populations (*individual selection*); narrow your attention to genes in related individuals (*kin selection*); or widen

your attention to groups within populations (*group selection*). With your choice, you are characterizing *the units of organization at which the heritable variation resides* and which may be sorted by selection. The second assumption concerns the *mechanisms by which selection among the units occurs*. For natural selection, any one of thousands of features of the social and ecological circumstances in which individuals live may favor or disfavor some individuals because of their trait variants. The third assumption specifies the *components of fitness* on which selection acts. Individuals are favored or disfavored only on the basis of their fitness; moreover, "fitness is relative," meaning that raw survival or raw numbers of offspring do not indicate one's fitness because fitness is always relative to others in the population. Components of fitness can be characterized in coarse or fine terms: Staying alive is a key fitness measure. Number of mates is another component of fitness. Other components of fitness also fall in the category of "reproductive success," which investigators estimate using a variety of measures such as the number of eggs laid or fertilized, of offspring born, or of offspring that survive to reproductive age, or the percentage of eggs surviving to adulthood (a measure of parents' likelihood of having grandchildren). Having high fitness means having longer lives or more offspring than others in the population.

Sexual Selection Is a Kind of Natural Selection

Under the broad heading of natural selection, the concept of *sexual selection* (Darwin, 1859, 1871) focuses on processes through which individuals in sexually reproducing species have differential access to mates (egg producers for sperm producers, and sperm producers for egg producers). In this context, "female" refers to egg producers and "male" refers to sperm producers. Sexual selection is a concept that many evolutionary biologists think explains sex differences in behavior. Now you will learn to cast your own sexual selection hypotheses. You need to assert the three assumptions (Gowaty, 2011, 2014): one about the level of selection, one about the mechanism(s) by which the trait variants in the level of selection are favored or disfavored (i.e., selected, sorted), and another about the components of fitness through which the mechanisms of selection operate. In sexual selection, the level of selection is *within-sex within a population*, that is, among males in a population or among females in a population. The mechanisms are limited to *intersexual interactions* (between different-sex individuals) or to *intrasexual interactions* (between same-sex individuals). Usually the selective forces are via "mate preferences" that individuals have for different-sex individuals or competitive interactions that occur between same-sex rivals. So mate preferences indicate affiliative interactions that can produce a selection pressure that sorts among same-sex individuals on the basis of their behavior toward potential mates. Male-male or female-female competitive interactions like fights are agonistic interactions, and these too can produce selection pressures among males when males fight over access to mates or otherwise compete or among females when females fight over access to mates or otherwise compete.

Two things should be apparent: First, the selection in sexual selection happens within a sex. That is, selection sorts same-sex individuals on the basis of trait variants. Second, the mechanisms that exert selective pressure are social interactions either of mate choice (between different-sex individuals) or of competitive interactions (between same-sex individuals). That means that sexual selection happens only within a population of interacting individuals, not between individuals in different populations. With respect to fitness components, biologists thinking about sexual selection usually posit that the mechanisms act on within-sex trait variants via the effects of mate choice or same-sex competition on variation in *number* of mates or the *quality* of mates that individuals of the sex under selection have. Those thinking about sexual selection then posit that individuals in the sex under selection have a greater number of mates or better quality mates (Altmann, 1997), either of which may increase individual reproductive success.

Keep in mind that both sexes can be under sexual selection at the same time. Just because one sex is experiencing selection does not mean the individuals in the other sex could not also be under sexual selection, too. For example, an important component of sexual selection relative to mate choice is that the interaction between different-sex individuals has potential fitness effects on both of them. Most evolutionary biologists have been interested in what happens with male-male sexual selection vis-à-vis the relative fitness of males (Arnold, 1994; Bateman, 1948). They have paid far less attention to female-female sexual selection vis-à-vis the relative fitness of females. The mechanism of mate choice is actually about sexual selection among the females in a population as well as selection among the males in a population. You should practice making simultaneous arguments about females and males who interact and how those interactions could affect sexual selection among females *and* among males; you also should practice looking for such arguments wherever you read claims about sexual selection in the literature.

SEXUAL CONFLICT IS SEXUAL SELECTION ACTING JOINTLY ON TWO SEXES

Sexual conflict is a theoretically difficult topic in modern evolutionary biology. Sexual conflict occurs when the fitness interests of the sexes conflict (Gowaty, 2018b). Take, for example, sexual assault in which a man attempts to kiss a woman or grope her genitals, or even copulate with her against her will. The calculation of who is a winner and a loser *in evolutionary terms* is challenging for more than one reason. To start, dealing with this issue demands of us the ability and willingness to distinguish our consideration of whether an assaultive interaction confers any within-sex fitness advantage or disadvantage ("winning" and "losing" as formal evolutionary terms) from our consideration of the psychological, moral, and legal dimensions of behavior—dimensions that can lead to quite different connotations of "winning" and "losing." We don't need a neat resolution among those meanings. We do benefit from understanding how the meanings shift depending on their conceptual context.

Assuming we come to grips with what *winning* and *losing* mean in the context of evolutionary theory, we can turn to how sexual conflict is about sexual selection within each sex (Gowaty, 2010)—specifically, the *within-sex* variation in fitness that occurs when one woman is raped and one man is the rapist. The questions that *sexual selection* raises are as follows: (1) Is the rapist a winner *among other males* in a population (e.g., has more offspring, lives longer), including those who do and do not rape? (2) Is the raped woman a loser (e.g., has fewer offspring, shorter lifetime) *among other females* in a population, including those who are sexually assaulted and those who are not?

These, of course, are much harder questions to answer than the psychological, moral, and legal questions we usually ask. I bring up these questions in sexual selection to make two points. One is the fact that what happens in our legal system may be a poor guide to answering questions of how behavior affects *fitness* (a relative measure of reproductive success or survival that varies between 0 and 1). The second is that in either mate choice or sexual conflict, there are two questions: One is about *female fitness relative to other females* in the population, and one is about *male fitness relative to other males* in the population. Both of these questions fall under sexual selection.

MECHANISMS OF INHERITANCE

Evolution by natural selection and sexual selection occurs whenever the trait variants sorted by selection are *heritable*. Offspring inherit the traits of their parents via several mechanisms (Jablonka, Lamb, & Zeligowski, 2014). We sometimes call these mechanisms of inheritance *mechanisms of information transfer between generations*. *Genes* are perhaps most familiar. Genes are functional base-pair sequences within DNA inherited from our genetic parents. It turns out that there are other important ways for us to inherit traits from our parents. *Epigenetic processes*—chemical modifications to alleles on chromosomes—affect "gene regulation," which means that just because we have a gene does not mean that it expresses. Epigenetic effects determine whether a gene is "turned on"—actively expressing—or "turned off," as though it were not there. Importantly, epigenetic modifications are common throughout the life span of humans and other animals, and are *environmentally induced* (e.g., through "maternal effects," through teaching and learning, and through stress or diet or even air pollution; Salk & Hyde, 2012; Schagdarsurengin & Steger, 2016), and in some cases are *heritable*. Developmental variation, including many of the changes experienced during puberty, is the result of epigenetic changes in our DNA: Ecological forces induce many of these epigenetic effects.

Mechanisms of heredity also exist above the cellular level. *Behavior* is another mechanism of information transfer between and within generations—and therefore is a mechanism of heredity. You no doubt gained new skill traits by mimicking your elders, or watching others, or being trained to play a musical instrument. Another mechanism of heredity—of information transfer between and within generations—is associated with our *symbolic communications*, such as oral and written histories. In other words, many mechanisms of information transfer between generations can produce "heritable traits" on which natural selection can occur to produce evolutionary change—differential trait frequencies between generations. If traits are not somehow heritable, selection will not produce evolution or, as Darwin called it, "descent with modification."

Proximate and Ultimate Causes

For generations, biologists spoke at cross-purposes, often confusing themselves and each other, and sometimes fighting over "the cause" of this or that trait. Along the way, consensus arose so that biologists realized that *how* and *why* questions are different, complementary questions about biological phenomena. *Proximate causes* are those that answer the "how" questions, providing the mechanistic ways that traits work. So, for example, a gene that influences trait expression is a partial answer to *how* the trait expresses. Hormones that at puberty cause breast development, for example, are proximate explanations for how breasts change during the teen years, how breasts change during pregnancy and lactation, and how breast tissue and breast shape change with menopause. The hormonal variation that occurs over a lifetime gives us an answer to the *mechanistic* question of *how* breasts change. *Ultimate causes* are those that answer the "why" questions about the *function* of a trait, which is usually a guess about the benefit of traits arising by natural selection. A trait may arise by chance, for example. Or processes of selection producing adaptive advantage or disadvantage may answer the why question of the cause of a trait.

Excellent resources for further understanding of the mutable proximate causes of gendered behavior—that is, the *mechanistic* bases of how sex differences and similarities arise—are the works of Anne Fausto-Sterling

(2000, 2012) and Melissa Hines's *Brain Gender* (2005; see also Chapter 11). This chapter concerns the *ultimate* causes and the *functional significance* of traits. The goal is to explore the *why* questions of the evolutionary origins of behavioral sex differences and similarities. I first delve into classical sociobiological explanations for sex differences in behavior, and then I contrast those classical ideas and their predictions with ideas and predictions from the switch point theorem (Gowaty & Hubbell, 2009, 2010, 2012, 2013).

THE CLASSICAL SOCIOBIOLOGICAL ARGUMENT FOR THE ORIGINS OF SEX DIFFERENCES IN BEHAVIOR

The classical argument centers on morphological differences between the sexes that some believe to be essential sex differences (but probably are not; Gorelick, Carpinone, & Derraugh, 2016). The argument has the form "Sex differences predict sex differences." This argument is correlational and inductive—that is, the argument does not have the strong form of hypothetico-deduction, in which an hypothesis depends entirely on its assumptions. In other words the assumptions of a hypothetico-deductive hypothesis form the hypothesis.

The classic argument starts with the idea that genetic females and males have different costs of reproduction (COR), which results in selection for differential reproductive decision making and associated behaviors in females and males. There are two related ideas. The first idea is the evolution of gamete size asymmetries, that is, *anisogamy* (Parker, Baker, & Smith, 1972). Anisogamy refers to the differences between ova and sperm in morphological size and motility, the evolution of which set the stage for the evolution of sex differences in being *choosy* or *indiscriminate* about mating. In most sexual organisms, sperm are very small compared to ova, suggesting that more parental resources are needed to produce one egg compared to one sperm. The argument from anisogamy is that females produced relatively large, immobile ova, whereas males produced many small, mobile sperm. The ova, it was said, emphasized the accumulation of resources that would later be the source of nutrients for any developing zygote. The small, agile sperm, it was said, emphasized sperm-sperm rivalry over access to the resource-rich ova.

The originators of the anisogamy argument proved mathematically that the differences in gamete size and morphology could indeed lead to *disruptive selection* on gamete sizes. The authors then made another, less formal *ad hoc* inference and said that these gamete differences—differences associated with the roles of ova-providing resources and of sperm competing over access to the resource-accruing ova—produced selection favoring "choosy" behavior in the ova-producing sex (females) and "indiscriminate" behavior in the sperm-producing sex (males). And thus, some say, choosy females and indiscriminate males have existed ever since. The selection idea justifying choosy females and indiscriminate males was a correlational add-on to the original mathematically deduced anisogamy argument for the evolution of *morphological* differences in gamete sizes. In other words, the association of choosy and indiscriminate mating *behavior* with gamete size was not part of the mathematical argument that described how disruptive selection on gamete sizes would come about. It was a qualitative *ad hoc* statement.

The second COR idea—*parental investment* (Trivers, 1972)—came from observations of mammals like us. When a female copulates, she risks having to gestate a fetus for some time (in humans about 9 months), and then she begins lactation and nursing of slowly developing (*altricial*) babies. Even after lactation has ended, mammal mothers often must care for offspring for years. In contrast, when a male copulates, he risks the energetic costs of producing sperm, getting a female to allow copulation, and ejaculating sperm—a relatively small cost compared to females. These sex differences in COR became the justification for two companion ideas: Sexual selection among females, who have "more to lose" from a copulation than males typically do, will favor females who are choosy, coy, and relatively chaste in their mating behavior. In contrast, sexual selection among males, who have less to lose from choosing poor-quality mates than females typically do, will favor males who are indiscriminate, competitive, and profligate in their mating behavior.

Like most natural selection arguments, both COR ideas have three assumptions: First, they assume that within populations, there was between-individual variation in heritable traits—say, in this case, behavioral tendencies to be choosy or indiscriminate about mating. Second, they assume that differences between individuals in the cost of reproduction had fitness consequences—specifically, that choosy males were selected against because less choosy males had more mates, or indiscriminate females were selected against because they mated with males with whom they were unlikely to produce high-quality offspring. In this hypothetical example of selection in action, the males most likely to produce the most offspring were those who were indiscriminate and mated with as many females as possible, and the females who were most likely to produce the highest quality offspring—the ones most likely to survive and have offspring who then also had offspring—were those that were choosy. In that regard, the flow of assumptions and their predictions seem to make good evolutionary sense. But it makes good evolutionary sense only if we can in real time see the work of selection. In fact, in most cases it is very hard to see selection in action even in naturalistic field observations and in laboratory experiments unless an observer can demonstrate the veracity of all three assumptions.

These ideas make so much sense to some readers that they suspect that past selection associated with anisogamy and parental investment honed and mostly eliminated the original within-sex variation in choosy and indiscriminate behavior. Such readers "believe" that almost invariably males are indiscriminate and females choosy. For them, the ideas are proof enough. *But that is not how science works.* Put aside—for the moment—the problem that these two ideas seem like a good excuse for the double standard, something that may say quite a lot about why these ideas blossomed after 1950 (see Gowaty, 2018). Science demands sound evidence. In the case of selection arguments, one must try to demonstrate all three links in the syllogism of selection. Without that, one only has correlation, and as you know, correlation is not causation. And, as you will shortly see, there are alternative hypotheses that we must consider in any quest to understand sex differences and similarities in behavior.

The linchpin in the classical argument about the origin of sex differences in reproductive behavior was a mid-20th-century paper by Angus J. Bateman (1948), who reported a huge experiment using 65 different small populations of fruit flies (*Drosophila melanogaster*). Bateman predicted that in these small populations, males would have more variation in their numbers of mates than females and that males with more mates would have more offspring; as a consequence, the number of offspring would be more variable among males than among females. This pattern would imply that evolutionary potential was greater in males than in females. Finally, he also predicted that the overall number of offspring would depend more on number of mates for males than for females.

Robert Trivers (1972), the originator of the parental investment idea, made Bateman's 1948 paper—and "Bateman's principles"—famous. And many modern investigators claim that their data are consistent with Bateman's principles. For them, sex differences in the dependence of reproductive success on numbers of mates explain why males act as randy, indiscriminate cads and females as coy, choosy "gold diggers." They are persuaded that the answer to our gendered mate choices resides entirely with Bateman-like sex differences in variability in fitness, with females being more similar to each other in reproductive success than are males. That belief, coupled with the evolutionary tenet of selection acting on heritable variability, leads to the conclusion that males continue to evolve far more than do females. Males, then it is said, are more powerful in evolution than females, according to this line of reasoning.

Fitness variation does generally seem to be greater in males than in females, and greater variation in number of offspring does appear to be associated with greater variation in number of mates for males than for females. The veracity of these results in terms of the classical model depends, however, on whether its assumptions are met in studies of sex differences in the dependence of number of offspring on *number* of mates. What if female-female sexual selection is not over number of mates, but *quality* of mates? If that were so, the appropriate analysis is not of sex differences in the association of *number* of mates with reproductive success. The appropriate analysis requires investigation, for each sex separately, of the relevant fitness components—that is, *components of fitness in females* hypothetically associated with the mechanisms of *sexual selection among females*, and the *components of fitness in males* hypothetically associated with mechanisms of *sexual selection among males*. Note that these suggested analyses are arguments that are different from the classical arguments about the relative COR for *females as compared to males*.

As far as I know, no one has done those analyses. Moreover, Bateman's paper is riddled with inferential and statistical errors (Snyder & Gowaty, 2007), as well as fatal methodological and logical flaws (Gowaty, Kim, & Anderson, 2012, 2013). Most of these serious errors have gone unrecognized by generations of professors and graduate students (see Gowaty, 2018). Fortunately, in recent years investigators found Bateman's original lab notebooks containing his raw data, which are now available for appropriate analysis. The title of the forthcoming paper (Hoquet et al., in preparation) says it all—"Bateman's data are inconsistent with Bateman's principles." The persistence of Bateman's principles despite mistakes and flaws in the original paper speaks to the psychological and sociological credulity of some modern students of sex differences in behavior (Gowaty, 2018).

What is needed, then, are carefully constructed observations and experiments to find out whether females are always choosy and males are always indiscriminate. *Do the data of nature match the predictions of anisogamy and parental investment theories?* As a scientist studying the origins of sex differences in behavior, my job has been to find out how the data do or do not match the predictions of theory. I have spent years studying, in female and male subjects, whether females are more likely to be choosy and males are more likely to be indiscriminate. My studies in several species of fruit flies and in mice have shown that females are often as indiscriminate as males and males are often as choosy as females (Anderson, Kim, & Gowaty, 2007; Drickamer, Gowaty, & Wagner, 2003; Gowaty, Drickamer, & Schmid-Holmes, 2003; Gowaty, Kim, Rawlings, & Anderson, 2010; Gowaty, Steinichen, & Anderson, 2002, 2003; Moore, Gowaty, & Moore, 2003).

FLEXIBLE INDIVIDUAL BEHAVIOR IS AN ALTERNATIVE HYPOTHESIS TO THE CLASSICAL MODEL FOR THE ORIGINS OF SEX DIFFERENCES IN BEHAVIOR

In the opening to this chapter, I announced:

Being gendered is a life-long *process of becoming*... Behaving in ways typical of females or males, or typical of both, or typical of neither, expresses a developmental (ontogenetic) process of continually becoming.

This claim comes from *The Theory of Mating* (Gowaty & Hubbell, 2009, and in progress), a series of formal deductive analytical models that demonstrate mathematically that individual flexibility will more reliably enhance fitness in an enormous range of environments compared to fixed (invariant) sex-specific patterns of reproductive decision making. The mathematical model derived from mating theory described here is the switch point theorem (SPT).

Figure 4.1 depicts a scenario for the evolution of individuals who can modify their behavior in response to changes in key parameters of the environment (Gowaty & Hubbell, 2009, 2010, 2012, 2013). In this scenario, changes in an individual's physical and social circumstances *can induce in real time*—not over generations—changes in the individual's behavior, specifically reproductive decision making. The key selection idea is this: Given variable life-history contexts, selection favors individuals who can and do change the way they behave to achieve a better fit to their changing circumstances. Darwin himself likely would have approved of the SPT, which proves mathematically that in most situations, a fixed mating strategy—whether choosy or indiscriminate—would be selected against. That is, individuals who did not change their behavior as their ecological situations changed would have left fewer descendants than those that can and do change. The SPT starts with individuals, not members of a sex category, and the inducing variables in the SPT act on individuals—as though blind to their sexes—and, in that sense, the SPT is *sex neutral*.

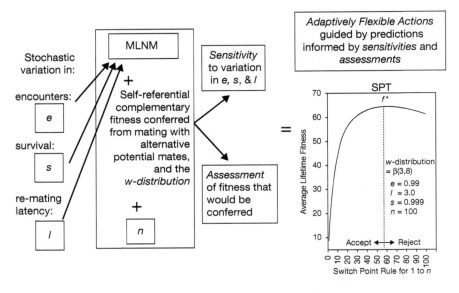

Figure 4.1 A scenario for the evolution of individually adaptive flexibility in reproductive decision making with quantitative predictions of actions and fitness. The scenario shown here is reproduced from Gowaty and Hubbell (© Patricia Adair Gowaty). It shows the assumptions of the analytical solution of the switch point theorem (SPT) that calculates the *switch point*, which describes for an individual—not sexes— the individual's expected lifetime number of mates and how many potential mates in a population will be acceptable or not in a particular circumstance (Gowaty & Hubbell, 2009). The analytical solution to the point along the *x*-axis of ranked potential mates in the graph on the right (#1 indicating highest fitness) at which Accept switches to Reject (indicated by *f**) can be found by evaluating the likelihood of encountering potential mates (probability *e*) and the likelihood of surviving to encounter potential mates again (probability *s*), and, if the individual is no longer a virgin, taking into account the length of the period of required postmating timeout before becoming receptive to mating again (indicated by "*l*" in the figure). The axis of ranked potential mates is unique to each individual in a population, meaning that individuals of one sex may each rank the individuals of the opposite sex differently. This means that according to the SPT, there is seldom a "best babe" or "best hunk" in a population.

The SPT posits that chance (stochastic) events in individual life histories that affect individuals' encounters with potential mates or the likelihood of their continued survival (for instance, potential mates that an individual randomly bumps into or events that alter the odds of the individual's survival), as well as evolved capacities of individuals to be sensitive to their own life-history circumstances, contribute to an individual's likelihood of behaving in a choosy or indiscriminate way at any particular point in time. An important parameter in SPT is the w-distribution, which we assume individuals learn about during development before they are receptive to mating. The *w-distribution* is the distribution of fitness values in a population of mating or potentially mating individuals. The w-distribution is a theoretical construct; it is based on a *matrix* (a grid of columns and rows that define cells) that, although impossible to measure in any real-world situation, is assumed to have measureable empirical effects and in that sense is testable. The cells in the matrix contain the fitness values for every female mated to every male and every male mated to every female. Note that because females vary, their achieved fitness with males will vary and vice versa. The w-distribution is a useful metric, and if we imagine that individuals in a population know something about the w-distribution, their reproductive decisions will be enhanced. For example, imagine that the w-distribution is highly right skewed (values clumped close to 1), meaning that no matter with whom a female or male mates, she/he will reap high fitness. In such a circumstance, there would be little margin in waiting for a better mate, that is in *acting choosy*. Instead, individuals may *mate on encounter*, as though indiscriminate. On the other hand, if the w-distribution is flat, meaning that there is very large variation in the likely fitness conferred by any mating, individuals who "wait for a better mate"—acting as if choosy—are likely to gain greater fitness rewards.

Here's how to think about what the SPT theorem does: First, imagine that before there was natural selection to accept or reject potential mates, there was stochastic (chance) variation in encounters with potential mates (e) and with decision makers' likelihood of survival (s). Express survival and encounters as probabilities. Second, imagine that an individual's encounter probability and survival probability influence the expected *mean* lifetime number of mates (a measure of reproductive success for an individual) and the *variance* in lifetime number of mates (a measure of the variation in reproductive success among individuals in a population). Both of these measures are important for evolutionary inferences. Third, imagine that in a population of n potential mates of varying quality, there are up to n different fitness qualities among the potential mates ($<n$ in a more homogeneous population). Fourth, make the reasonable informal assumption that mate assessment is self-referential, meaning that individuals may take their own variation into account when ranking potential mates in a population, while also using information that they learned during development about themselves. Fifth, hypothesize that individuals update their information as e, s, n, and w-distribution change in real time, to predict adaptive acceptance and rejection of potential mates. The SPT says that individuals who are flexible—sometimes waiting to mate (as if "choosy") and sometimes mating on encounter (as if "indiscriminate") thereby maximize their instantaneous contributions to lifetime fitness.

The predictions of the SPT are quantitative. You are invited to consider the nuances later. In the meantime, it is useful for you to know that one's expected lifetime number of mates will be higher in general when long-term survival is likely (high s) rather than unlikely (low s). Similarly, individuals with higher encounter rates, e, will have a higher expected lifetime number of mates than when e is low. If you understand something about how probability works, you are ahead of the game in the SPT. For instance, a high chance of rain might be announced on the evening news—and yet it doesn't necessarily rain. So even when one has a high s or a high e, one could—by chance—die tomorrow or never encounter another potential mate.

The probabilities of s and e also affect the movement of the switch point along the axis of all potential mates ranked for fitness quality (i.e., along the x-axis in the right-hand graph in Figure 4.1, with the best potential mate—#1—on the left end, at the origin of the axis). Higher s and e mean in general that the switch point will be toward the left. That is, with good prospects for a long life and plenty of mate encounters, the individual should hold out for high-quality mates; accept few, reject many. If these probabilities decline, the switch point will move toward the right, meaning that more potential mates fall into the acceptable category; fewer would be rejected. The distribution of fitness also affects the switch point: If the w-distribution is skewed toward high-quality mates, most potential mates will be acceptable, no matter what an individual's *s* or *e* is. Under such circumstances, most potential mates will boost lifetime fitness, so the mating decision rule would be to mate on encounter, as though "indiscriminate."

Something important you might notice when comparing the classical model to the SPT concerns the legacy of selection *in past generations*. In the classical model, selection in past generations favored different traits in females and males, and those traits were assumed to manifest in the behavior of contemporary individuals. In the SPT, selection in past generations favored flexible individuals who were sensitive to environmental changes and modified their behavior in response to those changes. The SPT predicts that flexibility is adaptive and the rules of the SPT show why *flexibility* is adaptive in almost all demographic circumstances, so that differences in the behavior of contemporary individuals reflect differences in their ecological and social circumstances.

Although both classical theory and the SPT are about Darwinian selection, the SPT does things that classical theory could never do. Among the absolute, can't-get-around-it essentials of mating are that to mate *you must be alive* and *you must encounter a potential mate*. The SPT starts with the absolute essentials and expresses those essentials as stochastic (chance) probabilities. It assumes further that *chance effects on life span and mate encounters are certainties*, and *these probabilities have huge effects on an individual's expected mean lifetime mating success and reproductive decision making*. The SPT models the real world better than the classical model does, because the SPT assumes that individuals live in variable environments, and that the "best fit" individuals will be ones who evaluate their circumstances (perhaps unconsciously) and change their behavior (again, perhaps unconsciously) to fit their particular and unique circumstances.

LIMITATIONS

The value of the SPT does not depend on it being complete and true. However, it is a theorem, and it is a mathematically proven theorem, and that is meaningful. Like all mathematically proven theorems, it cannot be rejected. It might not work in some systems, which is different from a rejection of the theory. For example, Newtonian mechanics do not work in some non-Earth bound systems, but do work reliably on Earth. Thus, the questions you should ask about the SPT include whether its assumptions are met in systems of mating decisions in the real world. It is hard to argue with its essentials: One must be alive to mate and one must encounter potential mates. As students of psychology, you can imagine the kinds of observations or experiments that would enable you to test the reliability of its predictions.

The matrix on which the w-distribution is based represents what we assume individuals "know" about the likely fitness benefits of a particular reproductive decision—either to wait to mate or mate on encounter. The assumption about the w-distribution is the most vulnerable in the theory because we know so little about the mechanistic basis of evaluating potential mates, not to mention that there are fewer than 10 measured w-distributions from either captive or wild populations. We—the scientific community—know almost nothing about the w-distributions of populations, although because they have been described in field and lab populations, w-distributions can be empirically measured.

Humans have long known that outbreeding produces the healthiest offspring. Known as "hybrid vigor" in old literature, today we talk about potential genetic parents' complementarity with respect to genes that code for certain proteins related to immune function, and we hypothesize that the more variable is the parental dyad (more complementary to each other having different immune coding genes), the healthier their offspring will be. Because healthy offspring are more likely to live long and prosper, parents who produce them will likely have future descendants and high lineage success.

EVOLUTIONARY ORIGINS OF GENDERED BEHAVIOR AND THE POTENTIAL FOR INTERDISCIPLINARY INQUIRY

According to the SPT, there is nothing so like a female as a male and nothing so like a male as a female. Whether it is a genetic female or a genetic male, a fruit fly with, for instance, dim prospects for surviving and encountering a mate will mate relatively indiscriminately, whereas a fly with better prospects for future survival and encounters with potential mates will be relatively choosy. Most (not all) psychologists are interested in humans. Does the SPT apply to people? *Homo sapiens* evolved and are evolving; humans, like flies, are animals. So, in theory, human behavior is amenable to evolutionary analysis. In deciding for yourself the relevance of the SPT to people, it will be helpful to remember that in the SPT, *environment* is broadly defined as encompassing physical (e.g., climate, topography, availability of fresh water, etc.) and social (e.g., population density, friendship networks, cultural norms, etc.) circumstances. In the SPT, culture is not "outside" of nature or an "alternative" to "biology." It follows from the SPT that, for instance, the double standard, which creates different developmental contexts for children assigned to different sex categories, is likely to generate "sex differences" in mating strategies—for example, if daughters are not allowed the opportunity to meet and greet potential mates as often as sons. It also follows from the SPT that more egalitarian contexts will result in girls/women and boys/men inhabiting more similar environments and therefore behaving more similarly.

From the SPT come insights remarkably consistent with the ideas of theorists in sociology and psychology who argue against sex/gender invariants, such as "boys will be boys." Consistent with the SPT, some theorists in psychology and sociology argue that culturally imposed rules codifying what children are allowed to learn and to do constrain their future development, cutting off opportunities for individuals in any sex category. Also like the SPT, some theorists view gendered behavior as flexible throughout the life span. The new evolutionary theory is not the same as sociological or psychological theories, but it shares with them an emphasis on flexible, contingent behavioral expression. These theories share a view of behavioral sex differences as deriving not from some binary essence passed down across generations but rather from dynamic interplay between flexible individuals and their life circumstances.

Consensus on the flexibility and environmental contingency of expressions of gender creates opportunities for new thinking across disciplines. Psychologists know how to study processes important in the SPT, such as monitoring the environment, evaluating potential mates, and transmitting information within and across generations. Sociologists know how to study social institutions, organizations, and movements that comprise important features of individuals' circumstances. Research combining the expertise of biologists, psychologists, and sociologists will provide robust outcomes in tests of the SPT predictions.

As a biologist, I find it daunting to consider the prospects of getting the kind of evidence for humans that would allow strong causal inferences about evolution. For practical and ethical reasons, researchers working with humans cannot randomly assign babies or adults to experimental populations to see how mate choices or fitness are affected. Also, assessing some constructs—such as number of sexual encounters and differential survival—is tricky in humans. Self-report measures, for instance, are vulnerable to people lying about, forgetting about, or differently defining sexual encounters. How diverse groups of scholars might navigate these challenges to bridge disciplines remains to be seen.

CONCLUSION

This chapter aimed to help you to understand and think critically about theories and data regarding the evolution of gendered behavior. It hopefully made clear why you should not assume that all contemporary evolutionary theories posit fixed, innate, "hard-wired" sex differences or other reductionist or deterministic accounts of behavior. Nonetheless, as you read the literature, you will likely encounter debates about evolutionary processes and mechanisms, even among scholars who agree that social context shapes behavior. The tools that this chapter has offered may enable you to make sense of those debates by considering the assumptions theorists make, as well as dissecting their arguments and evidence.

REFERENCES

Altmann, J. (1997). Mate choice and intrasexual reproductive competition: Contributions to reproduction that go beyond acquiring more mates. In P. A. Gowaty (Ed.), *Feminism and evolutionary biology* (pp. 320–333). New York, NY: Springer.

Anderson, W. W., Kim, Y. K., & Gowaty, P.A. (2007). Experimental constraints on mate preferences in *Drosophila pseudoobscura* decrease offspring viability and fitness of mated pairs. *Proceedings of the National Academy of Sciences of the United States of America, 104*, 4484–4488.

Arnold, S. J. (1994). Bateman principles and the measurement of sexual selection in plants and animals. *American Naturalist, 144*, S126–S149.

Bateman, A. (1948). lntra-sexual selection in *Drosophila*. *Heredity, 2*, 349–368.

Crews, D. (2012). The (bi)sexual brain. *EMBO Reports, 13*(9), 779–784.

Darwin, C. (1859). *The origin of species by means of natural selection*. London, UK: John Murray.

Darwin, C. (1871). *The descent of man, and selection in relation to sex*. London, UK: John Murray.

Drickamer, L. C., Gowaty, P. A., & Wagner, D. M. (2003). Free mutual mate preferences in house mice affect reproductive success and offspring performance. *Animal Behaviour, 65*, 105–114.

Fausto-Sterling, A. (2000). *Sexing the body: Gender politics and the construction of sexuality*. New York, NY: Basic Books.

Fausto-Sterling, A. (2012). *Sex/gender: Biology in a social world*. New York, NY: Routledge.

Gorelick, R., Carpinone, J., & Derraugh, L. J. (2016). No universal differences between female and male eukaryotes: Anisogamy and asymmetrical female meiosis. *Biological Journal of the Linnean Society, 120*(1), 1–21.

Gowaty, P. A. (2010). Forced or aggressively coerced copulation. In M. Breed & J. Moore (Eds.), *Encyclopedia of animal behavior* (pp. 759–763). Oxford, UK: Academic Press.

Gowaty, P. A. (2011). What is sexual selection and the short herstory of female trait variation. *Behavioral Ecology, 22*, 1146–1147.

Gowaty, P. A. (2014). Standing on Darwin's shoulders: The nature of selection hypotheses. In Hoquet T. (Ed.), *What's left of sexual selection?* New York, NY: Springer.

Gowaty, P. A. (2018a). Biological essentialism, gender, true belief, confirmation biases, and skepticism. In C. Travis (Ed.), *APA handbook of the psychology of women* (pp. 145–164). Washington, DC: American Psychological Association.

Gowaty, P. A. (2018b). Sexual conflict theory. In H. Callan (Ed.), *International encyclopedia of anthropology* (pp. 1–6). New York, NY: John Wiley & Sons.

Gowaty, P. A., Drickamer, L. C., & Schmid-Holmes, S. (2003a). Male house mice produce fewer offspring with lower viability and poorer performance when mated with females they do not prefer. *Animal Behaviour, 65*, 95–103.

Gowaty, P. A., & Hubbell, S. P. (2009). Reproductive decisions under ecological constraints: It's about time. *Proceedings of the National Academy of Sciences of the United States of America, 106*, 10017–10024.

Gowaty, P. A, & Hubbell, S. P. (2010). Killing time: A mechanism of sexual selection and sexual conflict. In J. Leonard & A. Cordoba-Aguilar (Eds.), *The evolution of primary sexual characters in animals* (pp. 79–96). New York, NY: Oxford University Press.

Gowaty, P. A., & Hubbell, S. P. (2012). The evolutionary origins of mating failures and multiple mating. *Entomologia Experimentalis et Applicata, 146,* 11–25.

Gowaty, P. A, & Hubbell, S. P. (2013). Bayesian animals sense ecological constraints to predict fitness and organize individually flexible reproductive decisions. *Behavior and Brain Sciences, 36,* 215–216.

Gowaty, P. A., Kim, Y.-K., & Anderson, W. W. (2012). No evidence of sexual selection in a repetition of Bateman's classical study of *Drosophila melanogaster. Proceedings of the National Academy of Sciences of the United States of America, 109,* 11740–11745.

Gowaty, P. A., Kim, Y.-K., & Anderson, W. W. (2013). Mendel's law reveals fatal flaws in Bateman's 1948 study of mating and fitness. *Fly, 7,* 28–38.

Gowaty, P. A., Kim, Y. K., Rawlings, J., & Anderson, W. W. (2010). Polyandry increases offspring viability and mother productivity but does not decrease mother survival in *Drosophila pseudoobscura. Proceedings of the National Academy of Sciences of the United States of America, 107,* 13771–13776.

Gowaty, P. A., Steinichen, R., & Anderson, W. W. (2002). Mutual interest between the sexes and reproductive success in *Drosophila pseudoobscura. Evolution, 56,* 2537–2540.

Gowaty, P. A., Steinichen, R., & Anderson, W. W. (2003). Indiscriminate females and choosy males: Within- and between-species variation in *Drosophila. Evolution, 57,* 2037–2045.

Hines, M. (2005). *Brain gender.* New York, NY: Oxford University Press.

Hoquet, T., W. C. Bridges, P. A. Gowaty (submitted). Bateman's data are inconsistent with Bateman's Principles. PeerJ (in review).

Jablonka, E., Lamb, M. J., & Zeligowski, A. (2014). *Evolution in four dimensions, revised edition: Genetic, epigenetic, behavioral, and symbolic variation in the history of life.* Cambridge, MA: MIT Press.

Moore, A. J., Gowaty, P. A., & Moore, P. J. (2003). Females avoid manipulative males and live longer. *Journal of Evolutionary Biology, 16,* 523–530.

Morris, J. A., Jordan, C. L., & Breedlove, M. (2004). Sexual differentiation of the vertebrate nervous system. *Nature Neuroscience, 7,* 1034–1039.

Parker, G. A., Baker, R., & Smith, V. (1972). The origin and evolution of gamete dimorphism and the male-female phenomenon. *Journal of Theoretical Biology, 36,* 529–553.

Roughgarden, J. (2013). *Evolution's rainbow: Diversity, gender, and sexuality in nature and people.* Berkeley: University of California Press.

Salk, R. & Hyde, J. S. (2012). Contemporary genetics for gender researchers: Not your grandma's genetics anymore. *Psychology of Women Quarterly, 36,* 395–410.

Schagdarsurengin, U., & Steger, K. (2016). Epigenetics in male reproduction: Effect of paternal diet on sperm quality and offspring health. *Nature Reviews Urology, 13,* 584–595.

Snyder, B. F., & Gowaty, P. A. (2007). A reappraisal of Bateman's classical study of intra-sexual selection. *Evolution, 61,* 2457–2468.

Trivers, R. (1972). Parental investment and sexual selection. In B. Campbell (Ed.), *Sexual selection and the descent of man* (pp. 139–179). Chicago, IL: Aldine Press.

PART II

Contemporary Avenues
of Inquiry

E ach of the 10 chapters in this section takes up a topic of contemporary relevance in the scholarship on gender, sex, and sexuality. Each chapter is a concise overview of a conceptual approach and a body of knowledge. The chapters range widely on a number of dimensions. Some focus in tightly on a closely linked set of empirical investigations; others endeavor to synthesize a more diverse group of investigations. Yet others focus on bodies of theory that have been important sources of knowledge, whereas others focus on emerging methods for studying social life. Together, these chapters showcase the diversity of topics, questions, and approaches that characterizes the psychological study of gender, sex, and sexualities.

5

Gender and Sex(ualities)

A Cultural Psychology Approach

TUĞÇE KURTIŞ AND GLENN ADAMS

I n this chapter, we describe a cultural psychology approach to the study of gender and sex(ualities). A cultural psychology approach refers not only to the exploration of cross-group diversity or a description of psychological patterns observed in "other" settings but also (and more profoundly) to the examination of the sociocultural and historical bases of psychological experience in any given setting. Associated with this approach is a conception of culture not as membership in rigidly bounded groups, but rather as engagement with *explicit and implicit patterns of historically derived and selected ideas and their material manifestations in institutions, practices, and artifacts* (Adams & Markus, 2004, based on Kroeber & Kluckhohn, 1952, p. 357). Although approaches vary, cultural psychology perspectives generally highlight the mutual constitution of psyche and culture (Shweder, 1990): how person-based structures of experience exist in a dynamic relationship with socially constructed affordances (i.e., qualities of an object or environment that allow performance of an action; see Gibson, 1977) embedded in the structure of everyday worlds.

THE CULTURAL CONSTITUTION OF GENDER
AND SEXUAL EXPERIENCE

One direction of the mutual constitution of psyche and culture is the *cultural constitution of psychological experience*. Applied to the topic of gender and sex(uality), this idea emphasizes that the experience of gender and sex(uality) is not simply the "natural" unfolding of genetic potential. Instead, this experience requires engagement with particular sociocultural affordances and reflects the incorporation—literally, "taking into the body"—of templates for gender and sexual experience deposited over historical time in the structure of everyday cultural worlds.

As an example, consider the medical assignment of sex (at birth or even during prenatal screening) based on the appearance of genitalia. The binary gender system currently prevalent in Western countries recognizes and requires assignment to one of two gender categories: male or female. In turn, this assignment to gender category structures lives. It forms the basis for expectations about toys, childhood activities, clothing, possible careers, and the people whom one should find romantically attractive, love, and marry (Basow, 2006). However, as many as 1.7% of births are of infants with ambiguous external genitalia (Fausto-Sterling, 1993). Although some communities embrace such people as a "third gender" (see Zimman & Hall, 2009), the typical response in Western contexts since at least the 1950s has been surgical alteration of genitalia to conform to binary categories (see Chapter 3). The basis for assigning an infant to a sex category is not necessarily chromosomal identity, but instead bears the impact of sex-role stereotypes (Diamond, 2010). Specifically, in Western high-income countries, the male-female binary defines males by their ability to penetrate and defines females by their ability to procreate. Whether doctors assign an infant with an XY pair of chromosomes to the male sex category depends on the presence of an "adequate" penis that in adulthood will be capable of performing vaginal penetration. If medical personnel judge that the XY infant lacks an "adequate" penis, then it is not uncommon for them to assign the infant to the female sex category and then surgically alter the infant's genitalia into a more normative female appearance. In contrast, medical personnel have typically assigned XX infants who have reproductive capacity to the female sex category, regardless of the appearance of genitalia. If medical personnel consider an XX infant's "phallus" too large, they typically have surgically minimized it, even if this procedure reduces future capacity for satisfactory sexual experiences. The point is that sex categories are not just natural but also are social constructions (Kessler & McKenna, 1978).

Another example that illuminates the cultural constitution of gender concerns changes over time in notions of what it means to be a woman or man in any given society. Researchers in the 1970s found that, by and large, female college students reported more feminine traits, male college students reported more masculine traits, and one third of both male and female students were androgynous (i.e., they endorsed a balance of masculine and feminine traits; Spence & Helmreich, 1978). A meta-analysis of studies examining students' scores on femininity and masculinity scales based on samples from more than 50 college campuses in the United States since the 1970s revealed significant increases over time in the endorsement of masculine traits by women, in the incidence of androgyny among women, and (to a lesser extent) in the incidence of androgyny among men (Twenge, 1997). Other researchers have similarly found that US college women reported engagement in more masculine-typed and less feminine-typed behaviors than their mothers (Guastello & Guastello, 2003). Researchers linked these changes in gender-related characteristics to broad societal changes in this era. In recent decades, girls and women in many social groups in the United States have been afforded more opportunities to develop and practice agentic skills, assertiveness, and independence, particularly in educational, occupational, and sports domains. Greater engagement in these male-stereotypic activities might account for the observed increase in endorsement of masculine traits and of androgyny among young women. In sum, these examples reveal the extent to which cultural affordances scaffold the experience of gender.

THE PSYCHOLOGICAL CONSTITUTION
OF GENDERED REALITIES

The other direction of the mutual constitution of person and culture concerns the *psychological constitution of cultural worlds*. Applied to the topic of gender and sex(uality), this idea emphasizes that cultural traditions of gender and sexuality are not timeless collective traits; instead, they are psychological products. In the course of everyday experience, people continually reproduce gendered worlds onto which they inscribe, objectify, and realize (literally, "make real," see Berger & Luckmann, 1966; Moscovici, 1984) particular beliefs and desires regarding gender and sexuality.

A focus on the psychological constitution of gendered reality resonates with various influential perspectives on the performative character of gender (Butler, 1990; West & Zimmerman, 1987). To say that gender is a performance is not to claim that a person has unfettered agency to choose or opt out of hegemonic gender regimes. Instead, the point is that people constitute gender categories and their meaning through their everyday action. People perform gender daily when they decide what to wear in the morning, remove or retain facial hair, sit on a subway with arms and legs close together or far apart (Vrugt & Luyerink, 2000), and use or avoid coarse language (Newman, Groom, Handelmann, & Pennebaker, 2008). Similarly, people perform gender in interpersonal relationships, at school, and at work through their embodiment and enactment of socially constructed gender scripts in ways that often reinforce (but occasionally resist or redefine) particular ways of doing gender and sexuality. For instance, within settings where homosexuality is stigmatized, boys and men often do not work or play in domains that are culturally coded as "feminine" nor act in ways that are culturally coded as "effeminate" in order to avoid homosexual stigma and to appear heteromasculine (heterosexual and masculine) to their peers (Anderson, 2005; Epstein, Kehily, Mac an Ghaill,

& Redman, 2001; Kimmel, 1994; McGuffey & Rich, 1999; Williams, 1995). Through such daily and repetitive performances, people not only reproduce social constructions of gender but also reinforce normative understandings of (hetero)sexuality.

Besides these individual performances or acts of doing gender, people also (re)produce gendered realities through engagement in cultural artifacts, environments, and practices. For instance, we produce or consume children's books portraying girls doing household chores (e.g., cooking and cleaning) and children's books showing boys using tools or building things (Burn, 1996). We build or use gendered public bathrooms that assume a binary gender scheme and ignore the needs of people who do not fit this scheme (Herman, 2013). We pile a disproportionate amount of childcare and household responsibilities on women, despite the considerable increase in women's participation in the labor force (Coltrane, 2000). We design or endorse policies that oppose or embrace same-sex couples, marriage, and family; in that way, we uphold or challenge heteronormativity (Hopkins, Sorensen, & Taylor, 2013). In other words, we deposit our particular, socially constructed understandings, beliefs, and desires about gender and sex(uality) into the structure of everyday cultural worlds we inhabit. As we act according to particular beliefs or desires regarding gender and sexuality, our gendered performances reproduce and naturalize some ways of doing gender and sexuality and extend these into the future. At the same time, our nonperformance of other possibilities—clothes that we did not wear, careers that we did not pursue, sexual interests on which we did not act—contributes to the silence, invisibility, and absence of otherwise viable ways of doing gender and sexuality.

IMPLICATIONS FOR FEMINIST SCHOLARSHIP

The mutual constitution framework of cultural psychology resonates with social constructionist accounts that are the prevailing approach in much of feminist theory and gender studies in the social sciences (Berkowitz, Manohar, & Tinkler, 2010). Consistent with social constructionist accounts by feminist scholars, a cultural psychology analysis proposes that gender and sex(uality) are socioculturally arranged and (re)produced in the course of everyday activity. Cultural psychology analyses deviate from the postpositivist versions of feminist psychology that predominate in the United States in their close attention to and interpretation of sociocultural diversity in the experience of gender and sex(uality).

The majority of work on gender in postpositivist psychological science draws disproportionately on experience in what cultural psychologists have referred to as WEIRD settings—that is, Western, educated, industrialized, rich, and (supposedly) democratic settings (Henrich, Heine, & Norenzayan, 2010)—characteristic of Eurocentric global modernity. Dominant traditions of *hegemonic* psychological science draw upon forms of knowledge and ways of being rooted in European and American experience and, through the exercise of colonial power, elevate them as default standards for global humanity and academic work. Judged against these standards, the dominant traditions of psychological science position sociocultural diversity in gender and sex(uality) as the deviation of cultural Others from the norm. This tendency to regard the experience of cultural Others as deviant or suboptimal is especially relevant to discussions of gender-based oppression in the Majority World, that is, among the 85% of humankind associated with such labels as "developing world" or "third world" (Kağıtçıbaşı, 1995). Dominant perspectives of hegemonic psychological science, including work that aspires to feminist goals, sometimes imposes understandings about gender oppression informed by experience in WEIRD spaces as prescriptive standards for "universal" gendered oppression across diverse local settings. One problem with this approach is that universal understandings in such accounts (e.g., regarding "gender" or "oppression") may be ill fitting across local contexts. Another problem is that this approach treats a wide range of practices across diverse Majority-World settings—including polygamy, arranged marriage, and veiling—as unambiguous evidence of "gender oppression" and denial of women's rights (e.g., to self-expression) rather than an embrace of other worthwhile moral goods (Menon & Shweder, 1998). One example is the tendency to regard the practices of arranged marriage as patriarchal impositions that curtail women's (and men's) self-expression, rather than a continuum of practices that de-emphasizes the narrow and volatile bliss of romantic love in favor of broader and more enduring relational well-being. In extreme cases, the imposition of Eurocentric norms portrays women in Majority-World spaces as powerless or ignorant victims who are at risk of "death by culture" (Narayan, 1997) in ways that demand imperialist intervention. A cultural psychology analysis, informed by perspectives of intersectionality theory and transnational feminism, can serve as an antidote to universalizing discourses, whether of hegemonic psychological science or of feminist scholarship, that have their roots in WEIRD cultural spaces (Adams, Kurtiş, Salter, & Anderson, 2012).

Intersectional Accounts: Diversity of Gender(ed) Experiences

A key framework that seeks to disrupt universalizing and essentialist constructions of gender is *intersectionality theory* (see Chapter 2, this volume). Numerous scholars have noted the extent to which forms of feminism rooted in White, middle-class experience ignore or misunderstand various forms of racial, classed, imperial, and neocolonial oppression that people experience across Majority-World spaces (e.g., hooks, 1981; Liebert, Leve, & Hui, 2011; Lugones & Spelman, 1983). In response to these concerns, scholars working from perspectives of Black feminist thought and critical race theory (especially Crenshaw, 1991) developed the concept of intersectionality as a means to challenge monolithic accounts of experience. In contrast to unidimensional conceptions of identity and identity-based oppression, intersectional analyses situate experience within a complex web of power relations at the intersections of social categories such as gender, race, ethnicity, class, ability, and sexual orientation (e.g., Crenshaw, 1991; Hurtado, 1996). Rather than drawing on essentialist and monolithic conceptions of gender and gender-based oppression, they propose that gender (and gender-based oppression) must be understood in relation to these other social locations (e.g., Crenshaw, 1994).

Another key framework that disrupts universalizing and essentialist constructions of gender and sex(ualities) comes from LGBT and queer perspectives, which you read about in Chapter 3. A key insight from these accounts concerns the extent to which categories of normative and deviant sexualities (e.g., heterosexuality and homosexuality) are socially constructed and vary across time and space. These accounts further reveal a variety of sexual and gender identities (e.g., transsexuals, bisexuals, drag queens, lesbians, gay men, queers, heterosexuals, and so on) that go beyond binary constructions and provide people with greater flexibility in how they define themselves.

Transnational Feminist Accounts: Challenging Hegemonic Standards

Consistent with the framework of intersectionality, transnational feminisms reject universalized claims about "women" and emphasize instead the diversity and multidimensional character of gendered experience. Similar to intersectional accounts that attend to marginalized voices within WEIRD settings, transnational feminisms draw on silenced perspectives of people in the Majority World to reveal alternate subjugated knowledges.

Writing more than 25 years ago, Mohanty (1991) drew upon postcolonial critiques of intellectual imperialism (e.g., Fanon, 1963; Said, 1978) to reveal the extent to which neocolonial and Orientalist discourses have positioned the West as culturally superior and bolstered self-representations of Western women as relatively liberated (e.g., Mohanty, 1991; Narayan, 1997). More recently, some feminist work has assumed that globalization, which often serves as a code word for modernization or Westernization, will enable women's empowerment in the Majority World (e.g., Gray, Kittilson, & Sandholtz, 2006; Moghadam, 2007). Such assumptions ignore the contradictory and often less than empowering consequences of globalization on women around the world (see Chow, 2003; Hawkesworth, 2006; Kempadoo, 2004). In contrast, transnational feminist theorizing draws upon the experiences of people in Majority-World settings as a productive intellectual standpoint from which to observe and theorize typically obscured forms of everyday gender oppression that operate in Western settings (Grabe, 2013).

Whereas feminist psychologists have begun to incorporate the concept of intersectionality into their work, transnational feminist perspectives remain notably absent from psychological theory and research. One reason for this is the disproportionate extent to which psychological research draws upon experience in WEIRD settings. Another reason concerns the inattention to decolonial perspectives (e.g., Grosfoguel, 2002; Mignolo, 2009) that privilege the standpoint of people in Majority-World spaces, even within otherwise critical formulations of psychology. In an effort to incorporate insights from transnational feminisms into psychological theory and research, we have previously articulated the possibility of a transnational feminist psychology (Kurtiş & Adams, 2013, 2015). Central to a transnational feminist psychology are two decolonizing strategies of cultural psychology (Adams, Kurtiş, Salter, & Anderson, 2012). The first decolonizing strategy is to normalize manifestations of gender and sexuality in diverse Majority-World spaces, manifestations that hegemonic accounts often portray as deviant or suboptimal. The second decolonizing strategy is to denormalize manifestations of gender and sexuality that hegemonic discourse treats as standards of optimal functioning. We apply these strategies to rethink conceptions of gender oppression in personal relationships. The example that follows from our research on experience of relationship at the intersection of gender and culture illustrates our use of these strategies.

AN ILLUSTRATION: CARE AS SILENCE AND SACRIFICE

An influential strand of thought in feminist psychology has emphasized in essentialist terms how universal conditions of women's experience (e.g., predominance in caregiving roles) promote characteristically "relational" tendencies of self-understanding and interpersonal relationships that lead women to desire and create intimacy-focused, high-disclosure forms of connection (e.g., Belenky, Clinchy, Goldberger, & Tarule, 1986; Gilligan, 1982). Judged against this standard, one might look with suspicion at patterns in many Majority-World settings in which women appear to sacrifice personal well-being in the context of oppressive relationships that burden them with obligations of care, lead them to focus on service to others at the expense of self, and require their silence to maintain domestic harmony (e.g., Jack & Ali, 2010). From these perspectives, women's experiences of care, service, and silence within Majority-World communities might appear as prototypical examples of rampant patriarchy and gender-based oppression, which force women to suppress their desires, opinions, and other forms of self-expression in service to male power.

This construction of care, service, and silence as a manifestation of patriarchal oppression sometimes elicits patronizing responses. Concerned intellectuals and practitioners in WEIRD settings sometimes experience a sort of righteous indignation about the oppressive treatment of their Majority-World sisters that motivates them to intervene on their behalf. In extreme cases, this motivation has led those with otherwise anticolonial politics to call for neocolonial military violence to "save brown women from brown men" (Spivak, 1999, p. 93; see also Stabile & Kumar, 2005). In less extreme cases, this motivation to intervene on behalf of oppressed Majority-World sisters leads researchers and practitioners to engage in *epistemic violence*. *Epistemic violence* refers to processes by which scholars and practitioners in WEIRD settings understand their particular ways of knowing and being as the pinnacle of human development, present these ways of knowing and being as universal standards for all humanity, impose these standards on Other societies, and subjugate Other ways of knowing and being in the process.

Our own engagement with these ideas arose in the context of research by the first author on silence among women in Turkish settings. The initial inspiration for this work was *Silencing the Self Theory* (STST; Jack, 1991), which conceptualizes women's silence in dating/mating relationships as evidence of gender oppression. STST proposes that women

inhibit self-expression or action when these are likely to produce conflict with partners, which leads to women's "loss of self" (Jack, 1991).
Similarly, STST proposes that patriarchal societies socialize women to
take on burdens of care that cause them to sacrifice their own aspirations
and silence their own desires in service to others. Some studies have associated women's self-silencing in dating/mating relationship with a wide
variety of negative health outcomes, most notably depression (e.g., Duarte
& Thompson, 1999; Jack & Dill, 1992; Witte, Sherman, & Flynn, 2001).
From this perspective, an emphasis on silence (in the service of harmo-
nious relationships and obligations of care) is a gendered phenomenon
that disproportionately threatens women's well-being. In what follows,
we describe Kurtiş's consideration of STST among women in Turkish settings. As you will see, drawing on the perspectives of transnational feminism and cultural psychology led her to question the generality of STST,
as well as conventional understandings of care and silence among women.

Care and Silence as Authentic Expression
of Relational Selves

The first decolonizing strategy that Kurtiş employed was to *normalize* the
Other patterns that STST has portrayed as abnormal. Without denying
that particular relationship practices in various Majority-World spaces
may have oppressive consequences, a normalizing strategy asks scholars
to rethink ways in which these patterns of relationship may be beneficial. Rather than presuming that practices of care, service, and silence are
deficits in relationality or signs of universal gender oppression (e.g., self-
sacrifice), one can consider other possibilities. They may, for example, be
features of maintenance-oriented forms of relationship that are attuned
to everyday realities and are productive of broader well-being within cultural worlds of *embedded interdependence*: conceptual and material realities that promote a sense of rootedness in context (see Adams et al., 2012).

Evidence to support this idea comes from a study of women in Turkish
settings (Kurtiş, 2010), which scholars associate with cultural worlds of

interdependence (e.g., Kağıtçıbaşı, 1973). The women who participated in this study completed measures of self-silencing, relationship satisfaction, and depression. Consistent with the normalizing strategy—but contrary to theory and research in North American settings—Turkish women's scores on the self-silencing measure were unrelated to depression and were positively related to their reported relationship satisfaction.

An interview study of a different group of Turkish participants helped Kurtiş to understand how what looks like self-silencing might instead be a form of self-expressive restraint. The interviewees noted that silence served as a tool to preserve or affirm relationship quality. In fact, they considered silence to be a better tool for expression of an authentic self—constituted to a large extent by the experience of relational embeddedness—than direct forms of disclosure that implied distance from partners or risked the long-term pain of conflict for the short-term gain of expressing momentary annoyances. Likewise, interview responses revealed that participants experienced care as duty and obligation congruent with—and not opposed to—authentic manifestations of self. Rather than oppressing or subordinating oneself to the requirements of the relationship that results in "self-sacrifice" or "loss of self," duty-based care allowed a woman to express or realize her authentic self. Although this research is still underway, the results are consistent with the idea that in certain cultural settings, silence and care are not antithetical to authentic personal desires and do not necessarily constitute a threat to (women's) well-being. In fact, in such settings, silence and care may even be expressive of authentic personal desires and promote well-being.

Expression-Oriented Relationality as Neoliberal Individualism

Besides rendering as normal patterns of action that Minority-World psychologists often consider as pathological or suboptimal, a second decolonizing strategy is to "denaturalize" patterns that scholars in European and American contexts consider as standards of optimal functioning and gender justice. Applied to the present case, the denaturalizing strategy proposes that expression-focused, intimacy-rich, high-disclosure patterns of growth-oriented relationality are not intrinsically superior. Instead, such patterns reflect engagement with neoliberal individualism associated with cultural worlds of *abstracted independence.* Cultural worlds of abstracted independence involve conceptual and material realities that afford an experience of bounded separation or insulation from physical and social contexts (see Adams et al., 2012). As some theorists have pointed out, worlds of high relational mobility (e.g., Yuki & Schug, 2012) do not afford the sense of inherent commonality and interdependence that is associated with stable networks of kin and place-based relationship. In such worlds, people feel compelled to create intimacy and the basis for emotional connection through processes of mutual disclosure (Oliker, 1998; Schug, Yuki, & Maddux, 2010).

Rather than regard neoliberal individualism as the optimal form of relationality, Kurtiş's cultural psychology analysis linked expression-oriented relationality and the neoliberal individualist sense of abstraction from context to what one decolonial theorist called "the coloniality of being" (Maldonado-Torres, 2007). The coloniality of these ways of being is evident in two features. First, the coloniality of these ways of being is evident in processes of violence required to afford abstraction from context. As both postcolonial and feminist scholars have suggested, the sense of freedom from constraint and abstraction from context has its foundations in colonial and patriarchal domination (e.g., Shaw, 2000). A sense of ontological separation of individuals from context became possible and remains typical for a privileged few whose appropriation of others' labor—whether in the gendered domestic household, in the racialized violence of slavery, or in exploitative economic arrangements (e.g., feudalism, capitalism)—provided them with the surplus of time and energy to explore personal desires and pursue their dreams (Coltrane, 2000). As such, this experience of being is a manifestation of domination and injustice because the associated sense of freedom from constraint is unavailable to people in less privileged positions, who constitute the vast majority of humanity.

Second, the coloniality of this experience of being is evident in its consequences for reproduction of domination. It encourages retreat into personal liberation (via self-expression and growth), privatization of public space, and narrowing of relational obligation at expense of broader community care or service. In other words, this way of being limits conditions of possibility for broader sustainable well-being (Becker & Marecek, 2008). As such, the exercise of abstracted independence not only reflects but also reproduces the marginalization of people in less privileged positions (Shaw, 2000). From this perspective, conceptions of gender justice that prescribe equal enjoyment of growth-oriented relationality for women (at least, those with enough power to take advantage of resulting opportunities) may result in the reproduction of racial, ethnic, and class domination in the name of gender equality.

To summarize this section about decolonizing strategies, we return to the example that inspired it. First, a characterization of Turkish women's experience as an example of self-silencing is problematic to the extent that it projects a pathologizing construction of Other patterns that is at odds with local experience. What some observers interpret as a form of inhibition and self-sacrifice that puts women at risk for depression may instead constitute active self-direction toward authentic goals of nurturing the connections that provide meaning and security throughout the life course. Second, the imposition of hegemonic understandings as a universal prescription is problematic to the extent that it induces women (and people in general) to forgo broader relational security in pursuit of more narrowly defined self-development based on individualistic and androcentric models of self. Although these hegemonic forms may be associated with momentary experiences of happiness, they can have negative consequences if they lead people to forgo obligations and disinvest in broader relational connections that may provide security and sustenance at other points of the life course.

CONCLUSION: LIBERATORY IMPLICATIONS OF A CULTURAL PSYCHOLOGY ANALYSIS

To conclude this cultural psychology analysis of gender and sex(uality), we consider implications for feminist theory, research, and pedagogy.

Consistent with social constructionist approaches to feminist scholarship, a cultural psychology analysis illuminates the extent to which the experience of gender and sex(uality) emerges and gets reproduced through engagement with particular sociocultural affordances. One contribution of a cultural psychology analysis is its attention to marginalized experiences of the vast majority of humanity. Resonating with intersectionality theory, a cultural psychology analysis emphasizes diversity and dynamism in the experience of gender and sex(uality). Resonating with transnational feminist perspectives, a cultural psychology analysis draws upon experiences of people in Majority-World settings to rethink taken-for-granted notions of optimal functioning and "liberated" behavior. In this sense, a cultural psychology analysis provides a means of "thinking through others" (Shweder, 1991, p. 101), not in the sense of pondering until one comes to an accurate account of "diverse" others, but more profoundly in the sense of rethinking phenomena from the epistemic position of others. Centering the everyday experiences of people in Majority-World settings provides a privileged standpoint from which to illuminate issues of gender and sexual justice that Minority-World perspectives obscure. In particular, it can illuminate how even psychologists who work toward feminist-informed science can inadvertently endorse and propagate androcentric modes of being, associated with an individualist experience of abstraction from context, if we do not sufficiently interrogate the WEIRD foundations of our work.

An especially important view that such a standpoint affords concerns a more human(e) vision of personhood and justice. Rather than pathologizing Majority-World settings as sites of ignorance and victimization that need rescue via neocolonialist interventions, a cultural psychology analysis proposes that feminist workers can fruitfully learn from the experiences of people inhabiting such spaces. For instance, everyday experience in various Majority-World spaces can provide insights about relationality and the development of sustainable ways of being that derive from a foundation of embeddedness (Kurtiş & Adams, 2013). These insights can serve to cast into bold relief the costs of individualistic neoliberal ontology.

How does one apply insights of a cultural psychology analysis to teaching? One of our primary pedagogical goals as instructors of cultural psychology is to prompt students to critically evaluate their beliefs of what is natural and good (Kurtiş & Adams, 2016). Rather than condemning Other cultural practices as backward or ignorant, we encourage students both to understand the worlds in which those practices might make sense and to rethink the necessity or value of their own practices, which seem to be natural or normal. This approach is important when, as invariably happens in classroom discussions of cultural diversity, students encounter practices (such as honor killing, genital cutting, polygyny, arranged marriage, or restrictions on women's education, dress, mobility, and sexuality) that arouse their indignation and demand attention as apparent instances of social injustice.

When concerns regarding gender-based oppression appear to collide with concerns about cultural imperialism, we turn to the two decolonizing strategies of a cultural psychology analysis (Adams et al., 2012). Following the normalizing strategy, we emphasize perspectives of marginalized Others and encourage students to learn about the worlds that these individuals inhabit. This enables students to better appreciate the larger systems and historical context that shape apparently pathological ways of being. Equally important, we model a stance of epistemic humility, which involves both a recognition that one can have only partial knowledge of the human experience and an openness to learning from Other ways of being. We hope this encourages students to resist responses of paternalistic superiority that are often prevalent in academia and elsewhere. Following the denaturalizing strategy, we draw upon the perspective of people in marginalized settings as an epistemological standpoint for students to gain critical consciousness (Freire, 1970/1993) about the cultural and historical foundations of their own experience. The epistemological standpoint of oppressed others provides an invaluable pedagogical tool to illuminate how the lifestyle of privilege that our students take for granted is the ongoing product of racialized colonial violence and also contributes to the gender-based oppression that is the source of their indignation and concern. To cite just one example, we challenge students to consider (rather than overlook) links between their habits of consumption in the service of self-expansion and the systemic violence—including environmental degradation, erosion of public institutions, and crushing poverty—that have an especially negative impact on the lives of women in the Majority World.

In conclusion, a cultural psychology analysis shifts the emphasis from an inward-looking celebration of "freedom of choice" and "empowerment" to a recognition that the contemporary global order and associated ways of being are the product of racial and colonial violence. By offering students such an analysis, we can more effectively confront the epistemic privilege of WEIRD spaces and more adequately serve the interests of the majority of humanity. Rather than liberating a privileged few to better participate in the ongoing domination of the marginalized many, a cultural psychology analysis can illuminate lurking forms of racial and colonial privilege in a good deal of feminist scholarship and provide students with models of personhood and social relations that are more consistent with broader feminist goals of human liberation.

REFERENCES

Adams, G., Kurtiş, T., Salter, P. S., & Anderson, S. L. (2012). A cultural psychology of relationship: Decolonizing science and practice. In O. Gillath, G. Adams, & A. D. Kunkel (Eds.), *Relationship science: Integrating across evolutionary, neuroscience and sociocultural approaches* (pp. 49–70). Washington, DC: American Psychological Association.

Adams, G., & Markus, H. R. (2004). Toward a conception of culture suitable for a social psychology of culture. In M. Schaller & C. S. Crandall (Eds.), *The psychological foundations of culture* (pp. 335–360). Mahwah, NJ: Lawrence Erlbaum Associates.

Anderson, E. (2005). *In the game: Gay athletes and the cult of masculinity*. Albany, NY: State University of New York Press.

Basow, S. A. (2006). Gender role and gender identity development. In J. Worell & C. Goodheart (Eds.), *Handbook of girls' and women's psychological health* (pp. 242–251). New York, NY: Oxford University Press.

Becker, D., & Marecek, J. (2008). Dreaming the American dream: Individualism and positive psychology. *Social and Personality Psychology Compass, 2*, 1767–1780.

Belenky, M. F., Clinchy, B. M., Goldberger, N. R., & Tarule, J. M. (1986). *Women's ways of knowing: The development of self, voice and mind*. New York, NY: Basic Books.

Berger, P. L., & Luckmann, T. (1966). *The social construction of reality: A treatise in the sociology of knowledge*. Garden City, NY: Anchor Books.

Berkowitz, D. D., Manohar, N. N., & Tinkler, J. E. (2010). Walk like a man, talk like a woman: Teaching the social construction of gender. *Teaching Sociology, 38*, 132–143.

Butler, J. (1990). *Gender trouble: Feminism and the subversion of identity*. New York, NY: Routledge.

Burn, S. M. (1996). *The social psychology of gender*. New York: Mcgraw-Hill, Inc.

Chow, E. N. (2003). Gender matters: Studying globalization and social change in the 21st century. *International Sociology, 18*, 443–460.

Coltrane, S. (2000). Research on household labor: Modeling and measuring the social embeddedness of routine family work. *Journal of Marriage and the Family, 62*, 1208–1233.

Crenshaw, K. W. (1994). Mapping the margins: Intersectionality, identity politics, and violence against women of color. In M. A. Fineman & R. Mykitiuk (Eds.), *The public nature of private violence* (pp. 93–118). New York, NY: Routledge.

Crenshaw, K. (1991). Mapping the margins: Intersectionality, identity politics, and violence against women of color. *Stanford Law Review, 43*, 1241–1299.

Diamond, M. (2010). Intersexuality. In E. J. Haeberle (Ed.), *Human sexuality: An encyclopedia*. Retrieved from http://www.hawaii.edu/PCSS/biblio/articles/2010to2014/2010-intersexuality.html.

Duarte, L., & Thompson, J. (1999). Sex differences in self-silencing. *Psychological Reports, 85*, 145–161.

Epstein, D., Kehily, M., Mac an Ghaill, M., & Redman, P. (2001). Boys and girls come out to play: Making masculinities and femininities in school playgrounds. *Men and Masculinities, 4*, 158–172.

Fanon, F. (1963). *The wretched of the earth*. New York, NY: Présence Africaine.

Fausto-Sterling, A. (1993). The five sexes: Why male and female are not enough. *The Sciences, 33*, 20–25.

Freire, P. (1970/1993). *Pedagogy of the oppressed*. New York, NY: Continuum.

Gibson, J. J. (1977). The theory of affordances. In R. Shaw & J. Bransford (Eds.), *Perceiving, acting, and knowing: Toward an ecological psychology* (pp. 67–82). Hillsdale, NJ: Erlbaum.

Gilligan, C. (1982). *In a different voice*. Cambridge, MA: Harvard University Press.

Grabe, S. (2013). Psychological cliterodectomy: Body objectification as a human rights violation. In M. Ryan & N. Branscombe (Eds.), *The SAGE handbook of gender and psychology* (pp. 412–428). London, UK: SAGE.

Gray, M. M., Kittilson, M. C., & Sandholtz, W. (2006). Women and globalization: A study of 180 countries, 1975–2000. *International Organization, 60*, 293–333.

Grosfoguel, R. (2002). Colonial difference, geopolitics of knowledge, and global coloniality in the modern/colonial capitalist world-system. *Review, 25*, 203–334.

Guastello, D. D., & Guastello, S. J. (2003). Androgyny, gender role behavior and emotional intelligence among college students and their parents. *Sex Roles, 49*, 663–673.

Hawkesworth, M. (2006). *Globalization and feminist activism*. Lanham, MD: Rowman & Littlefield.

Henrich, J., Heine, S. J., & Norenzayan, A. (2010). The weirdest people in the world? *Behavioral and Brain Sciences, 33*, 61–83.

Herman, J. L. (2013). Gendered restrooms and minority stress: The public regulation of gender and its impact on transgender people's lives. *Journal of Public Management & Social Policy, 19*, 65–80.

hooks, b. (1981). *Ain't I a woman? Black women and feminism.* Cambridge, MA: South End.

Hopkins, J. J., Sorensen, A., & Taylor, V. (2013). Same-sex couples, families, and marriage: Embracing and resisting heteronormativity. *Sociology Compass, 7*, 97–110.

Hurtado, A. (1996). *The color of privilege: Three blasphemies on race and feminism.* Ann Arbor: University of Michigan Press.

Jack, D. C. (1991). *Silencing the self: Women and depression.* Cambridge, MA: Harvard University Press.

Jack, D. C., & Ali, A. (2010). *Silencing the self across cultures: Depression and gender in the social world.* New York, NY: Oxford University Press.

Jack, D. C., & Dill, D. (1992). The Silencing the Self Scale: Schemas of intimacy associated with depression in women. *Psychology of Women Quarterly, 16*, 97–106.

Kağıtçıbaşı, Ç. (1995). Is psychology relevant to global human development issues? *American Psychologist, 50*, 293–300.

Kağıtçıbaşı, Ç. (1973). Psychological aspects of modernization in Turkey. *Journal of Cross-Cultural Psychology, 4*, 157–174.

Kempadoo, K. (2004). *Sexing the Caribbean: Gender, race, and sexual labor.* New York, NY: Routledge.

Kessler, S. J., & McKenna, W. (1978). *Gender: An ethnomethodological approach.* New York, NY: John Wiley.

Kimmel, M. (1994). Masculinity as homophobia: Fear, shame and silence in the construction of gender identity. In H. K. Brod (Ed.), *Theorizing masculinities.* Thousand Oaks, CA: Sage.

Kroeber, A. L., & Kluckhohn, C. K. (1952). *Culture: A critical review of concepts and definitions.* New York, NY: Random House.

Kurtiş, T., & Adams, G. (2013). A cultural psychology of relationship: Toward a transnational feminist psychology. In M. Ryan & N. Branscombe (Eds.), *Handbook of gender and psychology* (pp. 251–269). London, UK: Sage.

Kurtiş, T., & Adams, G. (2015). Decolonizing liberation: Toward a transnational feminist psychology. *Journal of Social and Political Psychology: Special Thematic Section on Decolonizing Psychological Science, 3*, 388–413.

Kurtiş, T., & Adams, G. (2016). Decolonial intersectionality: Implications for theory, research, and pedagogy. In K. Case (Ed.), *Intersectionality pedagogy: Complicating identity and social justice* (pp. 46–59). New York, NY: Routledge.

Kurtiş, T. (2010). *Silencing the self and depression among Turkish women* (Unpublished master's thesis). Department of Psychology, University of Kansas, Lawrence, KS.

Liebert, R., Leve, M., & Hui, A. (2011). The politics and possibilities of activism in contemporary feminist psychologies. *Psychology of Women Quarterly, 35*, 697–704.

Lugones, M., & Spelman, E. (1983). Have we got a theory for you! Feminist theory, cultural imperialism and the demand for "the woman's voice." *Women's Studies International Forum, 6,* 573–581.

Maldonado-Torres, N. (2007). On the coloniality of being. Contributions to the development of a concept. *Cultural Studies, 21,* 240–270.

McGuffey, S., & Rich, C. (1999). Playing in the gender transgression zone: Race, class, and hegemonic masculinity in middle childhood. *Gender & Society, 13,* 608–610.

Menon, U., & Shweder, R. A. (1998). The return of the "White Man's Burden": The moral discourse of anthropology and the domestic life of Hindu women. In R. A. Shweder (Ed.), *Welcome to middle age! (and other cultural fictions)* (pp. 139–188). Chicago, IL: University of Chicago Press.

Mignolo, W.D. (2009). Epistemic disobedience, independent thought, and decolonial freedom. *Theory, Culture, and Society, 26,* 159–181.

Moghadam, V. (Ed.) (2007). *From patriarchy to empowerment: Women's participation, movements, and rights in the Middle East, North Africa, and South Asia.* Syracuse, NY: Syracuse University Press.

Mohanty, C. T. (1991). Under Western eyes: Feminist scholarship and colonial discourses. In C. Mohanty, A. Russo, & L. Torres (Eds.), *Third world women and the politics of feminism* (pp. 333–358). Bloomington: Indiana University Press.

Moscovici, S. (1984). The phenomena of social representations. In R. M. Farr & S. Moscovici (Eds.), *Social representations* (pp. 3–69). Cambridge, UK: Cambridge University Press.

Narayan, U. (1997). *Dislocating cultures: Identities, traditions, and third-world feminism.* New York, NY: Routledge.

Newman, M., Groom, C. J., Handelman, L. D., & Pennebaker, J. W. (2008). Gender differences in language use: An analysis of 14,000 text samples. *Discourse Processes, 45,* 211–236.

Oliker, S. J. (1998). The modernization of friendship: Individualism, intimacy, and gender in the nineteenth century. In R. G. Adams & G. Allan (Eds.), *Placing friendship in context: Structural analysis in the social sciences* (pp. 18–42). New York, NY: Cambridge University Press.

Said, E. W. (1978). *Orientalism.* New York, NY: Vintage.

Schug, J., Yuki, M., & Maddux, W. (2010). Relational mobility explains between—and within-culture differences in self-disclosure to close friends. *Psychological Science, 21,* 1471–1478.

Shaw, R. (2000). "Tok af, lef af": A political economy of Temne techniques of secrecy and self. In I. Karp & D. A. Masolo (Eds.), *African philosophy as cultural inquiry* (pp. 25–49). Bloomington: Indiana University Press.

Shweder, R. A. (1991). *Thinking through cultures: Expeditions in cultural psychology.* Cambridge: Harvard University Press.

Spence, J. T., & Helmreich, R. L. (1978). *Masculinity and femininity: Their psychological dimensions, correlates, and antecedents.* Austin, TX: University of Texas Press.

Spivak, G. C. (1999). *A critique of postcolonial reason: Toward a history of the vanishing present.* Cambridge, MA: Harvard University Press.

Stabile, C. A., & Kumar, D. (2005). Unveiling imperialism: Media, gender, and the war on Afghanistan. *Media, Culture, & Society, 27*, 765–782.

Twenge, J. M. (1997). Changes in masculine and feminine traits over time: A meta analysis. *Sex Roles, 36*, 305–325.

Vrugt, A., & Luyerink, M. (2000). The contribution of bodily posture to gender stereotypical impressions. *Social Behavior and Personality, 28*, 91–103.

West, C., & Zimmerman. D. H. (1987). Doing gender. *Gender & Society, 1*, 125–151.

Williams, C. L. (1995). *Still a man's world: Men who do "women's" work.* Berkeley: University of California Press.

Witte, T., Sherman M. F., & Flynn, L. (2001). Silencing the self and the Big Five: A personological profile of silent women. *Psychological Reports, 88*, 655–663.

Yuki, M., & Schug, J. (2012). Relational mobility: A socio-ecological approach to personal relationships. In O. Gillath, G. E. Adams, & A. D. Kunkel (Eds.), *Relationship science: Integrating evolutionary, neuroscience, and sociocultural approaches* (pp. 137–152). Washington, DC: American Psychological Association.

Zimman, L., & Hall, K. (2009). Language, embodiment, and the "third sex." In D. Watt & C. Llamas (Eds.), *Language and identities* (pp. 166–178). Edinburgh: Edinburgh University Press.

6

Discursive Psychological Approaches to the (Un)making of Sex/Gender

NGAIRE DONAGHUE

Method is theory in disguise.

—Edwards, Ashmore, and Potter (1995)

O ver the past 150 years, psychologists have asked many questions and developed many theories about sex and gender. For the most part, psychological research into sex/gender has been conducted using the traditional research methods of psychology: quantitative measurement combined with experimental, quasi-experimental, correlational, and/or longitudinal research designs. Despite the incredibly varied research questions posed across the vast body of psychological research using these traditional methods, there is a common factor: the assumed existence (and importance) of sex/gender as a natural and obvious category is the starting point of this research. The long tradition of "sex-differences" research in psychology involves the recruitment of groups of women and men and the measurement of psychological characteristics of interest—such as intelligence or neuroticism or political leaning or interest in sports—in order to determine whether these characteristic are more strongly associated with one or other sex/gender. Longitudinal studies measure the development of characteristics in girls/women and boys/men, sometimes over very long periods of time, to explore the similarities and differences in the trajectories of girls and boys as they negotiate various developmental periods or life transitions. Despite the valuable insights that can be gained from research of this type, the privileging of sex/gender as a basic category (ignoring both its problematic status as a binary category as well as the myriad sociocultural factors that are confounded with it), works to reinforce the status of sex/gender as a fundamental source of difference (Hare-Mustin & Marecek, 1992).

Throughout this chapter, I use the term "sex/gender" as a hybrid concept, rather than the individual terms "sex" and "gender." Since the late 1970s, psychologists have tried to use language to mark the boundaries of a distinction between biological and cultural aspects of sex and gender. "Sex" has been used to refer to biological differences between males and females, and "gender" to refer to the cultural constructs of femininity and masculinity and to the women and men, boys and girls who are assumed to exhibit those qualities (Unger, 1979). But the usefulness of this distinction has broken down as sex/gender scholars increasingly come to grips with the issue that questions of how biological and cultural forces combine to shape aspects of human form/ability/capacity/preference/orientation are themselves fundamentally contested. Deciding to refer to something as an aspect of "sex" or an aspect of "gender" is neither self-evident nor inconsequential. It assumes that we can neatly separate the biological from the cultural despite mounting evidence of their profound enmeshment (Fausto-Sterling, 2012). I use the term "sex/gender" in an effort to acknowledge this complexity and to avoid building assumptions about the sources of human similarity and difference into sex/gender scholarship.

Discursive psychologists question the taken-for-granted status of the categories that are used to classify and investigate human experience (Potter & Edwards, 1996). Instead of assuming the "reality" of sex/gender and conducting empirical investigations into the qualities that characterize "each" of the sexes, discursive psychologists investigate how the concepts of "sex" and "gender" are constructed through their use in both scientific and everyday contexts. For discursive psychologists, there are no "pregiven" meanings attached to the categories of sex/gender. What these categories mean, what they signify, is a matter of negotiation and consensus. In this chapter, I explore how discursive psychologists have challenged the various assumptions underlying traditional sex differences research, and I consider some alternate approaches to asking questions about sex/gender based on discourse analysis.

The understanding of sex/gender as a social construct is central to discursive approaches. But although a social constructionist approach to meaning (including, but not limited to, the meanings of sex/gender) is a key feature of these approaches, it is not unique to them. Much quantitative psychological research proceeds from an understanding of gender (if not sex) as a social construct—that is, as a set of beliefs about the characteristics associated with "each" sex that are socioculturally specific and historically changeable (Unger, 1979). But despite this general agreement, there are important differences: nondiscursive social constructionist work tends to conceptualize social construction in more abstract terms, as something that *has already* happened, as a high-level sociocultural process that has provided people with the concepts that they then use in their day-to-day lives without needing to think too much about them. In theory, socially constructed concepts can always be subject to de/reconstruction. In practice, however, apart from discursive psychologists, psychologists usually treat them as stable social forces that have effects on people that can be reliably measured using psychometric instruments (such as tests and questionnaires) and used to draw meaningful insights into and predictions about people's past and future behaviour and experience.

In contrast, discursive psychologists conceptualise social construction as something that *is always happening*. Discursive approaches are primarily concerned with the language-use practices by which sex/gender are continually produced and reproduced as consequential social categories and made relevant in everyday life. Discursive psychologists ask how people use these constructs flexibly as ways of understanding and accounting for their own behaviour and that of others. Of particular concern are questions concerning how talk around sex/gender renders some types of experiences, actions, and ways of being intelligible and "natural" and others as "weird," "abnormal," or "wrong." A primary aim of discursive approaches is to uncover how various elements of social discourse work together to form a kind of cultural logic that shapes and constrains the actions and experiences of women and men in ways that reproduce and naturalize particular constructions of sex/gender.

WHAT IS DISCOURSE?

Discourse is a slippery concept. As with many contested concepts in the social sciences, the answer to the question "What is discourse?" depends on whom you ask. There are two major approaches to analysing discourse within psychology that have developed over the past 30 years. One is the more "macro" critical discourse analysis approach emerging from the work of scholars influenced by Marxian and Foucauldian theories. The other is what we might think of as a more "micro" discursive psychology approach that has its roots in ethnomethodology and critiques of measurement within psychology. In the section that follows, I consider these two traditions separately in order to make clear some of the key differences in how they conceptualise discourse and approach its analysis. However, these approaches have much in common, and in practice many psychologists who use discourse analytic methods adopt elements from both traditions.

"Macro" Discursive Approaches

"Macro" discourse analytic approaches have come into psychology largely through the critical psychology movement (Fox & Prilleltensky, 1997; Ibañez & Iñiguez, 1997; Parker, 1992). Critical psychology has its roots in the critical social theories developed in the mid-20th century by scholars such as Theodore Adorno, Max Horkheimer, Erich Fromm, and Herbert Marcuse. These scholars, heavily influenced by Marxist theorists, were centrally concerned with the relationships between ideology and subjectivity. They argued that the subjects of Western liberal democracies come to be understood—and, crucially, to understand themselves—in ways that make existing systems of social order and structures of privilege and oppression seem "natural" and inevitable functions of human nature. In this critical theory tradition, discourses are socially shared ways of thinking and speaking about certain topics or objects (including people). There is a sense in which a discourse can become a kind of entity, can be pointed to as a "thing" that has certain features and that can be understood as having currency in a certain sociohistoric context. For example, later in this chapter we will see how a version of evolutionary psychology has become "a discourse" that has increased in public visibility in Western societies over the past decade, and that has become available as a mainstream and commonsense way of accounting for certain observable differences in the lives of women and men. The grounding of "macro" discursive approaches in critical social theory directs attention to a fundamental question of ideology: Who benefits by the things we believe? What interests are served by the things that we take to be true about sex/gender? What modes of being in the world are made possible and "natural," and what kinds of alternatives are made strange, unthinkable, and abject?

These kinds of questions are also central elements of the poststructuralist theories of Michel Foucault (1972, 1994). For Foucault, discourse is a manifestation of power. That is, power operates in the ways that we conceptualise and speak about the objects that inhabit our societies (including people) and the relations between them. When a group of people comes to understand its own circumstances and the issues that affect it in terms that make the existing social order appear as natural, inevitable, and correct, then those people are likely to consent to its terms, minimising the need for those in power to engage in coercive control to maintain their advantaged position. This form of governance-through-consent is a central plank of the neoliberalism that has increasingly come to characterise

Western democracies over the past several decades (Rose, 1996). It illustrates the high stakes involved in promoting certain discourses over others. What we understand to be "natural" is what we (are more likely to) accept. Discourses, in this view, set the terms on which we live. Discourses that naturalise sex/gender as something that arises straightforwardly from human biology serve to normalise features of social life that might otherwise be more readily seen as instances of sex/gender-based injustice, such as the disproportionate number of men killed and injured in military service or the unequal burden of infant and elder care that falls to women.

In this "macro" understanding of discourse, discourses of sex/gender draw together scientific "facts," professional expertise, cultural representation and practices, institutional rules, and "raw" experience into a powerful edifice that simultaneously prescribes what is normal, correct, moral, or beneficial and provides the means through which deviations from these prescriptions are exposed and regulated. But more than simply influencing our thinking about the world, discourse shapes our subjectivity—our perceptions of the world around us and our private experiences of self are all made possible, and thus fundamentally shaped, by the discourses in which they/we are constituted. What it means, what it *feels like*, to be "a woman" or "a man" is, in this view, the result of the uncountable numbers of messages that we receive from the world around us—about how we should think, feel, and act; what is expected of us; and what we are excused from—that are the manifestation of the discourses within which we come to understand ourselves. Another way of understanding this is Foucault's famous dictum: systems produce subjects. Although there are multiple possible ways of being that can be accommodated within any given discourse, not every possibility is available—the actions of any person are produced and understood within the frame of reference provided by the discourse. The intelligible possibilities for personal identity and action that are provided within a particular discourse are known as *subject positions*. A common goal of much discursive work within this "macro" perspective is to identify various subject positions that are available within a particular discourse.

This understanding of discourse as inexorably part of the manifestation and reproduction of power is why discursive work is so widely understood as *critical psychology* and why discourse analysis is so fundamental to poststructuralist-informed analyses of sex/gender. Discourse is power in action, and to appreciate fully how various constructions of sex/gender work to reproduce entrenched patterns of privilege and oppression, we must look at how these are produced in language. But, crucially, even though discourses are suffused with power, they are never all encompassing. As Foucault emphasized, there is always some possibility of resistance, as other competing discourses find expression, often initially among those who have been marginalised or made abject by the dominant discourses. A major focus of critical psychology is to explore how alternate discourses are constructed and mobilised to counter the forces of dominant discourses and to make available alternate subject positions. For example, Irmgard Tischner and Helen Malson (2011) explored how discourses around femininity and fatness work together to construct a situation in which claims to successful feminine identity are impeded for "fat" women. Certain subject positions are culturally intelligible at the intersection of discourses of femininity and body size, only a few of which garner social approval. Furthermore, access to them may be restricted by other factors, such as age, "race," and sexuality. However, Tischner argues that the development of discourses of resistance, such as fat acceptance discourse, can open up the possibility of new, resistant subject positions that expand the range of possibilities for positive identity as a "fat" woman. Fat acceptance discourse, which challenges assumptions about (ill) health and (im)morality that are often attached to "fat" bodies, provides an alternate framework within which "fat" bodies can be understood and begins to render intelligible a wider range of subject positions, including "fit and fat," or "large and proud," or "big is beautiful."

"Micro" Discursive Approaches

The second major approach to the study of discourse, which I characterise as a "micro" discursive approach, comes out of work by scholars associated with the Discourse and Rhetoric Group at Loughborough University in the United Kingdom. This "micro" discursive psychology works with a definition of discourse that involves "all forms of spoken talk and written text" (Tuffin, 2005, p. 87). Scholars who adopt this perspective are less interested in the nature of "macro"-level discourses in the Foucauldian sense, and more concerned with the specific ways in which people use language to formulate the things that they say. Discursive psychologists study language use ranging from informal, everyday conversation among people, through various forms of institutional interactions (such as those between doctors and patients, for example) as well as more formal communications such as those found in print and electronic media. This focus is useful in that it captures the important idea that social understandings are continuously produced and reproduced across any and all contexts of social life. Micro-discursive approaches are particularly concerned with exploring how speakers construct their talk in ways that enable them to achieve their interactional goals, such as providing logical, reasonable, and moral accounts of their own actions, and presenting their own viewpoints as natural and sensible. For example, Nigel Edley and Margaret Wetherell's (1999) classic study of young men talking about their relationships with young women showed how the men were able to construct a position for themselves as being committed to egalitarian values as regard gender even while also describing many specific ways in which they expected to maintain traditional sex/gendered divisions of labor in their future relationships.

Discursive psychologists point to "interpretative repertoires" (Potter & Wetherell, 1987) or "commonplaces" (Billig, 1996), which are taken-for-granted statements, a kind of "commonsense" that a speaker can appeal to without needing to provide any further explanation. These interpretative repertoires are similar in some ways to the Foucauldian meaning of "discourse," in that they exist in the wider culture, rather than as individual "beliefs," and have a sense of "out-thereness" to them that transcends any particular instance of talk. The identification of such interpretative repertoires is an important goal of some discursive psychological analyses. For example, in their study of men's views about feminism, Edley and Wetherell (2001) found that the men whom they studied drew on two distinct interpretative repertoires about feminists. In one repertoire, feminists were constructed as reasonable women who simply (and understandably) felt that they deserved equal treatment to men. A second repertoire, by contrast, portrayed feminists as unfeminine women who were angry with men (supposedly for rejecting them), who blamed men for any dissatisfaction with their lives, and who were invested in punishing men and spoiling their fun. Edley and Wetherell showed how these two repertoires combined to construct a "Jekyll and Hyde" view of feminism, in which the "reasonable" desires of women for equal opportunities to men were "taken too far" by some feminists in ways that "inevitably" put men offside and caused them to become wary of feminism more generally.

"Micro" discursive researchers are particularly interested in exploring how interpretative repertoires are actually used by speakers and to what ends. This interest serves to keep their research grounded in the action-orientation of language. In the example mentioned earlier, Edley and Wetherell showed how men used the contrast between the "reasonable" and "extreme" repertoires of feminists to position themselves as egalitarian, even while engaging in substantial criticisms of women seeking equality. One participant (William) illustrates this positioning:

> WILLIAM: Well, it depends on what kind of feminism. If it's the extreme kind, I've got no time for it at all because I think they do women's issues a real disservice.

This extract show how William makes use of the "Jekyll and Hyde" repertoires regarding feminists not only to express a (negative) view about feminism but also to *position himself* as someone who really does care about and support women's rights: he claims to object to feminism because it harms women's actual interests, thereby bolstering his own claim to egalitarianism.

For "micro" discursive psychologists, every instance of talk is both *situated* and *occasioned*. That is, it occurs in a context, for a reason. These contexts and reasons are important parts of any analysis of how socially shared ideas (interpretative repertoires, discourses) are deployed in any given situation (Edwards & Potter, 1992).

One of the pragmatic differences between the "macro" and "micro" approaches to discourse analysis outlined earlier concerns the kind of data that is considered to be suitable for analysis. A central feature of "micro" discursive psychology is its commitment to the principle that social categories or concepts are important to understanding social interactions only to the extent that the participants in those interactions actually use them. The emphasis on action-orientation in language means that it is important that the situations in which discourse is analysed are natural and meaningful for the participants. In this view, it is not appropriate for a researcher to bring to the data her or his own ideas about what is likely to be important. Rather, the researcher should attend to the concepts and categories that are made relevant by the participants. Concepts such as sex/gender should only be used in analysing an interaction to the extent that they are "oriented to" by the speakers themselves (Stokoe & Smithson, 2001). This distinction is referred to as a distinction between members' (i.e., the actual participants in an interaction) and analysts' (i.e., the researchers) categories. The distinction reflects the intellectual roots of "micro" discursive psychology in ethnomethodology, which is a research method that is committed to understanding the actions of members of a social group entirely on their own terms, without importing systems of meaning from outside the group.

To avoid "contaminating" data with the agenda of the analyst, discursive psychologists have a strong preference for naturally occurring data. Naturally occurring data have been memorably defined as data that would pass "the dead psychologist test"—that is, if the psychologist who was planning the analysis were hit by a bus, would the data still exist? Examples of naturally occurring data include everyday conversations between friends, interactions between service providers and clients (such as in doctors' offices or on telephone help lines), and political debates. Unfortunately for the would-be analyst, there is often no record of these kinds of interactions, and although occasionally the participants may agree to their recording, the most accessible forms of naturally occurring data for analysis in psychological studies tend to be in written form (such as newspaper articles, blog posts and comments, and social media posts). For pragmatic reasons, however, studies are often conducted with focus groups (and, more rarely, interviews) in which participants are invited to talk about the issues that the analyst wishes to study. In these situations, it is considered important for the analyst to participate as little as possible and to try to facilitate a "natural" discussion among participants. For "macro" discourse analysts, however, the interactional pragmatics of the situation are not a key feature of the analysis, and therefore naturally occurring data are not considered so important. Researchers using this approach not only make use of focus groups but also may present group members with materials (such as newspaper articles or video clips) illustrating the issues of interest in order to stimulate discussion among participants.

KEY DIFFERENCES BETWEEN DISCURSIVE AND TRADITIONAL PSYCHOLOGY

The emphasis on the action-orientation of language in discursive approaches highlights an important break with traditional psychological methods and theories. Traditional psychologists treat language largely as a descriptive medium—it is used, albeit imperfectly, as a means by which people attempt to convey their inner thoughts and feelings to others. In this view, the things that are of interest to psychologists are understood as located in the minds of individuals, and language is seen as providing a window through which to peer into internal psychological processes. Furthermore, the psychological objects that are described through language are seen as largely durable and coherent. That is, people's attitudes, values, beliefs, and intentions are understood as stable attributes that can be measured; these measurements can be used to predict future behavior and experience. Inconsistencies in people's attitudes or beliefs are generally seen as reflecting problems with the tools that have been developed to measure them. Discursive psychologists, by contrast, see language as a constructive process, rather than a descriptive one. In other words, certain kinds of actions are achieved and certain kinds of experiences are enacted by the things people say. Inconsistencies in "attitudes" or "values" from this perspective are not *errors*, but rather are seen as *features* of discourse, features that show how language practices are shaped by the circumstances in which they occur. For discursive psychologists, people don't "have" attitudes so much as they take up attitudes in line with their interactional agendas in various situations. Or, as Jonathan Potter puts it, attitudes are *per*formed rather than *pre*formed (Potter, 1998, p. 246).

Despite some differences that we have seen earlier, all discursive approaches to the study of sex/gender have key elements in common. For discursive psychologists, sex/gender is something that exists in the social world; that is, it is a property not of the mind/body but of culture, and it is therefore to be studied not in the minds of individuals, but in the social encounters and media contexts of everyday life. Critical discursive psychologists are especially concerned with how people "speak themselves and others into being" by drawing on culturally available meanings, including sex/gendered meanings. We can see an example of how consequential language can be for identity—and how hotly contested issues of language and meaning can become—by looking at some of the issues emerging from the rapid mainstreaming of transgender issues in contemporary Western culture.

Much of the mainstream public discourse around transgender issues relies on and reproduces the idea that transgender women and men were "born into the wrong body." Although many trans activists welcome the increasing visibility of transgender issues as a means of reducing transphobia and asserting the right of all people to live according to the sex/gender with which they identify, there are many ways in which the oversimplifications and exclusions perpetuated in this mainstream discourse can be problematic. In particular, the emphasis in popular discourse on transgender women and men transitioning from "one" gender to "the other" has been criticised for the way it reinforces essentialist beliefs about sex/gender dimorphism (e.g., Nagoshi, Brzuzy, & Terrell, 2012). And because most sympathetic treatments of transgender issues are associated with progressive politics, this particular version of transgender identity, in which people are either (and only) female or male, works to reify and naturalise gender without provoking the same level of critique that is often raised against essentialist and binary views of gender in other more conservative contexts. This mainstream formulation marginalises other forms of gender (non)identification, such as are represented by the terms "nonbinary" or "genderqueer." These latter identifications challenge the status of sex/gender as a binary categorisation and instead emphasise the idea of gender as a spectrum and/or the idea of sex/gender identifications and presentations as fluid. However, despite the recognition of diverse forms of transgender identification within transgender and feminist communities, these complex and nuanced issues are largely missing from public discourse. Despite good intentions, the mainstream "born in the wrong body" discourse can be seen as contributing to the reproduction of regressive and essentialist social understandings of sex/gender, even while promoting (a form of) social inclusion for trans individuals. Emerging social issues such as this can provide insight into how certain discourses come to prominence in social life, and they can reveal the struggles and the stakes involved in shaping how the issue comes to be understood.

DISCOURSE AND THE CULTURAL LOGIC OF POSTFEMINISM: CHOICE, EMPOWERMENT, AND BIOLOGISM

Many feminist scholars working to understand sex/gendered relations and experience in the contemporary West are concerned with understanding how a widespread consensus that Western high-income societies are now "postfeminist" has arisen (Gill, 2007; McRobbie, 2009). "Postfeminism" is a contested term, but it is often used to signal a constellation of beliefs, including the putative "pastness" of feminism's legitimate concerns; a resurgence of interest in previously eschewed "traditionally feminine" pastimes and pleasures; and the notion that embracing femininity and feminine sexuality is "empowering" for young women. A key feature of postfeminism is the apparent "taking into account" of feminism while at the same time stripping away its political force for social change. In the following section I consider some examples of discourse analytic work that show how a range of social discourses weave together to provide powerful support for postfeminist cultural logic of sex/gender.

Choice Feminism, "Confidence," and "Empowerment"

At the heart of postfeminist culture is the assertion that women and men may have the same rights and opportunities and yet nevertheless make different "choices"—a discourse that has come to be characterised as "choice feminism." Choice feminism allows the plentiful evidence that professional, family, and social life remains strongly organised along gendered lines to be understood as simply a benign reflection of different preferences and priorities of women and men, rather than as evidence of continuing sexism. Many feminist scholars have used discourse analysis to demonstrate how the notion of "choice" functions as a bottom-line argument that cannot be easily countered. (See, for example, Braun, 2009; Stuart & Donaghue, 2012.) The emphasis on "choice" brings issues of sex/gender firmly into the neoliberal framework of individualism and freedom. So long as women and men are living in ways that they have "chosen" for themselves, by what right can those "choices" be questioned? Yet by positioning women and men as choice makers, other factors involved in these outcomes are minimized. For example, critiques of systemic and structural barriers that differentially reward and punish women and men for various actions and ambitions fade away under the relentless logic of individual freedom of choice.

Yet despite its power, sometimes "choice feminism" does encounter problems. Discourse analysis has been used to explore how a wider range of discursive resources can be marshaled in order to "shore up" choice-based explanations in instances where they might otherwise be seen to fall short. One companion discourse that has recently become a focus of attention concerns "confidence" and the distinctively gendered ways in which it is used (e.g., Gill & Orgad, 2015). According to Gill and Orgad (2015), a "confidence cult(ure)" has arisen across a wide and diverse range of sites that aim to promote the "empowerment" of women and/or girls. Gill and Orgad show how this discourse underwrites and reinforces the claims of choice-centric postfeminism. Ranging across domains as diverse as workplace achievement, body image, political engagement, international development, and even domestic violence, Gill and Orgad demonstrate how women are exhorted to understand their exclusion or oppression in terms of their own timidity and/or self-sabotage and to overcome these deficits by engaging in a range of self-transforming practices designed to increase their confidence.

Gill and Orgad (2015) provide detailed discourse analyses of material from two case studies: one concerning the workplace, the other, body image. The first involves analyses of advice contained in two bestselling career advice books addressed to women. A common formulation across these texts is the assertion that women have the same abilities and opportunities as men, but that they often unfortunately lack the confidence to fully "lean in" to their careers (Sandberg, 2013). It is this lack of confidence to make bold choices that is said to account for the underrepresentation of women at senior levels of corporate life, academia, and in government. By exhorting women to stop engaging in self-criticism and "just be more confident," this discursive framing encourages women to understand their lack of success in terms of their own shortcomings and marginalises continuing concerns about hostile workplace culture, unconscious bias, and outright sexism as factors contributing to the underrepresentation of women in public life.

Similarly, material from the second case study shows the continuity of key aspects of "confidence" discourse in a seemingly disparate domain. Gill and Orgad's discourse analysis of beauty industry advertisements (including print advertisements and online videos) shows how women's feelings of dissatisfaction and shame about their bodies are constructed as an unfortunate result of their own faulty perceptions, unnecessary perfectionism, and negative practices (such as engaging in "fat talk"). The miserable relationships that many women have with their bodies are understood as arising from their own mistaken thinking. The "solution" is simply to "choose" to feel more confident. Taken together, these two examples show how "confidence" discourse works as a counter to potential claims of sexism, by providing an account of how even outcomes that woman wouldn't willingly "choose" (such as "under"-achievement at work and body dissatisfaction) can be understood as flowing from their own actions—actions that are constructed as suboptimal because the lack of "confidence" undermines women's abilities to make the most "empowering" "choices" in their own interests. In this way, an account of women's dissatisfaction is produced that deflects attention and blame away from social or institutional sexism and locates the responsibility for change with individual women themselves.

Evolutionary Psychology as Discourse: The Renaturalisation of Biological "Sex" Differences

The rapid rise in profile of evolutionary psychology in recent years provides another pertinent example of how a discourse can enter into public consciousness and reshape the terms in which issues around sex/gender are understood. One of the many achievements of feminism in Western high-income societies in the period from the 1960s through the 1980s was the increasing acceptance of the view of masculinity and femininity as cultural constructs that were manifest in the behaviour and experiences of women and men largely as a result of gendered socialisation practices, rather than a "natural" expression of (putatively) dimorphic biological sex. This uncoupling of people's attributes, capacities, and preferences from their biological sex was a major plank in the political project of fighting for equal opportunities for women and men, and in the removal of both hard institutional barriers and soft social barriers to the participation of women and men across an expanded range of social roles. However, alongside the gains of the feminist movements, there has been a conservative pushback against decoupling of gendered behaviour from biological sex. The mass movement of women into public life, while cheered in many quarters, was also derided as "unnatural" and dysfunctional, just as the adoption by men of more egalitarian attitudes and nurturing roles has been transformed by detractors into a maligned figure of ridicule—the Sensitive New-Age Guy, who is portrayed as a hapless and unappealing loser.

Increasingly, as the backlash against feminism has gained momentum, claims about extensive and consequential differences between women and men have been recruited into the debate as a kind of clinching argument against which there can be no effective reply. The version of evolutionary psychology that has been taken up in public discourse puts several ideas into play. First, by identifying different adaptive challenges for ancestral men and women, it uses scientific research to legitimize belief in widespread and far-reaching biological differences between the sexes. For example, the theory of differential parental investment argues that because women have a lower maximum number of possible offspring than men and bear a heavier cost of reproduction (9 months gestation and infant care, at a minimum), it is likely that they have differentially evolved characteristics that allow them to optimise their different interests (Buss, 1996). Men, it is argued, will have more reproductive success if they are strongly sexually motivated and choose partners who are highly fertile; women, conversely, need to maximise the survival chances of each of their (fewer potential) offspring and so will have more success if they are more selective and choose "high-quality" partners who are able to provide resources that will assist in the successful rearing of those offspring to maturity. Many evolved sex differences in psychological characteristics are argued to flow from these asymmetric adaptive pressures, including a "natural" orientation to aggressive competition for status and jealousy among men and a more nurturing and selfless disposition among women (Buss, Larsen, Westen, & Semmelroth, 1992). Although there is scant evidence of a "hard-wired" basis for these orientations (see Grossi, Nash, & Parameswaran, 2014), popular versions of evolutionary psychology provide a potentially compelling narrative that appears to provide simple answers to some of the complex issues around the continuing push for sex/gender equality.

We can see these evolutionary psychology discourses in action in everyday life. Laura Garcia-Favaro's (2015) discourse analysis of contemporary

women's magazines and their associated websites shows how evolutionary arguments pervade the advice given to and by young women in
these sites. She analysed more than 2,000 interactions between readers
(mostly young women) on the magazines' online discussion boards in
which women express negative feelings about their male partners' use
of pornography. These women's reports of feeling hurt, disappointed,
and worried about the implications of their partners' actions were over-
whelmingly responded to with assertions that men's interest in pornography is an immutable "fact of life." Comments such as "women and men
are different, science says so"; "Men are biologically programmed to find
an attractive mate using a visual reference"; and "Men are wired to be
sexually attracted to more than one woman" show the pervasiveness of
the idea that male and female brains are equipped with fundamentally
different "wiring" and "programming."

But beyond providing an account that dismisses the women's hurt
feelings and relational concerns, evolutionary psychology discourse also
undergirded the advice given to women as to what they should do in
response to these "facts of life." Garcia-Favor shows how the taken-for-
grantedness of men's immutable desire for sexual novelty gave rise to
advice that women must adapt to this reality and must "work on themselves" in order to accommodate their partners if they want their relationships to be successful. Women were encouraged to cultivate a sense
of gratitude that their partner was content to use pornography rather
than seeking other sexual partners, to take a hard look at their own (presumed low) self-esteem and "get some confidence," and to "get over it."
Interestingly, Garcia-Favaro pointed out how some of this advice was even
acknowledged by the advice giver as "sexist" and "unfair" (e.g., "I know
this advice may sound harsh or even a little sexist"), but this was presented
as an irrelevant concern in the face of the unarguable fact that "men are
not the same as women (shock horror)." This analysis shows how evolutionary discourse can accommodate objections about aspects of gender
relations that are unfair and yet make these objections seem irrelevant by
engaging the idea that biological imperatives are no one's "fault."

If differences between women and men are "hard-wired," then the terms of the political debates around sex/gender are upended. Evolutionary discourse provides a cultural logic that works to make sense of the postfeminist conceit that women and men's lives are different only because—and only to the extent that—they *choose* them to be. If women and men have different "hard-wiring" and different "programming," as evolutionary psychology discourse would have it, how could it be surprising (or objectionable) that they would make different choices? In this way, the insertion of evolutionary discourse into public understandings of sex/gender accounts for and "naturalises" sex/gender differences, and thus apparently does away with the need for any political response to them (see also Donaghue, 2015). Crucially, popular versions of evolutionary psychology achieve this political outcome discursively. By providing a narrative framework that putatively explains why sex/gender differences might have come to exist, it sidesteps the need to provide actual evidence of the biologically based differences in psychological processes that it postulates.

Taken together, the "confidence" discourse and the evolutionary psychology discourse work to powerfully promote the "choice"-centric rationality of postfeminism. When faced with the obvious differences in the social distribution of rewards and responsibilities along sexed/gendered lines (as well as other identity categories), concerns about the fairness of these outcomes can be assuaged by the reassurance that these differences simply reflect people's different "choices." Popular evolutionary psychology discourse further shores up this analysis by providing pseudo-scientific explanations as to why it is "natural" for women and men to make very different choices, and "confidence" discourse further suggests that when women make "choices" against their best interests, it is because they lack the necessary confidence to "choose" a more "empowered" way of living. These discourses work together to direct attention and blame for any sex/gender-based injustice away from any systemic issues or any consideration of whose interests are served by this state of affairs; the only level at which accountability can be directed under the neoliberal logic of postfeminism is the "choice"-making individual.

CONCLUSIONS

Discursive psychology brings the study of sex/gender into the language practices of everyday life. Its key strength lies in its engagement with questions of ideology and power. By asking what functions are served by various discursive formulations, discursive psychologists show how existing social relations and social structures are rendered as "natural" in ways that reproduce the privileges and oppressions of members of those societies as simply logical consequences of individual actions.

Despite its many contributions to scholarly understandings of sex/gender, discursive psychology nonetheless has remained largely on the margins of mainstream psychology. The emphasis on natural language practices rather than on the "measurement" of psychological attributes means that discursive studies are often critiqued as unscientific (notwithstanding that observation and close description of phenomena are key activities of the natural sciences). In media coverage of psychological research, there is a status given to quantitative studies that is often withheld from qualitative work, a bias in favour of what Potter and colleagues have termed "quantification rhetoric" (Potter, Wetherell, & Chitty, 1991). The relatively small sample sizes that characterise many discursive studies sometimes lead others to claim that their findings are "anecdotal." Discourse analysis is not, however, aimed at making claims about individuals or populations; it is aimed at identifying culture-level patterns of talk that can reveal the cultural logics that members of these cultures use to understand and regulate themselves and others. (See Magnusson & Marecek, 2015, for an extended discussion of these issues.) Furthermore, one of discursive psychology's great strengths—its close consideration of issues of power—is seen in some quarters as a liability; discursive studies are all too frequently dismissed by some critics as "political" (assumed to be a bad thing), "subjective," and "biased." Although discursive psychology has produced trenchant critiques of these terms themselves, dismissive attitudes toward discursive psychology from within mainstream psychology make it very difficult to shift the epistemological terms of public debate for a wider audience. One of the challenges for discursive psychologists working on issues around sex/gender is to find more effective ways of explaining the value of our work to policy makers and to funding bodies.

Despite these challenges, discursive psychology provides critical insights into the reproduction of ideologies around sex/gender in the everyday practices of social life. Close attention to the myriad ways in which discourses of sex/gender are deployed across a wide range of social contexts and their intersections and interdependencies with other elements of political discourses can provide a deep understanding of how power operates in these social contexts. It also holds the possibility of locating potential sites of resistance, weakness, or gaps in the edifices constructed by dominant discourses, where critical counterdiscourses may find a toehold and begin to provide new and different possibilities for being in the world. If sex/gender is made of discourse, then discursive resistance may also be the straightest path to its unmaking.

REFERENCES

Billig, M. (1996). *Arguing and thinking: A rhetorical approach to social psychology.* Cambridge, UK: Cambridge University Press.

Braun, V. (2009). "The women are doing it for themselves." The rhetoric of choice and agency around female genital "cosmetic surgery." *Australian Feminist Studies, 24,* 233–249.

Buss, D. M. (1996). Paternity uncertainty and the complex repertoire of human mating strategies. *American Psychologist, 51,* 161–162.

Buss, D. M., Larsen, R. J., Westen, D., & Semmelroth, J. (1992). Sex differences in jealousy: Evolution, physiology, and psychology. *Psychological Science, 3,* 251–255.

Donaghue, N. (2015). The "facts" of life? How the notion of evolved brain differences between women and men naturalises biological accounts of sex/gender. *Australian Feminist Studies, 30,* 359–365.

Edley, N., & Wetherell, M. (1999). Imagined futures: Young men's talk about fatherhood and domestic life. *British Journal of Social Psychology, 38,* 181–194.

Edley, N., & Wetherell, M. (2001). Jekyll and Hyde: Men's constructions of feminism and feminists. *Feminism & Psychology, 11,* 439–457.

Edwards, D., Ashmore, M., & Potter, J. (1995). Death and furniture: The rhetoric, politics and theology of bottom line arguments against relativism. *History of the Human Sciences, 8,* 2–9.

Edwards, D., & Potter, J. (1992). *Discursive psychology.* London, UK: Sage.

Fausto-Sterling, A. (2012). *Sex/gender: Biology in a social world.* New York, NY: Routledge.

Foucault, M. (1972). *The archeology of knowledge.* London, UK: Tavistock.

Foucault, M. (1994). Technologies of self. In P. Rabinow & N. Rose (Eds.), *The essential Foucault* (pp. 145–169). New York, NY: The New Press.

Fox, D., & Prilleltensky, I. (1997). *Critical psychology: An introduction.* London, UK: Sage.

Garcia-Favaro, L. (2015). "Porn trouble": On the sexual regime and travels of postfeminist biologism. *Australian Feminist Studies, 30,* 366–376.

Gill, R. (2007). Postfeminist media culture: Elements of a sensibility. *European Journal of Cultural Studies, 10,* 147–166.

Gill, R., & Orgad, S. (2015). The confidence cult(ure). *Australian Feminist Studies, 30,* 324–344.

Grossi, G. S., Nash, K. A., & Parameswaran, G. (2014). Challenging dangerous ideas: A multi-disciplinary critique of evolutionary psychology. *Dialectical Anthropology, 38,* 281–285.

Hare-Mustin, R. T., & Marecek, J. (1992). *Making a difference: Psychology and the construction of gender.* New Haven, CT: Yale University Press.

Magnusson, E., & Marecek, J. (2015). *Doing qualitative research: A learner's guide.* Cambridge, UK: Cambridge University Press.

McRobbie, A. (2009). *The aftermath of feminism: Gender, culture and social change.* London, UK: Sage.

Nagoshi, J. L., Brzuzy, S. I., & Terrell, H. K. (2012). Deconstructing the complex perceptions of gender roles, gender identity, and sexual orientation among transgender individuals. *Feminism & Psychology, 22,* 405–422.

Parker, I. (1992). *Discourse dynamics: Critical analysis for social and individual psychology.* London, UK: Routledge.

Potter, J. (1998). Discursive social psychology: From attitudes to evaluative practices. *European Review of Social Psychology, 9,* 233–266.

Potter, J., & Wetherell, M. (1987). *Discourse and social psychology: Beyond attitudes and behaviour.* London, UK: Sage.

Potter, J., Wetherell, M., & Chitty, A. (1991). Quantification rhetoric—cancer on television. *Discourse & Society, 2*(3), 333–365.

Rose, N. (1996). *Inventing ourselves: Psychology, power, and personhood.* Cambridge, UK: Cambridge University Press.

Sandberg, S. (2013). *Lean in: Women, work, and the will to lead.* New York, NY: Random House.

Stokoe, E. H., & Smithson, J. (2001). Making gender relevant: Conversation analysis and gender categories in interaction. *Discourse & Society, 12,* 243–269.

Stuart, A., & Donaghue, N. (2012). Choosing to conform: Discursive constructions of choice in relation to feminine beauty practices. *Feminism & Psychology, 22,* 98–121.

Tischner, I., & Malson, H. (2011). 'You can't be supersized?' Exploring femininities, body size and control within the obesity terrain. In E. Rich, L. Monaghan, & L. Aphramor (Eds.), *Debating obesity: Critical perspectives* (pp. 90–114). London, UK: Palgrave Macmillan.

Tuffin, K. (2005). *Understanding critical social psychology.* London, UK: Sage.

Unger, R. K. (1979). Toward a redefinition of sex and gender. *American Psychologist, 34,* 1085–1094.

7

Gendered Power

Insights From Power Basis Theory

I-CHING LEE AND FELICIA PRATTO

Since 2009, *Forbes* magazine has compiled annual lists of the most powerful individuals on the planet. The list includes politicians such as Vladimir Putin and Barack Obama, billionaires such as Bill Gates and Warren Buffett, religious leaders such as Pope Francis, and Internet entrepreneurs Larry Page and Mark Zuckerberg. Many people on the list are repeats from previous years (43.8% on the 2015 list were also on the 2010 list; Forbes, 2011, 2016). Furthermore, women repeatedly are very unlikely to be considered the most powerful individuals, occupying 7.4% of the slots in 2010 and 12.3% of the slots in 2015. In this chapter, we introduce a theory, power basis theory, to account for the stability of gender inequality in power, and how it explains women's difficulty in gaining power in gender-binary cultural systems. We illustrate how power basis theory generates hypotheses that can be tested at several levels of organization (individual, group, ecological) using survey and experimental methodologies and a variety of statistical techniques tailored to specific conceptual questions.

To account for different kinds of power, we redefine power and elucidate basic principles that govern power dynamics according to power basis theory (Pratto et al., 2011). Power basis theory holds that different kinds of survival needs each give rise to a different kind of power, such as access to consumable resources, wholeness (i.e., health in mind and body), knowledge, legitimate acceptance in a community, and the care of other people. Roles, individuals, and groups often command different kinds of power. For example, billionaires, gangsters, Internet entrepreneurs, judges, and charismatic leaders differ in terms of their primary kind of power. Billionaires' primary power is wealth, gangsters' is physical force, Internet entrepreneurs' is knowledge, judges' is legitimacy, and charismatic leaders' is relationships. The necessity of consumption makes access to and control of material resources a fundamental kind of power (e.g., Marx, 1904; Smith, 1793). The chronic necessity of wholeness makes it possible for healing, threatening, or inflicting harm (i.e., violence) to always be kinds of power (e.g., Jackman, 2001; Keegan, 1993; Mosca, 1896/1939). The necessity of interacting competently with one's environment makes knowledge a fundamental kind of power (e.g., Elliot & Dweck, 2006). The necessity of belonging to a community makes having prestige, status, or legitimacy (assuming also a functioning community) a fundamental kind of power (e.g., Domhoff, 1990; Jost & Major, 2001; Parsons, 1954). People's need for care from others is normally met by social affiliation or obligations among people (Goode, 1972; Pratto & Walker, 2004). Given that every person must satisfy all these needs to survive, controlling access to material resources, using violence, healing, sharing or withholding crucial information, stigmatizing others, destroying communities, legitimizing others, and reneging on obligations and fulfilling obligations are *each* critical power actions.

As specified in power basis theory, being able to have one's survival needs met means that one is empowered. Power basis theory defines power as a state of the relationship between people or groups and the ecological system in which they are embedded, rather than as an individual state (e.g., having agency) or a state of a social relationship (e.g., having autonomy, interdependence or dominance vis-à-vis another; see

Pratto, 2015, for a detailed examination of definitions of power). That is, whether a person is powerful is not defined by a person's possessions, nor is it defined as influence over another. Rather, it is defined by how well the person's capacities mesh with the affordance of that person's ecology for meeting the person's needs.

From this perspective, several factors affect how a person's needs may be satisfied by the ecology. The first factor is the ease of opportunities in the ecology that allow for need satisfaction. For example, individuals in a free society have more options to pursue opportunities to have their needs met than individuals in an authoritarian state do. Hence, people in a free society should have more power than individuals in an authoritarian state, other things being equal. Within the same society, some groups of individuals (i.e., dominant or privileged groups) may enjoy more opportunities to have their needs met than other groups of individuals (i.e., subordinate or stigmatized groups). The second factor is the degree to which the ecology makes possible the transformation of one kind of power into another. This phenomenon is called *power fungibility* in power basis theory. Suppose two people in different societies have the same amount of money, and it is adequate. If their two societies offer the same number of opportunities for individuals to fulfill their needs, a person in a society with a low living standard (L) may be more powerful than a person in a society with a high living standard (H), everything else being equal. Because the costs for the person L to transform one kind of power into another are lower than for person H, L is more likely to use her fortune to satisfy her material needs (one kind of power) and to transform it into satisfying her other needs (other kinds of power, such as attaining knowledge, becoming a philanthropist to be respected by the community, hiring body guards, hiring caretakers) more easily than H.

Power in power basis theory, then, has a crucial social facet: All the kinds of power may be fungible with each other through social transactions. That is, a person may be empowered with regard to one specific need, but she is in a better condition to be able to meet her other needs if she is able to transform one kind of power into other kinds of specific power. This is especially the case if she does not have to lose one kind of power to gain another. For example, being esteemed within a community can make more lucrative jobs available, such that her legitimacy is kept, and, at the same time, her esteem can be used to gain greater material resources. Likewise, the threat of violence or physical force can be used to require people to transmit material resources to others, as in the cases of governments using the possibility of imprisonment to enforce tax laws, colonial exploitation, and mugging. Conversely, people and groups with the least power sacrifice what they have to meet an acute survival need. Thus, the fungibility of their kinds of power is limited. For example, people with little power may offer their own labor in exchange for immediate resources and be forced to forego longer term opportunities (e.g., to be become educated) in order to survive the short term. Their need for an immediate income prevents "investing" in education that in the future might afford them better opportunities for income, safer jobs, more legitimacy within their societies, and so forth.

POWER BASIS THEORY AND GENDERED POWER

Applying power basis theory to understanding men's and women's power, we argue that whereas women and men are likely to achieve equality in some kinds of power (e.g., knowledge), it is more difficult for women to achieve equality in other kinds of power (e.g., as community leaders, in force). For this, we offer two explanations. First, the ecology may offer more opportunities for men (and more constraints for women) to gain some kinds of power. Attaining or exercising particular kinds of power (e.g., physical strength, legitimacy) may violate gender expectations (e.g., gender norms); thus, they pose challenges and risks to women who do so that are not imposed on men. Secondly, because powerful people are presumed to be men, the ecology may have more constraints for women to translate power in one arena to another arena (i.e., *power fungibility*) than for men. To test these two explanations, we examine evidence from survey and experimental data on group and individual levels, and on the constraints within one society, Taiwan, and globally.

On the Group Level

To test the two predictions made by power basis theory regarding gendered power inequalities, we first tested the stereotypes and ideals that people who self-identify as men and women ("participant sex") have about both men and women. Group stereotypes are descriptive gender norms, which paint a picture of what men and women are believed to be like, whereas gender ideals are prescriptive stereotypes, which describe what people think men or women should be like (Prentice & Carranza, 2002). In a study conducted in Taiwan, we randomly assigned participants to report how the gender groups are viewed in the society in terms of personality traits (52 young women and 32 young men, mean age = 20.3, SD = 1.2) or in terms of behaviors (also 52 young women and 32 young men, mean age = 20.8, SD = 2.2). In both samples, at least three words were measured to tap each kind of power except for knowledge behavior (two behaviors). For example, we asked how "knowledgeable" men and women are for a personality trait measure, and "how likely [men, women] are to attain an advanced degree" as a behavioral measure of knowledge power. To test what kinds of power reflect lay people's sense of power, we also measured participants' beliefs about men's and women's general power traits.

We tested whether men and women were perceived to differ on all dimensions of power together using repeated-measures ANOVA, and we also considered participant sex as a factor. As can be seen by the means in Table 7.1, participants perceived men to be more generally powerful, more knowledgeable, more forceful, and more resourceful than women. Participants also perceived men as more likely to attain advanced degrees (knowledge), to use force (force), to invest (material resource), to have useful networks and care for themselves rather than for others (relationship), and to lead the community (legitimacy) than women. The responses of these two groups of participants demonstrate that men are often perceived to have more power than women, and perceived gender differences are larger with regard to specific behaviors than for traits.

Pratto and Walker (2004) argued that obligatory relationships, such as being in parent–child relationships, are more of a power domain for women than for men. As such, women's having stronger obligations (e.g., to family) limits their ability to obtain other and more fungible forms of power. When we factor analyzed our stereotype data according to the proposed power dimension (i.e., obligatory power), we found partial support for this argument, in that women were perceived to be more protective, exploiting, popular, and well connected (loaded on one factor in trait ratings, Eigenvalue = 2.23, loadings > .45) than men. However, men were perceived to have good connections that can help them in the long run (i.e., networking behaviors) and behaviors that indicate that they would not sacrifice themselves for others. Although women are believed to have social skills and qualities that should assist them in developing relationships as measured in trait ratings, these relationships may not necessarily be instrumental as measured in behavior ratings (e.g., getting ahead in life) or in power fungibility. Consistent with our interpretation of the mean differences between the two types of measures, men's perceived relationship traits were associated significantly with general power traits $[r(82) = .35, p = .001]$, whereas women's perceived relationship traits were marginally associated with general power traits $[r(82) = .19, p = .08]$. This last finding shows that people perceive power in general to be the kind of power believed to characterize men more than women even in the relationship domain.

We also examined the ideals men and women have for their own gender. In addition to the specific power dimensions that we have discussed, we added a new power dimension, namely physical appearance. Human beings are motivated to extend themselves in time, such as to pursue longevity or to ensure that their genes or culture survives. Men and women value several other characteristics in potential mates more than they do physical appearance (e.g. "kind and understanding"; Buss & Barnes, 1986). However, in diverse societies (including Chinese societies), physical appearance is rated as more important for women as mates, more so in societies with relatively *high* gender equality (Buss, 1989; Chang et al., 2011; Schmitt, 2012). Why gender equality is associated with *greater* perceived importance of women's appearance is an interesting conundrum. A group of 91 Taiwanese women and 62 Taiwanese men reported

TABLE 7.1   GROUP PERCEPTIONS FOR MEN AND WOMEN AND IDEAL MEN AND WOMEN ON POWER TRAITS

Stereotypes/Power Words	Traits (from "0" highly unlikely ~ "4" highly representative)[a]		Behavior (from "0" highly unlikely ~ "100" highly likely)[a]	
Target Groups	Women	Men	Women	Men
General power (α = .79)	1.44[b] (1.28, 1.61)	2.80[b] (2.63, 2.97)	N/A	N/A
Knowledge (αs > .77)	2.02[b] (1.83, 2.21)	2.45[b] (2.26, 2.64)	57.15[b] (53.03, 61.27)	63.49[b] (59.37, 67.61)
Physical strength (αs > .85)	0.85[b] (0.66, 1.04)	2.75[b] (2.56, 2.93)	35.83[b] (32.07, 39.58)	59.22[b] (55.46, 62.97)
Resource (αs > .78)	1.56[b] (1.36, 1.75)	2.25[b] (2.06, 2.45)	53.34[b,c] (48.92, 57.77)	58.77[b,c] (54.35, 63.19)
Relationships[d] (α = .66)	3.44[b] (3.27, 3.60)	3.27[b] (3.01, 3.44)		
Networking (α = .75, 2 items)			52.79[b,c] (49.62, 55.96)	61.50[b,c] (58.33, 64.68)
Not sacrificing for others (α = .60, 3 items)			31.14[b,c] (34.18, 40.10)	47.78[b,c] (44.82, 50.75)
Community respect (αs > .69)	2.15 (2.03, 2.28)	2.18 (2.05, 2.30)	52.94[b] (49.17, 56.72)	65.55[b] (61.77, 69.32)
Sample size	84	84	84	84

NOTES: Means are shown with 95% confidence intervals shown in parentheses.

[a] Participants were randomly assigned to rate either trait measures or behavior measures; thus, they had the same sample size and gender breakdown.

[b] The Target Group main effect was significant.

[c] The Target Group x Participant Sex interaction was significant; significant differences were observed only among participants who were women.

[d] Two sets of behaviors were considered, networking (+) and sacrificing for others (–). The more one has networking ability and less obligations for others, the more one has relationship power. All comparisons in bold were significant at a level of $p < .05$.

how they would ideally view their own gender group (see sample and
method details in Lee, 2013; see the second and third columns in
Table 7.2). Ideal men and women were rated similarly on knowledge,
relationships, and legitimacy. However, consistent with our reasoning
that men would expect themselves to be more powerful than women,
ideal men were rated higher on traits reflecting general power, physical
strength, and resources, whereas ideal women were rated higher on traits
reflecting physical appearance. Overall, the findings suggest that although
men and women believe that ideals for men and women are similar on
some dimensions (e.g., knowledge), women think they should aspire
to be physically attractive (i.e., ideal women), whereas men think they

TABLE 7.2   MEN'S AND WOMEN'S SELF-EVALUATIONS AND IDEAL
EVALUATIONS FOR OWN SEX ON POWER TRAITS

Power Traits	Ideal Evaluations[a]		Self-Evaluations[a]	
	Women	Men	Women	Men
Powerful (αs > .74)	1.43 (1.26, 1.59)	2.35 (2.15, 2.55)	1.23 (1.02, 1.43)	1.58 (1.34, 1.83)
Knowledgeable (αs > .86)	2.43 (2.26, 2.61)	2.54 (2.34, 2.75)	1.76 (1.59, 1.93)	2.01 (1.80, 2.22)
Attractive (αs > .71)	2.56 (2.40, 2.73)	1.79 (1.59, 1.99)	1.34 (1.17, 1.52)	1.20 (0.99, 1.41)
Forceful (αs > .77)	0.90 (0.76, 1.03)	2.82 (2.66, 2.99)	1.21 (1.05, 1.37)	1.61 (1.42, 1.80)
Resourceful (αs > .62[b])	1.51 (1.34, 1.69)	2.43 (2.22, 2.64)	0.93 (0.78, 1.08)	0.94 (0.76, 1.12)
Popular (αs > .55[c])	2.47 (2.32, 2.62)	2.38 (2.20, 2.56)	1.78 (1.61, 1.95)	2.04 (1.83, 2.25)
Respected (αs > .81)	2.11 (1.92, 2.30)	2.30 (2.07, 2.53)	1.55 (1.39, 1.71)	1.69 (1.50, 1.89)
Sample size	91	62	91	62

[a] Same sample.
[b] α = .62 for self-evaluations and α = .76 for ideals-evaluations.
[c] α = .79 for self-evaluations and α = .55 for ideal-evaluations. Numbers in bold reached the
significance level of $p < .05$.

should aspire to be powerful, forceful, and resourceful (i.e., ideal men). Extrapolating from these findings, it may be that when women achieve equality in education, they devote more effort to transform education power into certain domains (e.g., beauty, relationships) than into others (e.g., resources and domains that require using force, such as joining in police force or army), if they wish to become ideal women. Men, conversely, do not find themselves in such a predicament because ideal men were not perceived to be particularly low on any of the power dimensions except for physical attractiveness, which may be largely determined by one's physical features.

On the Individual Level

We also tested how men and women actually perceive themselves with regard to different types of power traits. In the same sample in which participants rated the ideal for their own gender group, we asked participants to rate themselves (see Table 7.2 for sample sizes and results). Gender differences on self-ratings were only robust on general power and physical strength (see Table 7.2). Men perceived themselves to possess more general power traits than did women (M = 1.98 vs. M = 1.66, $p <$ .001). However, the gender difference on self-ratings for general power is much smaller than that for ideal men and women (M_D = 0.18, p = .04 vs. M_D = 0.46, $p <$ .001). A similar pattern was observed on ratings of traits reflecting physical strength.

Juxtaposing the findings from the group level and self-ratings, we found that there are small gender differences on the individual level, but large gender differences on prescriptive gender norms, and even larger gender differences on descriptive gender norms. There are two possible explanations for the findings. They may reflect the changing Taiwanese society. Taiwan has a Chinese culture, in which rigid gender norms may be prevalent in older generations but not in younger generations. Thus, young adults might report what they observe in the older generations for descriptive gender norms, but, due to social changes promoting gender equality, they may have adopted less gender-stereotypic prescriptive norms and beliefs about themselves. Alternatively or in addition, descriptive and prescriptive gender norms may be so interconnected that the gender hierarchy seems legitimate and normal. That is, even when young adults accept that men and women could ideally be alike, they may not believe that they are actually alike. We will examine more evidence to address this possibility later in this chapter.

To further understand perceptions of power from the observer perspective, we asked a group of 209 Taiwanese young adults (127 women) to read about one target person at a time (see sample and method details in Lee, 2012). Each participant read about a total of six targets (also described as young adults) who could be high or lower on specific kinds of power and who could be male or female. For example, a target high on knowledge was described to be a bright student at school who earned a PhD degree and teaches at a well-known university. The target's sex category was manipulated by the target's name and pronouns.

Although participants responded to male and female targets largely similarly, there were three reliable findings that have gender implications. First, observers consistently showed gender bias in favor of the male target over the female target when the target was described as receiving community recognition (on perceptions reflecting knowledge, relationships, resources, and status). The male target described as being respected in the community was rated more knowledgeable (on a scale of 0 "not at all" to 4 "completely", $M_M = 2.12$ vs. $M_F = 1.77$, $p = .03$), resourceful ($M_M = 2.54$ vs. $M_F = 2.07$, $p = .004$), popular ($M_M = 2.24$ vs. $M_F = 1.91$, $p = .03$), and respected ($M_M = 3.04$ vs. $M_F = 2.68$, $p = .03$) than his female counterpart, although the female target was described in *exactly* the same way as the male target. Second, women were rated more appealing and attractive than men across targets ($M_F = 0.97$ vs. $M_M = 0.66$, $p < .001$), except when descriptions regarding appearance were explicitly given (on various kinds of traits, $ps > .29$). Third, men were rated more forceful than women across targets ($M_M = 0.61$ vs. $M_F = 0.45$, $p < .001$), except when descriptions regarding force were explicitly given (on various kinds of traits, $ps > .50$).

These findings elucidate why sometimes gender biases occur and why sometimes they do not. First, some dimensions are more gender laden than others. Physical appearance and physical strength seem to be strongly gendered. They affect how people view themselves, expect their gender to be, and how they view others. Resource power and community recognition seem to be somewhat gendered. Resource power has a gendered aspect when people evaluate what is ideal for men and women and when they perceive others. Community recognition appears to be a gendered dimension when perceiving others.

In addition, target sex rarely affects observers on impressions that directly correspond to the specific features (e.g., the ratings of targets who were "respected" regarding community respect), but target sex does often affect observers on impressions that do not correspond to the specific features (e.g., the ratings of "resourceful" on targets who receive community respect). That is, when observers view leaders in a community, they tend to view male leaders as respected *and* resourceful, whereas the female leaders are respected but not necessarily viewed as resourceful, even though perceivers were not given information on the levels of the leaders' resources. This association between the two power dimensions in the absence of any evidence of the link supports our argument that "*power fungibility*" could account for men's and women's different kinds of power.

Societal Constraints

The aforementioned research findings provide evidence for our explanations of why women have difficulty in gaining power compared to men. We further investigated whether the predicament women experience may be caused by constraints in the social ecology. To this aim, we examined beliefs that may prohibit women gaining specific kinds of power (e.g., gaining a job), as well as beliefs about women transforming one kind of power into other kinds of power (relationship translating to economic power) in Taiwan. Because the discrepancies between descriptive and prescriptive gender norms we observed earlier may be due to generational differences, we examined whether societal constraints upheld by individuals differ by generations. We also tested for urban/ rural differences to examine the effect of ecology on power dynamics. We analyzed the data from a representative sample collected in Taiwan in 2012 (Chang, Tu, & Liao, 2014) and found that respondents tended to prioritize women's responsibilities in family and consider infant care more important than paid jobs for women. Older generations (aged 45 to 98), those who reside in rural (less modern) areas, and men were more likely to endorse these beliefs than younger generations (aged 19 to 44), those who reside in urban areas, and women, respectively. The geographic area x sex interaction indicated that in rural areas, men are more likely than women to agree that mothers' having jobs is bad for preschool children; this is not the case in urban areas. Gender differences across age groups were stable. The lack of the gender and age interaction suggests that although young people do not endorse these beliefs as strongly as older people, men are more likely to endorse these beliefs than women regardless of their ages.

More important, regression analysis shows that these beliefs were found to reliably correspond to men's and women's hours per week doing domestic chores, having a paid job, and income levels among cohabiting and married heterosexual individuals. After controlling for age and years of receiving education, men who believed that "men's responsibility is earning money and women's is caring for the family and its members" were less likely to do domestic chores, standardized $B = -.14$, $p = .001$, whereas their female counterparts with such a belief were more likely to do domestic chores, $B = .12$, $p = .01$. Women with such a belief were also more likely to care for family members, $B = .10$, $p = .03$ and earn less, $B = -.11$, $p = .01$. Furthermore, women who believe that wives' having full-time jobs is bad for family life were less likely to have a job, $B = -.14$, $p = .001$, and if they do have a job, they earn less, $B = -.12$, $p = .005$. These gender beliefs did not predict men's job status and income.

Our last study investigated societal constraints by comparing nations. In particular, we examined how gender equality in one domain may be translated into gender equality in other domains (i.e., *power fungibility*) by comparing all nations for which data are available to each other ($k = 175$). In other words, in this analysis we can consider the nation to be the ecology (and it is the statistical case). To measure constraints in the ecology, we used social freedoms and comparative wealth of the economy.

As a measure of societies' freedom, we used the Societal Freedom Index computed by Freedom House (2016), which evaluates freedom and rights enjoyed by the individuals according to the Universal Declaration of Human Rights (i.e., political rights and civil liberties) in each nation. The Purchasing Power Parity Index is one of the World Bank's (2016) development indicators, which takes into account the relative cost of living and inflation rates in comparison with income levels. If a society enjoys very little freedom, it may be difficult for a person to transform one kind of power into another. If a society's purchasing power parity is high, then competition with others may make it more expensive for a person to transform one kind of power into another.

We used each nation's gender equality in education from 2010 to see whether, based on multiple regression analysis, it statistically predicts measures of gender equality in all of power basis theory's power domains 5 years later. The first thing to note in the Table 7.3 results is that except for one measure (i.e., sexual violence committed by non partners since age 15), each of the 2015 gender equality measures was predicted by measures of ecological affordances and/or freedom. This suggests that social ecologies are important for inhibiting or enabling gender equality. The second thing to note is that even controlling for these ecological measures, as expected, they were moderated by purchasing power parity, which is the interaction term ($E \times P$), and freedom, which is the interaction term ($E \times F$) in Table 7.3. Whenever separate data for men and women were available, we used those. For example, women's (men's) expected education in 2015 was predicted by women's (men's) actual education in 2010. According to the United Nations Development Programme's data (2010, 2015), gender equality in actual high school attainment in 2010 predicted gender equality in actual and expected high school attainment in 2015 (standardized Bs [$k = 141$] > .74, $ps < .001$, see Table 7.3). However, the association between actual high school attainment in 2010 and 2015 was stronger in societies with lower

TABLE 7.3   GENDER EQUALITY ACROSS DOMAINS PREDICTED BY EDUCATION ADVANCES IN 2010, FREEDOM INDEX, AND PURCHASING POWER PARITY INDEX: STANDARDIZED REGRESSION COEFFICIENTS

Gender Equality Indices	Education[a]	Freedom	PPP[b,c]	E × F	E × P
Actual education attainment in 2015	.89***	.14***	.04	N/A	−.50***
Expected education attainment in 2015	.74***	.14*	.06	N/A	−.44***
Labor participation in 2015	.01	.36***	−.06	N/A	N/A
Income in 2015	.08	.37***	−.14	N/A	N/A
Women in the parliament in 2015 (%)	.03	.12	.24*	N/A	N/A
Life expectancy	.49***	.05	−.21*	N/A	−.32***
Sexual violence committed by non partners since age 15[d]	.21	.04	.23	N/A	N/A
Sexual violence committed by current or past partners for the last 12 months[d]	−.04	−.32**	−.40**	−.21*	.35**

[a] Education in 2010.
[b] Purchasing power parity (PPP, in international dollars).
[c] The freedom and PPP indices were correlated moderately, $r (k = 175) = −.45$; thus, we refrain from creating an interaction term involved with both indices.
[d] The higher the scores, the lower the gender equality observed. In addition, the numbers across countries varied by the data collection year.
*$p < .05$
**$p < .01$
***$p < .001$

DATA SOURCES: United Nations Development Programme's data (2010, 2015); http://unstats.un.org/unsd/gender/vaw/; https://freedomhouse.org/report/freedom-world/freedom-world-2010; http://siteresources.worldbank.org/DATASTATISTICS/Resources/GNIPC.pdf

purchasing power parity (see the differential points in Figure 7.1, Panel A). In addition, consistent with our reasoning of ecological constraints for women regarding power fungibility, gender equality in high school education in 2010 did not translate into gender equality in labor participation, income, nor political power (i.e., women in the parliament) in 2015, $ps > .17$. These results show that reducing differences between men and women in education does not translate into reducing differences between men and women in other domains.

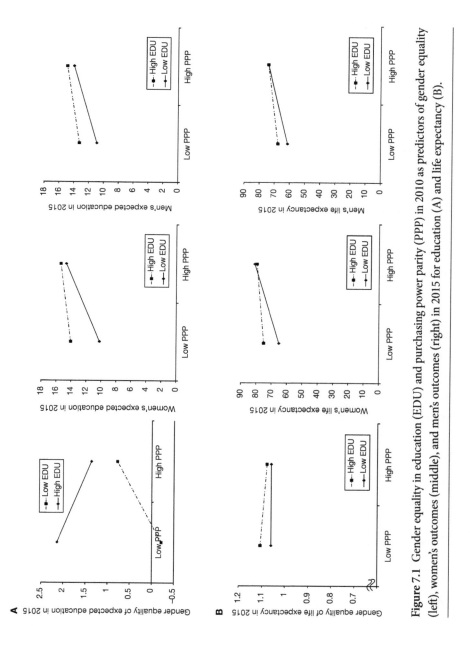

Figure 7.1 Gender equality in education (EDU) and purchasing power parity (PPP) in 2010 as predictors of gender equality (left), women's outcomes (middle), and men's outcomes (right) in 2015 for education (A) and life expectancy (B).

There was only one exception concerning when gender equality in education was transformed into domains other than education: life expectancy. Women typically lived longer than men; this gender difference was larger in nations with greater educational equality (e.g., Russian Federation, Lithuania) than in nations with less educational equality (e.g., Swaziland, Mali). Moreover, this pattern was more obvious for women in nations with *lower* purchasing power parity than women in nations with higher purchasing power parity (see Figure 7.1, panel B). The finding is consistent with our reasoning that purchasing power parity is a constraint in one's ecology that reduces power fungibility. Similar patterns were also observed in how gender equality in education transforms into sexual violence committed by current or past partners (see the last row of Table 7.3). That is, gender equality in 2010 education predicted *less* sexual violence committed by current or past partners in 2015 only in societies with less purchasing power parity.

Moreover, consistent with our reasoning, when women live in a society that offers greater protections of rights and liberties, they are more likely to advance in education and job markets, and they are less likely to suffer from sexual violence in intimate relationships (see the third column of Table 7.3). However, there is an interaction between gender equality in education and the degree of freedom offered by the society. As seen in Figure 7.2, women who gained higher education (the dotted line) appeared to suffer less sexual violence by current or past partners only in societies that offer members high personal rights and freedom.

GENERAL DISCUSSION

The inequalities between women and men in leadership roles, control of resources, family roles, and victimization by violence are often noted. A useful and overarching way of understanding such findings is why women and men on average have unequal power. As we have explained here, a more detailed understanding of what this means

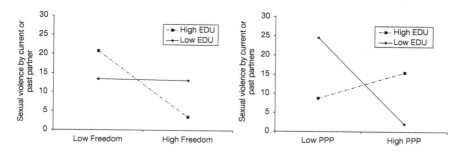

Figure 7.2 Sexual violence by current or past partners in 2015 predicted by gender equality in education and societal freedom (left) and purchasing power parity (right) in 2010.

requires acknowledging two things: (1) that there are separate domains of power for men and women, and (2) that even when women have power of a given sort, it often is not as empowering for them as power generally is for men because it is more difficult for women to use power in the forms they have to get power in other forms. This is due to what social context affords for them.

We saw several kinds of evidence for this. First, the complementarity of descriptive and prescriptive gender norms solidifies power differentials between men and women. We found that people do perceive and also expect men and women to differ in the kinds of power they have. Men are perceived and expected to have more physical strength and resources than women. Men's actions are also perceived to command community respect and establish and maintain relationships that serve their goals. Conversely, women are expected to be physically attractive and perceived to have characteristics that should allow them to establish or maintain relationships more easily than men. And this was the case despite the fact that their self-described differences were much narrower than stereotypic expectations. The fact that both descriptive and prescriptive stereotypes are widely shared means that anyone who tries to differ from them may be pressured by subtle or even overt disapproval for violating social norms. Or such a person may lose public approval for violating norms.

Second, reducing the power differential between men and women is difficult because people hold beliefs that curtail women's power fungibility. In the survey of Taiwanese opinion, we saw that stereotypes about gender roles and gender role prescriptions may serve as legitimizing myths that regulate women's behaviors and liberate men from certain obligations. For example, men who endorse women prioritizing family over paid work also performed less housework. The prescriptive belief about women not only makes men's lives easier, it constrains women by requiring more of their time and energy. If women gain approval for their expertise and contributions in the "private" sphere of family, this constrains what other avenues of power might be open to them.

Third, obstacles in the ecology may also limit power fungibility for women. Comparing nations of the world, we saw that aspects of the social ecology influenced the fungibility of power for men and women. When there was more educational equality for boys and girls in a given year (2010), there was also more equality between men and women 5 years later in education, in life expectancies, and in intimate relationships, but this was only the case in societies where living standards are low or in societies that offer personal rights and freedom.

Future Research Directions

Given that we have found evidence consistent with the idea that ecologies can influence gender differences in power fungibility, studying people's beliefs and norms about the use of power by women and men in several other societies would be an important extension of our first three studies. Follow-on research also could utilize experimental methods other than the one used here to test hypotheses based on power basis theory (see Pratto, Pearson, Lee, & Saguy, 2008). Other questions also are unanswered by our work so far. First, the correlational evidence for obstacles in the ecology regarding power fungiblity, though it has the strength of ecological validity, does not allow strong causal inferences. We are not able to rule out possible alternative explanations such as a third variable or reverse causality. Second, future research should ascertain the causality between gender stereotypes and the differential levels of power fungibility between men and women. Lastly, the evidence for power fungibility comes primarily from young adults in a culture with a dominant construction of gender as binary. Future researchers should examine whether the findings could be applied to other cultures and delve into power relations among groups in nonbinary gender frameworks.

Remedies

Considerable feminist work has expanded the positive choices women have: physical autonomy, advanced education, economic autonomy, control over family timing and size, and freedom from violence and coercion by intimate partners. Some of this work was surely intended to have ripple effects, expanding women's options beyond the immediate domain of change (e.g., the family). Our theoretical and empirical analyses suggest that another important feminist project is to increase power fungibility for women—otherwise such ripple effects will not occur. This is especially the case because having obligations in families often comes with heavy responsibilities, and when these are not shared with partners, women are hampered from many other opportunities.

Our data suggest that economic and political contexts should be taken into account in developing policies and family practices that can increase women's power in all arenas. The following seem to us to be implementable in most societies. In school or programs for children, teaching all children skills for household chores and child care would enable all to do them, as well as changing "facts" children observe about gender differences. Exposure to families in which everyone performs care work, even in books, can also help change norms. In every country, the wrongness of sexual and intimate partner violence should be taught in culturally appropriate frameworks, and prosecution of such crimes and equal standing of women in the court must accompany the moral persuasion. Spreading the availability of birth control and good pre- and postnatal health care remain important.

At levels of organization above family and intimate relations, simple election rules, such as requiring all parties to run female and male candidates, can dramatically increase women's representation in political leadership. Now that gender parity in education has become widespread, internships and programs directly connecting schools with employers to recruit women employees or provide self-employment advice could be implemented. In wealthier countries, employers should ensure equal pay and encourage male workers especially to care for family members when the needs arise; employee productivity and loyalty will then follow. Not marginalizing part-time work may appeal to families who would like a parent to be home with small children, and high-quality care for infants and children is important to parents' feeling comfortable that having paid jobs is not bad for their children. Along with this, the benefits of preschool and good childcare should be demonstrated to the grandparent generation so that they do not pressure the younger adults to maintain unequal gender role norms. In countries with poorly functioning governments, community relationships are an important resource for women as well as their families and communities. The rapid advance of gender parity in secondary education demonstrates that gender equality can be realized if we do not stop there.

Despite the uphill battles that many women have faced around the world, more and more women have become the leaders of nations and organizations. The courage, strengths, and creativity expressed by those women (e.g., Angela Merkel, Sonia Sotomayor, Tsai Ing-wen, Aung San Suu Kyi, Michelle Obama, Monica Lozano) make power fungible and inspire younger women to break through.

ACKNOWLEDGMENTS

The research reported in this chapter was supported by two grants (MOST 98-2410-H-004-026-, MOST 99-2410-H-004-095-MY2) from the Ministry of Science and Technology, Republic of China.

REFERENCES

Buss, D. M. (1989). Sex differences in human mate preferences: Evolutionary hypotheses tested in 37 cultures. *Behavioral and Brain Sciences, 12,* 1–14.

Buss, D. M., & Barnes, M. (1986). Preferences in human mate selection. *Journal of Personality and Social Psychology, 50,* 559–570.

Chang, L., Wang, Y., Shackleford, T. K., & Buss, D. M. (2011). Chinese mate preferences: Cultural evolution and continuity across a quarter of a century. *Personality and Individual Differences, 50,* 678–683.

Chang, Y.-W., Tu, S.-H., & Liao, P.-S. (2014). 2012 Taiwan Social Change Survey (Round 6, Year 3): Gender (C00223_2)[Data file]. Available from Survey Research Data Archive, Academia Sinica. doi:10.6141/TW-SRDA-C00223_2-1

Domhoff, G. W. (1990). *The power elite and the state.* New York, NY: Aldine de Grutyer.

Elliot, A. J., & Dweck, C. S. (Eds.). (2006). *Handbook of competence and motivation.* New York, NY: Guilford.

Forbes. (2011). The world's most powerful people 2010. http://www.forbes.com/lists/2011/20/powerful-people_2010.html

Forbes. (2016). Inside the 2015 Forbes billionaires list: Facts and figures. http://www.forbes.com/sites/kerryadolan/2015/03/02/inside-the-2015-forbes-billionaires-list-facts-and-figures/

Freedom House (data retrieved on August 31, 2016). Freedom in the world: 2010. https://freedomhouse.org/report/freedom-world/freedom-world-2010

Goode, W. J. (1972). The place of force in human society. *American Sociological Review, 37,* 507–519.

Jackman, M. R. (2001). License to kill: Violence and legitimacy in expropriative social relationships. In J. T. Jost & B. Major (Eds.), *The psychology of legitimacy* (pp. 437–467). New York, NY: Cambridge University Press.

Jost, J. T., & Major, B. (Eds.) (2001). *The psychology of legitimacy.* New York, NY: Cambridge University Press.

Keegan, J. (1993). *The history of warfare.* New York, NY: Knopf.

Lee, I.-C. (2012). An introduction of power basis theory: Definition of power and fungibility. *Chinese Journal of Psychology, 54,* 203–217.

Lee, I-C. (2013). Perceptions of success and life satisfaction: A gender examination in Taiwan. *Journal of Applied Social Psychology, 43,* 446–455.

Marx, K. (1904). *A contribution to a critique of political economy.* New York, NY: International Publishers.

Mosca, G. (1896/1939). *The ruling class: Elements of political science.* New York, NY: McGraw-Hill.

Parsons, T. (1954). An analytical approach to the theory of social stratification (1940). In *Essays in sociological theory* (pp. 69–88). New York, NY: Free Press.

Pratto, F. (2016). On power and empowerment. *British Journal of Social Psychology, 55,* 1–20.

Pratto, F., Lee, I-C., Tan, J. Y., & Pitpitan, E. V. (2011). Power basis theory: A psycho-
    logical approach to power. In D. Dunning (Ed.), *Social motivation* (pp. 191–222).
    New York, NY: Psychology Press.

Pratto, F., Pearson, A. R., Lee, I. C., & Saguy, T. (2008). Power dynamics in an exper-
    imental game: Individual and collective effects of the use of "force." *Social Justice
    Research*, *21*, 377–407.

Pratto, F., & Walker, A. (2004). The bases of gendered power. In A. H. Eagly, A. Beall,
    & R. Sternberg (Eds.), *The psychology of gender* (2nd ed.) (pp. 242–268). New York,
    NY: Guilford.

Prentice, D. A., & Carranza, E. (2002). What women and men should be, shouldn't be,
    are allowed to be, and don't have to be: The contents of prescriptive gender stereo-
    types. *Psychology of Women Quarterly*, *26*, 269–281.

Schmitt, D. P. (2012). When the difference is in the details: A critique of Zentner and
    Mitura (2012) "Stepping out of the caveman's shadow: Nations' gender gap pre-
    dicts degree of sex differentiation in mate preferences." *Evolutionary Psychology*, *10*,
    720–726.

Smith, A. (1793). *An inquiry into the nature and causes of the wealth of nations* (7th ed.).
    London, UK: A. Strahan & T. Cadell.

United Nations Development Programme (2010). Human development report
    2010: 20th anniversary edition. New York, NY: UNDP.

United Nations Development Programme (2015). Human development report
    2015: Work for human development. New York, NY: UNDP.

World Bank (2016). Gross national income per capita 2010, Atlas method and PPP.
    Available from http://siteresources.worldbank.org/DATASTATISTICS/Resources/
    GNIPC.pdf

8

Gender Stereotypes and Stereotyping

A Cognitive Perspective on Gender Bias

MONICA BIERNAT AND AMANDA K. SESKO

Gender stereotypes—the beliefs people hold about the personal attributes of members of gender categories (women and men, girls and boys)—are at the heart of a cognitive perspective on gender. Stereotypes function as expectations about qualities females and males have (e.g., women are warm and communal, men are agentic) and how females and males differ quantitatively (e.g., men are expected to be more aggressive and ambitious than women). Specific beliefs about women and men may or may not reflect reality—that is, actual trait, experiential, or behavioral differences between sex categories. What is most important to the cognitive perspective is that stereotypes, whether "accurate" or not, function as expectations, guiding perception and judgment.

In this chapter, we delve into the theoretical and empirical literature on gender stereotypes to describe how gender stereotypes are conceptualized and measured, how these group-level stereotypes affect judgments of and behaviors toward individual women and men, and the implications

of those judgments and behaviors for equitable policies and social institutions, such as schools and workplaces. We highlight both the *assimilative* influence of gender stereotypes, whereby perceivers judge individual
women and men consistently with gender stereotypes, and their *contras-
tive* influence, whereby stereotypes serving as comparative standards of
judgment may produce counterstereotypical outcomes. We also emphasize the importance of context in understanding the effects of stereotypes and the importance of considering gender in combination with
other demographic categories. The chapter ends with some consideration
of *self*-stereotyping effects. A caveat is worth mentioning here: Much of
the research we consider is based on US university student samples, and
although the findings *may* apply broadly, additional research is needed
across cultural contexts and across diverse groups of individuals in those
contexts.

THE CONTENT OF GENDER STEREOTYPES

Determining the content of gender stereotypes has typically involved
explicitly asking participants to rate males and females on a list of characteristics. In an early study, college students were asked to "list behaviors, attitudes, and personality characteristics which they considered to
differentiate men and women" (Rosenkrantz, Vogel, Bee, Broverman, &
Broverman, 1968, p. 287). Any characteristic that was listed more than
once was then presented to a new sample of participants who were asked
to "imagine that you are going to meet a person for the first time and
the only thing you know in advance is that the person is an adult male/
female." They then indicated the extent to which they expected each attribute to characterize an adult male/female on 1–7 rating scales. Of the 122
attributes, 41 were judged by at least 75% of respondents to differentiate
women and men. Male traits included *aggressive, independent, competitive, adventurous, dominant, self-confident*, and *ambitious*; female traits
included *gentle, aware of others' feelings, neat, tactful*, and *expresses tender
feelings*. Similar findings have emerged over time and across cultures (e.g.,

Williams & Best, 1980). In short, these attribute sets reflect beliefs about men's "agency" (e.g., self-assertion, self-expansion) and women's "communality" (e.g., connection to others).

These associations are also evident at the *implicit* level, in both women and men (Rudman & Glick, 2001). Rather than asking participants to indicate their explicit beliefs about women and men, the Implicit Association Test (IAT) measures speed of categorizing female and male names alongside, for example, communal and agentic adjectives (see Nosek, Greenwald, & Banaji, 2006, for a description of the IAT). When female names and communal adjectives (such as *communal* and *cooperative*) are categorized by pressing the same key on a computer keyboard, and male names and agentic adjectives (such as *independent* and *competitive*) are categorized by pressing the same key, reaction times are faster than when the opposite pairings occur (male/communal; female/agentic). Thus, at explicit and implicit levels, gender stereotypes reflect the communal = female, agentic = male distinction.

Alternate terms that reflect this distinction include "instrumentality" and "expressiveness" (Spence & Buckner, 2000) and, more recently, "competence" and "warmth" (Fiske, Cuddy, Glick, & Xu, 2002). Indeed, the latter authors propose a broad "Stereotype Content Model" (SCM), based on the idea that competence and warmth are two key dimensions along which all social evaluation occurs. From a functional perspective, "people want to know others' intent (i.e., warmth) and capability to pursue it (i.e., competence)" (Fiske et al., 2002, p. 879). The SCM suggests that perceived status and power contribute to high competence beliefs: High-status groups tend to be perceived as competent, low-status groups as relatively incompetent. Independent of this, perceived competitiveness contributes to low warmth perceptions: Groups that compete with others for resources are seen as low in warmth; those that do not pose such a threat are seen as high in warmth. Competence perceptions are typically measured by asking judges to rate the extent to which groups are "viewed by society" as *competent, confident, independent, competitive,* and *intelligent*; perceived warmth is assessed with the traits *tolerant, warm, good natured,* and *sincere*. Note that this approach assesses people's *knowledge*

of cultural stereotypes rather than their personal *endorsement* of stereotypic beliefs.

According to the SCM, stereotypes of groups can vary on these dimensions, producing a 2 × 2 matrix: Some groups are stereotyped as high in
both competence and warmth (e.g., our in-groups and close allies), some
are stereotyped as low in both (e.g., poor people), and some have mixed
content—high on one dimension and low on the other. Gender stereotypes seem to reflect this mixed content—men are stereotyped as competent but not warm; women as warm but not competent, a "paternalistic"
stereotype. In studies in which groups are rated on these dimensions, the
group "homemakers"—a subgroup of women—falls most squarely into
this high-warmth/low-competence space. However, presumably because
of their higher status and higher competitiveness, business women are
perceived as high in competence but low in warmth, the typical "male"
pattern.

Another theoretical perspective, social role theory (SRT), suggests that
stereotypes derive from the kinds of roles in which we typically see and
encounter group members (Eagly & Wood, 2012). For example, women's
greater involvement in paid and unpaid care for children may give rise to
the stereotype that women are "communal," whereas men's greater involvement in high-status work roles may lead perceivers to assume that men are
"agentic." In a clever study designed to test this hypothesis experimentally,
participants read about two fictional groups from another planet, one
described as made up of 80% "child raisers" and 20% "city workers" (the
female analog) and the other with the opposite role distribution (the male
analog; Hoffman & Hurst, 1990). Participants then rated the groups on a
set of agentic and communal traits. The male-analog group was judged
more agentic/less communal than the female-analog group, particularly
when the two groups were characterized as different "species" versus different "subcultures."

In a more recent test of SRT involving real groups, Koenig and Eagly
(2014) demonstrated that beliefs about the occupational roles in which
groups are overrepresented predict the content of group stereotypes (on
the agency/communality dimensions). For example, White women were

perceived as overrepresented in roles such as nurses and homemakers (and were judged high in communality), and White men in roles such as CEOs and politicians (and were judged high in agency).

The content of gender stereotypes has remained fairly stable over time (Haines, Deaux, & Lofaro, 2016), but both the stereotype content model and social role theory suggest the *potential* for dynamism and change in the content of gender and other stereotypes. For the SCM, stereotypes should change as groups change in status and competitiveness; for SRT, change should follow groups' redistribution into social roles. With increases in women's labor force participation, for example, stereotypes of women have shifted—and are projected to shift in future years—in the direction of increased agency (Diekman & Eagly, 2000). But women still maintain heavy involvement in domestic roles and in communal occupations, and therefore the shift in perceived communality is less marked. Men's roles have changed less; men have not entered female-dominated roles and occupations to the extent that women have entered male-dominated occupations (Croft, Schmader, & Block, 2015), and perceivers project less change in attributes of the typical man (Diekman & Eagly, 2000). When research participants are explicitly told that a group's dominant roles will be shifting in the future, stereotypes do change (Koenig & Eagly, 2014).

The examples discussed thus far highlight *White* women and men, and indeed the "default" race/ethnicity seems to be White when research participants (often predominantly White themselves) think of the typical man or typical woman (Merritt & Harrison, 2006). Researchers have increasingly paid attention to the fact that individuals identify as members of multiple categories at the same time, and that gender, race/ethnicity, age, sexual orientation, and other categories intersect, producing divergent stereotype content. For example, Ghavami and Peplau (2012) asked participants to "list at least 10 characteristics that are part of the current cultural stereotypes" (p. 116) of groups that varied in gender and race/ethnicity. For example, participants considered "Black women" or "Black men," though for comparison, some participants also nominated stereotypes of the nonintersecting groups (e.g., "Blacks," or "women"). Unique stereotype content was evident for gender x race/ethnicity groups that was not merely the result of adding the content of the individual gender and ethnicity categories. Black women, for example, were described as *confident, aggressive, assertive*, and *not feminine*—attributes that clearly distinguish them from "women." Consistent with the "White default" idea, stereotypes of "women" and "men" overlapped more with stereotypes of "White women" and "White men" than other ethnic categories (Ghavami & Peplau, 2012).

Theoretically, the pattern reported by Ghavami and Peplau (2012) should hold for intersections of target social identities in very different cultural (sub)groups, but whether it does is an empirical question. Testing the hypothesis in other cultural settings would mean adapting the methods in a way that is ecologically valid. For instance, in other contexts, "Black" would not refer to Americans of African descent but to other racial/ethnic groups (e.g., Aboriginal peoples in Australia). Stereotype content of the same group may also vary across cultural context (e.g., "Black women" in Somalia may be stereotyped differently than "Black women" in the United States). Every study is bound by its context, and the fact that most of the studies we review in this chapter were conducted in North America should raise some questions about generalizability. There is much room for additional cross-cultural research on gender stereotypes; by varying study contexts and particulars, we can better test theories and determine their limits and boundary conditions.

GENDER STEREOTYPING: APPLYING GROUP-LEVEL STEREOTYPES TO INDIVIDUALS

Gender stereotypes reflect beliefs about women and men as groups, but they also have important implications for how we perceive, evaluate, remember, and behave toward *individual* women and men. Stereotyping refers to the application of a group-based belief to an individual, and the research literature points to the many ways that stereotypes matter for individual outcomes.

Stereotypes Affect Construal and Memory

Stereotypes serve as expectations that allow us to anticipate and predict our social environments, and much research suggests that we often see and remember what we expect to see (Olson, Roese, & Zanna, 1996). Classic research by developmental psychologists has documented this tendency with regard to gender stereotypes in young children. Martin and Halverson (1983) showed 5- to 6-year-old children pictures of males and females enacting gender stereotype-consistent behavior (e.g., a boy playing with a toy train) or stereotype-inconsistent behavior (e.g., a girl sawing wood). When memory was tested 1 week later, children were roughly three times as likely to misremember—to reverse the actors' sexes—when the original pictures showed stereotype-inconsistent than stereotype-consistent activities (e.g., the girl sawing wood was misremembered as a boy). Furthermore, children were more confident of their memories when they remembered stereotype-consistent pairings, even when these were in error. These effects held for both boys and girls, and regardless of the child's explicit endorsement of gender stereotypes.

Stereotype-consistent memory effects can also be seen in the kinds of inferences people make about ambiguous behavioral information. Dunning and Sherman (1997) exposed college students to 50 brief descriptions of male or female actors. For example, participants read that "Jane (or Bill) administered medicine to a patient." Recognition memory was later assessed by asking participants whether slightly altered sentences had or had not appeared in the original set. Some sentences were altered to include a stereotype-consistent interpretation. For example, "Jane, *the nurse* (or Bill, *the doctor*) administered medicine to a patient," whereas others were altered to be stereotype inconsistent. Participants were more likely to falsely recognize stereotype-consistent construals (29%) than stereotype-inconsistent construals (17%). This effect held regardless of participants' gendered beliefs, suggesting the "generality of stereotype-driven" inferences (Dunning & Sherman, 1997, p. 467).

The use of gender as a recall cue may also bias memory. In one study, undergraduate participants first considered the college application of an

Asian American female and were later asked to recall information from the application, including the student's math SAT score (Pittinsky, Shih, & Ambady, 2000). Before the recall, participants were either cued to the applicant's gender ("Please answer the following questions for the female high school student") or her ethnicity ("the Asian high school student"), or were given no cue. Consistent with stereotypes of women and Asians, those cued with gender remembered a lower math SAT score than those in the control condition, who in turn remembered a lower SAT score than those cued with race/ethnicity.

These distinct research paradigms demonstrate that gender stereotypes exert an assimilative effect on memory, leading perceivers to remember and distort information in a stereotype-consistent direction. Intersections of gender and race/ethnicity may also affect memory at a broader level— memory for people's faces and contributions to conversations. Sesko and Biernat (2010) tested the hypothesis that because Black women are viewed as atypical of their race and gender categories, they are relatively *invisible* such that their faces go unnoticed and their voices unheard. One study used a "who said what" paradigm, in which participants heard a mocked-up conversation among Black and White women and men (depicted via photographs), and were later asked to match each statement with the person who said it. Participants made more memory errors about Black women than any other group, incorrectly attributing their statements to others and misattributing others' statements to them. Invisibility of this sort may be particularly likely for those who are members of multiple subordinate groups (Purdie-Vaughns & Eibach, 2008).

Stereotypes Affect Judgment and Evaluation
of Individual Others

Perhaps the most commonly examined effect of stereotypes is their influence on judgments of women and men. These studies often rely on a simple paradigm: Participants are exposed to information about a (fictitious) target person—a behavioral description, a résumé—and the gender of this person is varied via a name, photo, or use of pronouns. Participants are then asked to evaluate the target, perhaps rating him or her on overall favorability or on stereotype-relevant trait dimensions (warmth and competence), or making a hiring or school admission decision.

The key prediction in this research is *assimilation*—individual women will be judged more communal/warm and less agentic/competent than an identically described man. A more nuanced prediction is also derived from role congruity theory (Eagly & Karau, 2002) and the "lack of fit" model (Heilman, 1993). These perspectives recognize the importance of context and suggest that women will be evaluated as less competent than men in "masculine" settings (e.g., in male-dominated jobs), but more competent than men in "feminine" settings.

A number of studies have demonstrated that women are devalued relative to men when they are considered as applicants for "masculine" jobs. In one study, academic psychologists were sent the curriculum vitae (CV) of a biopsychologist, identified as either female ("Karen Miller") or male ("Brian Miller"; Steinpreis, Anders, & Ritzke, 1999). The CV was either that of a new PhD seeking a faculty position or a more advanced faculty member seeking tenure, and participants were asked to indicate whether they would recommend hiring/tenuring. Both women and men recommended new PhD Brian for hiring more often than the identical Karen (roughly 74% of the time versus 29% of the time), though the tenure case did not show evidence of gender bias—Brian and Karen were recommended for tenure at equivalent, high rates (about 81% of the time). The authors note that this may have been due to the high quality of the tenure-case CV: "A superb record may indeed function as a buffer for gender bias" (Steinpreis et al., 1999, p. 524; see also Williams & Ceci, 2015).

In a more recent study, researchers sent science faculty members an application for a lab manager position from John or Jennifer, an undergraduate student (Moss-Racusin, Dovidio, Brescoll, Graham, & Handelsman, 2012). Evidence of pro-male bias emerged on all dependent measures: John was judged more competent, more likely to be hired and mentored, and deserving a higher salary than the identically credentialed Jennifer, by both female and male faculty members.

THE DOUBLE BIND FOR WOMEN

Gender stereotypes define women as communal and nonagentic, and individual women often get judged in this manner. But what happens when women *do* display agency and/or *do not* behave communally? The double bind for women reflects the fact that women may be penalized for being nonagentic (i.e., they lose "competence" points and respect) but also penalized for being agentic (i.e., they lose "likeability" points).

For example, Rudman (1998) documented a pattern of "backlash" against self-promoting women. Participants viewed a videotape of a (supposed) practice job interview of a male or female candidate who behaved in either a self-promoting or self-effacing manner. Self-promoters were judged more competent than self-effacers, whether male or female. But self-promoting women were judged less likeable than self-promoting men, *and* as less hireable. Thus, self-promotion may enhance perceived competence, but women in particular suffer backlash from using this strategy.

Other forms of self-promotion may trigger similar responses. For example, women are penalized more than men for the expression of anger, another form of agency. In one relevant study, mock juror participants engaged in a virtual (online) deliberation in a murder trial (Salerno & Peter-Hagene, 2015). No other jurors were actually present; instead, comments from five supposed others were rigged such that four always agreed with the decision expressed by the participant, and one was a holdout, expressing the opposite verdict preference. This holdout was also manipulated to be either male or female and to express her or his opinion with either no emotion, with fear, or with anger. The influence of the holdout was operationalized as the extent to which the participant lost confidence in her or his initial verdict. In the "no –emotion" and "fear" conditions, confidence did not change from pre- to postdeliberation, regardless of the holdout's gender. But when anger was expressed, the male holdout exerted significant influence—making jurors doubt their initial verdict—whereas the female holdout had the *opposite* effect: An angry female holdout led jurors to be *more* confident in their initial opinion.

These data and others suggest that when women act agentically, they may gain respect but lose in other ways, such as likeability. Explicit assurances of likeability are needed to overcome this effect, placing an added burden on women. But being "too feminine" can be problematic as well (e.g., being a mother; Fuegen, Biernat, Haynes, & Deaux, 2004). This paints a picture of women needing to walk a "tightrope" at work, facing pushback for masculine behavior and pressure to behave in feminine ways (e.g., taking on "caretaker" or "office mom" roles at work) but also penalties for doing so (Williams & Dempsey, 2014). There is some evidence, however, that Black women may be less subject to this form of backlash at work, perhaps because of the more masculinized stereotypes of this group. For example, Livingston, Rosette, and Washington (2012) found that White female (and Black male) leaders who expressed dominance were penalized, but Black female (and White male) leaders who did the same were not. Though our focus here has been on the double bind for women, it is worth noting that men may also face backlash at work for behaving in feminine ways (e.g., advocating for others; Bosak, Kulich, Rudman, & Kinahan, 2016).

FAILURE TO RECOGNIZE FEMALE EXPERTISE

Another literature has highlighted the failure to even recognize female expertise in masculine domains. In one study, researchers asked participants to complete a decision-making task in which they had to rank-order 12 items according to their usefulness in surviving an Australian bushfire (Thomas-Hunt & Phillips, 2004). This task is perceived as male-typed, but when compared to expert decision makers, women and men tend to perform equally well. Business undergraduates first completed the task alone and then were randomly placed into 3- to 5-person groups charged with coming to a joint decision. Prior to the group discussion, an "expert" was identified in each group—the person who had *actually* scored the best in their individual decisions. In roughly half the groups, this person was male, and in the other half, female.

By comparing the final group decision to members' initial decisions, researchers could determine the influence each member had on the final group outcome. Not only were women less influential overall, but female *experts* were less influential than female nonexperts, whereas male experts were more influential than male nonexperts. Groups with female experts performed less well than groups with male experts precisely because they failed to use the female expert's knowledge to their advantage. Similar anti-female bias emerged in a study focusing on the stereotype of men as better at math than women, where high-performing women were less likely to be hired to perform math tasks than comparably performing men (Reuben, Sapienza, & Zingales, 2014).

Alongside the failure to appreciate women's expertise in masculine domains is the tendency to harshly critique their mistakes. In one study, a female police chief who made a mistake (dispatched too few police to a community protest) was judged less competent and less deserving of status than a male police chief who made the same mistake (Brescoll, Dawson, & Uhlmann, 2010). Indicating that this pattern was due to the perceived lack of fit between gender and job, male leaders in a counterstereotypical role (e.g., male president of a women's college) were judged more harshly for making a mistake than female leaders.

In the preceding section, we discussed the finding that dominant Black women may face less backlash in leadership roles than White women. At the same time, Black women may be subject to heightened penalties for failure, perhaps because stereotypes about competence deficiencies are stronger for Black than White women (Rosette & Livingston, 2012). It may be important to distinguish between *agentic deficiency* assumptions and *agentic penalty* as they differentially affect women from varying ethnic groups (see Rosette, Koval, Ma, & Livingston, 2016).

SHIFTING STANDARDS

The research described thus far points to an assimilative influence of stereotypes, such that individual women and men are judged consistently with overall gender stereotypes. But group-based expectations may also serve as a standard against which individuals are compared, resulting in contrast effects. For example, a man who cries at work may be judged *more emotional* than a crying woman (Fischer, Eagly, & Oosterwijk, 2013), perhaps because he is evaluated relative to a lower expectation of emotionality. Indeed, the shifting standards model suggests that on stereotype-relevant dimensions, individuals will be judged relative to within-group standards (Biernat, 2012). Because it is easier to surpass a low than high standard, this opens the door to contrast effects—under some circumstances, women may be judged more agentic than men, or men may be judged more emotional than women, because they are judged relative to lower within-sex category standards.

This tendency to shift standards is possible because of the subjectivity of language. Many descriptors have no absolute, objective meaning. Instead, what it means to be "competent" or "warm" varies depending on the context and on whom is being described (Huttenlocher, Higgins, & Clark, 1971). A man and woman might both be labeled "competent" or "emotional," but we may mean different things by these labels. Based on shifting standards, "competent" may mean something *objectively less competent* when applied to a woman than a man, and "emotional" may imply something *objectively more emotional* when applied to a woman than a man.

Methodologically, evidence of a shifting standards effect can be gleaned if gender-based judgment patterns look different when shifts in standards are prevented—when the judgment language is more *objective* or *common rule* in nature. Imagine, for example, judging men and women's heights on a subjective "short" to "tall" rating scale, or in objective units—feet and inches. Inches are stable measurement units and therefore are not prone to within-group adjustment of meaning and contrast effects. In studies that prompted participants to judge the heights of women and men in either subjective or objective units, objective judgments showed assimilation to the stereotype (i.e., men were judged taller than women), whereas subjective judgments showed null or reverse (contrast) effects (i.e., women were judged equal to or taller than men; e.g., Biernat et al., 1991).

Shifting standards effects imply "for a . . ." thinking. *For a woman,* a height of 5'7" is "tall," but *for a man,* it might be considered "short." Evidence of shifting standards has also been documented in domains more relevant to gender stereotypes regarding agency/competence. For example, Biernat and Kobrynowicz (1997) asked participants to consider a male or female applicant for a masculine "chief of staff" or feminine "executive secretary" position. Judgments were made on either subjective rating scales or in objective rating units (e.g., assigned letter grade or percentage score). In objective judgments, the gender that fit the job was judged most competent: Men were judged better than women in the chief of staff position, and women were judged better than men in the executive secretary position. But in subjective judgments, these patterns were reversed: *For a woman*, Katherine was perceived as a pretty good chief of staff candidate, although she was not rated as objectively good as Kenneth.

Other studies have found that female applicants were more likely than male applicants to be placed on a "short list" in a search for a "chief of staff," but they were less likely to be hired (Biernat & Fuegen, 2001). Moderately athletic-looking female softball players received more praise than comparable male players for getting a hit but were less likely to be chosen to be on a co-ed team, to play an infield position, or to bat early in the lineup (Biernat & Vescio, 2002). These findings suggest that researchers should be thoughtful about how they measure evaluative judgments—objective measures and bottom-line decisions may reveal assimilation to stereotypes, but subjective measures may mask or reverse these tendencies, underestimating the influence of stereotypes.

Gender Stereotypes Affect Attributions

Stereotypes also affect the *attributions* or explanations for women and men's behavior and performance. One key dimension of attributions is their *locus*: Outcomes may be attributed to internal/dispositional causes or to external/situational causes. For example, failure at a task can be attributed to internal causes such as a lack of skill, or to external causes such as bad luck or task difficulty. Independent of locus, some causes are more stable than others (e.g., low ability versus low effort; see Weiner, 1985).

WHAT IS SKILL FOR MEN IS LUCK FOR WOMEN

In a classic study, Deaux and Emswiller (1974) asked participants to make attributions for the successful performance of a woman or man on a female or male sex-typed task (e.g., identifying objects such as a mop or a wrench, respectively). On the male-typed task, women's successful perfor-mance was attributed to luck but men's to skill; no attributional differences emerged on the female-typed task. A meta-analysis found target gender differences in attribution to be small overall (Swim & Sanna, 1996), but on masculine tasks, men's failures tend to be attributed to unstable causes (low effort and bad luck), whereas women's failures tend to be attributed to stable causes (task difficulty and low ability, ds from .13 to .40).

She's Emotional, He's Having a Bad Day

Gender stereotypes may affect which emotions are attributed to males and females. For instance, Hess, Adams, Grammer, and Kleck (2009) asked participants to guess the gender of a series of computer-generated androg-ynous faces displaying different emotions. Angry faces were more likely to be rated as male, and happy faces as female.

Gender stereotypes about emotion also affect causal attributions regarding the source or origin of emotions. Women are perceived as lack-ing the ability to control emotions and thus are perceived to *be emotional*, whereas men are perceived to *have emotions* (for reviews, see Brescoll, 2016; Shields, 2013). In other words, attributions for women's emotions tend to rely on essentialist explanations (dispositional causes—it's part of her, she can't control it), whereas men's emotions are attributed to the sit-uation. These attributions have consequences for the workplace: Brescoll and Uhlmann (2008) found that a female leader who expressed anger was judged to be "out of control," but a male leader who did the same was not. This attribution was used to justify awarding the female leader less pay, power, and status.

Attributing Credit Where It Is Due

When a successful work product is produced by a team, gender stereo-types may prompt perceivers to give less credit to women's ability and con-tributions. Heilman and Haynes (2005) asked participants to read about a work team (one man, one woman) who had successfully completed an investment portfolio. Across three studies, participants rated the female team member as less competent, less likely to have taken a leadership role,

and less influential in the team success than the male team member. This
pro-male bias was not evident when clear information about the female
employee's past or current contribution was provided, but work settings
often include team efforts in which individual contributions are ambiguous. Interestingly, this pattern of gender bias appears to be stronger for
White women than Black women, perhaps due to stereotypes of higher
agency for Black than White women, or because Black women's "invisibility" protects them from some forms of gender bias (Biernat & Sesko, 2013).

APPLYING STEREOTYPES TO THE SELF

Self-Stereotyping

In addition to influencing our judgments of others, gender stereotypes
may affect judgments of the self. *Self-stereotyping* occurs when individuals perceive themselves as group members and subsequently incorporate group stereotypes into their self-concepts (e.g., Hardie & McMurray,
1992). Self-stereotyping research is rooted in social identity theory, which
posits a need to positively differentiate one's in-group from the out-group
(Tajfel & Turner, 1986); taking on in-group stereotypes may serve this
function. Self-stereotyping increases with cognitive accessibility of the
group membership (Hogg & Turner, 1987). Some have suggested that
because of women's lower status relative to men, gender is more salient
for women and thus women are more likely to self-stereotype (Cadinu &
Galdi, 2012).

The general methodology used to study self-stereotyping is to either
manipulate category salience or to measure degree of identification with
a group, and then to assess the extent to which individuals endorse group
stereotypes as self-descriptive. For example, Oswald (2008) found that
when gender stereotypes were made salient, female participants reported
more liking for, and more favorable perceptions of their abilities in, traditionally feminine domains (e.g., nurse, teacher). In a similar study,
Sinclair, Hardin, and Lowery (2006) found that Asian women—whose

gender is associated with poor math ability, but whose ethnicity is associated with good math ability—evaluated their math ability more favorably when their ethnicity was made salient, but their verbal ability more favorably when their gender was made salient.

Other research has investigated how individuals negotiate both the positive and negative attributes associated with a single social identity. Oswald and Chapleau (2010) asked female university students to indicate how characteristic positive and negative gender-related personality traits were of themselves, their closest friend, women in general, and university students (an in-group control). They found that positive traits were endorsed for the self, closest friends, and women in general (and less so for university students). But negative traits were rated as most descriptive of women in general, followed by university students, and least for self and closest friends. This reflects a kind of *selective self-stereotyping*, which allows individuals to admit the reality of negative stereotypes (by attributing them to the group as a whole), while protecting the self from hits to self-esteem (by denying their self-relevance; Biernat, Vescio, & Green, 1996).

Stereotype Threat

A large literature has emerged on the phenomenon of *stereotype threat*: "being at risk of confirming, as self-characteristic, a negative stereotype of one's group," often evident in performance decrements when group membership or the stereotype itself is made salient (Steele & Aronson, 1995, p. 797). Early research focused on the stereotype of women as less competent than men at math. Spencer, Steele, and Quinn (1999) told participants that a math test they were about to take was either gender-fair—women and men perform equally well—or that it shows gender differences in performance (anticipating participants would assume men outperform women). When told there were gender differences, women performed less well than men, but when told the test was gender-fair, women and men performed equally. When no information was provided, women also underperformed relative to men. In fact, simply making gender salient

before a task produces stereotype threat effects. This suggests that stereotypes need not be explicitly stated; rather, the threat is "in the air" (Steele,
1997), affecting subsequent performance (for a review, see Spencer, Vogel,
& Davies, 2016).

The self-stereotyping and stereotype threat literatures indicate that individuals may adopt stereotypical behaviors and attributes of their groups,
wittingly or not. Self-categorization as a group member may facilitate
assimilation to these stereotypes (especially positive ones), and the threat
of confirming negative group stereotypes may paradoxically increase the
likelihood of behavioral assimilation.

FUTURE DIRECTIONS

This chapter began with a description of the content of gender stereotypes,
followed by a brief sampling of research demonstrating how these stereotypes affect the way we perceive individual women and men as well as
ourselves. However, we do not want to suggest that perceivers *only* pay
attention to gender, or that gender overrides the impact of other information perceivers have about others. Individuating information, for example,
can convey that job applicants have terrific versus terrible credentials, or
that they are kind versus horrid. This information carries a lot of weight
in judgment, regardless of gender. One meta-analysis of studies involving
simulated hiring found that gender accounted for roughly 4% of the variance in hiring, whereas qualifications accounted for 35% (Olian, Schwab,
& Haberfeld, 1988). Nonetheless, holding information constant—as in
virtually all of the studies reviewed here—gendered beliefs lead to differential outcomes for women and men.

We know less about other aspects of the impression formation process,
such as: how people revise their impressions of women and men over time,
after gaining new information; how gender stereotyping effects accumu-
late, as multiple perceivers offer their impressions; and how the act of gender stereotyping may strengthen gender stereotypes, making them more
likely to be applied in the future. Researchers studying stereotyping and

prejudice have examined strategies to reduce negativity and change group stereotypes (for a review, see Paluck & Green, 2009) but we know less about effective interventions to reduce stereotyp*ing*—the application of stereotypes to individuals—especially outside the lab. One recent effort to train managers to "interrupt bias" (in recruiting, hiring, and evaluating employees) is an interdisciplinary working group developed by law professor Joan Williams (see biasinterrupters.org). This group (of which the first author is a member) is currently engaging with companies to execute experimental tests of intervention effectiveness, measurable via reduced gender and race inequities in hiring, performance evaluation, and promotion.

Throughout this chapter, we have drawn attention to the intersections of gender and race, noting, for example, that stereotypes of Black women may mean they face different outcomes than White women and Black men in work settings. But there are considerable gaps in the literature when it comes to examining gender in conjunction with other racial/ethnic groups, and with other social categories such as sexual orientation, age, national origin, and social class (see Chapter 2, this volume, on intersectionality). Race itself may be gendered, such that we categorize people differently by race depending on their gender (Johnson, Freeman, & Pauker, 2011), and perceived social class confounds with race may play out differently for women and men (Neuberg & Sng, 2013). The research literature on stereotypes has also relied upon an exclusively binary view of gender, but more work is needed on the intersections of sex categories and gender identity as they affect stereotyping, and on perceptions of nonbinary individuals (see Chapter 3; Richards et al., 2016). We look forward to new stereotyping research that incorporates and reflects the changing social landscape.

REFERENCES

Biernat, M. (2012). Stereotypes and shifting standards: Forming, communicating, and translating person impressions. In P. Devine, A. Plant, P. Devine, & A. Plant

(Eds.), *Advances in experimental social psychology*, Vol. 45 (pp. 1–59). San Diego, CA: Academic Press.

Biernat, M., & Fuegen, K. (2001). Shifting standards and the evaluation of competence: Complexity in gender-based judgment and decision making. *Journal of Social Issues, 57,* 707–724.

Biernat, M., & Kobrynowicz, D. (1997). Gender-and race-based standards of competence: Lower minimum standards but higher ability standards for devalued groups. *Journal of Personality and Social Psychology, 72,* 544–557.

Biernat, M., Manis, M., & Nelson, T. E. (1991). Stereotypes and standards of judgment. *Journal of Personality and Social Psychology, 60,* 485–499.

Biernat, M., & Sesko A. K. (2013). Evaluating the contributions of members of mixed-sex work teams: Race and gender matter. *Journal of Experimental Social Psychology, 49,* 471–476.

Biernat, M., & Vescio, T. K. (2002). She swings, she hits, she's great, she's benched: Implications of gender-based shifting standards for judgment and behavior. *Personality and Social Psychology Bulletin, 28,* 66–77.

Biernat, M., Vescio, T., & Green, M. (1996). Selective self-stereotyping. *Journal of Personality and Social Psychology, 71,* 1194–1209.

Bosak, J., Kulich, C., Rudman, L., & Kinahan, M. (2016). Be an advocate for others, unless you are a man: Backlash against gender-atypical male job candidates. *Psychology of Men & Masculinity,* doi:http://dx.doi.org/10.1037/men0000085.

Brescoll, V. L. (2016). Leading with their hearts? How gender stereotypes of emotion lead to biased evaluations of female leaders. *The Leadership Quarterly, 27,* 415–428.

Brescoll, V. L., Dawson, E., & Uhlmann, E. L. (2010). Hard won and easily lost: The fragile status of leaders in gender-stereotype-incongruent occupations. *Psychological Science, 21,* 1640–1642.

Brescoll, V. L., & Uhlmann, E. L. (2008). Can an angry woman get ahead? Status conferral, gender, and expression of emotion in the workplace. *Psychological Science, 19,* 268–275.

Cadinu, M., & Galdi, S. (2012). Gender differences in implicit gender self-categorizations lead to stronger gender self-stereotyping by women than by men. *European Journal of Social Psychology, 42,* 456–551.

Croft, A., Schmader, T., & Block, K. (2015). An underexamined inequality: Cultural and psychological barriers to men's engagement with communal roles. *Journal of Social Psychology Review, 19,* 343–370.

Deaux, K., & Emswiller, T. (1974). Explanations for successful performance on sex-linked tasks: What is skill for the male is luck for the female. *Journal of Personality and Social Psychology, 29,* 80–85.

Diekman, A. B., & Eagly, A. H. (2000). Stereotypes as dynamic constructs: Women and men of the past, present, and future. *Personality and Social Psychology Bulletin, 26,* 1171–1188.

Dunning, D., & Sherman, D. A. (1997). Stereotypes and tacit inference. *Journal of Personality and Social Psychology, 73*(3), 459–471.

Eagly, A. H., & Karau, S. J. (2002). Role congruity theory of prejudice toward female leaders. *Psychological Review, 109,* 574–598.

Eagly, A. H., & Wood, W. (2012). Social role theory. In P. A. M. Van Lange, A. W. Kruglanski, & E. T. Higgins (Eds.), *Handbook of theories of social psychology* (pp. 458–476). London, UK: Sage.

Fischer, A. H., Eagly, A. H., & Oosterwijk, S. (2013). The meaning of tears: Which sex seems emotional depends on the social context. *European Journal of Social Psychology, 43*(6), 505–515.

Fiske, S. T., Cuddy, A. J., Glick, P., & Xu, J. (2002). A model of (often mixed) stereotype content: Competence and warmth respectively follow from perceived status and competition. *Journal of Personality and Social Psychology, 82,* 878–902.

Fuegen, K., Biernat, M., Haines, E., & Deaux, K. (2004). Mothers and fathers in the workplace: How gender and parental status influence judgments of job-related competence. *Journal of Social Issues, 60,* 737–754.

Ghavami, N., & Peplau, L. A. (2012). An intersectional analysis of gender and ethnic stereotypes: Testing three hypotheses. *Psychology of Women Quarterly, 37,* 113–127.

Haines, E. L., Deaux, K., & Lofaro, N. (2016). The times they are a-changing . . . or are they not? A comparison of gender stereotypes, 1983–2014. *Psychology of Women Quarterly, 40*(3), 353–363.

Hardie, E., A., & McMurray, N., E. (1992). Self stereotyping, sex role ideology, and menstrual attitudes: A social identity approach. *Sex Roles, 27,* 17–37.

Heilman, M. E. (1993). Sex bias in work settings: The lack of fit model. *Research in Organizational Behavior, 5,* 269–298.

Heilman, M. E., & Haynes, M. C. (2005). No credit where credit is due: Attributional rationalization of women's success in male-female teams. *Journal of Applied Psychology, 90,* 905–916.

Hess, U., Adams, R. B., Grammer, K., & Kleck, R. E. (2009). Face gender and emotion expression: Are angry women more like men? *Journal of Vision, 9*(12), 456–471.

Hoffman, C., & Hurst, N. (1990). Gender stereotypes: Perceptions or rationalization? *Journal of Personality and Social Psychology, 58,* 197–208.

Hogg, M. A., & Turner, J. C. (1987). Intergroup behaviour, self-stereotyping and the salience of social categories. *British Journal of Social Psychology, 26,* 325–340.

Huttenlocher, J., Higgins, E. T., & Clark, H. H. (1971). Adjectives, comparatives, and syllogisms. *Psychological Review, 78,* 487–504.

Johnson, K. L., Freeman, J. B., & Pauker, K. (2012). Race is gendered: How covarying phenotypes and stereotypes bias sex categorization. *Journal of Personality and Social Psychology, 102*(1), 116–131.

Koenig, A. M., & Eagly, A. H. (2014). Evidence for the social role theory of stereotype content: Observations of groups' roles shape stereotypes. *Journal of Personality and Social Psychology, 107,* 371–392.

Livingston, R. W., Rosette, A. S., & Washington, E. F. (2012). Can an agentic woman get ahead? The impact of race and interpersonal dominance on perceptions of female leaders. *Psychological Science, 23,* 354–358.

Martin, L. C., & Halverson, C. F. (1983). The effects of sex-typing schemas on young children's memory. *Child Development, 54,* 563–574.

Merritt, R. D., & Harrison, T. W. (2006). Gender and ethnicity attributions to a gender- and ethnicity-unspecified individual: Is there a people = white male bias? *Sex Roles, 54,* 787–797.

Moss-Racusin, C., Dovidio, J. F., Brescoll, V. L., Graham, M. J., & Handelsman, J. (2012). Science faculty's subtle gender biases favor male students. *PNAS Proceedings of the National Academy of Sciences of the United States of America, 109*(41), 16474–16479.

Neuberg, S. L., & Sng, O. (2013). A life history theory of social percep- tion: Stereotyping at the intersections of age, sex, ecology (and race). *Social Cognition, 31*(6), 696–711.

Nosek, B. A., Greenwald, A. G., & Banaji, M. R. (2006). The Implicit Association Test at age 7: A methodological and conceptual review. In J. A. Bargh (Ed.), *Social psychol- ogy and the unconscious: The automaticity of higher mental processes* (pp. 265–292). New York, NY: Psychology Press.

Olian, J. D., Schwab, D. P., & Haberfeld, Y. (1988). The impact of applicant gender compared to qualifications on hiring recommendations: A meta-analysis of exper- imental studies. *Organizational Behavior and Human Decision Processes, 41*(2), 180–195.

Olson, J. M., Roese, N. J., & Zanna, M. P. (1996). Expectancies. In E. T. Higgins & A. W. Kruglanski (Eds.), *Social psychology: Handbook of basic principles* (pp. 211–238). New York, NY: Guilford Press.

Oswald, D. L. (2008). Gender stereotypes and women's reports of liking and ability in traditionally masculine and feminine occupations. *Psychology of Women Quarterly, 32,* 196–203.

Oswald, D. L. & Chapleau, K. M. (2010). Selective self-stereotyping and women's self- esteem maintenance. *Personality and Individual Differences, 49,* 918–922.

Paluck, E. L., & Green, D. P. (2009). Prejudice reduction: What works? A review and assessment of research and practice. *Annual Review of Psychology, 60,* 339–367.

Pittinsky, T. L., Shih, M., & Ambady, N. (2000). Will a category cue affect you? Category cues, positive stereotypes and reviewer recall for applicants. *Social Psychology of Education, 4,* 53–65.

Purdie-Vaughns, V., & Eibach, R. P. (2008). Intersectional invisibility: The distinctive advantages and disadvantages of multiple subordinate-group identities. *Sex Roles, 59,* 377–391.

Reuben, E., Sapienza, P., & Zingales, L. (2014). How stereotypes impair women's careers in science. *Proceedings of the National Academy of Sciences, 111,* 4403–4408.

Richards, C., Bouman, W. P., Seal, L., Barker, M. J., Nieder, T. O., & T'Sjoen, G. (2016). Non-binary or genderqueer genders. *International Review of Psychiatry, 28*(1), 95–102.

Rosette, A. S., Koval, C. Z., Ma, A., & Livingston, R. (2016). Race matters for women leaders: Intersectional effects on agentic deficiencies and penalties. *The Leadership Quarterly, 27,* 429–445.

Rosette, A. S., & Livingston, R. W. (2012). Failure is not an option for Black women: Effects of organizational performance on leaders with single versus dual-subordinate identi- ties. *Journal of Experimental Social Psychology, 48,* 1162–1167.

Rosenkrantz, P. Vogel, S., Bee, H., Boverman, I., & Boverman, D. (1968). Sex-role ste-reotypes and self-concepts in college students. *Journal of Consulting and Clinical Psychology, 32,* 287–295.

Rudman, L. A. (1998). Self-promotion as a risk factor for women: The costs and benefits of counterstereotypical impression management. *Journal of Personality and Social Psychology, 74,* 629–645.

Rudman, L. A., & Glick, P. (2001). Prescriptive gender stereotypes and backlash toward agentic women. *Journal of Social Issues, 57,* 743–762.

Salerno, J. M., & Peter-Hagene, L. C. (2015). One angry woman: Anger expression increases influence for men, but decreases influence for women, during group delib-eration. *Law and Human Behavior, 39*(6), 581–592.

Sesko, A. K., & Biernat, M. (2010). Prototypes of race and gender: Invisibility of Black women. *Journal of Experimental Social Psychology, 46,* 356–360.

Shields, S. A. (2013). Gender and emotion: What we think we know, what we need to know, and why it matters. *Psychology of Women Quarterly, 37,* 423–435.

Sinclair, S., Hardin, C. D., & Lowery, B. S. (2006). Self-stereotyping in the context of multiple social identities. *Journal of Personality and Social Psychology, 90,* 529–542.

Spence, J. T., & Buckner, C. E. (2000). Instrumental and expressive traits, trait stereo-types, and sexist attitudes: What do they signify? *Psychology of Women Quarterly, 24,* 44–53.

Spencer, S. J., Logel, C., & Davies, P. G. (2016). Stereotype threat. *Annual Review of Psychology, 67,* 415–437.

Spencer, S. J., Steele, C. M., & Quinn, D. M. (1999). Stereotype threat and women's math performance. *Journal of Experimental Social Psychology, 35,* 4–28.

Steele, C. M. (1997). A threat in the air: How stereotypes shape intellectual identity and performance. *American Psychologist, 52,* 613–629.

Steele, C. M., & Aronson, J. (1995). Stereotype threat and the intellectual test per-formance of African Americans. *Journal of Personality and Social Psychology, 69,* 797–811.

Steinpreis, R. E., Anders, K. A., & Ritzke, D. (1999). The impact of gender on the review of the curricula vitae of job applicants and tenure candidates: A national empirical study. *Sex Roles, 41,* 509–528.

Swim, J. K., & Sanna, L. J. (1996). He's skilled, she's lucky: A meta-analysis of observ-ers' attributions for women's and men's success and failures. *Personality and Social Psychology Bulletin, 22,* 507–519.

Tajfel, H., & Turner, J. C. (1986). The social identity of intergroup behavior. In S. Worchel & W. Austin (Eds.), *Psychology of intergroup relations* (2nd ed., pp. 7–24), Chicago, IL: Nelson-Hall.

Thomas-Hunt, M. C., & Phillips, K. W. (2004). When what you know is not enough: Expertise and gender dynamics in task groups. *Personality and Social Psychology Bulletin, 30,* 1585–1598.

Weiner, B. (1985). An attributional theory of achievement motivation and emotion. *Psychological Review, 92,* 548–573.

Williams, J. C., & Dempsey, R. (2014). *What works for women at work: Four patterns working women need to know.* New York, NY: New York University Press.

Williams, J. E., & Best, D. L. (1980). *Measuring sex stereotypes: A multination study.* Newbury Park, CA: Sage.

Williams, W. M., & Ceci, S. J. (2015). National hiring experiments reveal 2:1 faculty preference for women on STEM tenure track. *Proceedings of the National Academy of Sciences, 112,* 5360–5365.

9

Psychoanalytic Theories of Gender

LESLIE C. BELL

Caucasian, cisgendered woman in her forties presents as a very traditionally gendered woman—full makeup, regularly colored and styled hair, and traditionally feminine clothing. She is also ambitious and successful in her career in a male-dominated field. She struggles, however, to prioritize her romantic relationships and has trouble being direct with her male romantic partners, even as she pushes forward in her career. She wishes that she were more skilled in what she terms "the domestic arts," but she isn't. A Filipino American, cisgendered man in his twenties is meticulously well groomed, from his neatly coiffed hair to his well-shined shoes. He loves his female fiancée very much, but he feels unappreciated by her. He expresses his frustration with her through passive aggression, with sighing and exasperated looks. He is responsible for most household chores, and he likes it that way because it keeps him in charge.

These two individuals enact their genders in both expected and unexpected ways. This man and this woman also feel, think, and act in ways that they wish they didn't. We might also consider a woman who holds strong feminist ideals yet finds herself wishing to be financially taken care of by a man and feels herself deserving of such care. Or a man who seems radically independent in most of the public world yet finds himself feeling like a dependent child in relation to his female boss; he wishes to please her and easily feels scorned by her.

How do we account for these seemingly inconsistent and conflicted representations of gender in which people find themselves acting, feeling, and thinking in ways that they wish they didn't? At the same time, how do we account for individuals who occupy their gender in more conventional ways? A useful psychology of gender needs to make sense of both the seemingly fixed and universal aspects of gender and the seemingly contradictory and individual aspects of gender. It should provide an explanation of gender's seeming intractability and universality, and of individuals' ability to manifest and experience gender in endlessly multiple ways. At the same time, a psychology of gender should make sense of the conflicted nature of gender, of the ways in which it is not always an easy fit and sometimes feels uncomfortable, and of the ways in which gender sometimes feels just right and as though it fits us perfectly.

This chapter shows the particular utility of psychoanalytic theory for understanding gender. Psychoanalytic theory has been concerned from its beginnings with questions of gender. I first describe what distinguishes psychoanalytic theory from other theories of human development and gender and outline Freud's initial contributions to the understanding of gender. I then describe the particular contributions and revisions to Freud's theory provided by feminist psychoanalytic theorists during the 1970s and 1980s. These theorists not only redressed some of the sexism in Freud's initial theories but also provided a way of understanding gender's seeming universality and intractability. Finally, I discuss more recent feminist psychoanalytic theorists influenced by postmodernism, queer theory, and the trans movement who argue for gender's particularity and fluidity, as well as for its universality and intractability.

Because psychoanalytic theory is generally generated by clinicians principally interested in the treatment of their particular patients, the evidence presented is drawn from clinical cases. That is, clinicians will describe the dilemmas, sufferings, and difficulties of their patients as evidence of the theory they propound, and they will use their patients' improvement as evidence of the theory's utility. Historically, psychoanalytic theory has been isolated from mainstream psychology in many parts of the world because of its reliance on concepts that are difficult to study using traditional empirical techniques and its seeming reliance on subjective rather than objective knowledge. As the field of psychology focused more exclusively on objectively measurable phenomena in representative samples, psychoanalysis's focus on the unconscious and on single cases came to seem unscientific and not worthy of exploration within research psychology (Hornstein, 1992). More contemporary branches of critical psychology and feminist psychology, however, have made use of the psychoanalytic concepts of the unconscious and subjectivity (Hollway, 2006; Hollway & Jefferson, 2000).

In this chapter I will present primarily clinical evidence in support of psychoanalytic theory. These are generally individual cases presented by psychoanalytic theorists that illustrate phenomena that clinicians have observed across their patients.

TRADITIONAL PSYCHOANALYTIC THEORY

Psychoanalysis occupies a both-and position as a mode of inquiry. On the one hand, it is a treatment providing a cure for the troubles that ail individuals and a process of discovering meaning that may be true for particular individuals. On the other, it may also generate insights that are characteristic of groups of individuals. Freud was, paradoxically, both a man of his time and a man ahead of his time when it came to sex and gender. Because many of Freud's patients were women and he was male, because he worked during the Victorian era in Europe during which gender prescriptions were quite rigid, and perhaps because of his own personal experiences of gender, Freud focused on differences between male and female development generally and the development of gender in particular (1905, 1925, 1931, 1932, 1937). Freud was perhaps the first "gender theorist" in his insistence that the sex category assigned at birth is not the same as acquired gender, that biology is not destiny, and that gender is made and not inborn. He did not go quite as far as subsequent theorists in making these claims, and at times his writing can sound deterministic, as though biology were in fact destiny. But the tools and insights he provided us with are invaluable in understanding gender in its universal and particular aspects.

Two of Freud's early findings that have endured and that are particularly important in the psychology of gender are the concept of internal conflict and the idea that we have an unconscious part of ourselves that motivates us but of which we remain unaware. These two findings are related and have important implications for our experiences of gender as contradictory and unexplained by our conscious desires and feelings.

Freud became intrigued by female patients who at the time were diagnosed with what was then called hysteria—that is, they exhibited physical and bodily symptoms like paralysis, shortness of breath, tics, and loss of sense of smell when there seemed to be nothing medically wrong with them (Breuer & Freud, 1895). They were generally assumed to be incurable or if curable, then by medical science. Freud believed there to be psychological meaning in the symptoms the women manifested. Along with his colleague Breuer and one of Breuer's patients, Anna O, Freud came upon the talking cure in which the patient simply talked, saying anything and everything that came into her mind in order to trace symptoms back to their origins. This is what came to be called "free association." Talking in this way sometimes enabled the therapist and patient to come to understand the origins of the patient's symptoms. When symptoms were fully understood and accounted for, they were often eliminated.

Freud and Breuer found that, from the point of view of a person's unconscious fantasies or beliefs, there is meaning in symptoms that may appear to be meaningless. An unconscious part of the mind reflects desires, wishes, and fantasies that are not conscious to us in our waking lives but which inform the ways that we think, act, and feel. In the case of Freud's patients, symptoms could be traced to meaningful experiences that caused such profound inner conflict that women developed physical symptoms to manage the conflict. For example, one patient could not tolerate the anger and resentment that she felt over having to tend her dying father. Another patient could not tolerate the shame and anger that she felt at having been sexually abused by her father's friend. They both developed physical symptoms rather than consciously experiencing such personally and socially unacceptable feelings. The concept of internal conflict helps to explain why the woman mentioned in the opening lines of this chapter may struggle to prioritize romantic relationships despite consciously wanting to—she cannot tolerate the feelings of dependency and helplessness that may arise in relation to her romantic partners, and so she keeps her focus on her work in which she seemingly has more control. The existence of an unconscious part of ourselves explains some of the contradictions that we feel in relation to our experiences of gender, such as why the radically independent man mentioned earlier may long for approval from his female boss.

Although the concepts of the unconscious and internal conflict are useful for the purposes of understanding gender, it is also true that psychoanalysts have been substantively interested in gender and sexuality from the inception of psychoanalysis and onward (Abraham, 1922; Bonaparte, 1956; Deutsch, 1943; Freud, 1905, 1920, 1925, 1931, 1932, 1937; Horney, 1926; Rivière, 1929). In particularly elastic moments in *Three Essays on the Theory of Sexuality*, Freud argued that while gender is always related to sexual object choice (that is, who people are sexually attracted to), neither fully causes the other (1905). Instead, he insisted that everyone, both men and women, are masculine and feminine, passive and active, and inherently bisexual in sexual orientation. He also argued that one's gender experience is not predictive of whom one loves. That is, a man may appear to be traditionally masculine in his presentation, but he may love men, and a woman may appear to be traditionally masculine in her presentation and also love men. Individuals may experience traditionally masculine and feminine aspects of themselves in relation to the same person, and they may seek out love objects that correspond to both traditionally masculine and feminine ideals.

As you read earlier, Freud held that gender was acquired, not inborn. In his view, the processes by which people became gendered took place early in a child's life. He first focused his attention on boys and the development of masculinity. Freud made the radical claim that men are made and not born, that boys' development into men who are "masculine" and heterosexual needs to be explained and is not inevitable or "natural." Freud sought to explain how boys, who are originally attached to their mothers, develop into men who identify with their fathers and are romantically attracted to women other than their mothers (if they are heterosexual). Freud identified important puzzles to be solved about male development. How do boys manage to sever their identification with their mothers when maternal figures are more central in children's early care than are their fathers? How and why does masculinity develop, given that it is usually women who are most centrally involved in childrearing? And how do boys shift their attachment from their mothers to other women? Why would a boy ever give up a mother's love, and his love for her?

Freud chose the myth of Oedipus to illustrate his theory of male development. He argued that myths and fairy tales often reflect a collective unconscious, something that is fundamentally true about human life but that remains generally hidden from conscious life, only to be told in story and fantasy form. Myths and fairy tales persist throughout time, argued Freud, because they reflect something essential in human experience. Freud proposed that boys face dilemmas, passions, and conflicts similar to those that Oedipus faced. In very simplified form, the story of Oedipus's life is that an oracle decreed that Oedipus would eventually kill his father and marry his mother. To prevent this fate from befalling them and him, Oedipus' parents sent him to live elsewhere. Nonetheless, as an adult, Oedipus unwittingly killed his father and married his mother. When he discovered this, he was so despairing and devastated that he gouged out both of his eyes. Freud took from the myth and from evidence in his clinical work with patients the idea that young boys unconsciously wish to marry their mothers and kill off their fathers so that they have no competition for their mothers' affection. Oedipus lived out this wish, but most men, Freud argued, merely have an unconscious wish and do not act on these desires. But men do require a way out of this dilemma, which Freud described as the resolution of the Oedipus complex.

According to Freud's theory, little boys desire to have their mother as their own love object. They are angry with their father for having their mother and wish to kill the father to be able to claim their mother as theirs. However, when boys are around 4–6 years old, they become aware of the differences between the sexes. Prior to this age, children do not differentiate themselves or others by sex, claimed Freud. At this age, the boy notices the absence of a penis in women and imagines that he could also be deprived of his penis. He fears that the father will take away his penis as punishment for desiring his mother and wanting to displace his father. The boy finds himself in a terrible dilemma here—without identification with the aggressor, he could be castrated by his father, but in order to identify with the aggressor, he must give up his attachment to his mother. What he gains is identification with his father and the capacity to love another woman later in life.

Later, Freud turned his attention to the development of femininity in girls. Freud argued that girls' development runs parallel to boys' development but also diverges from boys' development in some important ways (1925, 1931, 1932). The puzzles of female development, as Freud saw them, were as follows: How does femininity develop and why do women submit to its limitations? How do girls who grow up to become heterosexual shift their love from their mothers to their fathers and then to other men? Why would a girl ever give up a mother's love and her love for her mother? Because Freud believed that "mature" femininity involved an acceptance of the absence of a penis, and the clitoris for Freud was merely a childhood stand-in for the penis, he believed that "mature" women derived sexual pleasure from vaginal and not clitoral stimulation. He then wondered, how and why do girls change the genital organ from which they derive pleasure from the clitoris to the vagina?

Freud argued that girls, in complement to boys, desire to marry the father and kill the mother who is a rival for the father's affection. Girls spend their early lives attached to the mother in the same way as do boys. Between 4 and 6 years of age, however, girls recognize that they lack a penis and experience themselves as castrated and inferior to boys and men. They then feel contempt for their mothers and women generally because of their lack of a penis, and they blame the mother for their own lack. This contempt and anger at the mother fuel the girl's turning from her mother and toward her father as a love object. Upon realizing that she cannot have a penis, she gives up "active" sexuality based in the clitoris for "passive" sexuality based in the vagina and wishes for a child from the father as a substitute for a penis. She then has a similarly rivalrous relationship with her mother as does the boy with his father. A girl's identification with the mother is more complicated than is a boy's identification with the father, because the girl has not resolved her contemptuous and angry feelings at the mother, and because she holds her mother to be inferior.

The theory of the Oedipus complex has been rightly critiqued over the years by feminist theorists and gay and lesbian theorists, who argued that it holds the penis in too high regard, and that it assumes that maturity entails heterosexuality (Benjamin, 1988; Chodorow, 1978, 1992; Isay, 1990, to name a few). More recent research also shows that infants perceptually distinguish sex categories much earlier than Freud believed (Hock, Kangas, Zieber, & Bhatt, 2015) and that most female orgasms are based on clitoral stimulation. And yet many feminist and LGBT scholars have continued to rework rather than reject Freud's theory of the Oedipus complex because the compelling questions that Freud originally asked continue to need to be answered—How does gender identity develop? And how do children identify and disidentify with their parents? Futhermore, the psychoanalytic method that he developed for answering them remains among the most useful that we have for understanding the passions and discomforts of gender. Contemporary psychologists and social scientists interested in gender and sexuality have found useful Freud's attention to the family, the body, the unconscious, internal conflict, and internalization in the development of gender. They have modified and built upon Freud's theory to rid it of phallocentrism (that is, its overvaluing of the penis), to problematize its assumption of heterosexuality, to assert the subjectivity of the mother, and to rid the theory of its biological determinist bent.

FEMINIST PSYCHOANALYTIC THEORIES OF THE 1970s AND 1980s

Early feminist psychoanalytic theorists were clinicians who sought to redress the phallocentric focus of early psychoanalytic theory (Horney, 1926; Klein, 1928; Jones, 1927; Thompson, 1943). They made claims about girls' early knowledge of the vagina (Freud claimed girls were aware only of the clitoris), suggested that womb envy may be as powerful and plausible as penis envy, and argued for a distinct line of female development that differed from male development from early on, not only with the onset of the Oedipal stage. They based much of their thinking on clinical work with women patients whose lived experiences of their bodies and genders diverged widely from Freud's theory.

Feminists writing during the 1970s and 1980s in a number of countries, notably the United Kingdom, France, and the United States, turned to psychoanalytic theory because it addressed gender and sexuality, and because it seemed to account for the persistence of gender inequality, both in individual psyches and in cultural and social institutions, despite Western society's political and social commitment to gender equality. They took from Freud the premise that particular personality characteristics such as active and passive, and independent and dependent, do not universally differentiate the sexes. They accounted for how entrenched gender and gender inequality are by focusing on how these become lodged in and actually constitute the psyche.

In what follows, I have chosen to focus on those feminist psychoanalytic theorists whose work has been most grounded in clinical work but who still retained a focus on and interest in the interplay of the social and the psychological. Nancy Chodorow (1978) and Jessica Benjamin (1988) have had particularly far-reaching influence not only in the field of feminist psychology but also in the humanities and other social sciences.

They both trained as sociologists and as psychoanalysts, which has likely influenced their ability to speak to social scientists as well as clinicians. Interested readers may wish also to explore the work of French psychoanalytic feminist theorists, whose work has also had wide-ranging impact in the social sciences and the humanities (see, for example, de Cixous, 1976; Irigaray, 1977; Kristeva, 1969).

Chodorow and Benjamin used important concepts provided by psychoanalysis—the unconscious, internal conflict, the relationship between sexuality and gender, the role of early childhood experiences—to link the psychology of gender to the persistence of gender inequality. One of the central problems they addressed is that women, as the usual primary parent of children, occupy the difficult position of being all-important to children at the same time that they are devalued by society, and often by themselves. And children, in the process of development, may insist upon devaluing all that is feminine and maternal within themselves, both to defend against the mother's power and to assert their individuality. Girl children then have great difficulty in developing a feminine sense of self that is subjective and agentic, and boy children have difficulty relating to women without devaluing them.

At the time of Chodorow's early writing in the 1970s, much feminist thinking was concerned with the split between the public and private spheres in postindustrial societies in the West. That is, at the time when she wrote, men occupied the valued public sphere of work, politics, and culture; and women occupied the devalued private sphere of home and children. This split seemed central to gender inequality, and Chodorow (1978) worked to explain both its origins and its perpetuation. She did not, as did many feminist scholars at the time, look solely at social institutions such as the state and the economy, but examined the role of families and early childhood experiences in producing both individual and social gender. At the time of Benjamin's early writing, much feminist thinking was focused on how and why it is that men dominate women sexually (1988). Power differences between men and women in other domains of life, in her view, seemed to be traceable to the sexual domination of women by men, with gender inequality being created and perpetuated in the most private of places, the bedroom.

Chodorow posed the original question that paved the way for subsequent explorations and understandings of the role of mothering in perpetuating gender. How is it, she asked, that women come to want to be mothers, across diverse societies and in varied circumstances? Previously, women's mothering had been described as natural because it is women who give birth and lactate, but Chodorow sought to understand the psychology of mothering, the desire to mother and not just its physical logic based on women's possession of uteruses and mammary glands. In particular, if mothering is often a fundamental basis of gender inequality, why would women desire it? In Chodorow's view, of central importance to the issue of women's desire to mother is the question of boys' and girls' connection to and separation from their mothers. Chodorow argued that parenting arrangements in the late 20th century in Western high-income countries, in which women were primarily responsible for parenting and men went out to work in the public sphere and had limited parenting responsibilities, produced different personality structures in girls and boys. For both boys and girls, Chodorow argued that although mothers may be socially devalued, they are extremely powerful in children's eyes and experiences. Mothers are the primary figures in boys' and girls' early lives, and they are the people both boys and girls most profoundly need in their early lives. The puzzle for Chodorow then became this: How do boys and girls manage to connect to and separate from their own mothers, and why does this connection and separation look different in boys and girls? Freud also considered this question, but from a phallocentric perspective. He answered that boys fear the deprivation of the penis so they separate from the mother, and that girls are angry with the mother for having deprived them of a penis, so they too separate from her. Chodorow proposed a model of boys' and girls' development without relying on the importance of the penis.

Girls, in Chodorow's model, spend their early childhood with an experience of physical and psychological sameness and continuity with their mothers. Girls then must struggle intensely to attain a sense of separateness and individuation (a basic developmental task for both boys and girls) from their mothers through adolescence. Heterosexual relationships for women are unlikely to be deeply satisfying because of their conflicts over closeness and separateness (based on their relationships with their mothers) and because of men's unavailability for connection and intimacy (see later). Women then have a need for attachment beyond heterosexual relations with men even if they are heterosexual, and Chodorow argued that they therefore desire to become mothers and to develop close attachments to their children. The cycle—the reproduction of mothering—thus continues.

Boys, on the other hand, grow up with an early experience of continuity with their mothers and a later experience of difference from their mothers once they come to recognize bodily and social gender differences. Because of boys' experience of difference, they are more easily able to separate and individuate from their mothers. They identify with their fathers, who occupy the public sphere and turn toward material achievement in the outside world both as a means of achieving gender identity and as a means of freeing themselves from their mothers' power. Later in life, men will desire to love and be close to women in the private sphere, grounded in the safe position in the public sphere they occupy. Heterosexual activity and relationships for men will likely be a satisfying return to the primary oneness originally experienced with their mothers.

Benjamin drew upon Chodorow's premise that women's mothering is central in the development and perpetuation of gender inequality, and she used it to understand how men's domination of women is anchored in women as much as it involves male exercise of power. Other feminist scholars had explored the roots of male domination but had not pursued the question of female submission to domination. Benjamin drew upon psychoanalytic theory to answer such a question, because consciously women certainly do not want to be dominated (most of the time), and consciously most men do not want women to be reduced to less valuable human beings. But, in a familial constellation in which women are primarily responsible for child care and men base their identities in the public sphere of work, Benjamin argued that boys and girls experience their parents differently and so develop into dominant men and subordinated women. Children experience their fathers as exciting subjects and agents in the outside world, capable of action on their own behalf and able to act of their own desire. By contrast, they experience their mothers as passive and not capable in the outside world but able to nurture in the private sphere, objects of their fathers' desire but not in possession of their own. The mother's nurturing features are important but are socially denigrated and split off from the excitement of the father. Both boys and girls feel the desire for excitement as their own inner desire and then look to the exciting other (the father) for recognition of their desires. Both boys and girls seek what Benjamin termed "identificatory love" with the exciting father who appears to have freedom, autonomy, and desire.

Boys, in Benjamin's formulation, can see themselves as like the exciting father and so gain subjecthood and desire. And yet this comes at the price of their attachment to the mother and the qualities she possesses and engenders. They can achieve a certain form of subjectivity, but it is one that denigrates the qualities of women. Girls, who are left with mothers who are themselves objects of desire but not subjects, will find it impossible, according to Benjamin, to develop a sense of true subjectivity. Girls are generally not recognized by their parents as like the exciting father and are relegated to identifying with their mothers as objects.

Although these theories have been influential among feminist psychoanalysts, they have also received some criticism for their presumption of a heterosexual family formation in which both parents are present, the father is the primary breadwinner, and the mother is the primary caregiver. Given that only 28% of families in the United States today have this structure (Parker & Livingston, 2016), some have argued that 1970s and 1980s feminist psychoanalytic theory is not applicable to children and caregivers in other family formations. Chodorow and Benjamin, and others, have countered that, despite the proliferation of various family formations, it is still true that women are responsible for the bulk of caregiving to children. In 2011, mothers in the United States spent on average 14 hours per week caring for children, whereas fathers spent on average 7 hours per week (Parker & Livingston, 2016). And even in families in which the other parent is a woman, it is generally true that one parent is more a secondary parent who goes out into the world, who is less affiliated with the domestic sphere and caregiving responsibilities. Furthermore, Benjamin and others have argued that it is not essential to have two parents, nor two parents of different genders, in order to have these split experiences of autonomy and dependency (1995, 1998). Some of the dynamics and processes discussed by these authors may then hold true despite appearances to the contrary.

Chodorow and Benjamin also assumed that the pattern of development they described would in most cases lead to heterosexuality. If an individual did not experience heterosexual attraction, this indicated that something had gone awry during the individual's early childhood. Because we know same-sex attraction and bisexuality to be "normal" outcomes of child development that has not gone awry, others have argued for the inapplicability of Chodorow's and Benjamin's theories to children and adults who are gay, lesbian, bisexual, gender nonconforming, and transgendered.

Chodorow's and Benjamin's theories provided us with powerful tools for understanding gender's seeming universality and intractability. They helped to describe gender's origins in the individual as well as its reproduction in social and individual life. And they showed the ways that its location in individual psyches makes it particularly difficult to change—it is constitutive of the self and subjectivity more generally, so it does not respond to mere suggestion or teaching. By locating the development of gender not only in families but also in social structures that depend upon particular representations of gender, they further bolstered their arguments for gender's seeming entrenchment. Also their focus on pre-Oedipal development in boys and girls highlighted the importance of the primary caregiver and the primary caregiver's gender. However, their theories are somewhat overgeneralized, as clinical evidence suggests that individuals' experiences of gender sometimes fit general categories, but they sometimes also manifest themselves in idiosyncratic and personal ways. The seemingly universal experiences of gender they discussed are important but do not fully account for the range of gendered experience that psychotherapists witness clinically. Nor did they theorize the body and its relationship to sexuality, out of concerns to avoid biological determinism.

FEMINIST PSYCHOANALYTIC THEORY FROM
THE 1990s TO THE PRESENT

More recently, feminist psychoanalytic theorists have argued for an expansion of our understanding of healthy gender, and they conceptualize a post-Oedipal experience of gender in which individuals are neither rigidly experiencing gender in one objectively observable way nor experiencing gender fluidly only in a purely subjective way. Some theorists have also turned to problematizing masculinity as well as femininity. And finally, they have returned to a focus on the body and sexuality in understanding the psychology of gender, and they are able to do so without the biological determinism that feminist psychoanalysts of the 1970s and 1980s so assiduously avoided.

More recent feminist psychoanalytic theorists focus on understanding how we can be subject to the dichotomous categories of gender described and explained so convincingly by feminists of the 1970s and 1980s, and at the same time have some freedom from those categories. They do so by borrowing from postmodern and queer theorists such as Judith Butler (2004) and Gayle Salamon (2010). Queer and postmodern theorists argue that the dichotomous categories of masculine/feminine, subject/object, active/passive, contained/container, and autonomy/dependency constitute our selfhood at the same time that they severely limit it. These categories, and the splits they produce and inspire, require us to choose between being one thing or another and so circumscribe our capacity to be fully human.

Building upon queer and postmodern theory, more recent works such as those by Ken Corbett (2011), Virginia Goldner (1991, 2003), Adrienne Harris (1996), Muriel Dimen (1991), and Jessica Benjamin (1995, 1998) discuss and elaborate a post-Oedipal experience of gender in which the consolidation of gender is not solely an Oedipal achievement, a final arrival at a solid and fixed gender identity that is either man or woman and that corresponds to one's genital anatomy. This post-Oedipal experience of gender does not correspond to particular ages, as the Oedipal period does in Freud's original theory. Rather, it describes an experience of gender that some individuals may develop once they have a capacity for more flexibility and complexity in their self identities. More recently, theorists have recognized the value of Oedipal-level thinking about gender, in which rigid categories and dichotomies predominate, during childhood but not adulthood. The child, they argue, develops rigid and polarized categories of thinking that organize his or her experience—male and female, Black and White, can and cannot, subject and object, active and passive, and so on. It is developmentally appropriate that children should think using such categories. It is not developmentally appropriate, however, that adults should remain at this developmental stage. Theorizing about the post-Oedipal experience is heavily influenced by the ideas of the British psychoanalytic theorist Melanie Klein (1928), who argues that categorical splitting is characteristic of early developmental stages in childhood. When mobilized by adults, it may be used defensively, to ward off the difficulties of complexity. Several theorists argue that consolidating a stable gender identity is a developmental "accomplishment" that requires the activation of processes such as disavowal and splitting (Benjamin, 1995, 1998; Corbett, 2011; Goldner, 1991, 2003). It requires that we disavow and cut off parts of ourselves that could otherwise be expressed and experienced, because of our loyalty to rigid and dichotomous categories of gender. There is some evidence that rigid sex typing leads to behavioral inflexibility and difficulty adapting to unfamiliar situations for both men and women (Helson & Picano, 1990), certainly not a hallmark of mental health. And although men who occupy rigidly masculine categories of gender at least appear to benefit socially from doing so, Corbett (2011), Benjamin, and Chodorow have argued that what is conventionally taken to be "successful" masculinity involves a disavowal of surrender, relatedness, loss, and passivity—human qualities and experiences without which rigidly masculine men suffer personally.

Post-Oedipal experiences of gender involve the capacity to tolerate ambiguity and instability and to occupy multiple categories of gender. In the post-Oedipal period, one can experience oneself as both male and female, active and passive, penetrating and containing. In the post-Oedipal period, people may sometimes experience themselves as open, nurturing, and receptive, attributes socially coded as feminine, and may at different points experience themselves as penetrating and withholding, attributes socially coded as masculine.

Another post-Oedipal achievement entails a capacity to move back and forth between the inclusivity of the post-Oedipal period and the rigidity of the Oedipal period. That is, a man may at times experience himself to be both masculine and feminine, and at other moments to be exclusively masculine. Optimal well-being would be signaled by the capacity to move between these different experiences of gender in order to experience one's self most fully (Aron, 1995; Sweetnam, 1996). In either case, we find a very different picture of "healthy" gender than in previous psychoanalytic accounts, in which men and women were thought to achieve a singular and unified gender that held true for them across time and space. For the-orists writing today, the development and experience of gender continues throughout life and is not finished following the Oedipal period.

Feminists of the 1970s and 1980s shied away from using the body to understand the psychology of gender, in an effort to avoid the determin-ism characteristic of other bodily and biologically based theories. Today, however, feminist psychoanalytic theorists have at their disposal the ideas of postmodernism and queer theory, which situate the body within a social context. Postmodern theories understand the body to have different meanings and to evince different experiences depending upon the social forces that not only influence but also create a particular experience of the body. Queer theorists argue that bodies and what we do with them dur-ing sex certainly matter; otherwise, deviations from normative sexuality would not engender such hostility, fear, and discrimination (Butler, 1990, 2004; Sedgwick, 1990). To discuss gender and sexuality without consid-ering the body is, they argue, to be blind to the social significance of the body and what it does and does not do.

The trans and genderqueer (what in Chapter 3 we call nonbinary gen-der) movements have pushed the thinking in psychoanalysis, asking that psychoanalytic theorists conceive of masculinity and femininity as located in both men's and women's, mothers' and fathers' bodies. At the same time, the insistence by some in the trans movement that bodies matter—that gender identities and bodies are not always a match, and that having a change in one's body can result in a more comfortable experience of one's gender identity—has pushed psychoanalytic theory both forward and back to its roots. Diverse experiences within the trans and gender-queer communities challenge psychoanalytic theorists and practitioners to become more flexible in their own thinking about gender. That is, some trans and genderqueer individuals may have a nonbinary gender identity, which could include having no gender, having a mixed gender, being to some extent but not completely one gender, being of a specific additional gender, moving between genders, or disputing the gender binary of men and women altogether (see Chapter 3).

Contemporary psychoanalytic theorists are currently wrestling with the ways in which trans and genderqueer identities are, like all gender identities, some kind of compromise formation, that is, a symbolic representation of both a forbidden wish and the defense against the wish. They argue that trans and genderqueer identities are "simultaneously inventive and defensive" (Goldner, 2011), and they point to the ways in which trans identities may be experienced as paradoxical—both queering and ratifying gender at the same time (Hansbury, 2011; Saketopoulou, 2011; Suchet, 2011). Some psychoanalytic clinicians and theorists have also been placed in the complicated position of being gatekeepers for trans individuals who wish to pursue surgery, as gender-crossing surgery in the United States is not available without a psychiatric diagnosis, even as "cosmetic" surgeries to "improve" upon one's birth gender are commonplace and require no diagnosis.

Contemporary feminist psychoanalytic theory has returned to Freud's original insights about the fundamental importance of the body in the development of a gendered self, but theorists are now able to understand the body as both given and as constructed. That is, the body exists materially prior to the self and is prediscursive, but it is given meaning through its relationship to others and so it is also constructed. Rosemary Balsam returns to the insights of the original feminist psychoanalytic theorists such as Karen Horney and Helene Deutsch and expands upon them (2012). She argues that the female capacity to become pregnant and to give birth, and children's (both boys' and girls') experience of a pregnant mother are crucial to understanding women's (and men's) experiences of gender. Women's bodies, she argues, have a capacity to swell and contract, to loosen and to tighten, that she sees reflected in female patients' anxieties and concerns about how they occupy space relative to other women. Balsam is not arguing for a universal experience of or understanding of pregnancy and birth, but she is arguing that girl children and women have their own highly individualized reactions to these corporeal realities. Ken Corbett also returns to Freud's initial theorizing about the significance of the penis, but he focuses on boys' and men's joyful experiences of their whole bodies to propose a healthy and not defensive version of masculinity (2011). New understandings of genetic, biological, and chemical processes as multidirectional and multicausal—that is, that material bodies and even genes can be altered by environmental experiences, at the same time that material bodies and genes can influence the way an individual develops (Frost, 2011)—are helping to ease the way for feminist psychoanalytic theorists to return to the body in their understandings of gender. As feminist psychoanalytic thinking expands to include more complex understandings of the body, we see a growing convergence across fields that have often been viewed as irreconcilably opposed such as neuroscience, evolution, and psychoanalysis.

SUMMARY AND FUTURE DIRECTIONS

Psychoanalytic theories offer us a unique lens in understanding the psychology of gender. They do so by focusing attention on outside forces that broadly impact experiences of gender and internal forces that make meaning of gender in very particular ways. They are also unique in their long-standing interest in gender as constitutive of the self. Gender, in psychoanalytic thinking, has always been one of the principal axes of development, and gender differences and similarities have interested psychoanalytic thinkers from the beginning.

Although many late 20th-century and early 21st-century theorists have criticized Freud, as did his own contemporaries, for some of his sexist and phallocentric views on gender, it is nonetheless the case that many of his insights have stood the test of time and proven useful to other contemporary theorists. Many of his theories retain a flexibility characteristic of few psychological theories of his time.

Feminist psychoanalytic theorists of the 1970s and 1980s have developed an important reformulation of psychoanalytic theories of gender. They pointed to the significant role of gender in parenting, brought forward the importance of the mother–child relationship and attachment in the very early life of the baby, and argued that women's mothering and men's lack of involvement in child rearing create and perpetuate particular forms of gender and gender inequality. They also discussed the ways in which male and female gender are intertwined and co-created as they are often defined in opposition to one another. They provided compelling accounts of the ways in which gender is constitutive of both individual psyches and the culture at large.

Feminist psychoanalytic theories of the 1990s and beyond have furthered our understanding of gender by returning to Freud's most compelling early observations of gender—that it is related to but not determinate of sexuality, that it is influenced but not determined by sex, that it is informed by but not caused solely by the body, and that it is always mediated by the personal unconscious.

Psychoanalytic theorists are beginning to correct their historical overreliance on White, upper-middle-class women and men in the Global North as their primary subjects, but they could certainly go further. Psychoanalytic theorists could also further problematize both masculinity and heterosexuality. Psychoanalytic theorists are beginning to struggle with trans issues and the challenges they pose to a theoretical tradition with a decidedly ambivalent relationship to physical bodies. With exciting new developments in neuroscience, epigenetics, and transgender movements, psychoanalytic theorists could also do more to integrate the work of other disciplines and make their work known to other disciplines.

ACKNOWLEDGMENTS

Portions of this chapter are reproduced verbatim or with revision from the author's chapter in Beall, Eagly, and Sternberg (Eds.) (2004), *The psychology of gender* (2nd ed.), with permission from Guilford Press.

REFERENCES

Abraham, K. (1922). Manifestations of the female castration complex. *International Journal of Psychoanalysis*, III(Part 1), 1–29.

Aron, L. (1995). The internalized primal scene. *Psychoanalytic Dialogues*, 5(2), 195–237.

Balsam, R. (2012). *Women's bodies in psychoanalysis*. New Haven, CT: Yale University Press.

Benjamin, J. (1988). *The bonds of love: Psychoanalysis, feminism, and the problem of domination*. New York, NY: Pantheon Books.

Benjamin, J. (1995). *Like subjects, love objects: Essays on recognition and sexual difference*. New Haven, CT: Yale University Press.

Benjamin, J. (1998). *Shadow of the other: Intersubjectivity and gender in psychoanalysis*. New York, NY: Routledge.

Bonaparte, M. (1956). *Female sexuality*. Madison, CT: International Universities Press.

Breuer, J., & Freud, S. (1895). Studies on hysteria. *Standard Edition*, 2 (pp. 1–319). London, UK: Hogarth Press, 1953.

Butler, J. (1990). *Gender trouble: Feminism and the subversion of identity*. London, UK: Routledge.

Butler, J. (2004). *Undoing gender*. New York, NY: Routledge.

Chodorow, N. J. (1978). *The reproduction of mothering: Psychoanalysis and the sociology of gender*. Berkeley: University of California Press.

Chodorow, N. J. (1992). Heterosexuality as a compromise formation: Reflections on the psychoanalytic theory of sexual development. *Psychoanalysis and Contemporary Thought*, 15, 267–304.

Corbett, K. (2011). *Boyhoods: Rethinking masculinity*. New Haven, CT: Yale University Press.

Deutsch, H. (1943). *The psychology of women, Volume 1: Girlhood*. Allyn & Bacon.

de Cixous, H. et al. (1976). The laugh of the medusa. *Signs*, 1(4), 875–893.

Dimen, M. (1991). Deconstructing difference: Gender, splitting, and transitional space. *Psychoanalytic Dialogues*, 1(3), 335–352.

Freud, S. (1905). *Three essays on the theory of sexuality*. New York, NY: Basic Books, 2000.

Freud, S. (1920). The psychogenesis of a case of homosexuality in a woman. *Standard Edition*, 18 (pp. 145–172). London, UK: Hogarth Press, 1955.

Freud, S. (1925). Some psychical consequences of the anatomical distinction between the sexes. *Standard Edition*, 19 (pp. 241–258). London, UK: Hogarth Press, 1961.

Freud, S. (1931). Female sexuality. *Standard Edition, 21* (pp. 225–243). London, UK: Hogarth Press, 1961.

Freud, S. (1932). Femininity. In *New introductory lectures on psycho-analysis* (pp. 139–166). New York, NY: W.W. Norton, 1964.

Freud, S. (1937). Analysis terminable and interminable. *Standard Edition, 23* (pp. 209–254). London, UK: Hogarth Press, 1964.

Frost, S. (2011). The implications of the new materialisms for feminist epistemology. In H. E. Grasswick (Ed.), *Feminist epistemology and philosophy of science* (pp. 69–83). New York, NY: Springer.

Goldner, V. (1991). Toward a critical relational theory of gender. *Psychoanalytic Dialogues, 1*(3), 249–272.

Goldner, V. (2003). Ironic gender/authentic sex. *Studies in Gender and Sexuality, 4,* 113–139.

Goldner, V. (2011). Trans: Gender in free fall. *Psychoanalytic Dialogues, 21*(2),159–171

Hansbury, G. (2011). King Kong & Goldilocks: Imagining trans masculinities through the trans-trans dyad. *Psychoanalytic Dialogues, 21*(2), 210–220.

Harris, A. (1996). Animated conversation: Embodying and gendering. *Gender and Psychoanalysis, 1,* 361–383.

Helson, R., & Picano, J. (1990). Is the traditional role bad for women? *Journal of Personality and Social Psychology, 59*(2), 311–320.

Hock, A., Kangas, A., Zieber, N., & Bhatt, R. S. (2015). The development of sex category representation in infancy: Matching of faces and bodies. *Developmental Psychology, 51,* 346–352.

Hollway, W. (2006). Psychoanalysis in social psychological research. *The Psychologist, 19*(9), 544–545.

Hollway, W., & T. Jefferson. (2000). *Doing qualitative research differently: Free association, narrative, and the interview method.* London, UK: Sage.

Horney, K. (1926). The flight from womanhood. *International Journal of Psycho-Analysis, 7,* 324–339.

Hornstein, G. A. (1992). Return of the repressed: Psychology's problematic relationship with psychoanalysis, 1909-1960. *American Psychologist, 47*(2), 254–263.

Irigaray, L. (1977). *This sex which is not one.* New York, NY: Cornell University Press.

Isay, R. (1990). *Being homosexual: Gay men and their development.* New York, NY: Avon.

Klein, M. (1928). Early stages of the Oedipus conflict. *International Journal of Psychoanalysis, 9,* 167–180.

Kristeva, J. (1969). *Desire in language.* New York, NY: Columbia University Press.

Jones, E. (1927). The early development of female sexuality. *International Journal of Psycho-Analysis, 8,* 459–472.

Parker, K., & Livingston, G. (2016, June 16). 6 facts about American fathers. Retrieved from http://www.pewresearch.org/fact-tank/2016/06/16/fathers-day-facts/

Rivière, J. (1929). Womanliness as a masquerade. *International Journal of Psychoanalysis, 9,* 303–313.

Saketopoulou, A. (2011). Minding the gap: Intersections between gender, race, and class in work with gender variant children. *Psychoanalytic Dialogues, 21*(2), 192–209.

Salamon, G. (2010). *Assuming a body: Transgender and rhetorics of materiality.* New York, NY: Columbia University Press.

Sedgwick, E. (1990). *Epistemology of the closet.* Berkeley: University of California Press.

Suchet, M. (2011). Crossing over. *Psychoanalytic Dialogues, 21*(2), 172–191.

Sweetnam, A. (1996). The changing contexts of gender: Between fixed and fluid experience. *Psychoanalytic Dialogues, 6*(4), 437–459.

Thompson, C. (1943). "Penis envy" in women. *Psychiatry, 6,* 123–125.

10

Gender, Dispositions, Peer Relations, and Identity

Toward an Integrative Developmental Model

CAMPBELL LEAPER

In this chapter, I review and explore some of the ways that peer relations, group identity, and dispositional traits are possibly interrelated and contribute to children's gender development. In doing so, I seek to advance an integrative theoretical model of gender development that bridges a few complementary theories (see Leaper, 2011). In most instances, my arguments are based on existing research studies. However, I hypothesize some possible connections that may not yet have been directly tested. Most of the research studies upon which I base my proposals were conducted primarily or exclusively in Western industrialized countries. Accordingly, the reader is cautioned that some of these findings may not generalize to all cultural contexts (see Henrich, Heine, & Norenzayan, 2010). I will reiterate this point throughout the chapter.

PROLOGUE

Terminology

To begin, I review some of the terminology used in the chapter. I apply the term *gender* to refer to the categorization of self or others, for instance, as girls (or women), boys (or men), genderfluid, or genderqueer. I use the term *sex* (and the terms *female* and *male*) to refer more narrowly to processes associated with the person's genetic sex (based on the twenty-third pair of human chromosomes; most often XX or XY, allowing for other variants). *Gender development* encompasses processes at various levels of organization (e.g., physiological, cognitive-motivational, interpersonal, and sociocultural) that are associated with people's self-identified and/or assigned gender categories. These processes include identity and self-perceptions, attitudes and beliefs, values and preferences, behavioral expressions, and competencies. With few exceptions, the available research literature on gender development has focused on cisgender children (that is, children who identify with their assigned gender at birth). However, an increasing number of developmental psychologists are considering a wider range of gender identities.

Background

For much of my career as a research psychologist, I have considered how gender is constructed and socialized in the context of social relationships (e.g., Leaper, 2000, 2015). Some of my studies have examined these processes in parent–child interactions. However, I have been especially intrigued with the ways that gender is expressed and socialized in peer relationships—which is a major focus of this chapter.

Although I am especially interested in sociocultural influences, I recognize other factors additionally shape people's development. When I started my research career over three decades ago, I tended to downplay the impact of sex-related physiological processes (e.g., genes and hormones) on thinking and behavior. Over time, the cumulative scientific evidence has convinced me that sex-related physiology and anatomy partly contribute to gender-related variations in some behaviors (e.g., see Hines, 2013; Wood & Eagly, 2012). Moreover, I now recognize that acknowledging this point is neither equivalent to adopting a "biological essentialist" perspective of gender development nor incompatible with feminist gender-egalitarian goals for society. Even when sex-related physiology and anatomy are implicated, social and material environments still play a major role in accounting for variations in most behavioral outcomes. In some societies, technological and cultural changes have mitigated the functional importance of the most fundamental sex differences in physiology and anatomy (as reviewed later in the chapter). Also, environments influence genetic expression and aspects of neurophysiological development (see Chapters 4, 11, and 13).

Although I continue to focus on social factors in my own studies of gender development, I have reflected on how sex-related dispositional traits and physical characteristics might contribute to some gender-related variations in behavior during childhood. In this chapter, I explore some of these possibilities. I posit an integrative developmental model that addresses the possible interrelationships among sex-related traits (e.g., temperament, physical characteristics), group socialization, and identity during gender development in a given cultural context. To build my argument, I first review ways that gendered group processes shape children's identities and their motivation to enact and develop particular behaviors and competencies. Afterward, I describe evidence linking some sex-related physiological processes and physical characteristics to variations in particular behaviors. Finally, I propose how these two sets of processes might be interrelated.

PEER GROUPS, SOCIAL IDENTITIES, AND GENDER DEVELOPMENT

As explicated in social identity theory and research (Tajfel & Turner, 1979), belonging to a group commonly leads to a set of processes that shape how a person behaves and thinks. These include in-group bias (favoring the members and attributes associated with one's in-group), in-group assimilation (conformity to the in-group's norms), and out-group stereotyping (viewing out-group members as homogenous). I will highlight how these processes commonly occur in children's same-gender peer groups. Across many societies, most children affiliate primarily in same-gender peer groups throughout childhood and adolescence. Indeed, some psychologists have argued that same-gender peer groups may be the most important context for the socialization of gender during childhood in many cultures (e.g., Harris, 1995; Maccoby, 1998).

Emergence of Gender as a Social Identity

Around 3 years of age, most children begin to show an increasing preference for same-gender peers. In one study in the United States, the ratio of same-gender to mixed-gender interactions went from 3:1 at 4 years of age to 11:1 at 6 years (Maccoby, 1998). Researchers have observed childhood gender segregation across a range of societies (Whiting & Edwards, 1988). However, it was less prevalent in cultural settings where children had limited access to same-age peers (Harkness & Super, 1985).

Observational studies suggest that the initial emergence of gender segregation may be partly based on seeking out peers with compatible behavioral styles (Maccoby, 1998; Martin et al., 2011b). During early childhood, average gender differences are seen in self-control (girls higher), empathy (girls higher), activity level (boys higher), and play preferences (see Leaper, 2015). As they get older, children's social identities as girls or boys may take priority over behavioral compatibility as a motivating force toward gender segregation (Leaper, 2015; Martin et al., 2011b, 2013).

The gender self-socialization model (Tobin et al., 2010) offers possible explanations for the development of individual variations in how strongly people might identify with their gender in-group. Some indices of one's identification with an in-group include centrality (personal importance of group), self-perceived typicality (perceived similarity to other group members), and in-group ties (positive ties to other group members) (Leaper, 2015; Tobin et al., 2010). According to the self-socialization model, persons who strongly identify with their gender in-group will be more likely to emulate the stereotypes associated with the group and to expect others to do so. Also, when there is concordance between one's self-perceived attributes and the expectations for the in-group (e.g., a girl who likes dolls and sees most other girls liking dolls), a stronger gender identity will be more likely. However, for some children, there can be discordance between the expectations for a gender in-group and their self-perceived attributes (e.g., a girl recognizes that most girls like dolls, but she herself does not like dolls); if so, the person will be less likely to identify with the particular gender in-group (e.g., low in-group centrality or low self-perceived in-group typicality).

In general, the gender self-socialization model is premised on people's tendency to seek concordance across (1) their self-perceived attributes (e.g., "I like playing with dolls"), (2) their expectations about their gender in-group (e.g., "Girls like dolls"), and (3) their gender in-group identity (e.g., "I am a girl; I am like other girls"). As explored later in the chapter, this model may help us understand why children may or may not readily identify with the gender category assigned to them at birth.

Impact of Gender as a Social Identity

Affiliating with a same-gender peer group during childhood is associated with the social identity processes seen in most stable social groups (see Harris, 1995). First, social norms define these groups. For example, among youth in some US communities, researchers observed boys expressed relatively greater endorsement of dominance goals, whereas girls showed relatively more emphasis on prosocial goals (see Rose & Rudolph, 2006). Second, in-group bias has been demonstrated through children's tendency to evaluate peers more positively (e.g., likeability, having desirable traits) when the peers are from one's gender in-group. Finally, in-group assimilation pressures are commonly exerted in children's same-gender peer groups (see Leaper, 2015).

Because children are usually motivated to gain acceptance, they tend to conform to the group's norms (Harris, 1995; Tobin et al., 2010). To this end, as Martin and Fabes (2001) observed in the United States, preschool or kindergarten children's amount of time spent with same-gender peers predicted subsequent increases over 6 months in behaviors that were generally typical of their gender in-group (e.g., play preferences, activity levels, frequency of aggression).

Assimilation may occur over time in gendered peer groups as a result of several influences. First, peer groups provide children with opportunities and incentives to practice particular behaviors (see Bussey & Bandura, 1999). In many groups, this means encouraging behaviors typical of the in-group as well as avoiding behaviors that are more typical of any out-groups. Behaviors that are practiced are more likely to lead to feelings of self-efficacy and ultimately to greater competence (Bussey & Bandura, 1999). Furthermore, as children internalize the group's norms, these behaviors become more internally motivated (i.e., based on personal standards and interests) and less externally motivated (i.e., based on others' approval or disapproval). As a consequence, children's internalization of the group's norms has a self-regulatory function—as explicated in cognitive theories of gender development (e.g., Bussey & Bandura, 1999; Tobin et al., 2010).

Although most children affiliate primarily with same-gender peers in most cultures, there are certain contexts in some societies when cooperative mixed-gender interactions often occur (see Mehta & Strough, 2009). For example, based on studies mostly conducted in North America or Europe, these interactions typically take place in private settings when companion choices are limited (e.g., in children's homes) or in public settings when children can attribute contact to external causes (e.g., teacher-assigned, mixed-gender collaborations). If children violate these general conventions, they often risk peer rejection. When adults assign children to mixed-gender cooperative groups, however, the repeated contact can help reduce gender stereotyping (see Leaper, 2013).

In summary, peer groups can have a powerful socializing influence on children's development. Children tend to identify with their gender in-group, and same-gender peer groups commonly reinforce the norms associated with the in-group. In subsequent sections, I consider possible ways that dispositional traits and physical characteristics may play a role in this process.

SEX-RELATED VARIATIONS IN DISPOSITIONAL TRAITS AND PHYSICAL CHARACTERISTICS

As reviewed next, there are sex-related variations in some personality dispositions, such as particular temperamental traits, and possibly in intense interests. In addition, there are sex-related variations in physical characteristics, including anatomy and physical abilities. Although I am addressing some features where comparisons of females and males point to meaningful effect sizes, the reader should note that there is considerable similarity and overlap between females and males on most measures of behavior (see Hyde, 2005) and brain functioning (see Joel, 2016).

Dispositional Traits

Personality dispositions or traits refer to individual variations in behavioral tendencies. Two kinds of traits that I consider are children's temperament and intense interests. Temperament refers to characteristic patterns of emotional arousal, response, and regulation that emerge early in children's development and tend to remain stable across time and settings; also, these personality traits appear to be partly heritable (based primarily on evidence from twin studies; see Else-Quest, Hyde, Goldsmith, & Van Hulle, 2006). In addition to temperament, there is evidence that some (but not all) children may have dispositions toward strong interests in particular objects and activities. Gender-related variations in these two kinds of dispositions—temperament and intense interests—are reviewed next.

Among various temperamental traits that psychologists have identified, self-control and activity level are two facets associated with meaningful average gender differences in children (see Else-Quest et al., 2006, for a meta-analysis; culture and socioeconomic status were not significant moderators). First, on average, girls demonstrated greater self-control (e.g., attentional focus and impulse control; $d = .41$ [Cohen's d is an index of effect size reflecting the average difference between groups in standard deviation units]). Lower average self-control among boys may be partly related to a corresponding higher incidence of physical aggression (see Leaper, 2015). Second, on measures of activity level (i.e., energy expenditure in motor behavior), boys tended to score higher on average than did girls ($d = .33$). Although these average gender differences in temperament are indicated in childhood, there is considerable within-gender variation as well as overlap between girls and boys in their distribution of scores (i.e., some girls are highly active and some boys are highly self-controlled). Also, whereas temperamental traits are partly heritable, they are subject to environmental influences.

In addition to temperament, recent research suggests there may be sex-related variations in dispositions toward interests in particular objects and activities during childhood. Average differences in girls' and boys' relative interests in social stimuli (girls higher) and physical objects (boys average) have been observed as young as infancy (see Alexander & Wilcox, 2012; Leaper, 2015). Additional research suggests that some (but not all) children may have especially intense interests in particular stimuli and activities (DeLoache, Simcock, & Macari, 2007; Halim et al., 2014; Johnson, Alexander, Spencer, Leibham, & Neitzel, 2004). Unlike temperamental traits, there are only a few pertinent studies of intense interests, all of which were conducted in North America and Europe.

First, there may be some children who have very strong interests in objects and activities that are highly typical of their gender in-group. In one study, DeLoache and colleagues (2007) identified approximately one quarter of children as demonstrating "extremely intense interests" in objects and activities during early childhood (1 to 6 years of age). That is, interest levels were exceptionally strong and reliably expressed across time and settings among some children. Among boys, these extreme interests usually included toy vehicles, machines, dinosaurs, and balls. The only intense interest seen principally among girls was dress-up (also see Halim et al., 2014). Another observed pattern was that extremely intense interests were much more common among boys than girls (DeLoache et al., 2007; Johnson et al., 2004).

There are also other children who demonstrate extremely intense interests in objects and activities that are contrary to cultural expectations for their gender in-group; at the same time, they express low interest in objects and activities that are stereotypical for their gender in-group (Golombok et al., 2012; VanderLaan et al., 2015; Zucker, Bradley, & Sanikhani, 1997). For example, in these studies, some boys indicated strong preferences for dress-up and doll play rather than sports. Also, some girls strongly preferred sports and physical activity over doll play. These patterns were reliable for these children across time and settings (Golombok et al., 2012; VanderLaan et al., 2015). Also, intense counterstereotypical interests were more common among boys than girls (VanderLaan et al., 2015; Zucker et al., 1997).

The origins of extremely intense interests are unclear. Studies of children with congenital adrenal hyperplasia (CAH) illustrate how intense interests may occur in some rare cases. (See Chapter 11 for more detail about CAH.) In cases of CAH, a recessive gene triggers a high production of androgen hormones during prenatal development. Among genetic females (XX sex chromosomes) with CAH, this high exposure to prenatal androgens appears to influence the organization of the nervous system in ways that can alter behavior later in childhood. Girls with CAH tend to prefer physically active play and show less interest in doll play than girls without CAH (Hines, 2013). In contrast, genetic males (XY chromosomes) with CAH do not appear to differ from control boys. Genetic males (with or without CAH) are normally exposed to high levels of androgens during prenatal development. Thus, high levels of prenatal androgens may partly contribute to some children's preferences for certain play activities.

To be clear, I am not proposing that all extremely intense interests have the same etiology. The research on girls with CAH points to one possible influence (e.g., prenatal androgen exposure) that might lead to intense interests in some instances. However, there may be multiple developmental pathways leading to dispositions toward intense interests.

As noted earlier, temperamental traits appear to be partly heritable. Perhaps the same will be found for intense interests. Even when a trait is heritable, it emerges through the interaction of genes and environments. Environments strengthen or weaken initial predispositions that may be partly heritable. For example, consider temperamental dispositions in activity level for which there is a moderate average difference with boys higher than girls. The magnitude of this average difference appears to be small during early childhood and moderate in middle childhood (see Leaper, 2013, 2015). As described earlier, Martin and Fabes (2001) found that preschool children's amount of time with same-gender peers over the year predicted increases in preschool boys' activity levels and decreases in girls' activity levels. Thus, over time, children may have conformed to the average in-group tendency (i.e., boys became more active while girls became less active). That is, dispositions can be fostered through practice and encouragement; alternately, they can be weakened through lack of practice and discouragement (Martin et al., 2011a).

In summary, the research comparing girls and boys on certain temperamental traits and interests points to average differences between groups as well as within-group variations in how strongly children are inclined or disinclined toward expressing particular behaviors. Some children may be strongly disposed toward a behavior that is typical of their assigned gender in-group in a given culture (e.g., in United States: highly active boys; girls with intense interest in dress-up); some other children may be strongly inclined toward a behavior that is counterstereotypical of their assigned gender in-group (e.g., in the United States: highly active girls; boys with intense interest in dress-up play). However, most children may indicate weaker dispositions toward a given style or preference (e.g., moderately active children)—which may make them more malleable in response to opportunities and practice during development (Leaper, 2000).

Physical Characteristics

Some of the largest average differences between females and males are in physical characteristics. In addition to sex-related differences in genitalia and reproductive capacity, there are average differences in size and muscle mass (both greater in males) that increase from early childhood into adolescence (see Wood & Eagly, 2012). For example, in a meta-analysis (Thomas & French, 1985), average differences in strength were large in magnitude during childhood and were even larger in adolescence (e.g., for throwing distance: $d = 1.5$ in childhood and $d = 3.0$ in adolescence). Of course, motor performance can be dramatically improved through training and practice. Also, despite the large magnitude of average differences in size and motor performance, there is within-group variability and cross-group overlap in the distributions of females and males. For example, consider the average difference in height after puberty, when males are generally taller than females. Despite a very large effect size, some adult females are taller than the average height for adult males, and some males are shorter than the average height for females.

DISPOSITIONAL TRAITS AND PHYSICAL CHARACTERISTICS AS MODERATORS OF GENDER SOCIALIZATION IN PEER GROUPS

In this section, I speculate on ways that within-gender variations in dispositions and physical characteristics may moderate the gender socialization process. First, I will review some general ways that children interact with environments during development. Then I will consider possible ways that sex-related dispositions and physical characteristics might interact with children's experiences in peer groups during the course of gender development.

Transactional Processes During Development

Transactional or dynamic-systems models (e.g., Bronfenbrenner & Morris, 2006; Liben, 2017) emphasize how multiple levels of organization (e.g., intra-individual, individual, dyadic, societal, and ecological) interact and jointly shape children's development. There are three major ways that personal and environmental factors interact over the course of a person's life (see Leaper, 2013, 2015). Environments can be imposed on the child, evoked by the child, or selected by the child. Each is described next.

First, some environments are *imposed* on the child (Bussey & Bandura, 1999). For example, children generally do not choose their families, neighborhoods, schools, or classmates. These imposed environments are settings in which children learn the cultural practices of their community and the larger society (Rogoff, 1990). In these settings, children are commonly expected to perform certain activities and to avoid others (e.g., most boys play sports but avoid doll play). Most children respond positively to these influences, and their gender-normative interests become stronger over time (e.g., Martin & Fabes, 2001; Martin et al., 2011b). However, as noted earlier and discussed again later, some children resist pressures from imposed environments and do not conform to gender-role expectations.

Second, children may *evoke* environments. In this regard, certain dispositional traits may increase the likelihood that children express behaviors that elicit particular reactions from others (Scarr & McCartney, 1983). For example, consider the difference between children with highly active versus inactive temperaments. Physically active children may be more likely than sedentary children to attract other active children. In this manner, children may tend to attract similar peers who strengthen one another's behavioral dispositions. The reaction that children elicit for a particular behavior, however, partly depends on how others view the behavior in relation to the child's gender.

Finally, as children get older, they *select and create* particular environments that are compatible with their interests and behavioral dispositions (Bussey & Bandura, 1999; Scarr & McCartney, 1983). For example, during the preschool years, most children increasingly select same-gender peers who share similar activity interests (Martin et al., 2013). Also, researchers have observed that adolescents in the United States tend to affiliate in small peer groups or cliques based on shared interests (Brown & Klute, 2003). In turn, repeated involvement in these selected environments strengthens the individuals' dispositions and interests (e.g., Martin & Fabes, 2001).

Children's capacity to select particular environments depends on the availability of the environments, which often differs for girls and boys (Leaper, 2000; Wood & Eagly, 2012). In particular communities or societies, children may be formally excluded from certain opportunities based on their gender. For example, in some parts of the world, formal education is available only to boys (UNICEF, 2016). Alternately, there may be fewer chances for one gender to participate in an activity. For instance, girls in the United States did not have many options for athletic achievement until the passage of Title IX legislation in 1972 (National Coalition for Women & Girls in Education, 2012). However, once athletic opportunities became readily available, girls' participation dramatically increased (described later).

Gender-Related Variations in Dispositions and Peer Group Socialization

As previously reviewed, there are average differences between girls and boys in some dispositional traits. At the same time, there is variability within each gender. Some children may have strong dispositions that are compatible with gender-based cultural expectations. For instance, boys with active temperaments or an intense interest in balls may more readily adapt to the traditional emphasis on sports during boys' socialization. Also, girls who have an intense interest in dolls may more easily conform to the traditional emphasis on nurturance during girls' socialization. Other children may have strong dispositions that run counter to cultural expectations. This includes, for example, girls with strong preferences for physical activity and low interest in doll play (Ahlqvist, Halim, Greulich, Lurye, & Ruble, 2013) as well as boys with strong interests in dress-up and dolls and little interest in rough play (Golombok et al., 2012).

I propose that children with strong dispositions (e.g., temperaments, intense interests) and physical characteristics that are compatible with

cultural expectations for their gender in-group may function as anchors
or models that lead other children toward conformity. In general, most
children look to models in their environments to inform their understanding of desirable behaviors for their gender in-group (Leaper, 2015;
Tobin et al., 2010). Hence, individuals who are most representative of gender archetypes may be especially salient and influential models in their
gender in-group.

To illustrate, consider boys who are physically active and athletic. Sports
and athleticism are considered fundamental to cultural constructions of
masculinity in many industrialized cultures (Kidd, 2013). Also, athleticism is often one of the strongest predictors of popularity among boys
in the United States (e.g., Shakib, Veliz, Dunbar, & Sabo, 2011). To the
extent that boys associate physical activity and sports with their gender
in-group, they may be attracted to the highly active and athletic boys. That
is, boys with moderate activity levels may engage with the highly active
and athletic boys in sports and other physical activities; then, over time,
most boys affiliating in these same-gender peer groups may increase their
activity levels and physical competence (e.g., Martin & Fabes, 2001). In
succeeding years, boys with prototypical profiles (e.g., active, athletic) and
adequate social skills may have more influence on the gender-role norms
of their peer group (e.g., Farmer & Rodkin, 1996).

Although I am focusing on the impact of peer groups, other socializing
agents also affect children's gender development. The various microsys-
tems in many children's lives usually work in concert to reinforce their
beliefs and attitudes about gender. Children derive many of their conceptions about gender from media, family members, teachers, and school
curricula. For example, mass media provide pervasive images that link
masculinity with athleticism and femininity with sexual attractiveness (see
Mazzarella, 2015). In general, children bring cultural expectations regarding gender into their peer groups. These expectations may lead many
children to attribute higher status to gender-stereotypical in-group members, such as athletic boys or attractive girls (e.g., Becker & Luthar, 2007).

To some extent, peer groups may become more flexible during adolescence; this occurs in some industrialized societies when many youth

begin to affiliate in smaller peer cliques based on shared interests (Brown & Klute, 2003). Examples in some US communities include "the jocks," "the freaks," "the geeks," "the nerd," "the hipsters," and so forth. Within each clique, there may be individuals who function as prototypes that shape the group's norms. For example, the talented computer programmer may be viewed with special admiration in a "geek" clique. The increased availability of peer groups based on a broadening set of interests allows for greater flexibility in how youth explore their identities (including their gender identities). However, in some societies, children have few or no opportunities to explore different interest-based cliques; for example, they may be assigned by their parents to help in subsistence activities or infant care (e.g., Rogoff, Morelli, & Chavajay, 2010).

Thus far, I have been addressing ways that children with gender-typical characteristics that are culturally desirable may function as prototypes in the formation of norms in same-gender peer groups. If we consider behavioral dispositions and physical characteristics along a distribution from one end (e.g., highly active children) to another (e.g., very inactive children), most children will fall in the middle. They may be relatively malleable regarding their play interests. Hence, these children may be most susceptible to influences from peers (or adults).

Children may become popular models when they demonstrate strong dispositions consistent with culturally desirable expectations for their gender in-group. However, children with strong dispositions that are counterstereotypical (e.g., boys who prefer dress-up and dislike sports) may be stigmatized by their peers (Drescher & Byne, 2012; Tobin et al., 2010). This latter set of children may find they diverge too much from existing cultural gender norms to reconcile their strong personal interests with gaining the approval of their peers (and adults). Consistent with the previously described gender self-socialization model (Tobin et al., 2010), some gender-nonconforming children may not identify with the gender category assigned to them at birth if it is seen as highly discordant with their interests. Instead, they may identify with a different gender category or more than one gender category, or they may not identify with any gender category (Boskey, 2014).

The difference between children who resist versus conform to gender-normative expectations is compatible with Liben and Bigler's (2002) dual-pathways gender schema model. The term *gender schema* refers to the gender-related knowledge and beliefs that shape how people view and think about the world. In the attitudinal pathway, children use gender schemas to screen whether particular activities or objects are compatible with expectations for their gender in-group (e.g., "I am a girl; girls like dolls; therefore, I will play with this doll"). Alternatively, the personal pathway occurs when children's personal interests drive their choices. In the personal pathway, children may interpret the activity or object as gender-neutral or they may incorporate their interests into their gender schemas (e.g., "I like sports; I am a girl; therefore, it is OK for girls to like sports"). Liben and Bigler observed intraindividual variations; that is, gender schemas guided a given child's interests in some things but not others. Also, the researchers noted individual differences, with the attitudinal pathway being more common for some children while the personal pathway was more common for other children. This latter finding is especially pertinent to my integrative theoretical model.

I propose that children who do not have intense interests in a particular domain (e.g., a play activity) may be more susceptible to letting the attitudinal pathway shape their activity choices and gender beliefs regarding that domain. That is, they may be more prone to same-gender in-group assimilation. These children also may be the most amenable to adopting more flexible gender norms when exposed to a broader range of role models.

Conversely, children with intense interests that are not typical of their gender in-group may be more likely to follow the personal pathway. That is, their personal interests may override gender-stereotyped expectations. In such cases, these children may find it difficult to reconcile their interests with social pressures for gender conformity. Perhaps this is one reason that some children do not identify with the gender category assigned to them at birth. As highlighted in the gender self-socialization model (Tobin et al., 2010), children are less motivated to identify with a gender in-group if they do not view the attributes associated with the group as concordant with their own interests; instead, these children may identify with a different gender category (Olson, Key, & Eaton, 2015).

The model that I am advancing has implications for understanding the well-being of gender-nonconforming youth. Gender nonconformity has historically been characterized as a form of psychopathology in North America and many other parts of the world (see Drescher, 2015). Given the challenges that gender-nonconforming children commonly face in being accepted by their peers, family, and others, it should not be surprising that many of these youth experience distress such as depression and anxiety (Drescher & Byne, 2012). Some clinicians have pointed to these difficulties as a justification for assigning psychiatric diagnoses such as gender identity disorder or gender dysphoria to gender-nonconforming children (see Drescher, 2015). In turn, these children have been subjected to clinics for treatment designed to foster greater gender conformity (see Bryant, 2006). An increasing number of critics are contesting this perspective. They consider these labels and practices as forms of discrimination against those who do not conform to dominant cultural gender norms (Bryant, 2006; Olson, 2016). Accordingly, any adjustment difficulties associated with gender nonconformity reflect societal intolerance rather than inherent psychopathology (e.g., Bartlett, Vasey, & Bukowski, 2000; Drescher, 2015; Olson, 2016). In support of this proposition, researchers have found that peer rejection or bullying mediated associations between gender nonconformity and indices of adjustment such as self-esteem or depression (Jewell & Brown, 2014; Smith & Leaper, 2006; Olson, 2016; Zosuls, Andrews, Martin, England, & Field, 2016). Therefore, adjustment difficulties associated with gender nonconformity should become less prevalent as society develops greater tolerance and acceptance of gender diversity.

Sex-Related Variations in Physical Characteristics and Peer Group Socialization

As considered next, sex-related variations in physical characteristics may additionally moderate gender socialization within same-gender peer groups. To explore this possibility, I begin with a review of the biosocial model of gender differences and gender equality. According to Wood and Eagly's (2012) biosocial model, gender differences in behavior result from the interaction between physical sex differences and the economic and social-structural organization of the society. Based on their review of cross-cultural studies, the authors argued that average physical differences between females and males—particularly adult females' childbearing and nursing capacities and adult males' greater average size and strength—are related to the likelihood of patriarchy in a society. For example, in societies in which physical strength was an advantage in subsistence (e.g., some forms of hunting or farming), men's strength offered an advantage in providing food for the community (which confers status and power). Women were disadvantaged when nursing infants limited their ability to participate in these forms of subsistence. However, Wood and Eagly noted more gender equality in cultures when these sex-related physical differences were not tied to participation in the major forms of subsistence.

Indeed, in modern technological-information societies, physical strength is not needed to succeed in high-prestige occupations such as business, medicine, or engineering. Also, reproductive choice, affordable childcare, and supportive family-leave policies can make it easier for women and men to participate more equally in the paid workforce (see Wood & Eagly, 2012). Notably, Scandinavian countries are the best in providing these resources (Ray, Gornick, & Schmitt, 2008) while also ranking highest on cross-national indices of overall gender equality (World Economic Forum, 2016).

The biosocial model is helpful in explaining some of the ways that gender equality has increased in many societies over the last century. At the same time, it would be misleading to suggest that full gender equality has been attained in any society or that sex-related physical differences do not continue to constrain gender development. Many women do not have easy access to means of reproductive control. Also, affordable childcare and supportive family-leave policies remain out of reach for many parents. Finally, some men continue to use their greater physical strength to exert control and dominance (including sexual violence) in relationships with women.

Physical sex differences also continue to play a role during many children's gender socialization. Having greater strength and size than one's peers can give boys greater advantage in sports. This advantage is pertinent when considering the links between masculinity and athleticism in many cultures, as well as the high status of male athletes in many US schools and in the larger society (Kidd, 2013). Thus, boys who are athletic may help to define what their peers consider desirable models (i.e., the prototype model proposed earlier).

Of course, it is now more acceptable in much of US society for girls to participate in sports. Since the passage of Title IX legislation in the United States in 1972, the proportion of girls among students participating in school sports in the United States has jumped from only a few percentage points to approximately 40% in recent years (National Coalition for Women & Girls in Education, 2012). By comparison, the rate of sports participation for boys over this time period has remained approximately 50%. Despite this dramatic historical change in the United States (and many other countries), athleticism is not equally celebrated for girls and boys (or women and men). In many US schools, sports participation is more strongly tied to popularity among boys than girls (e.g., Becker & Luthar, 2007; Shakib et al., 2011). Also, even a casual perusal of sports coverage in the US media reveals that the focus is primarily on men (see Cooky, Messner, & Musto, 2015). The most popular sport in the United States is American football, and it is exclusively men at the university level and at the professional level (and usually boys-only at the high school level). Nonetheless, the dramatic changes previously described in girls' athletic participation signal ways that societal changes can lead to greater gender equity.

LOOKING FORWARD

I have posited an outline for an integrative developmental model of gender development that highlights the interrelated influences of sex-related dispositions and physical characteristics, peer group socialization, and

identities in a given cultural context. Weaving together a set of complementary theories and research areas, I proposed that sex-related dispositions (such as temperaments and intense interests) as well as physical
characteristics (such as body size and strength) affect the process of assimilation within same-gender peer groups. Individuals with dispositions
and physical characteristics that are compatible with culturally valued
gender-in-group prototypes in a particular community (e.g., the athletic boy or the fashionable girl) may function as anchors that set the
standards for other group members to emulate. Conversely, those with
dispositions and characteristics that are highly discrepant from the prototypes may find themselves unable or disinclined to adapt to the group's
norms. As a consequence, they may be rejected or withdraw from the peer
group and may disidentify with the gender associated with the group. If
gender-nonconforming children are rejected and have inadequate social
supports, they may be more susceptible to adjustment difficulties (e.g.,
anxiety, depression). However, a greater risk of adjustment difficulties
would not be expected in social environments that accept and promote
a greater range of gender identities and gender expressions. Finally, the
majority of children who do not have strong temperamental dispositions
or intense interests are likely to be most amenable to the social influences
of peer groups.

The integrative model is somewhat speculative, and many hypothesized
components require testing. For example, I base parts of my model on
the gender self-socialization model (Tobin et al., 2010), which hypothe-
sizes that individuals tend to seek concordance among their self-concepts,
group identity, and group stereotypes. Although the authors based their
model on empirical studies, they are careful to present the expected links
among these components as hypotheses. In addition, more research is
needed on the extent, consistency, and course of intense interests. Also,
the origins of these intense interests are not well understood.

Sex-related dispositions and physical characteristics may have somewhat
different impacts on the gender in-group assimilation of cisgender boys
and girls. In industrialized Western cultures, gender socialization tends
to be more rigid for boys than girls (Leaper, 2015). For example, there is

generally less tolerance of counterstereotypical activities in boys than girls (e.g., boys playing with dolls vs. girls playing sports). Correspondingly, boys have been more likely than girls to be referred to clinics for gender nonconformity (Bartlett et al., 2000; Bryant, 2006; Leaper, 2015).

A related point is that more attention needs to be paid to the experiences of gender-nonconforming children. With few exceptions, studies of children's gender development have considered only girls and boys and not children with nonbinary gender identities. Research on transgender and other gender-nonconforming children has focused mostly on the children's adjustment. However, developmental psychologists need to consider transgender and other gender-nonconforming identities as normal variations in human development (e.g., Olson et al., 2015).

Next, developmental researchers need to investigate more fully the intersection of children's gender identities with other group identities. (See Chapter 2 on intersectionality theory.) Whereas gender-differentiated groups are pervasive in children's lives, they are not the only basis by which children establish social identities. Individuals commonly form social identities based on memberships in multiple groups. The meaning of a social identity—such as gender—may vary across individuals based on the intersection with other social identities, such as their ethnicity/race (e.g., Piña-Watson, Castillo, Jung, Ojeda, & Castillo-Reyes, 2014), school sports team (e.g., Steinfeldt & Steinfeldt, 2010), or interest-based clubs (e.g., Mahoney, Larson, Eccles, & Lord, 2005).

Furthermore, across all of the topics that I addressed, research has been conducted primarily with youth from Western industrialized countries. Even if support for my model is found within these societies, the same patterns may not extend to different cultural settings (Henrich et al., 2010). For example, the model emphasizes the role of peer groups in children's gender socialization. However, in some societies, children have limited access to peers of the same age (e.g., Harkness & Super, 1985).

In my review, I have considered a dynamic set of processes underlying children's gender development. The integrative model may help us better understand variations in gender development within a given society as well as across different societies. In some places, societal attitudes about gender and sexuality have become more progressive. Nonetheless, life for girls and gender-nonconforming youth remains highly oppressive in many regions of the world (Rafferty, 2013; United Nations Human Rights Council, 2015). Even in relatively more gender-egalitarian societies, there is still a long way to go (see Liben, 2016). In the United States and other nations, children and adolescents (as well as adults) are commonly harassed and assaulted for gender nonconformity (see Leaper & Robnett, 2016). Many LGBTQ youth are targets of discrimination and moral disapproval. In addition, many cisgender and heterosexual children are teased when they do not conform to traditional gender roles. For example, in the United States, this sometimes includes boys who are not athletic and girls who are not considered attractive (see Leaper & Robnett, 2016).

School- and community-based programs can go a long way toward expanding students' conceptions of gender and fostering a positive climate in classrooms and other spaces. Examples include educational programs designed to increase teachers' and students' awareness of gender diversity, bias, and discrimination; training exercises on ways to make proactive responses to biased or hostile behaviors; and programs that foster cooperative alliances among heterosexual-cisgender and LGBTQ youth (see Leaper & Brown, 2014; Poteat et al., 2015; Ryan, Patraw, & Bednar, 2013). As individuals in a given society become more accepted for their gender nonconformity, the culture's notions of gender will broaden. Should such trends become widespread, society will benefit: Children will be able to freely pursue their interests and talents. The result may be more gender-egalitarian societies whereby adult roles are not rigidly constrained by people's genetic sex or their assigned gender at birth.

ACKNOWLEDGMENTS

My chapter greatly benefited from Jeanne Marecek's thoughtful feedback and editing suggestions.

REFERENCES

Ahlqvist, S., Halim, M. L., Greulich, F. K., Lurye, L. E., & Ruble, D. (2013). The potential benefits and risks of identifying as a tomboy: A social identity perspective. *Self and Identity, 12,* 563–581.

Alexander, G. M., & Wilcox, T. (2012). Sex differences in early infancy. *Child Development Perspectives, 6,* 400–406.

Bartlett, N. H., Vasey, P. L., & Bukowski, W. M. (2000). Is gender identity disorder in children a mental disorder? *Sex Roles, 43,* 753–785.

Becker, B. E., & Luthar, S. S. (2007). Peer-perceived admiration and social preference: Contextual corrleates of positive peer regard among suburban and urban adolescents. *Journal of Research on Adolescence, 17,* 117–144.

Boskey, E. R. (2014). Understanding transgender identity development in childhood and adolescence. *American Journal of Sexuality Education, 9,* 445–463.

Bronfenbrenner, U., & Morris, P. A. (2006). The bioecological model of human development. In W. Damon & R. M. Lerner (Eds.), *Handbook of child psychology: Volume 1: Theoretical models of human development* (6th ed., pp. 793–828). Hoboken, NJ: Wiley.

Brown, B. B., & Klute, C. (2003). Friendships, cliques, and crowds. In G. R. Adams & M. D. Berzonsky (Eds.), *Blackwell handbook of adolescence* (pp. 330–348). Malden, MA: Blackwell.

Bryant, K. (2006). Making gender identity disorder of childhood: Historical lessons for contemporary debates. *Sexuality Research & Social Policy: A Journal of the NSRC, 3,* 23–39.

Bussey, K., & Bandura, A. (1999). Social cognitive theory of gender development and differentiation. *Psychological Review, 106,* 676–713.

Cooky, C., Messner, M. A., & Musto, M. (2015). "It's due time!": A quarter century of excluding women's sports in televised news and highlight shows. *Communication & Sport, 3,* 261–287.

DeLoache, J. S., Simcock, G., & Macari, S. (2007). Planes, trains, automobiles—and tea sets: Extremely intense interests in very young children. *Developmental Psychology, 43,* 1579–1586.

Drescher, J. (2015). Queer diagnoses revisited: The past and future of homosexuality and gender diagnoses in DSM and ICD. *International Review of Psychiatry, 27,* 386–395.

Drescher, J., & Byne, W. (2012). Gender dysphoric/gender variant (GD/GV) children and adolescents: Summarizing what we know and what we have yet to learn. *Journal of Homosexuality, 59,* 501–510.

Else-Quest, N., Hyde, J., Goldsmith, H., & Van Hulle, C. (2006). Gender differences in temperament: A meta-analysis. *Psychological Bulletin, 132,* 33–72.

Farmer, T. W., & Rodkin, P. C. (1996). Antisocial and prosocial correlates of classroom social positions: The social network centrality perspective. *Social Development, 5,* 174–188.

Golombok, S., Rust, J., Zervoulis, K., Golding, J., & Hines, M. (2012). Continuity in sex-typed behavior from preschool to adolescence: A longitudinal population study of boys and girls aged 3–13 years. *Archives of Sexual Behavior, 41,* 591–597.

Halim, M. L., Ruble, D. N., Tamis-LeMonda, C. S., Zosuls, K. M., Lurye, L. E., & Greulich, F. K. (2014). Pink frilly dresses and the avoidance of all things "girly": Children's appearance rigidity and cognitive theories of gender development. *Developmental Psychology, 50,* 1091–1101.

Harkness, S., & Super, C. M. (1985). The cultural context of gender segregation in children's peer groups. *Child Development, 56,* 219–224.

Harris, J. R. (1995). Where is the child's environment? A group socialization theory of development. *Psychological Review, 102,* 458–489.

Henrich, J., Heine, S. J., & Norenzayan, A. (2010). The weirdest people in the world? *Behavioral and Brain Sciences, 33,* 61–135.

Hines, M. (2013). Sex and sex differences. In P. D. Zelazo (Ed.), *Oxford handbook of developmental psychology* (Vol. 1, pp. 164–201). New York, NY: Oxford University Press.

Hyde, J. S. (2005). The gender similarities hypothesis. *American Psychologist, 60,* 581–592.

Jewell, J. A., & Brown, C. S. (2014). Relations among gender typicality, peer relations, and mental health during early adolescence. *Social Development, 23,* 137–156.

Joel, D. (2016). VIII. Captured in terminology: Sex, sex categories, and sex differences. *Feminism & Psychology, 26,* 335–345.

Johnson, K. E., Alexander, J. M., Spencer, S., Leibham, M. E., & Neitzel, C. (2004). Factors associated with the early emergence of intense interests within conceptual domains. *Cognitive Development, 19,* 325–343.

Kidd, B. (2013). Sports and masculinity. *Sport in Society, 16,* 553–564.

Leaper, C. (2000). The social construction and socialization of gender. In P. H. Miller & E. K. Scholnick (Eds.), *Towards a feminist developmental psychology* (pp. 127–152). New York, NY: Routledge Press.

Leaper, C. (2011). More similarities than differences in contemporary theories of social development?: A plea for theory bridging. In J. B. Benson (Ed.), *Advances in child development and behavior* (Vol. 40, pp. 337–378). San Diego, CA: Elsevier Academic Press.

Leaper, C. (2013). Gender development during childhood. In P. D. Zelazo (Ed.), *Oxford handbook of developmental psychology* (Vol. 2, pp. 327–377). New York, NY: Oxford University Press.

Leaper, C. (2015). Gender and social-cognitive development. In R. M. Lerner (Series Ed.), L. S. Liben & U. Muller (Vol. Eds.), *Handbook of child psychology and developmental science* (7th ed.), *Vol. 2: Cognitive processes* (pp. 806–853). New York, NY: Wiley.

Leaper, C., & Brown, C. S. (2014). Sexism in schools. In L. S. Liben, & R. S. Bigler (Eds.), *Advances in child development and behavior* (Vol. 47): *The role of gender in educational contexts and outcomes* (pp. 189–223). San Diego, CA: Elsevier Academic Press.

Leaper, C., & Robnett, R. D. (2016). Sexism. In R. J. R. Levesque (Ed.), *Encyclopedia of adolescence* (2nd ed.). New York, NY: Springer. Advanced online version at http://link.springer.com/referenceworkentry/10.1007%2F978-3-319-32132-5_226-2

Liben, L. S. (2016). We've come a long way, baby (but we're not there yet): Gender past, present and future. *Child Development, 87,* 5–28.

Liben, L. S. (2017). Gender development: A constructivist-ecological perspective. In N. Budwig, E. Turiel, & P. D. Zelazo, (Eds.), *New Perspectives on Human Development* (pp. 145–164). Cambridge, UK: Cambridge University Press.

Liben, L. S., & Bigler, R. S. (2002). The developmental course of gender differentiation: Conceptualizing, measuring, and evaluating constructs and pathways. *Monographs of the Society for Research in Child Development, 67*(2), vii–147.

Maccoby, E. E. (1998). *The two sexes: Growing up apart, coming together.* Cambridge, MA: Belknap Press/Harvard University Press.

Mahoney, J. L., Larson, R. W., Eccles, J. S., & Lord, H. (2005). Organized activities as development contexts for children and adolescents. In J. L. Mahoney, R. W. Larson, & J. S. Eccles (Eds.), *Organized activities as contexts of development: Extracurricular activities, after-school and community programs* (pp. 3–22). Mahwah, NJ: Lawrence Erlbaum Associates.

Martin, C. L., & Fabes, R. A. (2001). The stability and consequences of young children's same-sex peer interactions. *Developmental Psychology, 37*, 431–446.

Martin, C. L., Fabes, R. A., & Hanish, L. (2011a). Gender and temperament in young children's social interactions. In P. Nathan & A. D. Pellegrini (Eds.), *The Oxford handbook of the development of play* (pp. 214–230). New York, NY: Oxford University Press.

Martin, C. L., Fabes, R. A., Hanish, L., Leonard, S., & Dinella, L. M. (2011b). Experienced and expected similarity to same-gender peers: Moving toward a comprehensive model of gender segregation. *Sex Roles, 65*, 421–434.

Martin, C. L., Kornienko, O., Schaefer, D. R., Hanish, L. D., Fabes, R. A., & Goble, P. (2013). The role of sex of peers and gender-typed activities in young children's peer affiliative networks: A longitudinal analysis of selection and influence. *Child Development, 84*, 921–937.

Mazzarella, S. R. (2015). Media and gender identities: Learning and performing femininity and masculinity. In D. Lemish (Ed.), *The Routledge international handbook of children, adolescents, and media* (pp. 279–286). New York, NY: Routledge/Taylor & Francis Group.

Mehta, C. M., & Strough, J. (2009). Sex segregation in friendships and normative contexts across the life span. *Developmental Review, 29*, 201–220.

National Coalition for Women & Girls in Education. (2012). *Title IX and athletics: Proven benefits, unfounded objections.* Retrieved online at http://www.ncwge.org/athletics.html

Olson, K. R. (2016). Prepubescent transgender children: What we do and do not know. *Journal of the American Academy of Child & Adolescent Psychiatry, 55*, 155–156.

Olson, K. R., Key, A. C., & Eaton, N. R. (2015). Gender cognition in transgender children. *Psychological Science, 26*, 467–474.

Piña-Watson, B., Castillo, L. G., Jung, E., Ojeda, L., & Castillo-Reyes, R. (2014). The Marianismo beliefs scale: Validation with Mexican American adolescent girls and boys. *Journal of Latina/o Psychology, 2*, 113–130.

Poteat, V. P., Yoshikawa, H., Calzo, J. P., Gray, M. L., DiGiovanni, C. D., Lipkin, A., Mundy-Shephard, A., Perrotti, J., Scheer, J. R., & Shaw, M. P. (2015). Contextualizing gay-straight alliances: Student, advisor, and structural factors related to positive youth development among members. *Child Development, 86*, 176–193.

Rafferty, Y. (2013). International dimensions of discrimination and violence against girls: A human rights perspective. *Journal of International Women's Studies, 14,* 1–23.

Ray, R., Gornick, J. C., & Schmitt, J. (2008). *Parental leave policies in 21 countries: Assessing generosity and gender equality.* Center for Economic and Policy Reearch. Retrieved online at http://paidfamilyleave.org/pdf/ParentalLeave21Countries.pdf

Rogoff, B. (1990). *Apprenticeship in thinking: Cognitive development in social context.* New York, NY: Oxford University Press.

Rogoff, B., Morelli, G. A., & Chavajay, P. (2010). Children's integration in communities and segregation from people of differing ages. *Perspectives on Psychological Science, 5,* 431–440.

Rose, A. J., & Rudolph, K. D. (2006). A review of sex differences in peer relationship processes: Potential trade-offs for the emotional and behavioral development of girls and boys. *Psychological Bulletin, 132,* 98–131.

Ryan, C. L., Patraw, J. M., & Bednar, M. (2013) Discussing princess boys and pregnant men: Teaching about gender diversity and transgender experiences within an elementary school curriculum. *Journal of LGBT Youth, 10* (1–2), 83–105.

Scarr, S., & McCartney, K. (1983). How people make their own environments: A theory of genotype-environment effects. *Child Development, 54,* 424–435.

Shakib, S., Veliz, P., Dunbar, M. D., & Sabo, D. (2011). Athletics as a source for social status among youth: Examining variation by gender, race/ethnicity, and socioeconomic status. *Sociology of Sport Journal, 28,* 303–328.

Smith, T. E., & Leaper, C. (2006). Self-perceived gender typicality and the peer context during adolescence. *Journal of Research on Adolescence, 16,* 91–103.

Steinfeldt, J. A., & Steinfeldt, M. C. (2010). Gender role conflict, athletic identity, and help-seeking among high school football players. *Journal of Applied Sport Psychology, 22,* 262–273.

Tajfel, H., & Turner, J. C. (1979). An integrative theory of intergroup conflict. In W. Austin & S. Worchel (Eds.), *The social psychology of intergroup relations* (pp. 33–47). Monterey, CA: Brooks/Cole.

Thomas, J. R., & French, K. E. (1985). Gender differences across age in motor performance. A meta-analysis. *Psychological Bulletin, 98,* 260–282.

Tobin, D. D., Menon, M., Menon, M., Spatta, B. C., Hodges, E. V., & Perry, D. G. (2010). The intrapsychics of gender: A model of self-socialization. *Psychological Review, 117,* 601–622.

UNICEF. (2016). *The state of the world's children 2016: A fair chance for every child.* New York, NY: United Nations Children's Fund (UNICEF).

United Nations Human Rights Council. (2015). *Discrimination and violence against individuals based on their sexual orientation and gender identity: Report of the Office of the United Nations High Commissioner for Human Rights.* Retrieved online at http://www.ohchr.org/EN/Issues/Discrimination

VanderLaan, D. P., Postema, L., Wood, H., Singh, D., Fantus, S., Hyun, J., Leef, J., Bradley, S. J., & Zucker, K. J. (2015). Do children with gender dysphoria have intense/obsessional interests? *Journal of Sex Research, 52,* 213–219.

Whiting, B. B., & Edwards, C. P. (1988). *Children of different worlds: The formation of social behavior.* Cambridge, MA: Harvard University Press.

Wood, W., & Eagly, A. H. (2012). Biosocial construction of sex differences and similarities in behavior. In M. P. Zanna & J. M. Olson (Eds.), *Advances in experimental social psychology* (Vol. 46, pp. 55–123). San Diego, CA: Academic.

World Economic Forum (2016). *The global gender gap report: 2016.* Retrieved online at http://www.weforum.org

Zosuls, K. M., Andrews, N. C. Z., Martin, C. L., England, D. E., & Field, R. D. (2016). Developmental changes in the link between gender typicality and peer victimization and exclusion. *Sex Roles, 75*(5–6), 243–256.

Zucker, K. J., Bradley, S. J., & Sanikhani, M. (1997). Sex differences in referral rates of children with gender identity disorder: Some hypotheses. *Journal of Abnormal Child Psychology, 25,* 217–227.

11

The Integrative Psychobiology of Early Gender Development

MELISSA HINES

Human gender-related behavior develops under the influence of a number of different factors, including genetic information on the sex chromosomes, gonadal hormones during early development, postnatal socialization by others, and self-socialization. Much of my own research has explored the role of early testosterone exposure in gender development, and in this chapter I discuss these hormonal influences and how they relate to genetic influences, socialization by others, and self-socialization, in shaping gender development. In addition, in discussing these influences, I focus primarily on childhood play behavior. I have chosen this focus because childhood play behavior shows large differences between the sex categories of boy and girl, to which children are assigned at birth. I will refer to these behavioral differences as *gender differences*. Also, childhood play behavior has been studied extensively, providing perhaps the best example of how a gender-related behavior can be influenced by a range of factors working together over time.

I begin the chapter with a review of the magnitude of gender differences in various aspects of human behavior. I then critically review the evidence that testosterone, during early development, contributes to gender differences in children's play. Following this review, I summarize evidence suggesting that early hormone influences work together with influences of external socialization and self-socialization to produce individual differences in gender-related play. I conclude by suggesting that an integrative developmental psychobiological perspective is useful in understanding the development of children's gender-typical play behavior, and that a similar perspective also may be useful in understanding the development of other gender-related behaviors.

HOW LARGE ARE GENDER DIFFERENCES IN HUMAN BEHAVIOR?

This question concerns the magnitude of differences, not their statistical significance. To say that a difference between group means in a study is *statistically significant* is to say that the difference is larger than would be expected if the population means were not actually different; a very small difference can be highly significant (i.e., a low probability event). *Effect size*, on the other hand, refers to *how large* a difference is, taking into account within-group variability. It can be represented as the difference between means, expressed in standard deviation units ("d"; Cohen, 1988). Behavioral differences where $d = 0.8$ or more are considered large, those of about 0.5 are considered moderate in size, those of 0.2 are considered small, and those less than 0.2 are considered negligible.

When effect sizes are calculated, most behaviors appear not to differ substantially for groups of human males (boys, men) and females (girls, women). (Also see Chapter 10 for effect sizes of some gender differences.) A review of meta-analytic results concluded that most gender differences in human behavior are small to negligible (Hyde, 2005). In addition, the size of some gender differences can vary with context. For example, a meta-analysis of studies of helping behavior concluded that there is a substantial gender difference favoring men when people know that they are being watched, but a negligible gender difference when they clearly are not being watched (Eagley & Crowley, 1986). Gender differences also can vary with age. Vocabulary provides an example of this variability. From about age 18 to 60 months, girls use more vocabulary words than boys do, but this gender difference is not apparent in younger or older individuals (Bornstein, Hahn, & Haynes, 2004). Importantly, even large effects are associated with considerable overlap between groups. For example, if $d = 0.8$ for a behavioral gender difference in childhood (a large effect size), a person guessing whether a child were female or male from the behavioral score has a one in three chance of being wrong. Also, mean gender differences, whether small or large, do not constitute evidence of immutable traits, or "essences," that distinguish females and males categorically as "kinds" of people. In addition, differences of any size and arising through any developmental pathway should be interpreted in light of the fact that males and females are more alike than different.

I now narrow the focus to some psychological characteristics for which consistent, moderate to large, gender differences have been found. These characteristics include gender identity, sexual orientation, children's play behavior, certain personality characteristics, and certain cognitive abilities. To put these differences in perspective, consider the size of the gender difference in adult height as a familiar reference point. Men are generally taller than women, but many women are taller than at least some men. For the gender difference in height, $d = 2.0$, and this gender difference is larger than almost all gender differences in human behavior. A few human behavioral characteristics show gender differences as large as, or larger than, that seen in height. They include gender identity, sexual orientation, and children's play behavior. Differences in personality characteristics and in cognitive abilities tend to be less than half the size of the sex difference in height. For personality traits, the specific inventory used to measure traits also can influence the size of the gender difference. For example, empathy and social dominance show large gender differences when assessed using Cattell's 16 Personality Factor questionnaire (Feingold, 1994), but small to moderate gender differences using other personality questionnaires

(Costa, Terracciano, & McCrae, 2001). Gender differences in personality traits also appear to be larger in Western Europe and North America than in Africa or Asia, perhaps because people in communal, rather than individualistic, cultures make attributions to their social relations instead of their personality (Costa et al., 2001).

Regarding cognitive abilities, the largest gender difference appears to be that in three-dimensional (3-D) mental rotation performance. Males show a moderate to large advantage over females on a speeded test that requires discriminating rotated images from mirror image rotations of a 3-D block figure (Linn & Petersen, 1985; Voyer, Voyer, & Bryden, 1995). Tests using two-dimensional figures show smaller gender differences. Measures of spatial perception, which require individuals to accurately position a stimulus (e.g., a line) within a distracting array (e.g., a tilted frame), show gender differences of moderate size (Voyer et al., 1995), and measures of spatial visualization, which involve complex, sequential manipulations of spatial information, show small to negligible gender differences (Linn & Petersen, 1985; Voyer et al., 1995). This last type of task requires, for example, identifying simple figures in complex designs, constructing specified shapes using blocks, or imaging what unfolded pages would look like when folded to form 3-D objects. In contrast to results for spatial abilities, females show moderate-sized advantages over males on measures of perceptual speed (Ekstrom, French, & Harmon, 1976; Feingold, 1988) and on measures of verbal fluency (Kolb & Whishaw, 1985; Spreen & Strauss, 1991).

Explaining Gender Differences in Human Behavior

Gender differences in human behavior are complexly determined, not "innate" or "hard wired." They arise from interactions among multiple contributing factors at many levels of organization (from subcellular to cultural). Those factors, at various points during development, directly or indirectly alter the probability of various developmental outcomes, and they are not always correlated. The factors that are involved include but are not limited to genetic information on the sex chromosomes; hormones produced by the gonads before, and perhaps shortly after, birth; socialization by parents, peers, teachers, and other individuals; and self-socialization based on cognitive understanding of gender. I next briefly describe these contributors as they emerge chronologically, beginning with genetic differences present from conception. More extensive treatment of this material can be found in Hines (2015); for that reason, referencing in this chapter is kept to a minimum. The information is summarized here to enable discussion of how the influences of early androgen exposure relate to or interact with other types of influences in shaping the development of gender-related behavior.

Humans typically have 46 chromosomes organized into 23 pairs in all the diploid cells (i.e., cells containing paired chromosomes) in their body. Twenty-two pairs are called autosomes. Chromosomes in the 23rd pair are called sex chromosomes. Each sex chromosome comes from a haploid cell (i.e., a cell containing single chromosomes) received from a gametic parent: The ovum provides an X chromosome, and the sperm provides either an X or a Y chromosome. In approximately 99% of live births, the sex chromosomes in all diploid cells are XX or XY; these are the highest frequency genetic variants. Low-frequency variants include XO (a total of 45 chromosomes), XYY (a total of 47 chromosomes), or mosaicism (e.g., some cells contain XO and some contain XY). Sex assignment at birth on the basis of genital anatomy is most often female for XX individuals and is most often male for XY individuals. However, as explored later, genital anatomy is not determined simply and directly by chromosomes nor, does it seem, is gender-related behavior at birth or during childhood. Developmental pathways from conception to birth and beyond yield varied developmental outcomes.

Although there is some evidence that genes on the X and the Y chromosomes have direct effects on later sex-related behavior in rodents (Arnold, 2009), there is no evidence to date for similar direct effects on human behavior. In addition, in both humans and other mammals, the main effects of the sex chromosome genes on behavior are indirect. A gene on the Y chromosome, called *SrY*, causes the primordial gonads, which are identical in all human embryos until approximately gestational Week 6, to develop as testes. Without *SrY*, the primordial gonads develop as ovaries. The testes, but not the ovaries, begin to produce testosterone at about Week 8. Consequently, testosterone concentrations are higher during gestation in gonadal males than in gonadal females, particularly from about Week 8 to Week 16 or 24 of gestation.

The human testes are again active shortly after birth, from about the first to the sixth month of infancy, producing another marked difference in hormones between typically developing girls and boys. The gonads then produce little or no hormones until puberty, when the testes and the ovaries are active. Hormones released during these two early periods of testicular activity, prenatal and neonatal, result in penile formation and growth, usually resulting in external genitalia labeled at birth as male. As I discuss in more detail later, hormone activity during these early periods also appears to influence some aspects of brain development and to exert enduring influences on behavior. These effects do not produce a "male brain" or a "female brain," however. Each child has a human brain with the potential to generate behaviors that, in the child's culture, may be considered more typical of one gender than of other genders. That is, the binary nature of sex chromosomes (X or Y) or gonads (ovaries or testes) does not "scale up" to binary brains (Crews, 2012).

Socialization also differs for girls and boys and plays a role in the development of gender-related behavior. For instance, parents decorate bedrooms differently for girls and boys, provide girls and boys with somewhat different toys, and dress girls and boys differently. Parents, as well as peers, teachers, and other individuals, including strangers, also treat boys and girls differently. Part of this different treatment involves positively reinforcing children for engaging in behavior that is viewed as appropriate for children of their sex. Sometimes children, particularly boys, are also discouraged from playing with toys viewed as inappropriate for their sex.

In addition to external socialization, children self-socialize gender-typed behavior, and this self-socialization is thought to relate to their emerging cognitive understanding of gender. Beginning at about 2 years of age, children label themselves in a gendered way, typically that they are a girl or a boy. Over the next 5 years or so this self schema expands to include belief that their gender will not change over time or if they engage in cross-gender activities. In addition, by about 4 years of age, they also come to value engaging in gender-typical behavior. Based on these processes, children self-socialize gendered behavior. For example, they are more likely to model the behavior of other individuals that share their gender identity and they are more likely to show interest in objects that have been labeled as being for their own gender than an other gender (Hines et al., 2016; Masters, Ford, Arend, Grotevant, & Clark, 1979). Similar processes have been observed in transgendered children; that is, children prefer objects associated with the gender with which they identify, regardless of whether that identity matches the sex category assigned at birth (Olson, Key, & Eaton, 2015).

Early Androgen Exposure and Human Gender-Related Play Behavior

The effects of testosterone on neurobehavioral sexual differentiation have been demonstrated in thousands of studies of numerous rodent species, as well as of nonhuman primates (Arnold, 2009; Hines, 2004; McCarthy, De Vries, & Forger, 2009). Researchers have found, for instance, that female offspring of rhesus monkeys who were treated with testosterone during pregnancy show increased male-typical sexual behavior and juvenile play behavior. Several general principles have emerged from this research, including the following:

- Exposing female animals to testosterone during early development increases male-typical behavior and reduces female-typical behavior.
- Removing testosterone from developing male animals reduces male-typical outcomes and increases female-typical outcomes.
- Estrogenic hormones, such as estradiol, do not have major feminizing effects during early development. Instead,

female-typical development occurs in individuals who have low
concentrations of testosterone and other androgens. In addition,
in rodents, testosterone is converted to estradiol within the
brain before exerting its masculinizing and defeminizing effects.
I mention these masculinizing and defeminizing effects of
estrogen largely to illustrate that hormones are not "masculine"
or "feminine." Instead, both males and females have androgenic
and estrogenic hormones.

- The effects of hormones on neurobehavioral development are
  linear. The size of the impact increases as dosage increases.
- Testosterone influences neurobehavioral characteristics that differ
  on average for males and females.

Studies investigating early testosterone exposure and later behavior in
nonhuman mammals use rigorous experimental procedures, such as
random assignment, to receive testosterone or placebo. These procedures generally are not ethical in human research. Researchers have,
however, investigated the behavior of people who were exposed to
unusual hormone environments during early development, because
they have uncommon genetic variants that alter levels of or sensitivity
to hormones. In addition, researchers have investigated links between
testosterone during early development and later behavior in typically
developing children. The next section of this chapter critically reviews
these studies.

Classical congenital adrenal hyperplasia (CAH) is an autosomal, recessive genetic variant that occurs in about 1 in 10,000 to 15,000 births
in Western Europe and North America (Merke & Bornstein, 2005).
Beginning prenatally, individuals with CAH have reduced cortisol production, usually due to low levels or none of an enzyme (21-hydroxylase)
that is necessary for cortisol synthesis. As a consequence, hormones that
typically would be used to produce cortisol are shunted into an androgen pathway. Female fetuses with classical CAH are exposed to elevated
androgens, with concentrations at midgestation similar to those of male
fetuses. In contrast, boys with classical CAH appear to have male-typical

androgen concentrations during gestation (Pang et al., 1980; Wudy, Dorr, Solleder, Djalali, & Homoki, 1999).

Girls with classical CAH are born at risk of dehydration and shock due to adrenal hormone insufficiency (aldosterone as well as cortisol), which can be life-threatening. They also often are born with urogenital anatomy (vagina and urethra are not separate) that can impair bladder function and with partially virilized external genitalia (e.g., fused labia, enlarged clitoris). Because assigning these newborns to a binary sex category on the basis of genitalia is difficult, these infants' genitalia are sometimes referred to as "ambiguous"; activists have advocated use of the term "intersex" so as to reduce the stigma associated with CAH. The sex assignment typically is as a girl.

The appearance of the external genitalia in girls with CAH raises the question at birth of whether, when, and how to intervene. Within the Western medical tradition, it has been common for girls with CAH to undergo urogenital surgery early in life. Early medical intervention for adrenal insufficiency and impaired urogenital functioning are relatively uncontroversial. The extent and timing of interventions for other reasons—for instance, sexual functioning or fertility later in life and, especially, cosmetic alteration of the external genitalia to appear more typical of girls—have complex cultural, psychological, and ethical dimensions and are the subject of debate and research.

Research has examined the possibility that, whatever decisions are made postnatally about medical intervention and rearing, prenatal exposure to high concentrations of androgens has altered brain development so as to increase the predisposition of girls with CAH toward male-typical behavior and away from female-typical behavior (Hines, 2015). Early reports using interviews, typically with mothers (who usually were the primary caregivers), to evaluate gender-related behavior reported that girls with CAH showed increased interest in toys and play activities typically preferred by boys, and reduced interest in toys and play activities typically preferred by girls (Ehrhardt & Baker, 1974; Money & Ehrhardt, 1972). Some researchers suggested that these findings might reflect perceptions, based on knowledge of the CAH, rather than changes in the actual behavior of the girls with CAH (Fausto-Sterling, 1992; Quadagno, Briscoe, & Quadagno, 1977).

This critique led to research that observed girls with CAH playing, instead of relying on interview data. An initial study observed girls and boys with and without CAH in a playroom with toys that were typically preferred by boys (e.g., toy vehicles), typically preferred by girls (e.g., dolls), and gender-neutral (e.g., books) (Berenbaum & Hines, 1992). Controls in this study were typically developing relatives (siblings or first cousins) of children with CAH, to provide some control for family background and genetic factors other than those causing CAH. Results showed the expected sex differences in toy preferences. Control boys played more with toys typically preferred by boys, and less with toys typically preferred by girls, than did control girls. Girls with CAH also played more with toys typically preferred by boys, and less with toys typically preferred by girls, than did control girls. As expected, there were no group differences in play with neutral toys, and no differences between boys with and without CAH in toy preferences. Similar findings were later reported for a subgroup of this sample at an older age by one author of the original study (Berenbaum & Snyder, 1995) and for a new sample of children with and without CAH by the other author (Pasterski et al., 2005). An independent research team has replicated the results for girls with and without CAH, but this replication study did not include boys (Servin, Nordenstrom, Larsson, & Bohlin, 2003).

Other studies have used questionnaires and interviews to assess toy interests, as well as other aspects of play, in children with CAH. These studies have been conducted in several locations in the United States and the United Kingdom, and in Canada, Germany, Japan, the Netherlands, and Sweden. The studies have used a range of assessment approaches and varied control groups, and have consistently found increased male-typical play and reduced female-typical play in girls with CAH, but not in boys with CAH, relative to same-sex controls (Hines, 2015).

CAH varies in degree, and the size of the difference in gender-related play between girls with and without CAH varies with its degree. Girls with the most extreme forms of CAH, as indicated by genotype, severity of adrenal insufficiency, or degree of genital virilization at birth, show the most marked increase in male-typical, and decrease in female-typical, play (Dittmann et al., 1990; Frisen et al., 2009; Hall et al., 2004).

Other low-frequency genetic variants that cause unusual hormone exposure during early development have not been studied as extensively as has CAH, perhaps because the other disorders occur even less frequently. There is some information, however, on complete androgen insensitivity syndrome (CAIS). Individuals with CAIS have XY sex chromosomes with an unusual variation on the X chromosome that codes for androgen receptors that do not bind with androgens (Grumbach, Hughes, & Conte, 2003). Unlike XX individuals, these XY individuals do not have another X chromosome with the more common allele for androgen receptor function, resulting in expression of the androgen-insensitive receptors in their cells (i.e., it is an X-linked recessive trait). Individuals with CAIS do have a Y chromosome with the SrY gene, so they develop testes, which typically are undescended at birth. At the usual developmental stage, their testes begin to produce testosterone and other androgens. However, because cells in their body tissues cannot respond to the androgens, they are born with external genitalia that are typical for a female, and they are assigned and reared as girls.

Given the evidence for the role of prenatal androgen exposure on childhood play behavior, the lack of functional androgen exposure before birth in children with CAIS would be expected to produce behavior that is more typical of girls and less typical of boys, compared to chromosomal males (XY) without CAIS. Indeed, individuals with CAIS have been found to show more girl-typical, and less boy-typical, childhood play compared to matched male controls, assessed retrospectively via a self-report questionnaire (Hines, Ahmed, & Hughes, 2003). Another study included girls with CAIS and another girl who, like the girls with CAIS, had XY chromosomes and had been born with female-appearing external genitalia due to low prenatal androgen exposure, but for another reason (impaired androgen biosynthesis) (Jurgensen, Hiort, Holterhus, & Thyen, 2007). Compared to male controls, these girls also showed increased girl-typical play and decreased boy-typical play, measured using a questionnaire completed by a parent. These findings resemble those from girls with CAH, in suggesting an androgenic contribution to male-typical childhood play. All of the XY females had been reared as girls, however, so their lack of effective androgen exposure cannot be separated from their female socialization in relation to their female-typical behavior. Notwithstanding this limitation, these results do show that girl-typical childhood play behavior can develop in individuals with a Y chromosome, given a lack of androgen exposure and/or female socialization. Sex chromosomes are not destiny. Rather, development of gendered behavior unfolds as a function of many probabilistic, graded events at many levels of organization at developmentally sensitive times.

Variability in Hormones in Typically Developing Children

Researchers also have examined whether variability in early hormone exposure among typically developing children is related to later gender-related play. Several approaches have been used, including measuring testosterone in maternal blood during pregnancy, in amniotic fluid during gestation, in umbilical cord blood at birth, and in blood, urine, or saliva during early infancy.

One study reported a significant, positive relationship between testosterone measured in amniotic fluid and male-typical play, assessed using the Pre-School Activity Inventory (PSAI: a parent report questionnaire), in girls and in boys (Auyeung et al., 2009). However, a similar study using a different parent report measure did not find significant relationships (Knickmeyer et al., 2005), nor did a study that measured play by observing children in a free play situation (van de Beek, Van Goozen, Buitelaar, & Cohen-Kettenis, 2009). It is not yet known whether the one positive finding is unreliable, or whether smaller samples or less sensitive measures account for the two negative results. Testosterone measured in amniotic fluid testosterone may not be a sufficiently sensitive or reliable measure of prenatal androgen exposure for detecting relationships to behavior, except perhaps in very large samples (Constantinescu & Hines, 2012).

Studies relating maternal testosterone during pregnancy to later gender-typed play also have produced inconsistent findings. One study found a relationship between maternal testosterone at midgestation and later PSAI scores, for girls, but not boys, in a general population sample of thousands of pregnant women and their offspring (Hines et al., 2002). Genetic factors were thought to contribute to the observation of a relationship in girls, but not boys. Testosterone is not thought to transfer from pregnant women to fetuses. Also, women pregnant with girls and boys have similar testosterone concentrations, suggesting that testosterone does not transfer from fetuses to mothers. Testosterone production is highly heritable in mothers and daughters, but not in mothers and sons, perhaps because girls and their mothers have in common that they produce testosterone in their adrenal glands and ovaries, whereas boys produce most of their testosterone in their testes. Thus, mothers with relatively high testosterone may have daughters with relatively high testosterone, perhaps explaining why maternal testosterone is only related to offspring behavior for girls. Although a second study did not see a similar relationship between maternal testosterone and daughters' gender-typed toy preferences (van de Beek et al., 2009), it used a different behavioral measure, and a much smaller sample, than the first study. As for the findings for testosterone in amniotic fluid, additional research could determine whether the positive report is unreliable, or whether the replication failure results from reduced power, for example, because of small sample size or weak behavioral measures.

Researchers also have related testosterone measured in urine samples during infancy to later gender-typical behavior. Testosterone in urine shows an early postnatal peak similar to that seen in research using blood samples (Kuiri-Hanninen et al., 2011; Lamminmaki et al., 2012). It peaks at about age 1 month and declines to baseline by about age 6 months. In one study, testosterone during this period of elevation, called mini-puberty, positively predicted male-typical play at age 14 months, assessed using the PSAI in boys (Lamminmaki et al., 2012). The correlation between testosterone and boy-typical play in girls also was positive, but it was not statistically significant. The children also were observed playing with toys. Girls played more than boys with a doll, and boys played more than girls with a truck. Testosterone positively predicted play with the train in girls, and negatively predicted play with the doll in boys. The significant relationships observed in this study involved small samples (15 boys for the PSAI, 22 girls for play with the train, 20 boys for play with the doll), however. I am not aware of attempts to replicate these findings.

VARIABILITY IN PHYSICAL CHARACTERISTICS IN TYPICALLY DEVELOPING CHILDREN

Researchers also have used physical characteristics that are influenced by androgens before birth to attempt to measure prenatal androgen exposure. The most popular approach of this type involves measuring the ratio of the length of the second digit to the fourth digit of the hand (2D:4D). The rationale underlying this approach is that this ratio is larger (i.e., closer to 1.0) in females than in males, and this sex difference is thought to result from prenatal androgen exposure (Manning, 2002).

Three studies have related 2D:4D to gender-typed play. One study (Honekopp & Thierfelder, 2009) found a significant, negative correlation between left-hand 2D:4D and PSAI scores in boys, but not girls, but no correlation for right-hand 2D:4D in either sex. This study is hard to interpret, because it did not use the standardized scoring system for the PSAI. Another study (Mitsui et al., 2016) found a significant, negative correlation between an average of left- and right-hand 2D:4D and PSAI scores in boys, but not girls. A third study (Wong & Hines, 2016) related 2D:4D to PSAI scores, as well as to observed play with sex-typed toys, on two occasions. Of 24 gender-related variables assessed, only one correlated significantly with 2D:4D, and results were inconsistent across the two assessment occasions. These findings were interpreted to suggest that 2D:4D is an insufficiently sensitive measure of early androgen exposure to produce consistent results for relationships to behavior. Other researchers also have concluded that finger ratios do not show consistent relations to early androgen exposure, and that they are not sufficiently sensitive to individual variability to provide reliable results in studies relating early androgen exposure to behavior (Berenbaum, Bryk, Nowak, Quigley, & Moffat, 2009; Constantinescu & Hines, 2012).

Other researchers have related aspects of the external genitalia, known to be influenced by testosterone and other androgens during early development, to play behavior. Anogenital distance (AGD), the distance from the anus to the genitalia, is larger in females than in males, and prenatal androgen exposure reduces AGD (Dean & Sharpe, 2013; Thankamony, Pasterski, Ong, Acerini, & Hughes, 2016). Penile growth from birth to 3 months postnatal relates to testosterone exposure at this time (Boas et al., 2006; van den Driesche et al., 2011), and it has been used as a measure of early postnatal androgen exposure (i.e., during mini-puberty).

In one study, penile growth from birth to age 3 months was used to estimate androgen exposure during mini-puberty, and AGD at birth was used to estimate prenatal androgen exposure (Pasterski et al., 2015). Both AGD at birth, and penile growth from birth to 3 months made significant, separate contributions to later gender-related behavior, assessed using the PSAI. I am not aware of any attempts to replicate these findings.

INTERACTIONS BETWEEN EARLY ANDROGEN EXPOSURE AND SOCIALIZATION

Extensive evidence shows that the social environment contributes to children's gender-related play, as do processes related to children's cognitions regarding gender. These social and cognitive influences are detailed in other chapters of this book (e.g., Chapters 9, 10, and 14). Here, I will explore how hormones, socialization, and cognitive processes might work together to influence children's gender-related play.

One approach to this question has involved studies of girls with CAH. These girls have unusual androgen exposure prenatally but are thought to be socialized largely like other girls. Their prenatal androgen exposure, however, could cause some differences from other girls in their socialization, particularly given that they show more boy-typical, and less girl-typical, behavior compared to other girls. Girls and women with CAH also have been found to show somewhat reduced female gender identity (Hines, 2015), and this could influence cognitive mechanisms involved in the development of gender-related behavior.

One way to study possible alterations in socialization involves observing girls with CAH as they play not only on their own but also with their parents. One such study found that girls with CAH showed gender-atypical toy preferences regardless of whether they played alone or with a parent (Servin et al., 2003). A second study examined parental responses to gender-typical and gender-atypical play in children with and without CAH (Pasterski et al., 2005), and it found greater parental encouragement of gender-typical play for girls with CAH than for girls without CAH. A third study used questionnaires to assess parents' encouragement of gender-typical and gender-atypical activities (Wong, Pasterski, Hindmarsh, Geffner, & Hines, 2012), and it found that parents recalled encouraging gender-atypical play more in their daughters with CAH than in their daughters without CAH. Overall, the results of these studies suggest that parents of girls with CAH, like other parents, encourage their children to engage in the activities that the children enjoy, even if this involves encouraging their daughters to engage in activities more typical of boys. When in a setting, such as the laboratory playroom, with easy access to girl-typical toys, however, they encourage their daughters with CAH to play with these gender-typical toys.

Girls with CAH also might show reduced responses to cues indicating gender-typical behavior. One study examined children's responses to gender labels identifying specific gender-neutral toys as for girls or for boys, and to male and female models choosing gender-neutral items (Hines et al., 2016). For the labeling protocol, children were taught, for example, that green balloons are for girls and silver balloons are for boys, or vice versa. For the modeling protocol, all of four male or all of four female models were seen choosing between items, such as pencils over pens, or toy squirrels over toy hedgehogs. As in prior research using these protocols, girls without CAH and boys with and without CAH on average showed verbal and/or behavioral preferences for the items that had been labeled as for their own sex, or that they had seen chosen by others of their own sex. In contrast, on average, girls with CAH did not. Instead, they showed equal interest in the items that were labeled as for girls or for boys, and equal interest in items they had seen being chosen by female and male models. These results suggest that girls with CAH show less sex-typed behavior not only because androgen has altered their neural circuitry prenatally but also because of how early neural changes alter their behavior, which in turn alters the social environment (e.g., parental encouragement of gender-atypical behavior) and self-socialization processes (e.g., responses to gender labels and to peer models on the basis of their sex).

Another question is whether individuals who are not subject to the same social and cognitive influences on gender-typical behavior seen in our society have sex-typed play or toy preferences. One approach to this question has been to examine the play behavior of nonhuman primates. As mentioned earlier, juvenile male rhesus macaques show more rough-and-tumble play behavior than do female rhesus macaques, and prenatal androgen exposure increases rough-and-tumble play in female macaques (Goy, 1978, 1981). In regard to toys, male and female vervet monkeys have been found to differ in their toy preferences, with female monkeys spending more time than male monkeys with toys like dolls, and male monkeys spending more time than female monkeys with toys like vehicles (Alexander & Hines, 2002). A second study of nonhuman primates, in this case rhesus macaques, replicated the finding of greater male than female preference for toys preferred by boys, in this case wheeled toys (Hassett, Siebert, & Wallen, 2008). These findings all suggest that sex-related toy preferences can develop in the absence of many of the social and cognitive processes that have been found to be influential in children. For instance, the nonhuman primates had no prior experience with the toys, had little to no referential language with which to communicate, and presumably had no cognitive understanding of gender as a cultural construct, particularly in relation to toys.

These studies raise new questions. For instance, what are the characteristics of children's toys that make them more or less appealing to male and female animals who have never seen the toys before? Could it be color, texture, or shape, or the affordance of movement? Humans share with nonhuman primates vital early attachment relationships; does variation in caregiver–infant dyadic interactions as a function of infant sex alter the offspring's later predisposition to prefer certain objects and peer activities? These are among the many questions that are currently being and could be investigated to understand how early development in complex primate societies unfolds, in the absence of uniquely human behaviors (e.g., symbolic language) and institutions (e.g., formal schooling).

TESTOSTERONE IN TYPICALLY DEVELOPING CHILDREN DURING INFANCY AND LATER GENDER-RELATED BEHAVIOR

Another area of active investigation is the influence of testosterone during the early neonatal period when androgens are elevated in boys, called *mini-puberty*. Although there is convergent evidence from children who developed in atypical hormone environments that androgens contribute to children's gender-related toy choices and other aspects of gender typed play, it is important to know whether androgen exposure within the usual range has similar influences. Answering this question has been challenging. Several approaches to studying the impact of normal variability in prenatal androgen exposure, including measuring testosterone in amniotic fluid and in maternal blood, and using finger ratios (2D:4D) as proxies for prenatal androgen exposure, have produced inconsistent results. All of these measures may be too unreliable to detect relationships between androgen exposure and later behavior, other than, perhaps, in very large samples of participants.

Unlike amniotic fluid, which is almost always available only in a single sample, taken at an uncontrolled time of day, testosterone can be measured repeatedly in samples taken from infants during the early postnatal testosterone surge and can be obtained under controlled conditions, using not only blood sampling but also noninvasive techniques such as urine or saliva sampling (Constantinescu & Hines, 2012). Thus, sampling during this early postnatal period could provide more definitive information on the impact of early androgen exposure on children's gender-typical toy preferences in the general population. In addition, because this approach is noninvasive, it could allow studies of large samples of children and thus enable research investigating interactions between early androgen exposure and social and cognitive influences on children's gender-related play behavior.

FUTURE DIRECTIONS IN INTEGRATIVE DEVELOPMENTAL PSYCHOBIOLOGY

Exposure to the hormone, testosterone, in early development appears to contribute to children's gender-related play behavior, including toy preferences. Research in several species using several methods supports this conclusion. However, it is important to resist interpreting evidence for a role of processes early in individual development (e.g., at conception, prenatal) and at low levels of organization (e.g., chromosomes and receptors) as supportive of reductionistic models of gendered behavior. No chromosome or gene ensures a particular genitalia phenotype at birth, much less a child's identity, behavior, or peer relationships years later. The relationship between sex chromosomes and varied—not predetermined—developmental outcomes at different points in development has been illustrated earlier. Models of gender development would benefit from incorporating gene x gene and gene x environment interactions, where "environment" is broadly conceived of as including the early hormonal environment, parents, peers, societal norms, and cultural artifacts (Salk & Hyde, 2012). Such models will integrate events at multiple levels of analysis across development.

Integrative frameworks are well suited to innovations in research on prenatal androgen exposure and gender development. One important future direction concerns the emergence of nonbinary gender identities in childhood. The research reviewed earlier has attended to both gender conformity and gender nonconformity and, to some extent, to gender identity. However, new scholarship is beginning to shed light on the complex nature of gender identity, particularly nonbinary identities (see Chapter 3). The emergence of gender identity and its relationship to prenatal and early neonatal developmental events as well as early childhood behavior are topics ripe for re-examination.

Another future direction concerns ways in which postnatal development proceeds similarly or differently as a function of cultural variables, including culture-specific beliefs about gender (e.g., see Chapters 5 and

14) and intersections of gender with other social identities, such as ethnicity and class (see Chapter 2). Since the initial research on early androgen exposure and later gender-related behavior, gender scholarship has
become more cross-cultural and global. Future conceptualizations of
the integrative psychobiology of gender development could benefit from
incorporating information from those growing literatures.

REFERENCES

Alexander, G. M., & Hines, M. (2002). Sex differences in response to children's toys
in nonhuman primates (*Cercopithecus aethiops sabaeus*). *Evolution and Human
Behavior, 23*, 467–479.

Arnold, A. P. (2009). The organizational-activational hypothesis as the foundation for
a unified theory of sexual differentiation of all mammalian tissues. *Hormones and
Behavior, 55*, 570–578.

Auyeung, B., Baron-Cohen, S., Chapman, E., Knickmeyer, R., Taylor, K., Hackett, G.,
& Hines, M. (2009). Fetal testosterone predicts sexually differentiated childhood
behavior in girls and in boys. *Psychological Science, 20*, 144–148.

Berenbaum, S. A., Bryk, K. K., Nowak, N., Quigley, C. A., & Moffat, S. (2009). Fingers as
a marker of prenatal androgen exposure. *Endocrinology, 150*, 5119–5124.

Berenbaum, S. A., & Hines, M. (1992). Early androgens are related to childhood sex-
typed toy preferences. *Psychological Science, 3*, 203–206.

Berenbaum, S. A., & Snyder, E. (1995). Early hormonal influences on childhood sex-
typed activity and playmate preferences: Implications for the development of sexual
orientation. *Developmental Psychology, 31*(1), 31.

Boas, M., Boisen, K. A., Virtanen, H. E., Kaleva, M., Suomi, A. M., Schmidt, I. M., . . .
Main, K. M. (2006). Postnatal penile length and growth rate corrrelate to serum
testosterone levels: A longitudinal study of 1962 normal boys. *European Journal of
Endocrinology, 154*, 125–129.

Bornstein, M. H., Hahn, C. S., & Haynes, O. M. (2004). Specific and general language
performance across early childhood: Stability and gender considerations. *First
Language, 24*, 267–304.

Cohen, J. (1988). *Statistical power analysis for the behavioral sciences* (Vol. 2). Hillsdale,
NJ: Lawrence Erlbaum Associates.

Constantinescu, M., & Hines, M. (2012). Relating prenatal testosterone exposure to
postnatal behavior in typically developing children: Methods and findings. *Child
Development Perspectives, 6*, 407–413.

Costa, P. T., Terracciano, A., & McCrae, R. R. (2001). Gender differences in personality traits across cultures: Robust and surprising findings. *Personality and Social
Psychology, 81*(2), 322–331.

Crews, D. (2012). The (bi)sexual brain. *EMBO, 13*(9), 779–784.

Dean, A., & Sharpe, R. M. (2013). Anogenital distance or digit length ratio as measures of fetal androgen exposure: Relationship to male reproductive development and its disorders. *The Journal of Clinical Endocrinology & Metabolism, 98*(6), 2230–2238.

Dittmann, R. W., Kappes, M. H., Kappes, M. E., Borger, D., Meyer-Bahlburg, H. F. L., Stegner, H., . . . Wallis, H. (1990). Congenital adrenal hyperplasia II: Gender-related behavior and attitudes in female salt-wasting and simple virilizing patients. *Psychoneuroendocrinology, 15*, 421–434.

Eagley, A. A., & Crowley, M. (1986). Gender and helping behavior: A meta-analytic review of the social psychological literature. *Psychological Bulletin, 100*, 283–308.

Ehrhardt, A. A., & Baker, S. W. (1974). Fetal androgens, human central nervous system differentiation, and behavior sex differences. In R. C. Friedman, R. M. Richart, & R. L. van de Wiele (Eds.), *Sex differences in behavior* (pp. 33–52). New York, NY: Wiley.

Ekstrom, R. B., French, J. W., & Harman, H. H. (1976). *Manual for kit of factor-referenced cognitive tests*. Princeton, NJ: Educational Testing Service.

Fausto-Sterling, A. (1992). *Myths of gender*. New York, NY: Basic Books.

Feingold, A. (1994). Gender differences in personality: A meta-analysis. *Psychological Bulletin, 116*, 429–456.

Feingold, A. (1988). Cognitive gender differences are disappearing. *American Psychologist, 43*, 95–103.

Frisen, J., Nordenstrom, A., Falhammar, H., Filipsson, H., Holmdahl, G., Janson, P. O., . . . Nordenskjold, A. (2009). Gender role behavior, sexuality, and psychosocial adaptation in women with congenital adrenal hyperplasia due to CYP21A2 deficiency. *Journal of Clinical Endocrinology and Metabolism, 94*, 3432–3439.

Goy, R. W. (1978). Development of play and mounting behaviour in female rhesus virilized prenatally with esters of testosterone or dihydrotestosterone. In D. J. Chivers & J. Herbert (Eds.), *Recent advances in primatology* (pp. 449–462). New York, NY: Academic Press.

Goy, R. W. (1981). Differentiation of male social traits in female rhesus macaques by prenatal treatment with androgens: Variation in type of androgen, duration and timing of treatment. In M. J. Novy & J. A. Resko (Eds.), *Fetal endocrinology* (pp. 319–339). New York, NY: Academic Press.

Grumbach, M. M., Hughes, I. A., & Conte, F. A. (2003). Disorders of sex differentiation. In P. R. Larsen, H. M. Kronenberg, S. Melmed, & K. S. Polonsky (Eds.), *Williams textbook of endocrinology* (Vol. 10, pp. 842–1002). Philadelphia, PA: Saunders.

Hall, C. M., Jones, J. A., Meyer-Bahlburg, H. F. L., Dolezal, C., Coleman, M., Foster, P., . . . Clayton, P. E. (2004). Behavioral and physical masculinization are related to genotype in girls with congenital adrenal hyperplasia. *The Journal of Clinical Endocrinology and Metabolism, 89*, 419–424.

Hassett, J. M., Siebert, E. R., & Wallen, K. (2008). Sex differences in rhesus monkey toy preferences parallel those of children. *Hormones and Behavior, 54*, 359–364.

Hines, M. (2004). *Brain gender*. New York, NY: Oxford University Press.

Hines, M. (2015). Gendered development. In R. M. Lerner & M. E. Lamb (Eds.), *Handbook of child development and developmental science* (7th ed.) (Vol. 3, pp. 842–887). Hoboken, NJ: Wiley.

Hines, M., Ahmed, S. F., & Hughes, I. (2003). Psychological outcomes and gender-related development in complete androgen insensitivity syndrome. *Archives of Sexual Behavior, 32*, 93–101.

Hines, M., Golombok, S., Rust, J., Johnston, K., Golding, J., & The, A. S. T. (2002). Testosterone during pregnancy and childhood gender role behavior: A longitudinal population study. *Child Development, 73*, 1678–1687.

Hines, M., Pasterski, V., Spencer, D., Neufeld, S., Patalay, P., Hindmarsh, P. C., . . . Acerini, C. L. (2016). Prenatal androgen exposure alters girls' responses to information indicating gender-appropriate behaviour. *Philosophical Transactions of the Royal Society: B, 371*(1688), 20150125.

Hönekopp, J., & Thierfelder, C. (2009). Relationships between digit ratio (2D: 4D) and sex-typed play behavior in pre-school children. *Personality and Individual Differences, 47*(7), 706–710.

Hyde, J. S. (2005). The gender similarities hypothesis. *American Psychologist, 60*(6), 581–592.

Jurgensen, M., Hiort, O., Holterhus, P. M., & Thyen, U. (2007). Gender role behavior in children with XY karyotype and disorders of sex development. *Hormones and Behavior, 51*, 443–453.

Knickmeyer, R. C., Wheelwright, S., Hackett, G., Taylor, K., Raggatt, P., & Baron-Cohen, S. (2005). Gender-typed play and amniotic testosterone. *Developmental Psychobiology, 41*(3), 517–528.

Kolb, B., & Whishaw, I. Q. (1985). *Fundamentals of human neuropsychology* (Vol. 2). New York: W.H. Freeman and Co.

Kuiri-Hanninen, T., Seuri, R., Tyrvainen, E., Turpeinen, U., Hamalainen, E., Stenman, U. H., . . . Sankilampi, U. (2011). Increased activity of the hypothalamic-pituitary-testicular axis in infancy results in increased androgen action in premature boys. *Journal of Clinical Endocrinology and Metabolism, 96*, 98–105.

Lamminmaki, A., Hines, M., Kuiri-Hanninen, T., Kilpelainen, L., Dunkel, L., & Sankilampi, U. (2012). Testosterone measured in infancy predicts subsequent sex-typed behavior in boys and in girls. *Hormones and Behavior, 61*, 611–616.

Linn, M. C., & Petersen, A. C. (1985). Emergence and characterization of sex differences in spatial ability: A meta-analysis. *Child Development, 56*, 1479–1498.

Manning, J. T. (2002). *Digit ratio: A pointer to fertility, behavior, and health.* New Brunswick, NJ: Rutgers University Press.

Masters, J. C., Ford, M. E., Arend, R., Grotevant, H. D., & Clark, L. V. (1979). Modeling and labelling as integrated determinants of children's sex-typed imitative behavior. *Child Development, 50*, 364–371.

McCarthy, M. M., De Vries, G. J., & Forger, N. G. (2009). Sexual differentiation of the brain: Mode, mechanisms, and meaning. In D. W. Pfaff, A. P. Arnold, A. M. Etgen, S. E. Fahrbach, & R. T. Rubin (Eds.), *Hormones, brain, and behavior* (Vol. 2, pp. 1707–1744). San Diego, CA: Academic Press.

Merke, D. P., & Bornstein, S. R. (2005). Congenital adrenal hyperplasia. *The Lancet, 365*, 2125–2136.

Mitsui, T., Araki, A., Miyashita, C., Ito, S., Ikeno, T., Sasaki, S., . . . Morioka, K. (2016). The relationship between the second-to-fourth digit ratio and behavioral sexual dimorphism in school-aged children. *PLoS ONE, 11*(1), e0146849.

Money, J., & Ehrhardt, A. (1972). *Man and woman: Boy and girl.* Baltimore, MD: Johns Hopkins University Press.

Olson, K. R., Key, A. C., & Eaton, N. R. (2015). Gender cognition in transgender children. *Psychological Science, 26*(4) 467–474.

Pang, S., Levine, L. S., Cederqvist, L. L., Fuentes, M., Riccardi, V. M., Holcombe, J. H., . . . New, M. I. (1980). Amniotic fluid concentrations of delta 5 and delta 4 steroids in fetuses with congenital adrenal hyperplasia due to 21-hydroxylase deficiency and in anencephalic fetuses. *Journal of Clinical Endocrinology and Metabolism, 51,* 223–229.

Pasterski, V. L., Geffner, M. E., Brain, C., Hindmarsh, P., Brook, C., & Hines, M. (2005). Prenatal hormones and postnatal socialization by parents as determinants of male-typical toy play in girls with congenital adrenal hyperplasia. *Child Development, 76,* 264–278.

Pasterski, V., Acerini, C. L., Dunger, D. B., Ong, K. K., Hughes, I. A., & Thankamony, A. (2015). Postnatal penile growth concurrent with mini-puberty predicts later gender-typed behavior: Evidence for neurobehavioral effects of the postnatal androgen surge in typically developing boys. *Hormones and Behavior, 69,* 98–105.

Quadagno, D. M., Briscoe, R., & Quadagno, J. S. (1977). Effects of perinatal gonadal hormones on selected nonsexual behavior patterns: A critical assessment of the non-human and human literature. *Psychological Bulletin, 84,* 62–80.

Salk, R., & Hyde, J. S. (2012). Contemporary genetics for gender researchers: Not your grandma's genetics anymore. *Psychology of Women Quarterly, 36,* 395–411.

Servin, A., Nordenstrom, A., Larsson, A., & Bohlin, G. (2003). Prenatal androgens and gender-typed behavior: A study of girls with mild and severe forms of congenital adrenal hyperplasia. *Developmental Psychology, 39,* 440–450.

Spreen, O., & Strauss, E. (1991). *A compendium of neuropsychological tests.* New York, NY: Oxford University Press.

Thankamony, A., Pasterski, V., Ong, K. K., Acerini, C. L., & Hughes, I. A. (2016). Anogenital distance as a marker of androgen exposure in humans. *Andrology, 4*(4), 616–625.

van de Beek, C., Van Goozen, S. H. M., Buitelaar, J. K., & Cohen-Kettenis, P. T. (2009). Prenatal sex hormones (maternal and amniotic fluid) and gender-related play behavior in 13-month-old infants. *Archives of Sexual Behavior, 38,* 6–15.

van den Driesche, S., Scott, H. M., MacLeod, D. J., Fisken, M., Walker, M., & Sharpe, R. M. (2011). Relative importance of prenatal and postnatal androgen action in determining growth of the penis and anogenital distance in the rat before, during and after puberty. *International Journal of Andrology, 34,* e578–e586.

Voyer, D., Voyer, S., & Bryden, M. P. (1995). Magnitude of sex differences in spatial abilities: A meta-analysis and consideration of critical variables. *Psychological Bulletin, 117,* 250–270.

Wong, W. I., & Hines, M. (2016). Interpreting digit ratio (2D: 4D)–behavior correlations: 2D: 4D sex difference, stability, and behavioral correlates and their replicability in young children. *Hormones and Behavior, 78*, 86–94.

Wong, W. I., Pasterski, V. L., Hindmarsh, P. C., Geffner, M. E., & Hines, M. (2012). Are there parental socialization effects on the sex-typed behavior of individuals with congenital adrenal hyperplasia? *Archives of Sexual Behavior, 42*(3), 381–391.

Wudy, S. A., Dorr, H. G., Solleder, C., Djalali, M., & Homoki, J. (1999). Profiling steroid hormones in amniotic fluid of midpregnancy by routine stable isotope dilution/gas chromatography-mass spectrometry: Reference values and concentrations in fetuses at risk for 21-hydroxylase deficiency. *Journal of Clinical Endocrinology and Metabolism, 84*, 2724–2728.

12

Contemporary Theory in the Study of Intimacy, Desire, and Sexuality

LISA M. DIAMOND

L ove and sex are powerful human experiences shaped by intersecting biological, cultural, and interpersonal factors, and intimate relationships provide significant sites for the enactment, reproduction, and negotiation of gender roles and identities across the life course. From the very first moments that girls and boys begin to experience compelling motivations to seek emotional and/or physical closeness with others, these urges necessarily prompt them to consider how they view themselves in relation to the object of their desire or affection. What are they supposed to do, or want, or be? What does the other person expect? What models of "typical" female or male behavior are available to guide them through these interactions? Parents? Friends? Church? Television? Social media? The vulnerability inherent in romantic and sexual relationships makes questions of gender—and gender role *violations*—particularly fraught.

The present chapter reviews contemporary theory and research on romantic love, sexual desire, and sexual orientation, highlighting some of the most intriguing recent developments and challenging future questions, and taking a fundamentally interdisciplinary approach that seeks to integrate different disciplinary perspectives (biological, evolutionary, psychological, cultural). A chief goal of the chapter is to move beyond many of the hackneyed and simplistic "nature/nurture" debates that continue to dominate work in this area, and to provide a forum in which different frames of reference—and the tensions between them—can be engaged to highlight the nuances and complexities of human experience. Along these lines, a note about terminology is in order: The vast majority of theoretical and empirical research on sex, love, and sexual orientation has been conducted with cisgender individuals in the United States (i.e., individuals whose gender identity and presentation match the sex category to which they were assigned at birth). Scholars are only now beginning to understand the unique experiences of *gender-variant* individuals (i.e., transgender individuals, gender-nonconforming individuals, and those who identify with multiple or changing genders). At the present time, their experiences are notably underrepresented in the research literature, and hence the terms "men" and "women" should be taken in this chapter to refer specifically to cisgender men and women. In many areas (such as attachment and pairbonding, addressed later), the experiences of gender-variant individuals may be similar to those of cisgender individuals, but such similarity should not be presumed without further research. One of the most important areas for future research involves the testing and refinement of US-based psychological research on cisgender men and women to a broader range of male-identified and female-identified individuals in non-US populations.

ROMANTIC LOVE AND ATTACHMENT

Although different cultures and historical periods have different interpretations and rules regarding intimate social ties, the *capacity* for humans to form intense emotional bonds to one another appears to be a cross-cultural universal that is a part of our evolved mammalian heritage. The dominant theoretical model governing contemporary research on adult romantic relationships is *attachment theory*. Attachment theory began as an evolutionary theory of infant–caregiver bonding, but in the mid-1980s social psychologists realized that this theory also aptly explained adults' feelings and behaviors toward romantic partners. Bowlby (1982) developed attachment theory to explain the powerful psychological relationship that normatively develops between human infants and their primary caregivers. Human infants are highly vulnerable and need extensive care during the first years of life, and Bowlby argued that the emotional and behavioral dynamics of the attachment system evolved to keep infants in close proximity to their caregivers in order to maximize their chances for survival. When an infant experiences distress, he or she automatically seeks proximity to the caregiver (via crying, reaching, clinging, etc.). This proximity and contact reassures and soothes the infant, and he or she comes to associate the presence of the caregiver with a psychological sense of safety and security. Over the course of repeated day-to-day physical care and contact, the infant develops a unique and emotionally primary bond to the caregiver, such that the caregiver is the infant's most preferred source of comfort, security, care, and closeness. When this occurs, the caregiver has become the infant's *attachment figure*.

Bowlby argued that the attachment system is operative across the entire life span, and other evolutionary theorists have argued that over the course of human evolution, the basic emotional dynamics of the infant–caregiver attachment system were "co-opted" to foster enduring emotional bonds between adult sexual partners. Such bonds promoted individual survival and reproduction by motivating men and women to stay together *after* sexual mating had been completed, thereby providing vulnerable infants with two parents to provide care and protection instead of just one (Mellen, 1982). Over the past 30 years, extensive research has supported the notion that the powerful feelings we typically call "romantic love" are actually adult versions of infant–caregiver attachment. Adult romantic attachments have been observed to show the same fundamental emotional and behavioral dynamics as infant–caregiver attachments: heightened proximity seeking; resistance to separation; and utilization of the partner as a preferred source of comfort, security, care, and closeness (Hazan & Zeifman, 1999). Biological research provides additional evidence for the links between adult attachment and infant–caregiver attachment: Studies of nonhuman mammalian species have shown that the distinctive proximity-seeking and separation distress associated with attachment formation—whether in infancy or adulthood—is mediated by the neurobiological reward circuitry of the mammalian brain, including endogenous opioids, dopamine, corticosterone, oxytocin, and vasopressin (reviewed in Carter & Keverne, 2002; Curtis & Wang, 2003).

Of course, the key difference between adult romantic attachment and infant–caregiver attachment is sexuality (Shaver, Hazan, & Bradshaw, 1988), given that sexual desire and behavior is a normal and typical part of adult attachment, but not infant–caregiver attachment. Yet although sexual desire is *normative* within adult romantic attachments, it does not appear to be *necessary* for such bonds to form. In the United States and many others cultures, adults report developing passionate emotional attachments with individuals to whom they are not sexually attracted or involved, and in some cultures these platonic bonds are recognized with rituals or ceremonies that testify to their social and emotional significance (reviewed in Diamond, 2003). Although modern observers might assume that any relationship of such emotional intensity must contain some erotic component (perhaps hidden or suppressed), there is no evidence for this presumption. Rather, the fact that some individuals develop intense but nonsexual attachments to one another may simply stem from the fact that the basic biobehavioral mechanisms underlying attachment formation originally evolved in the context of infant–caregiver bonds, for which sexual desire and behavior is irrelevant. Hence, although the intense, passionate intimacy of adult attachment may be *facilitated* by sexual desire and behavior (Hazan & Zeifman, 1994), it is not restricted to sexual partners.

This fact has profound implications for understanding the role of gender in romantic love. If the emotional, behavioral, and neurobiological dynamics of adult attachment are based in the infant–caregiver attachment system, then there is no reason to expect that our capacity to fall in love with another person depends on that person's gender. Infant–caregiver attachment is a fundamentally gender-neutral system: Both male and female infants (i.e., those with male-typical or female-typical external genitalia at birth, and hence male or female sex assignment) are capable of becoming attached to male or female caregivers. The chief characteristic driving the infant's attachment to the caregiver is the caregiver's availability and responsiveness, not the caregiver's perceived gender. Accordingly, it necessarily follows that adult attachment is similarly "gender neutral." Because adult attachment and infant–caregiver attachment share the same neurobiological architecture, gender cannot be "built in" to adult attachment if it is not "built in" to infant–caregiver attachment.

This, of course, flies in the face of most conventional assumptions about gender and romantic love. Specifically, it is commonly assumed that individuals are only capable of falling in love with individuals to whom they are sexually attracted, and that their sexual attractions are rigidly gender specific. For example, because heterosexual women are sexually attracted to men, it is assumed that they can only fall in love with men. Because lesbians are sexually attracted to women, it is presumed that they only fall in love with women. In essence, this point of view assumes that one's *sexual* orientation translates into a corresponding *romantic* orientation. Yet there is no evidence that romantic orientations exist. The truth is that individuals can form romantic attachments to just about anyone, regardless of the other person's gender or sexual desirability. As it happens, both the anthropological and historical literature are replete with descriptions of platonic same-sex "infatuations" between adults that were devoid of sexual interest and contact (reviewed in Diamond, 2003). Although some scholars have looked back on such cases and wondered whether the participants were "really" lesbian/gay, others have argued that this approach inappropriately projects modern Western notions of sexual identity onto individuals for whom such constructs do not apply (Blackwood, 2000). Questions of sexual identity and orientation are revisited later, but the important point here is to *distinguish* between romantic love and sexual desire, and to note that romantic love does not appear to be a fundamentally gender-oriented system. To the extent that most individuals do, in fact, only fall in love with partners of a particular gender (and partners to whom they are sexually attracted), this is due to cultural beliefs and social practices that structure their opportunities for intimate ties, and it is not a basic feature of human emotional bonding.

SEXUAL DESIRE

Sexual desire is a complex, multifaceted experience that has been notoriously difficult to define, operationalize, and study (reviewed in Diamond, 2012). Most scholars generally view sexual desire as "an interest in sexual objects or activities or a wish, need, or drive to seek out sexual objects or to engage in sexual activities" (Regan & Berscheid, 1995, p. 346). However, this definition lumps together two types of sexual desire that are not exactly the same: the urge to *seek out* sexual activity versus the ability to *become interested* in sexual activity after exposure to certain stimuli. In the primate literature, these two different types of sexual desire are respectively denoted *proceptivity* versus *receptivity/arousability* (Beach, 1976). One reason that it is important to distinguish between these two forms of desire is that they have different substrates: Proceptivity is directly regulated by gonadal hormones (testosterone in men and both testosterone and estrogen in women), whereas arousability is hormone independent (reviewed in Tolman & Diamond, 2001). This has particular importance for understanding *women's* experiences of sexual desire given that women undergo notable fluctuations in gonadal hormones over the course of the menstrual cycle, whereas men's gonadal hormone levels remain relatively stable. From an evolutionary perspective, women's proceptivity fluctuates cyclically because estrogen-related increases during ovulation ensured that women were strongly motivated to seek sex when they were able to conceive. Yet the fact that women can *become* sexually aroused at any point in the menstrual cycle underscores the fact that for humans (and other later-evolving primates and hominoids), sexual contact serves social and interpersonal functions as well as reproductive functions. Hence, although reproduction is obviously one function of sexual behavior, it is by far not the only one, and one of the hallmarks of the human species is our capacity to elaborate on basic urges (such as our motivations to seek food, shelter, and sexual release) by developing complex, culture-specific, individualized practices and preferences (such as highly specialized cuisines, diverse designs for human dwelling systems, and preferences for a range of different sexual practices and partners).

Another important difference between female and male sexual desire concerns concordance between subjective experience and physiological arousal. Sexual arousal involves a host of physiological sequelae ranging from blood flow to hormonal release to neurobiological activation, but these phenomena do not always neatly correspond to an individual's psychological experience of sexual desire. Most interestingly, women consistently show less correspondence between subjective desire and physiological arousal than do men (Chivers, Seto, Lalumiere, Laan, & Grimbos, 2010), for reasons that are not well understood. One possible explanation is that gender-specific cultural norms regarding masturbation in childhood and adolescence make it easier for boys than girls to "link up" their own experiences of subjective desire and genital arousal through self-exploration. Such exploration is considered typical behavior for boys, whereas it is more stigmatized for girls. Girls often receive the message from parents, peers, and the media that women have less interest in sex than men, and that it is the mission of respectable girls to *resist* the sexual advances of male partners (Fine, 1988), rather than to explore their own capacity for arousal and pleasure. The cultural factors encouraging girls to discount and dismiss their own capacity for sexual arousal continue to generate vociferous debate among youth advocates and developmental psychologists about the best way to encourage girls' sexual agency in a cultural climate that continues to commercialize and commodify their bodies and behaviors (Lerum & Dworkin, 2011).

An additional complication is the widespread assumption that all sexual desires revolve around *partnered* sexual behavior and are hence interpretable as desires for certain types of partners (male, female, blond, brunette, older, younger, etc.). This is perhaps most evident in the traditional conceptualization of sexual orientation, which is typically defined in Western culture as a stable sexual predisposition for same-sex partners, other-sex partners, or both types of partners. There are several shortcomings of this particular definition (addressed in more detail later), but one obvious problem is that it presumes that all sexual desires are experienced for (or triggered by) *other people*. This is not the case, and researchers such as Van Anders (2015) have critically expanded our understanding of sexual desire by highlighting distinctions between *solitary* sexual desires (which occur outside of a partnered context, and typically accompany masturbatory behavior) and *dyadic* sexual desires (which motivate individuals to seek partnered sexual activity). Van Anders's work shows that these different forms of desire have different subjective and hormonal correlates, and hence it is inaccurate to assume that all experiences of sexual desire revolve around the characteristics (most notably, the gender) of specific types of partners.

This insight is particularly important when considering sexual desires for unconventional sexual practices, such as sadomasochism, bondage and domination, voyeurism, exhibitionism, and desires that center on certain parts of the body. Historically, such desires have been viewed as forms of psychological dysfunction, but there is no scientific evidence that individuals with unconventional desires are fundamentally disordered in any way (reviewed in Kleinplatz & Diamond, 2013). After all, there are plenty of human activities that we might consider to be "extreme," painful, or even physically dangerous, such as high-altitude mountain climbing or skydiving, but society does not generally presume that the small group of individuals who reliably pursue such experiences are fundamentally pathological. Yet when individuals' *sexual* practices involve extremes of physical sensation or nonnormative relational practices, societies are quick to cast judgment on participants' mental health. Of course, definitions of "normal" versus "abnormal" sexual practices have changed dramatically over time, and they show great variability across different cultures (reviewed in Rubin, 1984). Hence, it is important to remember that social judgments of the "naturalness," respectability, and healthfulness of certain sexual practices are culturally bound. While certain sexual desires and practices may be less *common* than others, they are just as "natural" and just as much a part of the basic human capacity for diverse and flexible sexual expression.

SEXUAL ORIENTATION

Historically, sexual orientation has been viewed as a trait-like, genetically determined predisposition to experience sexual attractions for the same sex, the other sex, or both sexes. This predisposition has generally been thought to govern all aspects of sexual experience, such that individuals with exclusive same-sex attractions (i.e., those who are erotically attracted to individuals who present as the same sex as they themselves occupy, regardless of either individual's chosen sexual identity) have been presumed to experience exclusive same-sex sexual fantasies, exclusive same-sex romantic feelings, and exclusive enjoyment of same-sex sexual behavior. Sexual orientation has also been presumed stable over the life course, such that an individual's desire for same-sex versus other-sex partners expresses itself early in life and remains fundamentally unchanged and unchangeable over time.

We now know that this view of sexual orientation has significant limitations. Although it serviceably describes the experiences of some individuals with same-sex desires, it fails to adequately represent the diversity, complexity, and fluidity of human sexual expression. Notably, this traditional model of sexual orientation has performed particularly poorly in describing some of the unique experiences of women (Diamond, 2008b, 2016). Most early research on sexual orientation was conducted with predominantly or exclusively male samples, given that openly identified gay/bisexual men have historically been easier to identify and sample (Sell & Petrulio, 1996). Originally, this was not considered a substantive problem, given that sexual orientation was implicitly presumed to operate similarly for women and men. Yet over the years, research documenting gender differences in the development and expression of same-sex sexuality has called this presumption into question. For example, adult women appear particularly likely to report sizeable discrepancies among their attractions, romantic feelings, and sexual behaviors; to report a markedly late and abrupt onset of same-sex sexuality, often after heterosexual marriage; and to report fluctuations in their attractions, behaviors, and identities over time, sometimes triggered by single relationships (reviewed in Diamond, 2014).

The extent and basis of these gender differences are a matter of ongoing debate. Further complicating matters is the considerable role of cultural factors in shaping female and male sexuality, and specifically hindering women's abilities to freely articulate and act upon their own sexual desires. As long as women continue to gain social and sexual autonomy around the world, and as long as social acceptance of same-sex sexuality also grows, gender differences in the expression of same-sex sexuality may diminish. Yet at the current time, it remains difficult to know whether sexual orientations will continue to express themselves differently in men versus women, and whether the nature of these differences will change as our social constructions of gender continue to change.

Perhaps the most reliable difference between female and male same-sex sexuality concerns the prevalence of nonexclusive (i.e., bisexual) versus exclusive patterns of attraction. One recent review examined the prevalence of exclusive same-sex attractions versus bisexual patterns of attraction in 16 studies published between 2000 and 2016, each of which used a representative probability sample of adults, with sample sizes ranging from several thousand to several million participants (Diamond, 2016). These studies consistently found that women were more likely to report bisexual attractions than exclusive same-sex attractions, whereas men were typically more likely to report exclusive same-sex attractions than bisexual attractions.

What accounts for this reliable difference? What combinations of genetic and social differences between men and women may be involved? Some evidence suggests that women may have a stronger basic capacity for bisexual sexual arousal than do men. A series of studies examining sex differences in genital responses to sexual stimuli has found support for this view (Chivers, Rieger, Latty, & Bailey, 2004; Chivers, Seto, & Blanchard,

2007). Specifically, lesbian-identified and heterosexual-identified women show similar levels of genital arousal to their preferred sexual stimuli (same-sex for lesbians and other-sex for heterosexuals) and their nonpreferred sexual stimuli (other-sex for lesbians and same-sex for lesbians). Yet gay-identified and heterosexual-identified men show substantially stronger genital arousal to their preferred sexual stimuli than to their nonpreferred sexual stimuli. In essence, these findings suggest that even women who generally experience their sexual attractions as exclusively same-sex or exclusively other-sex possess a *capacity* for bisexual genital arousal, and that this capacity is greater among women than men.

Importantly, genital arousal does not always correspond to the subjective psychological experience of sexual desire, and women generally show less correspondence between patterns of genital and psychological arousal than do men (Suschinsky, Lalumiere, & Chivers, 2009). Hence, women who are capable of becoming genitally aroused to their "nonpreferred" gender may not necessarily perceive themselves as bisexual, if this capacity is not accompanied by a conscious and reliable experience of same-sex desire. This underscores the difficulty in operationalizing and measuring sexual orientation (Rieger, Bailey, & Chivers, 2005). Specifically, is it best conceived as a pattern of genital arousal, even if that arousal does not concord with conscious psychological desire? Is it, instead, best conceived as a pattern of conscious sexual attraction? If so, then how consistently must such attractions be experienced in order to "count" as evidence of an orientation? What role should we grant sexual behavior in assessing sexual orientation, given that behavior is heavily structured by culture and opportunity? Scholars have not reached consensus on these questions.

Another notable complication is the difference between the social meanings and social costs associated with same-sex and other-sex behavior for women versus men. Across different cultures and historical periods, women have been more seriously penalized than men for deviating from culturally traditional roles as wives and mothers (Faderman, 1981; Rich, 1980), potentially providing a compelling motive for women with same-sex attractions to pursue bisexual rather than exclusively same-sex behavior. Male bisexuality has also faced more cultural skepticism over the years than female bisexuality among scholars and laypeople alike, such that bisexually identified men are more likely than bisexually identified women to be dismissed as closeted or confused (Rieger et al., 2005). Hence, in addition to the possibility that bisexuality is more common among women than among men, it may also be easier for bisexual women than bisexual men to acknowledge and openly express their bisexuality, given that women's socialization has typically granted them more latitude to express affection with other women.

Before leaving the topic of bisexuality, it is important to note that bisexual patterns of attraction are substantially more common in *both* women and men than exclusive same-sex attractions, contrary to conventional wisdom (although rates of bisexual *identification* were much less common in previous generations than contemporarily, due to low cultural visibility of bisexuality and suspicion about its status within the lesbian and gay community as reviewed in Rust, 2000). Historically, it was assumed that sexual orientation came in two basic types—homosexuality and heterosexuality—and that bisexuals were an atypical "fringe" group comprised predominantly of individuals who were in the process of transitioning to a gay or lesbian identity or individuals who were temporarily experimenting with same-sex relationships (for reviews, see Diamond, 2008a; Rust, 1993, 2000). This view was largely attributable to the fact that early research on sexual orientation tended to recruit participants through gay/lesbian bars, organizations, events, businesses, and newspapers, all of which tended to underrepresent bisexually identified men and women.

Only now do scientists realize how these strategies have distorted our perceptions of the bisexual population. We now have access to large-scale, random, and representative data on the distribution of same-sex sexuality in the United States and other nations, and these studies reliably show that individuals with bisexual attractions outnumber individuals with exclusive same-sex attractions (Chandra, Mosher, Copen, & Sionean, 2011; Mosher, Chandra, & Jones, 2005). For example, one large-scale representative study of American adults (Mosher et al., 2005) found that 6% of American men and nearly 13% of American women reported attractions to both sexes, whereas 1.5% of men and .8% of women were exclusively attracted to the same sex (the same basic pattern emerged in Chandra et al., 2011). In the fourth wave of the National Longitudinal Study of Adolescent Health (during which participants were in early adulthood), 6.4% of men and nearly 20% of women reported same-sex attractions, and of these individuals, only 5% of women and 26% of men reported that these attractions were exclusively directed to the same sex. Given the historical underrepresentation of bisexuality in the research literature on sexuality and sexual orientation (reviewed in Diamond, 2008a), greater attention to this population is one of the most important priorities for future theoretical and empirical research on sexual orientation.

CHANGE OVER TIME

The historical notion of sexual orientation as a rigidly fixed trait has been challenged by a growing body of longitudinal evidence (reviewed in Diamond, 2016) showing that the specific distribution of an individual's attractions may shift over time, between exclusive homo/heterosexuality to bisexuality and vice versa (but rarely between exclusive homosexuality and exclusive heterosexuality). Importantly, such emergent changes should not be confused with *effortful* changes to extinguish same-sex attractions that some individuals seek through "reparative therapy," a form of therapy that is widely viewed to be both ineffective and psychologically damaging (APA Task Force on Appropriate Therapeutic Responses to Sexual Orientation, 2009).

Several examples illustrate the prevalence and magnitude of changes in sexual attractions: Savin-Williams, Joyner, and Rieger (2012) analyzed data from the National Longitudinal Study of Adolescent Health, which has been regularly tracking same-sex attractions and sexual identity in a random, representative sample of over 12,000 adolescents since 1994. At both the third wave of data collection (when respondents were between 18 and 24 years of age) and the fourth wave of data collection (when respondents were between 24 and 34 years of age) respondents described themselves as "100% heterosexual," "mostly heterosexual," "bisexual," "mostly homosexual," or "100% homosexual." Of the 5.7% of men and 13.7% of women who chose one of the nonheterosexual descriptors at wave three, 43% of the men and 50% of the women chose a different sexual orientation category 6 years later. Ott, Corliss, Wypijj, Rosario, and Austin similarly assessed change in sexual orientation in the "Growing Up Today Study" (GUTS) (Ott, Corliss, Wypij, Rosario, & Austin, 2011). This study includes over 13,000 youth who were the children of women who participated in the well-known Nurses Health Study II (NHSII), a prospective cohort study of over 116,000 registered nurses. Participants described themselves as "Completely heterosexual," "Mostly heterosexual," "Bisexual," "Mostly homosexual," "Completely homosexual," or "Unsure." Of the 7.5% of men and 8.7% of women who chose a nonheterosexual descriptor at age 18–21, 43% of the men and 46% of the women chose a different category by age 23.

Such findings show that longitudinal changes in sexual attractions are relatively common, and researchers must now tackle the difficult question of *why, how, and among which individuals* such changes occur. A number of studies finds that women are more likely to undergo changes in their attractions than men, but this might be attributable to the fact that women are more likely than men to be bisexual, and bisexual patterns of attraction show greater longitudinal change than exclusive patterns of attraction (Diamond, 2007, 2012; Ross, Daneback, & Månsson, 2012), perhaps because individuals may come into awareness of different aspects of their erotic spectrum as they move into and out of different environments and relationships (Weinberg, Williams, & Pryor, 1994). Furthermore, neurobiological research has documented numerous linkages between the neural substrates of sexual desire and the neural substrates of emotional attachment, making it possible that the formation of emotional attachments may facilitate unexpected changes in sexual desire (Diamond, 2003; Diamond & Dickenson, 2012).

Because sexual orientation has been presumed fundamentally stable up until this point, we lack a coherent body of theory that can help us to understand the causes and consequences of change in same-sex and other-sex attraction, and this is an important area for future research.

Dynamical systems theories provide one promising direction for study, given that they focus specifically on the underlying dynamics of complex variability in human experience over time. Dynamical systems approaches to social-behavioral phenomena belong to a larger family of theoretical perspectives seeking to replace deterministic models with an emphasis on dynamic person–environment interactions occurring over time (for review, see Granic, 2005). There are actually several different types of dynamical systems models (van Geert & Steenbeek, 2005), but at their core they all emphasize transformative, bidirectional, changing interactions among endogenous factors (such as genes, hormones, skills, capacities, thoughts, and feelings) and exogenous factors (such as relationships, experiences, cultural norms, family history, etc.). These models suggest that some complex experiences (such as patterns of same-sex and other-sex attraction) represent *emergent phenomena*, meaning that these patterns come into being through dynamic, unpredictable interactions among different elements in the system and may change if the constituent elements change.

Hence, dynamical systems approaches stand in direct contrast to essentialist, organismic models of development that presume that complex behaviors or experiences unfold progressively according to innate, deterministic programs. Whereas the organismic approach predicts relatively uniform trajectories with consistent onsets and outcomes, dynamical systems approaches maintain that developmental pathways are necessarily idiosyncratic, tweaked by long cascades of diverse interchanges between individuals and their changing environments. These models may be best equipped to help us understand the conditions under which sexuality may fluctuate and restabilize over time.

Another strength of dynamical systems theories is that they may be better able to make sense of discrepancies between individuals' self-ascribed sexual identities, attractions, and behaviors. The conventional conceptualization of sexual orientation gives the impression that the *only* individuals who authentically desire or enjoy same-sex sexual activity are those who were born with homosexual or bisexual orientations. Yet the research literature is replete with accounts of heterosexually identified individuals

who periodically engage in—and enjoy—same-sex sexual relationships. For example, a random representative sample of over 12,000 New
Zealanders over the age of 16 found that 3% of the respondents who considered themselves to be heterosexual reported having same-sex sexual
experience (Wells, McGee, & Beautrais, 2011). A representative sample of
over 3,000 Swedish high school students (Priebe & Svedin, 2013) found
that 13% of the heterosexually identified boys and 30% of the heterosexually identified girls reported some degree of same-sex attraction (1% of
the heterosexually identified boys and 2% of the heterosexually identified
girls also reported same-sex sexual behavior).

We could certainly conclude that such individuals are simply "closeted,"
and that they falsely maintain a heterosexual identification to escape
stigma and social rejection. Although this certainly accounts for some of
these cases, it is unlikely to explain all of them. Rather, it is more plausible
to assume that sexuality among all individuals retains some degree of plasticity and fluidity, and that any individual—regardless of his or her previous pattern of desire—may come to unexpectedly experience novel forms
of desire, whether for a limited or an extended period of time. The only
way to make sense of these experiences is to integrate investigations of
dynamic change into our theoretical models and empirical investigations
of sexuality. Dynamical systems theories can also help us to understand
the dynamics of sexual arousal and desire more generally, and the degree
to which they differ among men and women. For example, some scholars
have argued that the basic biopychological model of female sexual arousal
differs from male sexual arousal, and that female sexual arousal is fundamentally more circular and contextual in its emergence and expression.
Specifically, although male-based models of sexual desire have tended to
view sexual desire as an innate, automatic, drive-like force that influences
(but is not influenced *by*) sexual activity, research by Basson (2001) suggests that female sexual arousal is a more circular, responsive system, such
that sexual activity sometimes provides a trigger for the experience of
sexual arousal (rather than vice versa). This underscores the importance
of attending to processes of dynamic change in sexual desire and arousal
more generally.

DIRECTIONS FOR FUTURE RESEARCH

In the past, when researchers were confronted with individuals who showed discrepancies between their sexual identities and sexual behaviors, or individuals whose desires changed over time, the key question that researchers asked was "What is this individual's *true* sexual orientation? Is this a repressed lesbian or a confused heterosexual?" Yet now that we understand the dynamic nature of sexuality, and the probabilistic (rather than deterministic) nature of sexual orientation, this question makes little sense. The more pressing task for research is to understand the complex of social and biological forces that give rise to variability in sexual desire and behavior at different stages of life and within different social contexts.

In addressing these questions, it is important to adopt models of development that account for bidirectional patterns of influence. For example, psychologists have historically viewed the formation of a gay, lesbian, or bisexual self-concept as a process occurring *after*—and independently from—the development of one's sexual orientation. Yet it has become increasingly clear that the process of cognitively questioning one's sexual identity, and attaching different meanings to one's intimate experiences, can alter one's subjective experience of desire (Golden, 1996). Cass (1990) has elaborated this point in a cogent critique of the conventional notion that sexual orientation and sexual identity unfold according to totally independent processes, the former uniformly preceding the latter. Although Cass initially held this view herself, and used it as the foundation of her own widely used stage model of identity development, she eventually questioned the rigid distinction between orientation and identity. In her newer theorizing, she argues that the process of attaching meaning to one's same-sex attractions and behaviors, and developing a socially embedded self-concept centering on these experiences, fundamentally shapes subsequent experiences of same-sex desire and activity, "by narrowing opportunities for sexual/social/emotional expression, building attitudes that attach a fixed quality to identity and preference, reinforcing behaviors that are consistent with identity, and providing a system of rewards that encourages commitment to a particular mode of behavior" (p. 252).

In essence, Cass is highlighting the fact that sexual desires are not static properties but exist in dynamic interaction with individuals' attempts to interpret, label, and express them. Hence, whereas Cass's original stage model was characterized by an inexorable, unidirectional progression from early same-sex attractions and sexual activity to eventual identity adoption, her newer formulation suggests a cascading, recursive process through which identity, context, desire, and behavior mutually shape one another over time. Just as individuals' subjective sexual experiences directly inform the identities they choose to adopt (i.e., *I enjoy same-sex but not other-sex activity; therefore, I am gay*), the adoption of a socially embedded identity can feed back to shape the quality of one's sexual experiences, providing a cognitive frame that may alter the very phenomenology of erotic pleasure—for example, either amplifying or dampening it—and also altering its representation in memory. Once individuals consciously reflect on their sexual orientation and identity (a process that necessarily involves awareness of the cultural meanings and implications of same-sex sexuality), it is arguably impossible for them to experience same-sex and other-sex desire and behavior in precisely the same way. The very asking of the question, in a particular social context, necessarily influences the answer.

This is not a particularly novel idea: It is based in "cascade" models of human development, in which early traits and experiences continuously feed forward to shape individuals' changing skills, capacities, and propensities over time. When applied to sexuality, this view suggests that sexuality represents both the "output" of prior development and the "input" for forthcoming experience. In essence, sexuality is a moving target, continuously adapting and changing in response to an individual's cumulative succession of intimate feelings and experiences, and the socially embedded meanings attached to these experiences. Some individual's trajectories will gravitate toward increased stabilization, whereas others' will repeatedly splinter, diversify, and redirect. One of the most fascinating topics for future research concerns the complex interplay between cultural and biological factors, as well as the interplay between cells and organisms, and between organisms and social systems, which give rise to these different phenomenological trajectories.

Yet in order to conduct such research, we must adopt a broader life-span approach. As argued by McClintock and Herdt (1996), sexual desire does not simply switch on at puberty, but instead undergoes gradual development from childhood onward, reflecting a progressive interbraiding of biological, social, and psychological transitions experienced within changing social contexts. Observational data collected from parents and caretakers have consistently documented sexual interest and behavior in children as young as 2 years of age (reviewed in depth by de Graaf & Rademakers, 2011), yet our base of knowledge on these experiences, their normative developmental time course, and their phenomenology (from the child's perspective) is woefully limited, given that cultural taboos have made it difficult for researchers to systematically study these experiences (Lamb, 2013). In fact, the vast majority of published papers on childhood experiences of sexuality focus on the sexual *abuse* of children, rather than children's own volitional sexual activity (de Graaf & Rademakers, 2011). The lack of attention to normative features of childhood sexuality has severely hampered our basic understanding of life-span sexual development, and how it interacts with parallel developments in gender identity, attachment, social functioning, and cultural socialization. Investigating such topics is a priority for future research.

Another important area for future study concerns the experiences of gender-variant individuals. As noted earlier, the vast majority of contemporary research on love, sex, and sexual orientation has focused on cisgender individuals (i.e., those whose gender identity matches the gender to which they were assigned at birth). Yet one of the most important developments over the past several decades of research on gender and sexuality has been the increasing appreciation of the prevalence and diversity of fluid, nonnormative, and noncategorical forms of gender presentation and experience (Ekins & King, 1999; Halberstam, 2005; Roen, 2002). Contrary to the widespread assumption that gender-variant and/ or transgender individuals are distressed by, and hence seek to resolve and eliminate, discrepancies or ambiguities in their psychological experience and physical expression of gender, research has revealed that many of these individuals *embrace* their fluid, shifting, and ambiguous gender identifications, and do not seek unambiguous identification as male or female. For example, Gagné, Tewksbury, and McGaughey (1997) charted multiple forms of gender identity in their diverse sample of transgender participants. Although some sought a complete and clear-cut switch from one gender category to the other, others maintained various mixtures of male and female attributes, sometimes aided by the selective use of surgery and hormones and sometimes not. The diversity of contemporary transgender experience is reflected by the wide array of identity terms adopted by transgender youths and adults, including gender blender, gender bender, gender outlaw, gender queer, drag king/queen, trans, transgender(ist), and queer (Ekins & King, 1999).

In embracing the complexity and fluidity of their gender identities, transgender and gender-variant individuals pose an inherent challenge to traditional assumptions about "healthy" sexual and gender identity, and a key task for future research is to understand how their unique experiences with gender intersect with their experiences in sexually and emotionally intimate relationships. Of course, the notion that gender identity and sexual desire are fundamentally linked has a long history: In the 19th and early 20th centuries, it was widely believed that same-sex sexuality was caused by gender "inversion." This is no longer the current view, but the specific nature of links between gender and sexual identity remains to be fully understood. An individual's experience of same-sex and other-sex desire is necessarily connected to the social and interpersonal context of that individual's gender presentation and gendered experience, and changes in one domain necessarily shape the other in a dynamic and reciprocal fashion. Tracking such changes over time and across different social contexts and intimate relationships is a priority for future research.

CONCLUSION

Love, sex, and sexual orientation remain some of the most complex aspects of human experience, and our understanding of these domains has undergone radical changes over the past several decades, prompted by incisive scientific inquires that have uncovered previously hidden dynamics of these experiences among broader and increasingly diverse populations. Now that we have consistent evidence for "unconventional" experiences such as platonic romantic attachments, bisexuality, nonreproductive sexual practices, and longitudinal change in same-sex and other-sex desires, we can no longer afford to ignore these experiences. To the contrary, we must systematically integrate these phenomena into our own theorizing about love, sex, and gender. The next generation of research on these topics should continue to explore the intersecting dynamics of gender, intimacy, and eroticism as they shift across different cultural contexts and development epochs, reflecting the fundamental dynamism of human experience.

REFERENCES

APA Task Force on Appropriate Therapeutic Responses to Sexual Orientation. (2009). *Report of the task force on appropriate therapeutic responses to sexual orientation.* Washington, DC: American Psychological Association.

Basson, R. (2001). Using a different model for female sexual response to address women's problematic low sexual desire. *Journal of Sex & Marital Therapy, 27*(5), 395–403.

Beach, F. A. (1976). Sexual attractivity, proceptivity, and receptivity in female mammals. *Hormones and Behavior, 7,* 105–138.

Blackwood, E. (2000). Culture and women's sexualities. *Journal of Social Issues, 56*(2), 223–238.

Bowlby, J. (1982). *Attachment and loss: Vol. 1: Attachment* (2nd ed.). New York, NY: Basic Books.

Carter, C. S., & Keverne, E. B. (2002). The neurobiology of social affiliation and pair bonding. In J. Pfaff, A. P. Arnold, A. E. Etgen & S. E. Fahrbach (Eds.), *Hormones, brain and behavior* (Vol. 1, pp. 299–337). New York, NY: Academic Press.

Cass, V. (1990). The implications of homosexual identity formation for the Kinsey model and scale of sexual preference. In D. P. McWhirter, S. A. Sanders, & J. M. Reinisch (Eds.), *Homosexuality/heterosexuality: Concepts of sexual orientation* (pp. 239–266). New York, NY: Oxford University Press.

Chandra, A., Mosher, W. D., Copen, C., & Sionean, C. (2011). Sexual behavior, sexual attraction, and sexual identity in the United States: Data from the 2006–2008 National Survey of Family Growth. National Health Statistics Reports, March 3, 1–36.

Chivers, M. L., Rieger, G., Latty, E., & Bailey, J. M. (2004). A sex difference in the specificity of sexual arousal. *Psychological Science, 15,* 736–744.

Chivers, M. L., Seto, M. C., & Blanchard, R. (2007). Gender and sexual orientation differences in sexual response to sexual activities versus gender of actors in sexual films. *Journal of Personality and Social Psychology, 93*(6), 1108–1121.

Chivers, M. L., Seto, M. C., Lalumiere, M. L., Laan, E., & Grimbos, T. (2010). Agreement of self-reported and genital measures of sexual arousal in men and women: A meta-analysis. *Archives of Sexual Behavior, 39*(1), 5–56.

Curtis, T. J., & Wang, Z. (2003). The neurochemistry of pair bonding. *Current Directions in Psychological Science, 12*(2), 49–53.

de Graaf, H., & Rademakers, J. (2011). The psychological measurement of childhood sexual development in Western societies: Methodological challenges. *Journal of Sex Research, 48*(2–3), 118–129.

Diamond, L. M. (2003). What does sexual orientation orient? A biobehavioral model distinguishing romantic love and sexual desire. *Psychological Review, 110*, 173–192.

Diamond, L. M. (2007). A dynamical systems approach to female same-sex sexuality. *Perspectives on Psychological Science, 2*(2), 142–161.

Diamond, L. M. (2008a). Female bisexuality from adolescence to adulthood: Results from a 10 year longitudinal study. *Developmental Psychology, 44*, 5–14.

Diamond, L. M. (2008b). *Sexual fluidity: Understanding women's love and desire.* Cambridge, MA: Harvard University Press.

Diamond, L. M. (2012). The desire disorder in research on sexual orientation in women: Contributions of dynamical systems theory. *Archives of Sexual Behavior, 41*, 73–83.

Diamond, L. M. (2014). Gender and same-sex sexuality. In D. L. Tolman, L. M. Diamond, J. A. Bauermeister, W. H. George, J. G. Pfaus, & L. M. Ward (Eds.), *APA handbook of sexuality and psychology, Vol. 1: Person-based approaches.* (pp. 629–652). Washington, DC: American Psychological Association.

Diamond, L. M. (2016). Sexual fluidity in males and females. *Current Sexual Health Reports, 8*, 249.

Diamond, L. M., & Dickenson, J. A. (2012). The neuroimaging of love and desire: Review and future directions. *Clinical Neuropsychiatry, 9*(1), 39–46.

Ekins, R., & King, D. (1999). Towards a sociology of transgendered bodies. *The Sociological Review, 47*, 580–602.

Faderman, L. (1981). *Surpassing the love of men.* New York: William Morrow.

Fine, M. (1988). Sexuality, schooling, and adolescent females: The missing discourse of desire. *Harvard Educational Review, 58*(1), 29–53.

Gagné, P., Tewksbury, R., & McGaughey, D. (1997). Coming out and crossing over: Identity formation and proclamation in a transgender community. *Gender & Society, 11*(4), 478–508.

Golden, C. (1996). What's in a name? Sexual self-identification among women. In R. C. Savin-Williams & K. M. Cohen (Eds.), *The lives of lesbians, gays, and bisexuals: Children to adults* (pp. 229–249). Fort Worth, TX: Harcourt Brace.

Granic, I. (2005). Timing is everything: Developmental psychopathology from a dynamic systems perspective. *Developmental Review, 25*(3), 386–407.

Halberstam, J. (2005). *In a queer time and place: Transgender bodies, subcultural lives.* New York, NY: NYU Press.

Hazan, C., & Zeifman, D. (1994). Sex and the psychological tether. In D. Perlman & K. Bartholomew (Eds.), *Advances in personal relationships: A research annual* (Vol. 5, pp. 151–177). London, UK: Jessica Kingsley Publishers.

Hazan, C., & Zeifman, D. (1999). Pair-bonds as attachments: Evaluating the evidence. In J. Cassidy & P. R. Shaver (Eds.), *Handbook of attachment theory and research* (pp. 336–354). New York, NY: Guilford.

Kleinplatz, P. J., & Diamond, L. M. (2013). Sexual diversity. In D. L. Tolman & L. M. Diamond (Eds.), *APA handbook on psychology and sexuality* (pp. 245–267). Washington, DC: APA Press.

Lamb, S. (2013). Childhood sexuality. In D. L. Tolman & L. M. Diamond (Eds.), *APA handbook on psychology and sexuality* (pp. 415–432). Washington, DC: APA Press.

Lerum, K., & Dworkin, S. L. (2011). "Bad girls rule": An interdisciplinary feminist commentary on the report of the APA task force on the sexualization of girls. *Journal of Sex Research, 46*, 250–263.

McClintock, M. K., & Herdt, G. (1996). Rethinking puberty: The development of sexual attraction. *Current Directions in Psychological Science, 5*, 178–183.

Mellen, S. L. W. (1982). *The evolution of love*: San Francisco, CA: W.H. Freeman.

Mosher, W. D., Chandra, A., & Jones, J. (2005). Sexual behavior and selected health measures: Men and women 15-44 years of age, United States, 2002 (pp. 1–56). Advance data from vital and health statistics, no. 362. Hyattsville, MD: National Center for Health Statistics.

Ott, M. Q., Corliss, H. L., Wypij, D., Rosario, M., & Austin, S. B. (2011). Stability and change in self-reported sexual orientation identity in young people: Application of mobility metrics. *Archives of Sexual Behavior, 40*(3), 519–532.

Priebe, G., & Svedin, C. G. (2013). Operationalization of three dimensions of sexual orientation in a national survey of late adolescents. *Journal of Sex Research, 50*(8), 727–738.

Regan, P. C., & Berscheid, E. (1995). Gender differences in beliefs about the causes of male and female sexual desire. *Personal Relationships, 2*, 345–358.

Rich, A. (1980). Compulsory heterosexuality and lesbian existence. *Signs, 5*(4), 631–660.

Rieger, G., Bailey, J. M., & Chivers, M. L. (2005). Sexual arousal patterns of bisexual men. *Psychological Science, 16*, 579–584.

Roen, K. (2002). "Either/or" and "both/neither": Discursive tensions in transgender politics. *Signs, 27*(2), 501–522.

Ross, M. W., Daneback, K., & Månsson, S.-A. (2012). Fluid versus fixed: A new perspective on bisexuality as a fluid sexual orientation beyond gender. *Journal of Bisexuality, 12*(4), 449–460.

Rubin, G. (1984). Thinking sex: Notes for a radical theory of the politics of sexuality. In C. S. Vance (Ed.), *Pleasure and danger: Exploring female sexuality* (pp. 267–319). Boston, MA: Routledge and Kegan Paul.

Rust, P. C. R. (1993). Neutralizing the political threat of the marginal woman: Lesbians' beliefs about bisexual women. *Journal of Sex Research, 30*(3), 214–228.

Rust, P. C. R. (2000). Academic literature on situational homosexuality in the 1960s and 1970s. In P. C. R. Rust (Ed.), *Bisexuality in the United States: A reader and guide to the literature* (pp. 221–249). New York, NY: Columbia University Press.

Rust, P. C. R. (2000). *Bisexuality in the United States: A reader and guide to the literature*. New York, NY: Columbia University Press.

Savin-Williams, R. C., Joyner, K., & Rieger, G. (2012). Prevalence and stability of self-reported sexual orientation identity during young adulthood. *Archives of Sexual Behavior, 41*(1), 103–110.

Sell, R. L., & Petrulio, C. (1996). Sampling homosexuals, bisexuals, gays, and lesbians for public health research: A review of the literature from 1990 to 1992. *Journal of Homosexuality, 30*(4), 31–47.

Shaver, P. R., Hazan, C., & Bradshaw, D. (1988). Love as attachment: The integration of three behavioral systems. In J. Sternberg & M. L. Barnes (Eds.), *The psychology of love* (pp. 193–219). New Haven, CT: Yale University Press.

Suschinsky, K. D., Lalumiere, M. L., & Chivers, M. L. (2009). Sex differences in patterns of genital sexual arousal: Measurement artifacts or true phenomena? *Archives of Sexual Behavior, 38*(4), 559–573.

Tolman, D. L., & Diamond, L. M. (2001). Desegregating sexuality research: Combining cultural and biological perspectives on gender and desire. *Annual Review of Sex Research, 12*, 33–74.

van Anders, S. M. (2015). Beyond sexual orientation: Integrating gender/sex and diverse sexualities via sexual configurations theory. *Archives of Sexual Behavior, 44*(5), 1177–1213.

van Geert, P., & Steenbeek, H. (2005). Explaining after by before: Basic aspects of a dynamic systems approach to the study of development. *Developmental Review, 25*(3), 408–442.

Weinberg, M. S., Williams, C. J., & Pryor, D. W. (1994). *Dual attraction: Understanding bisexuality.* New York, NY: Oxford University Press.

Wells, J. E., McGee, M. A., & Beautrais, A. L. (2011). Multiple aspects of sexual orientation: Prevalence and sociodemographic correlates in a New Zealand National Survey. *Archives of Sexual Behavior, 40*(1), 155–168.

13

Integrating Evolutionary Affective Neuroscience and Feminism in Gender Research

LESLIE L. HEYWOOD AND JUSTIN R. GARCIA

For decades, feminist scholars have criticized theorizing rooted in the discipline of biology that "naturalized" (or "biologized"; Donaghue, 2015, Chapter 6, this volume) gendered phenomena. The concern has been with potential reductionism and determinism in dominant views of evolution, development, and neurophysiology—that is, implications that genetic bedrock or neural architecture creates sex differences, sharply limits flexibility in behavior, and explains, or even justifies, culturally structured gender inequalities. These feminist critiques took up the history and consequences of "nature versus nurture" thinking about gender, including the linkages in public discourse of "biology" with immutability and gender stereotypes, the incorporation of biological mechanisms into psychology, and the privileging of biological reductionism over cultural studies (Brescoll & LaFrance, 2004; Eagly & Wood, 2013b; Logan & Johnston, 2007).

Tensions between feminist and biological theories applied to human behavior generated extended debate (cf. Buss & Schmitt, 2011; Confer et al., 2010; Fine, 2010; Fisher, Garcia, & Sokol Chang, 2013; Gowaty, 1997; Heywood, 2013). The debate has been multifaceted, with threads focusing on, for instance, particular forms of evolutionary theorizing, the relationship between scholarly and popular discourses, and the relative appropriateness of scientific and humanistic methods of inquiry into human experience. Although many issues remain contentious, in recent years feminist researchers have been making a strong case for the integration of scientific insights into feminist paradigms. In "Feminism and Evolutionary Psychology: Moving Forward," feminist psychologists Alice Eagly and Wendy Wood (2013a) argue that:

> progress in research on gender requires a fundamental shift beyond the limitations that are now obvious in evolutionary psychology and classic feminist reasoning. We believe that a new theory is needed that departs significantly from these existing meta-perspectives. The evolutionary psychology assumptions are becoming untenable given conflicting data . . . Yet, classic feminist assumptions about the overriding importance of social environmental causation must integrate evolutionary processes in more complex models that account for biological, psychological, and social mediation of sex differences and similarities. (p. 553)

Theoretical innovations in evolution, development, and neuroscience point to ways of addressing long-standing tensions between scientific and feminist theory in a manner that honors and requires contributions from both. We have previously discussed the relevance and complementarity of the *extended evolutionary synthesis* to feminist theory (Garcia & Heywood, 2016), for instance, and reflect on it at the conclusion of this chapter. Here, we focus on the relevance and complementarity of *affective neuroscience* to feminist theory.

Recent developments in affective neuroscience represented by the work of Jaak Panksepp and Stephen W. Porges speak to how evolved mechanisms shared by all mammals, including humans, create a preconscious response to situational threat at the primary process level of basic emotion. This preconscious response in turn interacts with memory, cultural learning, and cognition to produce particular patterns that, when differentiated for gender, can demonstrate negative health outcomes. Here, we illustrate this interplay with the case of increasing rates of depression in teenaged girls in the contemporary United States (Mojtabai et al., 2016). To describe the way that particular cultural iterations of gender are internalized and inscribed at the neurophysiological level, there is clearly a need for feminist models that incorporate scientific research. Evolutionary affective neuroscience provides a strong framework for the case we examine here. Crucially for our argument, in a bidirectional circuit, "social environmental causation"—the nature of which can be elaborated from a feminist psychological and sociological perspective—triggers neurophysiological responses, and these in turn trigger affective responses which can be either positive or negative. An organism's affective response to its physical and social environments is an evolved capacity, and such adaptations are a central feature to evolutionary models of behavior stemming from strains such as behavioral ecology, cultural evolution, and social neuroscience. The neurophysiological responses to environments, if negative and ongoing, can contribute to a dysregulated depressive affect. The cultural catalyst → neurophysiological response → affective response chain that we trace helps provide an etiology that is consistent with both psychosocial arguments and the physiological mechanisms underlying human evolutionary biology and behavior. To Eagly's and Wood's (2013a) point that feminism needs to "integrate evolutionary processes . . . that account for biological, psychological, and social mediation of sex differences and similarities," we would suggest that integrative evolutionary neuroscience offers an account that, while not explicitly feminist, can be used productively in a feminist way.

Such an approach also lends itself to testable, and falsifiable, hypotheses. Here we provide a test case of how we can understand cultural inputs, neuroscience, and contemporary behavior from the integrated perspectives of both feminist psychology and evolutionary neurosciences. We

consider depression and its disproportionate incidence in women and
teenaged girls as compared with men and teenaged boys, at least in some
racial and ethnic groups, in Western high-income countries (Kuehner,
2017; Mojtabai et al., 2016).

At the same time that we investigate the disproportionate incidence of
depression in women and teenaged girls in Western high-income countries, we also acknowledge that "depression" is a remarkably slippery concept. The criteria for the psychiatric diagnosis of depression—which for
many can be quite severe and require medical and psychotherapeutic
intervention—have shifted over time, as have the everyday meanings of
the term (see Marecek, 2006). In North America and Europe, pharma-
ceutical companies have waged extensive marketing campaigns directed
to both physicians and the general public in order to boost sales of anti-
depressants (Whitaker & Cosgrove, 2015). These campaigns involve what
Monahan and Henry (2006) have called disease-mongering—that is,
expanding the range of experiences deemed to require treatment—as well
as assertions that depression is caused by "a chemical imbalance." At the
same time, some evolutionary scientists have argued that depression may
be an adaptive emotional response that can function to promote responsive changes in bodily systems, and they have likewise cautioned against
the overmedicalization of depression and questioned criteria for pharma-
cological treatment (Andrews & Thomson, 2009). Investigating cultural
inputs, therefore, requires researchers and clinicians to take into account
not only social stressors but also social meanings, such as what is recognized as an abnormal mood and what steps should be taken to rectify it.

We use the affective neuroscientific concept of "threat," which triggers
particular neurophysiological responses in everyone, in combination with
feminist analysis, to examine the contemporary cultural context of pervasive social media use, the "culture of confidence" (Gill & Orgad, 2015),
and the "pornification of everyday life" (Orenstein, 2016; Sales, 2016) as
environmental catalysts for neurophysiological responses that may lead
to increased rates of depression in teenaged girls (Mojtabai et al., 2016;
Steiner-Adair, 2013). These cultural trends may trigger the neurophysiological responses described by affective neuroscience, which are critical

if we wish to fully understand the health effects of social productions. In other words, engagement with social media and media culture more generally can be formulated as threatening in gendered ways. But *how* these things are a threat is explicable through feminist analysis.

Although not as immediately recognizable as a feminist tool, we will show how these recent developments in affective neuroscience, combined with a feminist perspective, offer precisely the kind of transdisciplinary interactionist model that Eagly and Wood (2013a; see also Wood & Eagly, 2012) call for that will "legitimately meld evolutionary and feminist perspectives and provide a model of human behavior that captures the cognitive and social capacities that enable human culture" (p. 554).

PRIMARY PROCESS AFFECTIVE SYSTEMS AND THE POLYVAGAL THEORY: AN INTRODUCTION AND LINKS TO DEPRESSIVE AFFECT

In "Psychology, Evolution, and the Traumatized Child," gender researcher Celia Roberts makes the case for the incorporation of an evolutionary neurophysiological theory also based in Porges's work into her feminist analysis. This integration of perspectives allows her to both explain the "persistence of behavioural and physiological patterns in neglected and abused children," and, more broadly, "new avenues for theorizing the entanglements of body, brain, and behaviour that are central to contemporary feminist thought" (Roberts, 2015, p. 377). We take a similar approach to integrating feminist theory with evolutionary affective neuroscience, using it, in this case, to help formulate an explanation for increased depression rates in adolescent girls.

A neurophysiological, affective approach to depression establishes the context for the cultural work that triggers its evolutionarily elaborated mechanisms. Psychobiologist Jaak Panksepp (1998, 2011) formulated depression as an elaborated response to the PANIC/GRIEF of separation anxiety that in turn leads to the failure of the basic motivational platform of the SEEKING system that manifests in depressive affect. Further,

the "brain-face-heart circuit" in psychophysiologist researcher Stephen
Porges's "Polyvagal Theory" (2009, 2011) is an evolved response to environmental contexts of threat or safety. The work of these affective neuroscientists provides evolutionary explanations of basic emotions and
brain structure and how and why they lead to, or fail to lead to, prosocial
engagement.

According to Panksepp (2009), there are seven basic brain systems at the
primary process level, located in subcortical brain regions, which humans
and other animals share. These systems include "SEEKING, FEAR, RAGE,
LUST, CARE, PANIC/GRIEF, and PLAY" (p. 1). Dopamine circuitry provides the mechanism through which all these complex cognitions eventually form. Dopamine is one contributing factor in a constellation that
includes electrochemical signals between neurons, neurochemical pathways, various emotions, and the brain and behavioral systems based on
those emotions. The behavioral patterns linked to those systems, such as
acquisition of "the material resources needed for bodily survival," are an
indissociable part of the "cognitive interests that bring positive existential
meanings into our lives" (Panksepp, 1998, p. 464).

Panksepp's capitalized designators for the systems he discusses are part
of his attempt to bridge neuroscience and psychology. As he explains,
"brain scientists are typically unwilling to use mentalistic words in discussing their empirical findings, and psychologists . . . are typically unable
to link the psychological concepts to brain functions . . . . Accordingly,
I use capitalized letters to highlight that I am focusing on certain necessary albeit not sufficient neural substrates for distinct types of emotional
processes" (1998, p. 90). In psychological terms, Panksepp works at the
primary-process level—the subcortical affective brain level instead of the
secondary process memory or emotional learning level, or the level of ter-
tiary process cognition. His research seeks to provide "a correct founda-
tional vision of how *primary process affects and emotion* are organized in
the brain, and how all of that relates to the massive cognitive plasticity of
the mammalian brain, especially the massive culture-induced plasticity
of the human brain" (2009, p. 3). Although the brain is made up of "core
executive networks for emotion" that are evolutionarily based "ancestral

tools for living" (p. 7), it also has an adaptive plasticity (changeability) that is, at the secondary process level, shaped by mechanisms of culture.

In particular, the "SEEKING" system is a catalyst for action. The brain contains a "foraging/exploration/investigation/curiosity/interest/expect-ancy/SEEKING system that leads organisms to eagerly pursue the fruits of their environment—from nuts to knowledge, so to speak" (1998, p. 104). It is important to Panksepp, according to whom these basic emotional circuits are shared by all mammals, including humans, that primary pro-cesses like SEEKING not be ignored or conflated with cognition because they "all figure heavily in the genesis of a variety of emotional or clinical disorders" (2009, p. 7).

The SEEKING system is what becomes suppressed in depression. According to Panksepp, "depression is intimately related to (1) sustained overactivity of the separation-distress PANIC/GRIEF system that can, if prolonged, lead to a downward cascade of psychological despair . . . and (2) the despair phase that follows the acute PANIC/GRIEF response which is characterized by abnormally low activity of the SEEKING sys-tem" (Panksepp & Watt, 2011, p. 5). Suppression of SEEKING is an impor-tant feature for an analysis of contemporary culture and its attendant effects. Extensive social media use, while ostensibly establishing prosocial connections, can actually lead to a sense of isolation and loneliness, so that "young adults with high social media use seem to feel more socially isolated than their counterparts with lower social media use" (Primack et al., 2017, p. 1). Panksepp linked social isolation to "overactivity of the separation-distress PANIC/GRIEF system" (Panksepp & Watt, 2011), which can be triggered by, for instance, people not responding to a given person's media posts, or, worse, by responding in negative or bullying ways. Because, as we develop further later, girls use social media more than boys and are more often the targets of bullying, Panksepp's under-standing of depression as a response to social isolation is important in explaining why depression rates have risen so quickly in the last few years among adolescent girls (Mojtabai et al., 2016).

Whereas Panksepp's work primarily concerns the subcortical regions of the central nervous system (CNS), and the SEEKING system is part of the initial CNS engagement that is directed toward environmental cues predictive of reward or danger, Porges's work examines how evolution has modified the structure of the autonomic nervous system (ANS) to specifically respond to these same environmental cues through a process he calls *neuroception*. Porges's polyvagal theory argues that in mammals, an individual's ANS response to environmental cues of safety or danger follows a phylogenetic hierarchy facilitated by neuroception: "a neural process, distinct from perception, that is capable of distinguishing environmental (and visceral) features that are safe, dangerous, or life-threatening" (Porges, 2009, p. 45). Porges identifies a "brain-face-heart circuit" in which an individual, through neuroception, reads cues of safety or danger in the faces of those around her/him, which has an effect on heart rate in particular but also on respiration and even more visceral features like digestion.

Neuroception precedes perception to influence body states, and the body states in turn trigger the primary process emotional circuits described by Panksepp. According to Porges, neuroception is an automatic, unconscious process that underlies any kind of engagement with the world outside of ourselves. Through neuroception, we interact with environmental contexts (and media use is an applicable context) with three neural circuits, in the following order:

1. The evolutionarily newest system, the social engagement system (SES), a parasympathetic neural circuit that is expressed in the newer myelinated vagus nerve (ventral vagal complex) that promotes prosocial behavior and helps maintain calm behavioral states. If we detect cues of safety, a vagal brake is applied that slows the heart rate and puts the body in "rest or digest" mode, and makes social engagement, cognition, and prosocial interaction with others possible.
2. If, however, we detect cues of danger, we react spontaneously with the evolutionarily older, sympathetic nervous system that supports fight/flight behaviors. This system mediates between the vagal circuit instrumental to the SES, and the older vagal circuit that initiates "freeze" responses.

3. If fight/flight fails, and we perceive ourselves to be in life-threatening conditions, we resort to this oldest vagal circuit, a parasympathetic circuit expressed in the unmyelinated vagus nerve that inhibits motion and is linked to disassociation in response to trauma—playing dead, and having an out-of-body sensation (Porges, 2009, 2011).

Responses start with the SES, but if real danger is sensed beyond that which a fight/flight response might address, we revert to the earliest evolved structural system characterized by the "freeze" response. Depression might be seen as an ongoing, chronic form of a freeze response, in which the individual withdraws from the world and ceases activity, thereby enacting an extended version of the "freeze."

In the next section we will use insights from feminist theory to establish the viability of a cultural context that, on unconscious levels, inculcates a "neuroception" of threat in teenaged girls in particular. This neuroception may initiate the third-level freeze response that Porges outlines, which in turn leads to the suppression of the SEEKING system; that suppression, in combination with the PANIC/GRIEF triggered by social isolation, can then be linked to the development of dysregulated affect. As Panksepp argued, sustained overactivity in the PANIC/GRIEF system in response to isolation causes "a downward cascade of psychological despair" that in turn triggers the "abnormally low activity of the SEEKING system," which is linked to depression (Panksepp & Watt, 2011, p. 5).

THE SOCIAL CONTEXT OF THREAT: DEPRESSION, SOCIAL MEDIA, AND TEENAGED GIRLS

Recently, psychiatrist Ramin Mojtabai and his colleagues (2016) questioned the degree to which rates of depression in US teens had increased over the past decade. They analyzed national data from interviews with more than 172,000 adolescents, finding that between 2005 and 2014, rates of depression showed a significant increase—an increase so robust that the results, if extrapolated to the general population of US adolescents, would show a half million more depressed adolescents in 2014 than in 2005. Fully three fourths of the depressed adolescents were girls. Mojtabai and his colleagues conclude that "the prevalence of depression in adolescents and young adults has increased in recent years" (p. 1), and they establish that:

> The trends in adolescents were different among boys and girls. This aligns with past studies that also found a larger increase in depressive symptoms in girls than boys in more recent years, and recent data on trends in suicide in the United States that identified a greater increase among adolescent girls and young women. Adolescent girls may have been exposed to a greater degree to depression risk factors in recent years. For example, cyberbullying may have increased more dramatically among girls than boys. As compared with adolescent boys, adolescent girls also now use mobile phones with texting applications more frequently and intensively and problematic mobile phone use among young people has been linked to depressed mood. (p. 6)

Although the authors begin to link the gender difference in depression rates to possible social factors, they conclude with the observation that "the causes of the observed trends remain elusive" (p. 6).

From a feminist perspective, the causes are perhaps not quite so "elusive." Psychologist Catherine Steiner-Adair, who has reviewed research on the effects of social media on sociality, relationships, and behavior (Steiner-Adair, 2013), said in an interview, "today's constant online connections—via texting, Facebook, Instagram, and Snapchat—can exacerbate that harsh focus on looks and other judgments from peers. The uptick in teen depression Mojtabai and colleagues found after 2011 could be evidence of that" (Neighmond, 2017). Furthermore, according to a 2015 study by the Pew Research Center, "aided by the convenience and constant access provided by mobile devices, especially smartphones, 92% of teens report going online daily—including 24% who say they go online 'almost constantly'" (Lenhart, 2015, p. 2). Girls use social media more extensively than boys: "teenage girls use social media sites and platforms—particularly visually-oriented ones—for sharing more than their male counterparts do. For their part, boys are more likely than girls to own gaming consoles and play video games" (Lenhart, 2015, p. 5). "Visually oriented" platforms include the ubiquity of the "sexy selfie" and girls' performative sexual self-productions via these means.

Recent research on sexting—the transmission of sexual images and messages via mobile phone or other electronic media—further supports these patterns. Using a national sample of single adults in the United States, Garcia and colleagues examined patterns of sharing of sexts (Garcia et al., 2016). The authors note that the primary risk for sexting is whether messages and images are shared, or trafficked, beyond the intended recipient; in the study, men were nearly twice as likely as women to share sexts. These issues may disproportionally affect young women who are highly engaged in social media use, in terms of the consequences of both sending and receiving sexual images as part of their expected interpersonal social media lives. The authors conclude that:

> we found that women were disproportionately concerned about how sexting could negatively impact their reputation, career, self-esteem, and current relationships and friendships. In a social context of persistent sexual double standards, women's concerns about being perceived as sexually hyperactive and indiscriminating, and the consequences of such stigmatization (Conley et al., 2013; Crawford & Popp, 2003 [both as cited by Garcia et al., 2016]), could explain their elevated concern. (p. 434)

A 2007 study commissioned by the American Psychological Association, "Report of the APA Task Force on the Sexualization of Girls," documents evidence of another link in the causal chain from a social environment saturated with sexualized social media to increased depression rates. The authors write that the research "links sexualization with three of the most common mental health problems of girls and women: eating disorders, low

self-esteem, and depression or depressed mood" (p. 23). They further argue
that "perhaps the most insidious consequence of self-objectification is that
it fragments consciousness. Chronic attention to physical appearance
leaves fewer cognitive resources available for other mental and physical
activities" (p. 21). In other words, if a girl focuses on appearance in order to
facilitate social acceptance and strengthen her social bonds, she has much
less mental energy to devote to coursework, extracurricular activities, or
other types of close relationships. Thus, sexualized self-making and sharing
through social media *becomes* her extracurricular activity. The APA Task
Force account of the pervasiveness of sexualization and sexualized self-
production and its attendant effects, along with the Pew Research study
that establishes the pervasiveness of this kind of activity (Lenhart, 2015),
might help explain the increased depression rates in teenaged girls documented by Motjabai et al. (2016), especially when combined with insights
concerning neurophysiological responses to threat.

Depression has long been empirically linked to gender. In an earlier review article of the clinical literatures, for instance, Piccinelli and
Wilkinson (2000) write "with few exceptions, the prevalence, incidence
and morbidity risk of depressive disorders are higher in females than in
males, beginning at mid-puberty and persisting through adult life" (p. 486).
The authors attribute this fact to "adverse experiences in childhood,
depression and anxiety disorders in childhood and adolescence, sociocultural roles with related adverse experiences, and psychological attributes related to vulnerability to life events and coping skills are likely to be
involved" (p. 486). More recent studies document a continuing gender gap
in depression rates, wherein "women are about twice as likely as men to
develop depression during their lifetime" (Kuehner, 2017, p. 146). Kuehner
links the prevalence gap to "the gender-related subtype of depression, of
which the developmental subtype has the strongest potential to contribute
to the gender gap" (p. 146), highlighting the importance of adolescence
in the gender gap question. However, she also writes, "limited evidence
exists for risk factors to be specifically linked" (p. 146). Her work shows
that not much has changed in the last two decades, when Piccinelli and
Wilkinson's (2000) literature review noted that "determinants of gender

differences in depressive disorders are far from being established and their combination into integrated etiological models continues to be lacking" (p. 486).

We argue that a neuroscience perspective informed by feminist theory that elucidates particular cultural trends can address this lack. On the one hand, porn production and consumption have been normalized in contemporary US culture. Feminist theorist Laura Garcia-Favaro, for instance, describes "the 'sexualization' of culture, where aesthetics, scripts, and values borrowed from pornography not only suffuse the media but have entered the everyday, together with a reassertion—and revalorization—of ideas about 'natural' sexual difference grounded in a heteronormative framing of gender complementarity" (p. 367). She finds that popular evolutionary discourses about sexual difference are reified in the user-generated content of women's online magazines in Spain and the United Kingdom, where women who expressed distress in relation to their (heterosexual) partners' consumption of pornography were routinely met with hostile, double-edged responses: Porn consumption was naturalized through comments such as "all blokes watch porn, it's a fact of life" (Garcia-Favaro, 2015, p. 368). The women's comments on the thread were "repeatedly interpreted as rooted in ignorance about the 'fact' that 'men are programmed differently to women,' and that 'their minds work in different ways'" (p. 368). That "difference" was then used to both normalize and naturalize porn consumption and to exhort women to construct themselves to look and perform like porn stars so as to "keep" their men.

Garcia-Favro quotes respondents who claim their views are based in science. In this group of respondents, porn and its messages (the normalization of male dominance and sexual violence against women) are articulated culturally as a scientific "fact." This particular claim is an example of what gender researcher Ngaire Donaghue points to as biologism in the discourses of sexual difference (Donaghue, 2015; Chapter 6, this volume). In this way, not only are the views of commentators on women's objections to and concerns about porn normalized, they are given a "truth-value" by the "science" of popularized notions of evolutionary psychology. In this way, the commentators both discredit and dismiss the women's concerns.

Importantly, these accounts of "male nature" leave out the prosocial side of human nature studied by evolutionary theorists in several disciplines, expressed, for example, as cooperation (e.g., Hrdy, 2009; Jordan, Hoffman, Nowak, & Rand, 2016), attachment (e.g., Bard, 2016; Carter et al., 2005), altruism (e.g., Brase, 2017; Wilson, 2016), and enduring romantic bonds (e.g., Fisher, 2016; Gray & Garcia, 2013). These prosocial behaviors provide evolutionarily informed hypotheses that are focused not on men's purported interest in low-investment sex but rather on the high degree of overlap between sexes/genders with regard to interest in developing and maintaining mutually reinforcing close relationships.

In tandem with the naturalization of porn consumption for men, Garcia-Favro identifies a second strain of response that argues that given the "reality" of how men are believed to monolithically be, the women who posted complaints about porn were then exhorted to "work on yourself" and make themselves into what can be described as porn star surrogates:

in addition to having more sex, elements of the compulsory sexual labor for women in relationships include performing a striptease, experimenting with sex toy's and costumes, and producing "sexy selfies" . . . exhort[ations] to "watch porn with him" and engage in the activities depicted in the material, together with whatever else men might want. (p. 373)

Garcia-Favro contextualizes this online discussion in a "postfeminist moment where gender polarity has not only been re-naturalised but also re-*eroticized*, and where pornography has not only been mainstreamed but also rebranded as liberating, chic, 'cool' for women" (pp. 373–374). Indeed, as journalist Nancy Jo Sales documents in her work on young women, media culture, and porn, "liking porn has become a trait associated with girls and women who are seen as cool and fashionable" (Sales, 2016, p. 38).

This aspect of media culture would not in itself be an issue if porn did not take the particular forms that it so often takes: "rape and gang rape are common scenarios in online porn . . . [W]omen are 'pounded,' 'railed,' and 'jack-hammered'. . . choking, slapping, and 'cum shots to the face' are standard moves" (Sales, p. 15). Although porn could ostensibly take many forms—say, in journalist Peggy Orenstein's words, "natural-looking people engaging in sex that is consensual, mutually pleasurable, and realistic," that is not, she writes, "what the $97 billion dollar global porn industry is shilling. Its producers have only one goal: to get men off hard and fast for profit. The most efficient way to do so appears to be by eroticizing the degradation of women" (Orenstein, 2016, pp. 27–28).

Debates in a variety of academic literatures continue regarding the influence of pornography (Ley, 2016; Orenstein, 2016; Tarrant, 2016), including whether feminist pornography can be actualized (e.g., Taormino, Shimizu, Penley, & Miller-Young, 2013). Here we are speaking specifically to what many consider the more misogynistic and violent forms of pornography. Consumption of this form of pornography likely bestows psychosocial effects on individuals and couples and, while pleasurable to some, is reaffirmation of sexuality as a space of female degradation and male authority, rather than one of mutual respect and reciprocal eroticism. Thus, it is this particular form of androcentric violent pornography that is likely then internalized and particularly problematic when teenagers are looking for guidance as to "how sex works." Because this form is what is most prevalent and easily accessed, "for many teenagers, porn seems to have become a form of sex ed[ucation]" (Sales, p. 16), and this form of sex education naturalizes both male dominance and violence as "facts of life" to which girls and women should habituate themselves and construct themselves toward. This has the effect of elevating, in Garcia-Favaro's (2015) words, "an unjust and injurious sexual regime th[at] disciplines women while privileging men. Ultimately, it establishes a brutally alienating framework for intimate relationality—and, indeed, human sociality" (p. 374).

Although researchers and pundits have long argued whether pornography use is associated with particular behaviors and attitudes, consensus seems to be building around problems with particular types of pornography. A recent meta-analysis by communication scientist Paul Wright and colleagues assessed a key question in this debate, the relationships between pornography consumption and committing actual acts of sexual aggression (Wright, Tokunaga, & Kraus, 2016). The meta-analysis, which included 22 general population studies from seven different countries using diverse research methods, found that pornography consumption was associated with sexual aggression among both men and women. Moreover, the authors suggest that "violent content may be an exacerbating effect" (p. 183). The authors conclude that:

> As with all behavior, sexual aggression is caused by a confluence of factors and many pornography consumers are not sexually aggressive. However, the accumulated data leave little doubt that, on the average, individuals who consume pornography more frequently are more likely to hold attitudes conducive to sexual aggression and engage in actual acts of sexual aggression than individuals who do not consume pornography or who consume pornography less frequently. (p. 201)

It is quite possible that the androcentric and violent scripts that characterize pornography are not only enacted by men and women in their own social lives, including sexual encounters and relationships, but they also become embodied, leading to physiological states that further endorse particular gender roles, both for those producing and those receiving such messages.

These findings, along with the work on the effects of sexualization and the normalization of gendered, pornographic, scripts, begin to elucidate a cultural context that could, on the level of neuroception, be perceived by many girls and young women as a threat, thereby leading to the dysregulation of affect that Porges and Panksepp outline. Knowledge of the neurophysiological mechanisms that underlie emotional response provides crucial insights for an integrated etiological model of depression in girls. Both the particular forms that contemporary pornography can take—the normalization of sexualized violence—and the particular forms that social media takes—SnapChat, Instagram, and related platforms for the production and consumption of "selfies"—assures that "many children experience the world as a never ending series of photo shoots, for public consumption" (Sales, 2016, p. 32). Crucially, those photo shoots are constructed within the context of a culture "permeated by a porn aesthetic" (Sales, 2016, p. 40). That aesthetic is linked to the normalization of violence directed toward women, and it is the aesthetic image girls model themselves upon in pervasive online interactions where they post sexualized shots of themselves for the reactions of their peers. This creates a day-to-day context in which one is judged more by one's peers than ever before. It is likely that self-sexualization in the context of pervasive judgment could be internalized—at the unconscious level of neuroception that is evolutionarily adapted to respond to cues of danger—as threatening.

Feminist theorists Rosalind Gill's and Shani Orgad's work adds another level of complication to this analysis, which helps make further sense of the way contemporary culture may function as a threatening environment to girls and women that in turn may serve to activate neural systems related to survival and dysregulated emotion. In their description of the contemporary "culture of confidence," *not only* are girls required to produce themselves as hypersexualized images, but this production is linked to the current preoccupation with girls' self-esteem. From the "lean in" culture of the workplace to the "love your body" discourses in popular media and public health, for girls and women, they argue, "to be self-confident is the new imperative of our time . . . exhortations to confidence are everywhere in education, in public health, in consumer culture, in a blaze of hashtags promoting female self-esteem, self-belief, and positive self-regard" (Gill & Orgad, 2015, p. 324).

Yet the ubiquitous apps and strategies offered to boost self-esteem fail to ask *why* girls and women are seemingly so deficient in this area, making the mission an individualized project of self-fashioning that places all the responsibility for said deficiencies on the individual girl. Much like the girl power and pro-sport discourses analyzed by gender researchers in the 2000s (Harris, 2004; Heywood, 2007), the "power" that girls were exhorted to access was one of self-construction and "choice" linked to the consumption of consumer goods and self-fashioning in the service of particular norms. Insidiously, with the advent of social media and technologies like smartphones in the century's second decade, constructing oneself through the use of codes derived from porn is one of the primary avenues to "confidence" offered to girls and women.

As Gill and Orgad (2015) write, "these internally focused and individualized strategies of psychic labor go hand in hand with a turning away from any account of structural inequalities or of the way in which contemporary culture may impact upon women's sense of self" (p. 333)—a culture that, in fact, "produces self-doubt, lack of confidence, shame and insecurity" (p. 339). The "culture of confidence" *seems* to be feminist in its emphasis on women's development of confidence, but it works by "denying and discrediting women's experiences" (p. 340) and placing the blame for any negative response to such experiences on them. It does so precisely by triggering the neural mechanisms that prompt survival responses and primary process responses that, when chronically triggered, result in dysregulated affects like depression. This creates a vicious circle wherein the social context of threat produces depression. The "culture of confidence" then tries to address this depression by blaming girls for their own lack of confidence. This blame invalidates the neurophysiological responses that are a valid reaction to a cultural context that devalues them on some very deep levels while seeming to elevate and care for them on others. In the context of the "brutally alienating framework for intimate relationality— and, indeed, human sociality" (Garcia-Favaro, 2015, p. 374) supported by the normalization of porn, a depressed affective response does not reflect some individual failure or flaw; it demonstrates a deep understanding of one's environment as threatening.

Depression researchers have yet to fully explore the way in which contemporary culture may impact upon a woman's sense of self, perhaps because medical/scientific literatures have up to this point remained largely separate from cultural analyses like those found in a feminist psychological and sociological approach. We argue that a transdisciplinary interactionist model allows for an integrative way of addressing how culture might impact a woman's "sense of self" on the neurophysiological level. As the work of Panksepp and Porges demonstrates, if one lives in a perpetual context of threat, one's affect will become dysregulated, with a number of consequences for relationships and health.

FUTURE DIRECTIONS

The current chapter focused on two particular models of evolutionary affective neuroscience, but there are other models of primary process affects and emotion (e.g., Barrett, 2017) that also lend themselves to integrative analyses. Our main point is that an understanding of the evolved neurophysiological mechanisms of emotion, along with the analysis of social environment informed by feminist theory, goes a long way toward explaining the increased prevalence of depression in girls that has baffled researchers focused on either the biological mechanisms or the social contexts rather than on the ways each of these informs the other.

The *extended evolutionary synthesis* (EES) is an emerging metatheoretical framework that further suggests new avenues of transdisciplinary integration in gender studies (Garcia & Heywood, 2016). EES emphasizes evolutionary processes that are less incremental and occur on time scales far shorter than traditionally have been considered ("fast evolution"). It also emphasizes the role of selective pressure on development-regulating processes ("EvoDevo"), context-dependent gene expression (epigenetics), neuroplasticity, and the existence of inheritance mechanisms in addition to natural selection (Jablonka & Lamb, 2006; Pigliucci & Muller, 2010; see also Gowaty, Chapter 4, this volume). The emphasis in EES on the potential for rapid transgenerational change, situational contingency, and changeability makes it inherently nonreductionistic and, therefore, particularly well suited to integration with a feminist analysis of culture and power (Garcia & Heywood, 2016).

Here, we use our case study of depressive affect to briefly illustrate how an understanding of evolutionary biology rooted in EES, affective neuroscience, and feminist theory might be integrated. Feminist analyses of media sexual socialization make important contributions to understanding ways in which humans create, maintain, or contest their own cultural environments—in EES terms, *human niche construction*. Gene expression across the life span is increasingly understood as a probabilistic, context-dependent *epigenetic* process. Feminist theory obviously provides a valuable lens on the socially structured contexts in which the expression of gene-linked depression may be gendered (gender x gene x environ-ment interactions; Salk & Hyde, 2012). Neuroplasticity is understood to be another mechanism by which many animals engage complex social ecologies. In articulating the mission of the new field of *cultural neuro-science*, Shinobu Kitayama and Jiyoung Park (2010) describe how *neural connectivity* is altered not by passive exposure to culture but rather by the embodied enactment of cultural ideologies and practices, the effects of which shape and depend on identity. That very neuroplasticity, and with it the ability for social and cultural experience to become embodied, is itself an evolved biological capability (Campbell & Garcia, 2009). For exam-ple, research on the role of cortical connectivity during adolescence in depression (Lichenstein, Verstynen, & Forbes, 2016) can be located within the EvoDevo framework, highlighting developmental experience and the resulting trajectory. Feminist insights into the normalization of pornogra-phy and its relation to self-sexualization among teenage girls can speak to how culture is (re)inscribed in brain function and behavior.

Many more such complex topics await transdisciplinary integrative approaches to gender and sexuality. We argue that these approaches are not reductionistic, instead invoking recursive processes across multiple levels of organization. They are *new materialisms* (Frost, 2014) that both "denaturalize" nature (by interrogating how naturalness is culturally con-structed and deployed) and "deculturize" culture (by examining the role of the prediscursive body in social relations). In so doing, this project takes seriously the dynamic interplays of human evolution, material bodies and physiology, feminist theory, social environments, and the cultural repre-sentations and performances of gender.

REFERENCES

American Psychological Association, Task Force on the Sexualization of Girls. (2007). *Report of the APA Task Force on the Sexualization of Girls*. Retrieved from http://www.apa.org/pi/women/programs/girls/report-full.pdf

Andrews, P. W., & Thomson, J. A. (2009). The bright side of being blue: Depression as an adaptation for analyzing complex problems. *Psychological Review, 116*, 620–654.

Bard, K. A. (2017). Dyadic interactions, attachment and the presence of triadic interactions in chimpanzees and humans. *Infant Behavior & Developmen, 48,* 13–19.

Barrett, L. F. (2017. *How emotions are made: The secret life of the brain.* New York, NY: Houghton Mifflin Harcourt.

Brase, G. L. (2017, January 26). Emotional reactions to conditional rules of reciprocal altruism. *Evolutionary Behavioral Sciences.* Advance online publication.

Brescoll, V., & LaFrance, M. (2004). The correlates and consequences of newspaper reports of research on sex differences. *Psychological Science, 15,* 515–520.

Buss, D. M., & Schmitt, D. P. (2011). Evolutionary psychology and feminism. *Sex Roles, 64,* 768–787.

Campbell, B. C., & Garcia, J. R. (2009). Neuroanthropology: Evolution and emotional embodiment. *Frontiers in Evolutionary Neuroscience, 1*(4), 1–6.

Carter, C. S., Ahnert, L., Grossmann, K. E., Hrdy, S. B., Lamb, M. E., Porges, S. W., & Sachser, N. (2005). *Attachment and bonding: A new synthesis.* Cambridge, MA: MIT Press.

Confer, J. C., Easton, J. A., Fleischman, D. S., Goetz, C. D., Lewis, D. M., Perilloux, C., & Buss, D. M. (2010). Evolutionary psychology. Controversies, questions, prospects, and limitations. *American Psychologist, 65*(2), 110–126.

Donaghue, N. (2015). The "facts" of life? *Australian Feminist Studies, 30*(86), 359–365.

Eagly, A. H., & Wood, W. (2013a). Feminism and evolutionary psychology: Moving forward. *Sex Roles, 69,* 549–556.

Eagly, A. H., & Wood, W. (2013b). The nature-nurture debates: 25 years of challenges in understanding the psychology of gender. *Perspectives in Psychological Science, 8*(3), 340–357.

Fine, C. (2010). *Delusions of gender: How our minds, society, and neurosexism create difference.* New York, NY: Norton.

Fisher, H. (2016). *Anatomy of love: A natural history of mating, marriage, and why we stray* (2nd ed.). New York, NY: W.W. Norton.

Fisher, M. L., Garcia, J. R., & Sokol Chang, R. (Eds.) (2013) *Evolution's empress: Darwinian perspectives on the nature of women.* New York, NY: Oxford.

Frost, S. (2014). Re-considering the turn to biology in feminist theory. *Feminist Theory, 15*(3), 307–326.

Garcia, J. R., Gesselman, A. N., Siliman, S. A., Perry, B. L., Coe, K., & Fisher, H. E. (2016). Sexting among singles in the USA: Prevalence of sending, receiving, and sharing sexual messages and images. *Sexual Health, 13*(5), 428–435.

Garcia, J. R., & Heywood, L. (2016). Moving toward integrative feminist evolutionary behavioral sciences. *Feminism and Psychology, 26*(3), 327–334.

Garcia-Favaro, L. (2015). Porn trouble. *Australian Feminist Studies, 30*(86), 366–376.

Gill, R., & Orgad, S. (2015). The confidence cult(ure). *Australian Feminist Studies, 30*(86), 324–344.

Gowaty, P. A. (Ed.) (1997). *Feminism and evolutionary biology: Boundaries, intersections and frontiers.* New York, NY: Chapman & Hall.

Gray, P. B., & Garcia, J. R. (2013). *Evolution and human sexual behavior.* Cambridge, MA: Harvard University Press.

Harris, A. (2004). *Future girl: Young women in the 21st century.* New York, NY: Routledge.

Heywood, L. (2013). The quick and the dead: Gendered agency in the history of western science and evolutionary theory. In M. L. Fisher, J. R. Garcia, & R. Sokol-Chang (Eds.), *Evolution's empress: Darwinian perspectives on the nature of women* (pp. 439–460). New York, NY: Oxford.

Heywood, L. (2007). Producing girls: Empire, sport, and the neoliberal body. In J. Hargreaves & P. Vertinsky (Eds.), *Physical culture, power, and the body* (pp. 100–120). New York, NY: Routledge.

Hrdy, S. B. (2009). *Mothers and others: The evolutionary origins of mutual understanding.* Cambridge, MA: Belknap Press.

Jablonka, E., & Lamb, M. J. (2006) *Evolution in four dimensions: Genetic, epigenetic, behavioral, and symbolic variation in the history of life.* Cambridge, MA: MIT Press.

Jordan, J., Hoffman, M., Nowak, M. A., & Rand, D. G. (2016). Uncalculating cooperation is used to signal trustworthiness. *PNAS Proceedings of the National Academy of Sciences of the United States of America, 113*(31), 8658–8663.

Kitayama, S., & Park, J. (2010). Cultural neuroscience of the self: Understanding the social grounding of the brain. *Social Cognition and Affective Neuroscience, 5,* 111–129.

Kuehner, C. (2017). Why is depression more common among women than among men? *The Lancet Psychiatry, 4*(2), 146–158.

Lenhart, A. (April 2015). Teens, social media, and technology: Overview 2015. Pew Research Center: 1–47.

Ley, D. J. (2016). *Ethical porn for dicks: A man's guide to responsible viewing pleasure.* Berkeley, CA: ThreeL Media.

Lichenstein, S. D., Verstynen, T., & Forbes, E. E. (2016). Adolescent brain development and depression: A case for the importance of connectivity of the anterior cingulate cortex. *Neuroscience and Biobehavioral Reviews, 70,* 271–287.

Logan, C. A., & Johnston, T. D. (2007). Synthesis and separation in the history of "nature" and "nurture." *Developmental Psychobiology, 49*(8), 758–769.

Marecek, J. (2006). Social suffering, gender, and women's depression. In C. Keyes and S. Goodman (Eds.), *Handbook of research on women and depression* (pp. 283–308). New York, NY: Cambridge University Press.

Mojtabai, R., Olfson, M., & Han, B. (2016). National trends in the prevalence and treatment of depression in adolescents and young adults. *Pediatrics, 138*(6), e 20161878.

Monahan, R., & Henry, D. (2006) The fight against disease mongering: Generating knowledge for action. *PLoS Medicine, 3*(4), e191.

Neighmond, P. (2017). Depression strikes today's teen girls especially hard. http://www.npr.org/sections/health-shots/2017/02/13/514353285/depression-strikes-todays-teen-girls-especially-hard

Orenstein, P. (2016) *Girls and sex: Navigating the complicated new landscape.* New York, NY: Harper Collins.

Panksepp, J. (1998). *Affective neuroscience: The foundations of human and animal emotions.* New York, NY: Oxford University Press.

Panksepp, J. (2009) Brain emotional systems and qualities of mental life: From animal models of affect to implications for psychotherapeutics. In D. Fosha, D. J. Siegel, & M. Solomon (Eds.), *The healing power of emotion: Affective neuroscience, development, and clinical practice* (pp. 1–26). New York, NY: Norton.

Panksepp, J., & Watt, D. (2011). Why does depression hurt? Ancestral primary-process separation distress (PANIC/GRIEF) and diminished brain reward (SEEKING) processes in the genesis of depressive affect. *Psychiatry, 74*(1), 5–13.

Piccinelli, M., & Wilkinson, G. (2000). Gender differences in depression: A critical review. *The British Journal of Psychiatry, 177*(6), 486–492.

Pigliucci, M., & Muller, G. B. (2010). *Evolution: The extended synthesis.* Cambridge, MA: MIT Press.

Porges, S. W. (2009). Reciprocal influences between body and brain in the perception and expression of affect. In D. Fosha, D. J. Siegel, & M. Solomon (Eds.), *The healing power of emotions: Affective neuroscience, development, and clinical practice* (pp. 27–54). New York, NY: Norton.

Porges, S. W. (2011). *The polyvagal theory: Neurophysiological foundations of emotions, attachment, communication, and self-regulation.* New York, NY: Norton.

Primack, B. et al. (2017). Social media use and perceived social isolation among young adults in the U.S. *American Journal of Preventive Medicine. 53*, 1–8.

Roberts, C. (2015) Psychology, evolution, and the traumatised child. *Australian Feminist Studies, 30*(86), 377–385.

Sales, N. J. (2016). *American girls: Social media and the secret lives of teenagers.* New York, NY: Knopf.

Salk, R. H., & Hyde, J. S. (2012). Contemporary genetics for gender researchers: Not your grandma's genetics anymore. *Psychology of Women Quarterly, 36*(4), 395–410.

Steiner-Adair, C. (2013). *The big disconnect: Protecting childhood and family relationships in the digital age.* New York, NY: Harper.

Taormino, T., Penley, C., Shimizu, C. P., & Miller-Young, M. (2013). *The feminist porn book: The politics of producing pleasure.* New York, NY: The Feminist Press at CUNY.

Tarrant, S. (2016). *The pornography industry: What everyone needs to know.* New York, NY: Oxford University Press.

Whitaker, R., & Cosgrove, L. (2015). *Psychiatry under the influence: Institutional corruption, social injury, and prescriptions for reform.* New York, NY: Palgrave Macmillan.

Wilson, D. S. (2016). *Does altruism exist? Culture, genes, and the welfare of others.* New Haven, CT: Yale University Press.

Wood, W., & Eagly, A. H. (2012). Biosocial construction of sex differences and similarities in behavior. In J. M. Olson & M. P. Zanna (Eds.), *Advances in experimental social psychology* (Vol. 46, pp. 55–123). London, England: Elsevier.

Wright, P. J., Tokunaga, R. S., & Kraus, A. (2016). A meta-analysis of pornography consumption and actual acts of sexual aggression in general population studies. *Journal of Communication, 66*, 183–205.

Categories, Gender, and Development

A Feminist Perspective

ELLIN K. SCHOLNICK AND PATRICIA H. MILLER

What is gender? In the past the simple answer was a dichotomy marking individuals as belonging to one of two gender categories, male or female. Developmentalists viewed gender development as learning which group one belonged to and what behaviors were associated with each group. A typical chapter on gender development would focus on delineation of the components of gender such as sex differences and debates about the origin of those differences. It would present accounts of the development of a gender identity as a male or a female as well as the consequences of personal gender identity throughout the life span. This chapter takes a different tack by contending that those scientific accounts of the study of gender are themselves a product of a gender *system* and its associated biases. How we think about gender categories is the product of implicit biases in the way we think. These biases arise from the gendered organization of society, the unequal allocation of power to various social locations (e.g., race, social class), and cultural beliefs about gender. Our gender biases pop up everywhere, even in unexpected places. Here, we will make a distinction between gender categories like male or female and a gender system that provides the meaning and evaluation of gender categories and their properties. This chapter explores two unexpected places: our definitions of categorical thinking—one of the tools for defining gender categories—and our accounts of human development.

The claim that gender biases are everywhere should not be surprising. Courses in abnormal psychology may lead students to consider that the definitions and boundaries of the normal and abnormal reflect cultural norms for behavior and the opportunities and constraints provided to individuals in different social locations. What is normal in one society may be considered inappropriate in another. It is not a great leap to question whether definitions of maturity, the pinnacle of "normal" development, also reflect sociocultural norms that include definitions of gender and gender categories. An important facet of human development is an increasing understanding of what it means to belong to a specific gender category and what membership in that category entails. We will argue that a society's definition of categories creates biases—toward a particular depiction of development and a binary gender category system. A different conception of categories of development and gender would change our understanding of development in general and would provide a different framework for exploring how gender categories and gender roles arise. Before developing this argument, it first is necessary to summarize some basic developmental themes and then Piaget's theory of development.

DEVELOPMENTAL PSYCHOLOGY AND PIAGET

The field of developmental psychology encompasses the study of change from conception onward. The disparity between the wide range and complexity of abilities and beliefs that adults possess and the repertoire of a newborn raises the question of how an individual gets from infancy to adulthood. What paths do individuals travel to reach the adult state and what factors shape those paths? With such a broad scope of inquiry, the choice of topics to study is enormous. Our central thesis is that this choice often is determined explicitly by theory and implicitly by politics. Piaget's theory can serve as an example of how researchers in Western high-income countries have constructed a selective framework for thinking about development and for describing the child's developmental path. We will then propose how this framework with its conceptual blinders influenced current concepts of gender and its development.

Piaget and Epistemology (Study of Knowledge)

The Swiss psychologist Jean Piaget (1970) has been one of the most influential theorists and investigators of children's development, especially the development of thinking. Early in his career, he was a member of Binet's laboratory, helping to develop IQ tests. He worked at a time when development was often defined by age, such as the "terrible twos." Often accounts of change lacked a strong theoretical connection between what happened at one age and what transpired at the next. Piaget introduced a range of tasks to study as indices of development and constructed an all-encompassing theory of what and how change occurs.

The particular choices Piaget made have been enormously influential in highlighting the importance of cognitive growth and defining its properties. The person whose developmental path Piaget tracked grows up to be an everyday epistemologist. Epistemologists are philosophers who offer an account of the nature and structure of different forms of knowledge, such as categories or if-then statements (e.g., "If a shape has four equal sides that meet at right angles, it is a square"). So when a child constructs knowledge for forming categories of colors, shapes, and types of animals, the child's knowledge is based on a set of rules the child has constructed that define what a category is. Piaget's theory and research traced the child's construction of the Western principles of logic, mathematics, and physics that we in Western societies consider to be the basis of rationality. He used these principles to provide a unifying frame that integrated all the changes that occur throughout childhood and adolescence and how the changes occurred. Piaget was tracing the emergence and growth of a little philosopher who used emerging consciousness of the methods of a scientific researcher and a logician to construct a view of the world.

Piaget and Universal Logic

This approach introduces a bias that deemphasizes variations in social experience and context. Its focus immediately narrows perspectives because logic and scientific thinking are assumed to be abstract, universal, and objective. For example, 2 + 2 = 4, no matter what is counted or who does the addition. Logical, mathematical, and scientific thinking leave out the question of "who" is thinking, because if logic and mathematics are universal, the gender, race, ethnicity, social class, nationality, and sexual orientation of the reasoner do not matter. The search for universal truths and general laws ignores the particularities of the social position of the individual seeking these laws and truths. It does not matter whether an individual had the opportunity to play with an abacus or use coins because the rules of addition are the same for everyone. Especially in the case of logic and mathematics, the methods of thinking are considered universally applicable across diverse contents and contexts. It does not matter what you count or where, 3 cents + 1 cent, 3 apples + 1 apple, 3 days + 1 day = 4. But do these methods of thinking about physics or mathematics also fit the study of social beings living in social structures? Scientific thinking privileges one way of discerning truth—through logic—and its nature leads to paying less attention to the conditions that have restricted certain groups' access to participation in the scientific enterprise. A more diverse scientific community might lead to more diverse perspectives on the choice of topics to be studied and explained (e.g., Rosser, 2012). Cognitive developmentalists' emphasis on logical thinking, inherited from Piaget, is fertile ground for critiques that argue instead that knowledge and ways of thought are socially situated and context dependent (Burman, 2008; Code, 2000; Lloyd, 1984; Walkerdine, 1988; see also Chapter 1).

In short, Piaget's theory of cognitive development contains a series of interconnected biases. It is a theory of the development of abstract logical and scientific thinking, not a theory of a socioemotional being living in a particular social structure. Additionally, Piaget based his ideas about the nature of developmental change exclusively on logical, mathematical, and scientific concepts, rules, and mechanisms. This chapter focuses on the set of rules underlying category logic, a key element in discussions of gender categories. Piaget's account of the growth of understanding of the logic of categorization is instructive because it provides an implicit framework for conceptualizing development in general. This in turn provides the groundwork for understanding social categories such as gender.

In the ensuing sections of the chapter we first describe Piaget's account of how children develop an appreciation of the logical structure of categories. We then explore how this framework shaped conceptualizations of development in general and the development of thinking about the social category of gender in particular. Next we identify how this framework introduces biases that lead to a selective, distorted view of concepts of gender categories and gender development. We then describe how one might conceptualize gender categories and their development differently when seen through a feminist lens. We conclude with suggestions for future feminist-based conceptualizing and research on genders as categories. Our goal is to show a pathway to a broader, more balanced account of gender concepts and the development of gender identity within developmental science.

THE CONSTRUCTION OF CATEGORIES
OF THOUGHT IN PIAGETIAN THEORY

Our categories are basic to how we represent the world—how we sort diverse items into groups of similar instances. Once formed, the construction of categories enables us to make generalizations. What we learn about one instance in a category might be applied to others in that group but not to other instances outside the group. For example, a child who observes that her brother is obsessed with videogames might assume that boys usually like playing with videogames but girls do not.

It matters that Piaget was working within the traditional logical framework of Western philosophy and science. He (Inhelder & Piaget, 1964) thus regarded categories as abstract entities that obeyed a set of logical rules regardless of the content of the category, such as circles and squares, lions and tigers, or males and females. What are those rules? The core rule is that members of the group possess common properties. Those properties are the basis for belonging in the group. For example, we learn that squares have four equal sides that meet at right angles. The number of equal sides defines the figure as a square and, conversely, all objects and only objects possessing those properties belong in that class regardless of whether the figure is drawn on paper or used to describe a downtown plaza. No circle has that shape. So class membership is exclusive (*only*), and the criteria for class membership are met by every member of the class (*all*). All squares, regardless of color or size, are equally "squared." What is said about one instance labeled a square is applicable to all others. This is why categories like these are called *equivalence categories*. Each member possesses the common property in the group and only members of the group have that property. The common properties defining the objects are definitional. The properties define the group.

These rules for forming a category are fixed; they are not dependent on the person who does the grouping or the context in which the group is constructed or the purpose for defining a category. If there is a category, there are common properties stipulating group membership. In the Piagetian analysis the strictures of homogeneity within categories and sharp boundaries of exclusion between categories apply to any category. Stereotypes reflect this kind of categorical thinking. Piaget had less interest in how we learn about particular equivalence categories than in children's growth in mastering the universal rules creating classical equivalence categories. In his view, these rules are fundamental to scientific thought. The structure of equivalence categories underlies scientific hypothesis testing of group differences, for example, comparing males versus females. Within-category differences are considered error variance.

IMPLICATIONS OF CATEGORIES
FOR CONCEPTUALIZATIONS OF DEVELOPMENT

Equivalence Categories Imply a Sequence of Stages

Equivalence categories with their "all-and-only" structure imply qualitative differences between categories. Infant behavior differs from the antics of the terrible twos, which differ from adolescents. In this view individuals are not a mixture of infants and toddlers. You fit either one stereotype or the other. This all-or-none characterization is also the basis for normative descriptions of developmental change—standards for what is normal and typical. Developmental steps or milestones can be interpreted as equivalence categories whenever mastery of each step is defined as all or none. For example, one might describe a child as behaving like a 2-year-old across the board. This all-or-none characterization is the foundation for stage theories, such as Freud's oral, anal, and genital stages or Piaget's sensorimotor, concrete, and formal stages of thought. Stage theories of development reflect equivalence categorical thinking. Stages are meant to be general frameworks of behavior, such that at each stage all children are thought to behave at approximately the same level of maturity in all interactions with all materials and in all settings. In addition, stages imply a set of norms for the age at which children should be in each stage.

Equivalence categories support not only the conceptualization of development as stage-like but also the idea that they occur in an invariant sequence. An example of these necessary universal paths of developmental change is children's mastery of the logic of equivalence categories and inclusion hierarchies. In Piagetian analyses, the rules for categorization shape the progression of category skill. A first step is when children realize that a group of diverse objects encountered are alike in some respect. (They could be called by the same name!) This leads to the realization that if *any* object has that property, it must belong in that group (the *all* rule). It follows that objects that don't have that property don't belong in the group (the *only* rule). It's like sorting laundry. A person looks for all the items that are shaped like feet while ignoring those with fingers. Until one discovers that a category is a group of instances with common properties dictating group membership, one cannot realize that all and only objects sharing the properties belong in the group. Mastery of the "all and only" rule for single categories provides the groundwork for the next level of understanding, the construction of inclusion hierarchies (e.g., red squares, squares, quadrilaterals). In these hierarchies, the lowest classes have many attributes in common, and then each higher class has fewer commonalities. Each narrower class forms the necessary foundation for the next broader step in a hierarchy that is headed toward increasing abstraction and generality—qualities highly valued in Western science and philosophy. In this way the development of categorical understanding proceeds in an invariant sequence.

The parallels between this sequential construction of category logic and a layperson's or stage theorist's conceptualizations of development are striking. Development is the ascent of a staircase of categories (i.e., each stage). Each step is a necessary precursor for the following step. For example, the search for personal autonomy that defines the behavior of toddlers is thought to lay the foundation for later self-control and independence, just as understanding counting is basic to arithmetic, which lays the foundation for understanding algebra. Development entails the increasing incorporation of "lower order" skills or rules (like addition) into higher order skills. The former provide the building blocks for broader abilities (like writing algebraic equations). Given the endpoint of development, the precursors of mature understanding are presumed to be self-evident because these precursors are required to reach the end state. In Piaget's view, the end goal of development is mature scientific thinking that includes the understanding of the rules for deductive inferences, or logical conclusions. Thus, construction of single categories lays the necessary foundations for category relations such as inclusion hierarchies (for example, males and females are gender categories) or conditional deductive statements like "If it's a truck, boys like to play with it." In sum, the forces that lead children to construct each next step are given by the underlying rule structure the child must master, rather than the social system. The rule structure defines the skill, orders the steps, and provides the opportunities to construct stable conceptual structures. Task analysis of end states takes the place of analyses of the situations in which particular skills and concepts might be deployed and of the various strategies that the child could use to acquire rules.

Critique of Equivalence Categorical Depictions of Development

The characterization of the content and sequence of development based on equivalence categories is problematical. Thinking of development in terms of stages goes hand in hand with thinking about an abstract generic child rather than particular individuals living in particular social settings. This type of thinking ignores human variability and the social factors that produce it. For example, despite the characterization of the "terrible twos," even a tempestuous toddler is a delight much of the time. Children differ temperamentally; some may never be difficult. Parents vary in their tolerance for unruly behavior, what they consider to be unruly, and how they handle the behavior. Children vary in their timing of developmental tasks as well. Some children's quest for self-assertion and control may occur much later than in most children, and children may return to issues such as assertion of independence repeatedly. In addition to de-emphasizing variation, the depiction of an abstract, universal child downplays intersections of age with social categories such as race, ethnicity, class, nationality, and immigration status (not to mention dramatic cultural differences from country to country!). Children of the same age vary greatly due to their particular social and economic circumstances. A developmental skill that is useful in one environment may not be useful in another one. The lack of attention to environmental influences may also occur because stages often imply that a biologically determined pathway and timetable during development produce the steps in development.

Stage models often presuppose that alternate developmental pathways are deviant because they are contrary to natural biological programming or to analyses of the necessary construction of skills. This assumption of a single path is shaky. The distinctive pathways taken by children raised in adverse circumstances may not be problematic and maladaptive, but they may instead be adaptive to local conditions (e.g., Frankenhuis & De Weerth, 2013). For example, skills that are adaptive in a consistent, predictable, privileged social environment may not be adaptive in an uncertain restricted environment. Additionally, although stage theorists depict development as progress toward a higher level of cognition and social behavior, it is not clear that higher is better. For example, theorists may consider the endpoint of asserting autonomy and independence to be a hallmark of maturity, but it could be argued that building the capacity for teamwork should be the valued endpoint of personal development. Moreover, theorists' choices of an endpoint and the opportunities to reach it may be gendered, especially when a culture provides certain experiences unequally to boys and girls. Who is allowed autonomy and independence? Which sex is encouraged, through particular types of toys, to be scientists or logicians?

Recent Categorical Approaches to Development

Many psychologists recently have turned away from describing qualitative stages as stepping-stones to development. Still, the stage narrative in academic developmental psychology continues today, for example, in work on a possible new stage of "emerging adulthood" between adolescence and adulthood (Arnett, 2015). There also are lingering traces of stage-category assumptions in the search for homogeneity in age-related performance and in the focus on universal uniform pathways of development. Moreover, the divorce of methods of measurement from the examination of real-world contexts and contents that may shape the child's acquisition and deployment of knowledge implies that the same outcome would occur in any context.

THEORY OF MIND

An example of these assumptions is the burgeoning field of research on "theory of mind," which explores children's understanding that people are psychological beings with different perspectives and goals. Often this research focuses on resolving debates about how early particular under-standings emerge, as in *the age* at which infants understand that people have intentions. The assumption is that all intentions are understood by all children at approximately the same age. In addition, theory-of-mind research examines across cultures the universality of a sequence of steps toward a preschool developmental end goal of understanding that peo-ple can have false beliefs because they lack critical information about an event or situation. Most assessments occur in similar laboratory settings. Researchers are beginning to consider contextual factors, such as fam-ily variables, including number of siblings and parental mental-state talk (Devine & Hughes, in press). However, they see these factors mainly as influences on *how early* a child acquires theory-of-mind concepts rather than on the settings in which the concepts are used or the goals to which the concepts are applied.

Essentialism

A recent strand of developmental research on children's attempts to explain actions of others implicitly draws upon equivalence categories. The research assumes that inherently all humans have a similar approach to explaining actions. That is, researchers assert that all humans assume people's actions and beliefs reflect the kind or category of person they are, their essence, as in "that's the way girls are." Gelman and her col-leagues (Cimpian, 2016; Gelman, 2003; Meyer & Gelman, 2016; Rhodes & Gelman, 2009) claim, "Our minds seem structured to facilitate the acqui-sition, retention, and manipulation of category information" (Cimpian, 2016, p. 102). In short, in this view, children inherently have a cognitive bias that creates explanatory essentialist categories. The researchers hold that children tend to pick up information about categories rather than an individual category member, and they are more accurate at remem-bering information about categories than about individual members. As early as infancy, according to this view, children are little theorists attuned to detecting categories, assigning an essence as the defining property of the category, and then deploying the rules for equivalence categories in making inferences about category members. They are said to deploy an

implicit essentialist theory that attributes to the diverse members of a
category an inherent, immutable essence defining the common features,
including the outward appearance of the category members. This essence
allows the categorizer to make generalizations. For instance, if one mammal has an esophagus, so will all the rest. Essences thus economize processing and foster induction. For instance, children might believe that boys
have a "boyness" essence that leads them to engage in rough, physical play.
In the Rhodes and Gelman (2009) study, 5-year-olds constructed categories of animals, artifacts, and gender, but not race, within an essentialist
framework. Categories like "boys" and "girls" were treated as equivalence
categories (e.g., "all boys do X"). The children considered people as either
male or female. Moreover, the children did not think it appropriate for
people from a different culture to draw different category boundaries.
For example, a boy could not be placed among the category of female
exemplars.

Developmentalists debate whether this essentialist bias applies to all
categories and at all ages and in all rearing environments. In older children, social categories like male and female begin to be treated differently.
Boundaries become fuzzier and crossovers are possible. Interestingly,
adolescents deal with social categories more flexibly if they come from
families that are highly educated, endorse progressive politics, and live
in a suburban environment, as opposed to those who live in conservative
communities. Notably, the category of race is more essentialized for those
in conservative communities (Rhodes & Gelman, 2009). Thus, contextual
factors such as the cultural or subcultural environment and the experiences that come with age seem to influence the tendency to form essentialist categories.

In summary, the legacy of Western logic, especially as instantiated in
Piaget's theory, propelled developmental psychology in a particular direction. Developmentalists have considered young children to be inborn theorists. The logic of equivalence categories in particular was expressed in
models incorporating universal stages and developmental sequences that
glossed over variation due to culture and place and history. The assumptions of equivalence categories still appear today in characterizations of

children's development and depictions of children's thinking as theory driven and naturally essentialist, dividing the world into essentialized equivalence categories.

Some developmentalists studying cognition now recognize within-child and between-child variability (e.g., Siegler, 2007), posit that aspects of cognitive development vary across different domains, such as mathematics versus reading (Gelman, 2015), and recognize multiple developmental paths in each domain (Frankenhuis & De Weerth, 2013). But the shift in focus to variability and to contextualization of changes in children's thinking has been slow. Moreover, there has been little spillover of a contextualized developmental approach to work on gender and gender role development where, as discussed later, equivalence categorical thinking pervades accounts of gender representations as distinctive binary categories.

IMPLICATIONS OF CATEGORIES FOR CONCEPTIONS OF GENDER ROLES AND THEIR DEVELOPMENT

In the preceding paragraphs we have shown how the use of equivalence categories to characterize development and concepts in general is problematical because it ignores the social contexts and variability among children. We now turn to the use of equivalence categories in characterizing how people think about gender categories. The starting point is that not all categories are alike in structure and content. If we understand the varied structure of categories, we may be able to discuss more varied forms of development and gender concepts and identity. Here we highlight a critical perspective, distinguishing equivalence categories from graded categories.

Equivalence categories obey the "all and only" rule in which all members of the category share a common property which other instances do not. Many feminist and queer theorists and activists have fought against the deployment of dichotomous equivalence classes to describe gender categorization in which the label "male" applies equally to all and only members of that category and "female" applies equally and exclusively to all members of that category.

Prototype Theory

There is an alternative. Cognitive psychologists, studying people performing cognitive tasks in controlled laboratory situations, have reported that most people do not impose an equivalence structure when they deal with a wide variety of categories. People's behavior may be better captured by the account provided by the prototype theory discussed by Eleanor Rosch (e.g., 1999). She distinguished between thinking with logical, equivalence categories and thinking based on prototype categories. We have been discussing equivalence categories. Take the contrast between boys and girls. When we assume all boys are alike, we are thinking of them within an equivalence category framework. But there is a different way to think about categories, one which uses *prototype categorization*. There is enormous variation among members of many different groups, including boys and girls. Within the category of birds, robins are much more typical of our notion of birds than are ostriches. Robins are a prototype of birds and have many more avian, bird-like properties than do ostriches. They are small creatures that sing and fly, unlike ostriches. Similarly, the label "dog" is more likely to evoke an image of a Labrador retriever than a Lhasa Apso. When people are asked to generate a list of birds, robins will be mentioned earlier and ostriches may fail to appear on the list. Memorizers are more likely to wrongly insert "robin" during recall of a list of birds than to insert "ostrich." In other words, there is within-category variability in the category of birds and many other categories of objects, animals, and social groups.

Prototype categories are defined by clusters of correlated features. Some instances possess more of them than do others. Those instances are the prototype that typifies the category. A robin is a typical bird. There may be no property that every member of the category possesses.

A robin may be the prototype for birds because it possesses most of the defining features of birds, whereas the large flightless ostrich is atypical. Therefore, a robin can stand for the whole category. Some instances are so atypical it is hard to put them in a particular category. Think of marsupials (opossums, koalas, kangaroos), which lack some key mammalian features focused on feeding offspring (e.g., during gestation the fetal marsupial is fed in a yolk sac, whereas most mammals are fed through the placenta). In other words, categories have a graded structure with some members more representative of the category than others because those representative members have more defining features. The graded structure of categories often presents problems in classification. Is a tomato a vegetable or fruit? Is a shark a mammal or a fish? Are kangaroos mammals?

Rosch attributes the structure of these graded categories to the structure of the world as it is encountered by individuals during their daily activities. The role of the observer is to detect that structure. Therefore, the observer will learn first about the prototype, such as robins for birds, which is sharply differentiated from prototypes in contrasting classes. Observers gradually learn about less typical creatures, such as ostriches, which may have few features defining their membership and some features that overlap with contrasting classes. In this way, children gradually learn about the graded nature of categories.

Prototypes of Gender Categories

There are two key elements of Rosch's analyses that are relevant to discussions about gender and development: (a) claims about the graded (according to typicality) structure of categories and (b) claims about the source of graded categories. The first claim provides a foundation for a feminist critique of the equivalence-category position that each gender category is a homogeneous category standing in opposition to its counterpart. The second claim is consistent with many feminist conceptual representations of social categories like gender.

The first claim suggests that gender categories are comprised of instances that vary in their resemblance to the category prototypes; there is no assumed equivalence of all members within the category (Fox, 2011). Category variability exists in a wide range of physical, social, and intellectual categories. If we recognize variability within classes of animals, vegetables, and minerals, we can recognize the variability within gender categories and the overlap between gender categories, which has been described in other chapters. We can view gender categories as graded structures. Some females are closer to the prototypic female than are others. Moreover, the typicality of individuals categorized as females shifts over the life course, because the number of category-typical features can vary over a lifetime. The cluster of biological and behavioral attributes people associate with each gender category can change. Thus, if children are using their representations of gender categories as a guide to defining their own development, a prototype view provides more leeway for development of their own identities, because a girl does not yet look like a prototypic woman.

In the second claim, Rosch asserts that the structure of the world determines how a perceiver groups instances. In her ecological view of concepts and categories, the "world" varies depending on where the perceiver is situated. The ability to sort objects into prototype categories by looking for instances with similar sets of correlated properties is intrinsic to human cognition. However, it is the perceiver's daily activities that determine which instances are included in one's categories and which category members are most central (Gabora, Rosch, & Aerts, 2008). Rosch notes that the context of daily life affects which properties are "learned, listed or expected in a category" (1999, p. 202). Many feminists agree (e.g., Burman, 2008; Miller & Scholnick, 2000). The environments of various people differ greatly. The ostrich is a more exotic bird in Alabama than in Africa, and thus would be a less prototypic bird in Alabama. People are positioned differently according to markers such as race, ethnicity, nation, gender, and social class and thus have different views of the objects and events in their environments. Many feminist scholars have challenged the idea that there is a "view from nowhere"; knowers are not interchangeable

(Harding, 2015). Each person has a particular perspective on the world, influenced by that person's social position and access to resources. The properties of gender categories considered to be highly prototypical may differ for women marginalized by society and women in the center who are privileged by society.

The structure of society will determine not only the content of gender categories but also whose categorizations matter. Some perspectives and voices are attended to more than others and become the socially accepted view. Therefore, society may influence whether gender categories are considered equivalence categories and what traits and behaviors are associated with each category.

Differences in social location can create great variations in the typicality and salience of gender categories. Among people who identify as female, a transgender woman may categorize gender differently than a woman who was a biological female since birth. The former may perceive transgendered women as more typical of the category female than does the latter, as well as the majority of society. As another example, a female physicist may be considered a more atypical exemplar of the female category in the eyes of some people than others and in some countries more than others. An example relevant to the salience of gender categories is that the nouns of some languages are gendered; a home (e.g., *casa*) is included in the category female in some languages but is not gendered at all in others.

HOW SHOULD GENDER BE REPRESENTED?

Many feminist scholars have criticized the exclusive, rigid boundaries inherent in assuming that all categories have an equivalence structure. The inappropriate imposition of equivalence structure onto categories has consequences that distort understanding of the world. In particular, category content may become exaggerated and polarized. This occurs in part because such categories lend themselves to an essentialist bias, especially in the social domain. For example, if boys are considered inherently interested in playing sports, then boys not interested in sports and girls interested in sports are not represented in the gender categories and the gender differences are exaggerated. Societies may institutionalize gender categories by creating two types of bathrooms (male and female), different elementary school uniforms for girls and boys, and so on. Cultures may exaggerate differences between categories and increase the salience of the categories through, for example, marketing (distinctive colors of clothing and toys for girls and boys; separate sections of toy stores or Internet merchant sites). Popular culture may emphasize contrasts in books published (e.g., *Men Are From Mars, Women Are From Venus*; Gray, 1993). Even scientific publications tend to focus on gender differences more than similarities. Language conventions (especially generic nouns such as "girls") may emphasize category differences and increase their polarity. So do phrases like "the opposite sex." In contrast, the representation of gender as a graded gender category is less likely to be distorted in these ways.

A second consequence of perceiving all social categories as equivalence groups is that the act of categorization often becomes entangled in a value system. People who dispute the assumed equivalence structure of specific categories are considered fuzzy thinkers or misinformed. Many arguments about stereotypes reflect disputes about the validity of equivalence and prototype categorizations. Using the structure of logical, equivalence categories lends itself to stereotypes, normative notions, and binary thought. It erases the differences within categories and diverts attention from the context for categorization. It also downplays the social-hierarchical nature of the social categories other than gender that intersect with gender. Social categories such as race, class, and migration status involve power differentials that cannot be separated from gender. Viewing gender as a graded category is less likely to lead to these outcomes.

The value system flowing from dichotomous equivalence categories also is seen in the valuing of one category in the binary over the contrasting category. The chosen category serves as the unmarked standard from which the other category deviates. The more valued and therefore the more privileged category is listed first: mind/body, reason/emotion, active/passive, and male/female. This is the case with gender categories, as seen in male privilege and power. The more valued category often becomes the norm. For example, people use the generic designation, such as "men," to discuss all humans, and what are supposed to be masculine traits, such as independence, autonomy, and mastery, become a universal goal of development (Code, 2000). The use of equivalence categories is not neutral. A graded gender category with its continuum of differences is less likely to result in these dichotomous value judgments and may be more realistic. Still, values may continue to operate in that some instances within each gender category may be considered "better" (i.e., more typical) exemplars than others in that category.

Essentialized, polarized, value-laden gender categories are problematic for understanding development. In social categories, including gender, one's own social category becomes the ingroup and other social categories are outgroups. This polarized aspect of these categories is important because even young children understand that membership in a social category entails the obligation not to harm other members of that category. In contrast, doing harm to members of the outgroup often is expected (Rhodes, 2013). Moreover, if equivalence categories are children's preferred way of carving up the world, they may be biased toward attending to and thinking about gender categories as equivalence groups, especially if they are salient within the culture in which the child lives. This tendency may make it more difficult for children to understand variation within each gender category or gender identities lying outside of the two categories. Their category structure seems to reflect their mental strategies more than the nature of objects themselves. Young children in particular, due to their limited processing capacity, may tend to form equivalence categories because it is cognitively less effortful to form simple dichotomous categories than more complex graded ones.

Given these problems with binary categories, some have proposed a continuum, a spectrum of gender, in place of categories (Barker & Richards, 2015). This challenges the entire gender binary by eliminating the two-category structure. Alternatively, there can be multiple gender categories. At one point, Facebook had 58 gender categories from which to choose. A main theoretical perspective challenging the gender binary is *gender queer theory*—an umbrella term including gender identities such as overlap of gender identities, fluctuating gender, and agender (Barker & Richards, 2015). Another approach is a dual identity perspective (Martin, Andrews, England, Zosuls, & Ruble, 2017): Researchers view children's gender identity as a multidimensional construct that includes children's perceptions of *how similar* they are to *both* male and female categories. This allows children to fall along a range of gender identities (e.g., high in both categories, high in one and low in the other). In the Martin et al. (2017) study, almost half the sample of US children age 5–10 felt similar to both genders or felt little similarity with either.

Thus, there are multiple ways of thinking about the gender system. The developmental question becomes: What causes children even to think about gender categories and the social gender system in terms of two equivalence categories? Gelman (2003) speculates that there is an inherent bias that facilitates processing by providing a simple rubric essentialism: to unite members of a group. Yet there are alternative societal explanations either for adopting essentialist stereotypes or for abandoning the equivalence strategy. We do know, for example, that children are more likely to infer an essentialist category when a generic label is provided for a category or when children lack certain social experiences, such as attending schools with diverse students (Diesendruck, 2013). The overall point is that categorizing often comes from human cognizers rather than from nature.

LOOKING TO THE FUTURE STUDY OF GENDER DEVELOPMENT

Whereas interdisciplinary women's, gender, and sexuality studies have made great strides in theorizing gender in recent years, these advances have had little impact on developmental psychology. In this chapter we drew on feminist perspectives to examine equivalence categories in conceptualizations of development and of gender. There are some lessons to be drawn for developmentalists, cognitive psychologists, and feminists. Many feminist psychologists and epistemologists trace the path from naming to norming to naturalizing (Code, 2000). Equivalence categories of development first delineated the categories through naming, and then they became normative, essentialized, and natural. We have illustrated how the deployment of equivalence categories pervades both earlier stage theories of development in many domains and more recent theories and research on children's thinking. Even children's categorical thought has become essentialized as involving an inherent cognitive bias. However, the equivalence template does not always fit. Equivalence categories have their limitations and are appropriate for only certain contents. Numbers in the equivalence category of even numbers are always divisible by 2, but gender or ethnic stereotypes can produce unreliable generalizations. The challenge for a developing child is figuring out which kind of representation, equivalence category or prototype category, works in a given situation and why it works. We argue that development in general and cognitive competence in particular involves an application process in which people must discern where a representation or representational strategy is appropriate or how to make it appropriate.

The use of an equivalence category has consequences. When one constructs a science in which there are fixed points of mastery that do not vary with the situation, one renders invisible the very forces that may help construct those points. We have offered an alternative way to conceptualize categories that addresses development and gender as socially constructed and situated. The challenge is that the traditional experimental and statistical methods often used to test the findings have not yet been tailored to this alternative. But the opportunities exist!

REFERENCES

Arnett, J. J. (2015). *Emerging adulthood: The winding road from the late teens through the twenties* (2nd ed.). New York, NY: Oxford University Press.

Barker, M. J., & Richards, E. (2015). Further genders. In C. Richards & M. J. Barker (Eds.), *The Palgrave handbook of the psychology of sexuality and gender* (pp. 166–182). New York, NY: Palgrave Macmillan.

Burman, E. (2008). *Deconstructing developmental psychology* (2nd ed.). London, UK: Brunner-Routledge.

Cimpian, A. (2016). The privileged status of category representations in early development. *Child Development Perspectives, 10*(2), 99–104.

Code, L. (2000). Naming, naturalizing, normalizing: The "child" as fact and artifact. In P. H. Miller & E. K. Scholnick (Eds.), *Toward a feminist developmental psychology* (pp. 215–237). New York, NY: Routledge.

Devine, R. T., & Hughes, C. (in press). Family correlates of false belief understanding in early childhood: A meta-analysis. *Child Development*.

Diesendruck, G. (2013). The development of a simple, but potentially dangerous, idea. In M. R. Banaji & S. A. Gelman (Eds.), *Navigating the social world: What infants, children, and other species can teach us* (pp. 263–268). New York, NY: Oxford University Press.

Fox, M. J. (2011). Prototype theory: An alternative concept for categorizing sex and gender. In R. P. Smiraglia (Ed.), *Proceedings from North American Symposium on Knowledge Organization*, Vol. 3 (pp. 151–159). Toronto, Canada.

Frankenhuis, W. E., & de Weerth, C. (2013). Does early-life exposure to stress shape or impair cognition? *Current Directions in Psychological Science, 22*(5), 407–412.

Gabora, L., Rosch, E., & Aerts, D. (2008). Toward an ecological theory of concepts. *Ecological Psychology, 20*, 84–116.

Gelman, R. (2015). Learning in core and non-core number domains. *Developmental Review, 38*, 185–200.

Gelman, S. A. (2003). *The essential child: Origins of essentialism in everyday thought*. New York, NY: Oxford University Press.

Gray, J. (1993). *Men are from Mars, women are from Venus: A practical guide for improving communication and getting what you want in your relationships*. New York, NY: Harper.

Harding, S. (2015) *Objectivity and diversity: Another logic of scientific research*. Chicago, IL: University of Chicago Press.

Inhelder, B., & Piaget, J. (1964). *The early growth of logic in the child: Classification and seriation*. London, UK: Routledge.

Lloyd, G. (1984). *The man of reason: "Male" and "female" in Western philosophy*. London, UK: Methuen.

Martin, C. L., Andrews, N. C. Z., England, D. E., Zosuls, K., & Ruble, D. N. (2017). A dual identity approach for conceptualizing and measuring children's gender identity. *Child Development, 88*(1), 167–182.

Meyer, M., & Gelman, S. A. (2016). Gender essentialism in children and parents: Implications for the development of gender stereotyping and gender-typed preferences. *Sex Roles, 75*(9–10), 409–421.

Miller, P. H., & Scholnick, E. K. (2000). Feminist theory and contemporary developmental psychology: The case of children's executive function. *Feminism & Psychology, 25*(3), 266–283.

Piaget, J. (1970). Piaget's theory. In P. H. Mussen (Ed.) *Carmichael's handbook of child development* (pp.703–732). New York, NY: Wiley.

Rhodes, M. (2013). How two intuitive theories shape the development of social categorization. *Child Development Perspectives, 7*(1), 12–16.

Rhodes, M., & Gelman, S. A. (2009). A developmental examination of the conceptual structure of animal, artifact, and human social categories across two cultural contexts. *Cognitive Psychology, 59*, 244–274.

Rosch, E. (1999). Principles of categorization. In E. Margolis & S. Laurence (Eds.), *Concepts: Core readings* (pp. 189–206). Cambridge, MA: Bradford Books, The MIT Press.

Rosser, S. V. (2012). The link between feminist theory and methods in experimental research. In S. N. Hesse-Biber (Ed.), *Handbook of feminist research: Theory and praxis* (2nd ed., pp. 264–289). Thousand Oaks, CA: Sage.

Siegler, R. S. (2007). Cognitive variability. *Developmental Science, 10*(1), 104–109.

Walkerdine, V. (1988). *The mastery of reason: Cognitive development and the production of rationality.* London, UK: Routledge.

Glenn Adams, PhD is Professor of Psychology and Director of the Cultural Psychology Research Group at the University of Kansas, USA. He served as a Peace Corps volunteer in Sierra Leone before earning his doctorate at Stanford University. His graduate training included two years of field research in Ghana, which provided the empirical foundation for his research on cultural-psychological foundations of relationship. He remains active in African Studies and in leadership of the Kansas African Studies Center. His current work applies a variety of interdisciplinary perspectives—including African Studies, critical race theory, and cultural psychology—to decolonize knowledge production in psychological science and to articulate models of development that promote sustainable ways of being for humanity.

Y. Gavriel Ansara, PhD is a Polycultural Psychotherapist and a Relationship and Family Counsellor at Imanadari Counselling and at his private practice, Ansara Psychotherapy, in Australia. He is Senior Research Consultant for Scotland's Equality Network and has been a policy consultant for Australian state and federal governments. His research on cisgenderism—the ideology that invalidates people's own understanding of their genders and bodies—received the 2012 American Psychological Association's Transgender Research Award. He also received the UK Higher Education Academy's 2011 National Psychology Postgraduate Research Award and the 2016 University of Surrey Vice Chancellor's Alumni Achievement Award for his contributions to standards and policies in international human rights and social justice.

Meg-John Barker, PhD is a senior lecturer in psychology at the Open University, UK. Their work on bisexuality, nonmonogamous relationships, sadomasochism, and nonbinary gender has appeared in numerous publications, including books published by Routledge and Palgrave, and they were cofounder of the journal *Psychology & Sexuality* and the Critical Sexology seminar series. They also write for general audiences, including their popular books *Queer: A Graphic History, Rewriting the Rules*, and *Enjoy Sex*, and their website www.rewriting-the-rules.com.

Leslie C. Bell, PhD is a psychotherapist and sociologist in private practice in Berkeley, California, USA. Her research focuses on young women's experiences of sexuality and relationships, and integrates psychoanalytic and sociological theories and methods. Her work has appeared in various academic and popular publications and has been frequently featured in the news media. She is the author of *Hard to Get: Twentysomething Women and the Paradox of Sexual Freedom* (University of California Press, 2013).

Monica Biernat, PhD is Distinguished Professor of Psychology at the University of Kansas, USA. Her research on stereotyping, prejudice, and social judgment has appeared in outlets such as the *Journal of Personality and Social Psychology, Advances in Social Psychology*, and *Personality and Social Psychology Bulletin*. She is author of the 2005 book, *Standards and Expectancies*, and a recipient of the American Psychological Association's Distinguished Scientific Award for Early Career Contribution to Psychology and the Association for Women in Psychology Distinguished Publication Award. She is currently editor of *Personality and Social Psychology Review*, coeditor of the Taylor and Francis series *Essays in Social Psychology*, and Executive Officer of the Society of Experimental Social Psychology.

Nancy K. Dess, PhD is Professor of Psychology at Occidental College in Los Angeles, California, USA. Her work on the relationship between emotion and eating, peace, and research ethics has appeared in peer-reviewed journals such as *Physiology and Behavior* and *PLoS ONE* and in edited volumes, including *Ethical Challenges in the Behavioral and Brain Sciences* and *Evolutionary Psychology & Violence: A Primer for Policymakers and Public Policy Advocates*, for which she was coeditor. She is a member of the American Psychological Association's Board of Scientific Affairs and has served as APA's Senior Scientist and on the editorial boards of the *International Journal of Comparative Psychology* and the *Archives of Scientific Psychology*. She is a Fellow of the American Psychological Association and the Association for Psychological Science.

Lisa M. Diamond, PhD is Professor of Psychology and Gender Studies at the University of Utah, USA. She studies the expression of sexual attractions and sexual identity over the life course, and the influences of early life experiences on later sexual development. Her 2008 book, *Sexual Fluidity* (Harvard University Press), describes the changes that she observed in the sexual attractions, behaviors, and identities of a sample of sexual-minority women that she has been following since 1995. Dr. Diamond is coeditor of the APA *Handbook of Sexuality and Psychology* and is a fellow of two divisions of the APA. She has published over 100 articles and book chapters and has been invited to present her research at over 60 universities and international conferences.

Ngaire Donaghue, PhD is adjunct Associate Professor in the School of Humanities at the University of Tasmania, Australia. Her work applies critical feminist approaches to questions concerning the relationships between cultural discourses around postfeminism and embodied subjectivity. This work has appeared in a wide range of journals, including *Feminism & Psychology, Sex Roles, Psychology of Women Quarterly, Women's Studies International Forum, Body Image, Fat Studies*, and *Australian Feminist Studies*, as well as being included in a number of edited collections. She currently serves as an associate editor for *Feminism & Psychology* and on the editorial boards of *Sex Roles* and *Fat Studies*.

Justin R. Garcia, PhD is Ruth Halls Associate Professor of Gender Studies & Associate Director for Research and Education at The Kinsey

Institute, Indiana University, Bloomington, USA. His research focuses on romantic and sexual relationships across the life course and attempts to integrate evolutionary and feminist theories. His work has appeared in a variety of disciplinary and interdisciplinary venues, and it has been frequently featured in the news media. He is coauthor of *Evolution and Human Sexual Behavior* (Harvard University Press, 2013) and coeditor of *Evolution's Empress: Darwinian Perspectives on the Nature of Women* (Oxford University Press, 2013).

Patricia Adair Gowaty, PhD is Distinguished Professor of Ecology and Evolutionary Biology, UCLA, and a Distinguished Research Professor Emerita, Odum Institute of Ecology, University of Georgia, Athens, USA. She is an evolutionary biologist who studied the social behavior of individuals and the fitness correlates in eastern bluebirds in the field for 30 years and *Drosophila* sp. for 15 years. She edited *Feminism and Evolutionary Biology* (Springer, 1997). She was President of the Animal Behavior Society in 2001. She is a Fellow of the AAAS, the Animal Behavior Society, and the American Ornithological Society. She is or has been an Associate Editor or on the Board of Editors for *American Naturalist, Animal Behaviour, Evolution, Behavioral Ecology and Sociobiology, Human Nature, EvoS, Integrative Zoology, Ecology and Evolution* (Wiley), and *PeerJ*.

Peter Hegarty, PhD is Professor of Psychology at the University of Surrey, Guildford, UK. His most recent work on norms that frame thinking about gender, race and events in historical time has appeared in *Cognition, Journal of Experimental Psychology: General, Memory Studies*, and *Psychology of Men and Masculinities*. He is the 2017–2018 Suzanne Tassier Chair of Gender and Human Rights at the Université libre de Bruxelles, Belgium.

Leslie L. Heywood, PhD is Professor of English, Gender, and Science Studies at Binghamton University, USA. She has published widely on third-wave feminism, including editing *Third Wave Agenda, Being Feminist, Doing Feminism* (Minnesota) and *The Women's Movement Today* (Greenwood Reference). Her work on women and sport is widely known, including *Built to Win: The Female Athlete as Cultural Icon* (Minnesota). Most recently, she has published in journals such as *Frontiers in Evolutionary*

Neuroscience, and *Feminism & Psychology*, focusing on neuropsychological approaches to gender and sport. She has served on the editorial boards of *The Journal of Sport and Social Issues, Evolutionary Behavioral Sciences*, and the *Gender and Popular Culture Series* for I.B. Tauris Books (UK). She has also published four books of poetry and a memoir.

Melissa Hines, PhD is Professor of Psychology at the University of Cambridge, Cambridge, UK, where she directs the Gender Development Research Centre. She is also a Fellow at Churchill College, University of Cambridge. She is author of the book, *Brain Gender*, published in 2004 by Oxford University Press, as well as of over 100 research articles. Her primary research focus is on how testosterone exposure during early development interacts with social and cognitive mechanisms to influence human gender development. She is a Past President of the International Academy of Sex Research and is a former Associate Editor of the journal *Hormones and Behavior*. Currently, she serves on the editorial boards of the journals *Hormones and Behavior* and *Biology of Sex Differences*.

Tuğçe Kurtiş, PhD is Assistant Professor of Psychology and the Women's Studies Program at the University of West Georgia. She completed her PhD in Social Psychology and a graduate certificate in African Studies at the University of Kansas. Drawing upon perspectives in cultural, feminist, and critical psychologies and interdisciplinary discussions in transnational feminisms, her research focuses on sociocultural constructions of subjectivity and relationality, which she examines through joint processes of voice and silence in interpersonal and collective experience. Her main objective as a social psychologist is to use psychological theory, research, and pedagogy as resources for global social justice.

Campbell Leaper, PhD is Professor and Department Chair of Psychology at the University of California, Santa Cruz, USA. His research concerns gender and sexism during childhood, adolescence, and adulthood. Topics addressed in his work include gender ideologies, social identity, self-concepts, language, social interaction, social relationships, media, academic achievement, and experiences with discrimination. In addition, he has conducted several meta-analyses and integrative reviews.

Professor Leaper has served on the editorial boards of *Child Development, Developmental Psychology*, and *Sex Roles*. He is cochair and organizer of the Biennial Gender Development Research Conference.

I-Ching Lee, PhD is Professor at National Chengchi University, Taiwan. Her work on gender, power, intergroup relations, cultural issues, and political psychology has appeared in *Psychological Bulletin, Personality and Social Psychological Bulletin, Journal of Cross-Cultural Psychology, PLOS One*, and *Feminism & Psychology*. She serves on the editorial boards for *Analyses of Social Issues and Public Policy, Indigenous Psychological Research in Chinese Societies, Journal of Education & Psychology*, and *Research in Applied Psychology*.

Eva Magnusson, PhD is Professor Emerita of Psychology at Umeå University, Sweden. Her work on family life and gender equality, gender in clinical psychology, and gender in work organizations has appeared in several books in Swedish and English and in journals such as *Feminism & Psychology* and *NORA: Nordic Journal of Feminist and Gender Research*. Eva has also published textbooks on the psychology of gender and on qualitative methods. She has previously served as head of women's and gender studies at Umeå University. She is currently an Associate Editor of the journal *Feminism & Psychology*.

Jeanne Marecek, PhD is William R. Kenan, Jr., Professor of Psychology Emerita at Swarthmore College in Swarthmore, Pennsylvania, USA. Her work has appeared in *American Psychologist, Psychology of Women Quarterly, Feminism & Psychology, Theory & Psychology*, and *Contributions to Indian Sociology*. She served as a Fulbright Scholar in Sri Lanka in 1988 and has engaged in research, teaching, and humanitarian work there since then. She is coauthor of *Making a Difference: Psychology and the Construction of Gender* (Yale University, 1990); *Gender and Culture in Psychology: Theories and Practices* (Cambridge, 2012); and *Doing Interview-Based Qualitative Research* (Cambridge, 2015). She is coeditor of the international journal *Feminism & Psychology*, as well as a Distinguished Reviewer for *Psychology of Women Quarterly* and a member of the editorial boards of *Qualitative Psychology* and *Qualitative Inquiry in Psychology*.

Patricia H. Miller, PhD is Professor of Psychology at San Francisco State University, USA. Her work on cognitive development and gender has appeared in developmental and feminist journals. She is author, coauthor, or coeditor of several books, including *Theories of Developmental Psychology, Cognitive Development*, and *Toward a Feminist Developmental Psychology*. She has served on several journal editorial boards and was an Associate Editor of *Child Development*. A Fellow of both the American Psychological Association and the Association for Psychological Science, she is a former president of Division 7 (Developmental) of APA. Her administrative positions have included Director of Women's Studies (University of Georgia), Head of Psychology (University of Georgia), and Associate Dean for Academic Affairs (University of Florida).

Felicia Pratto, PhD is Professor of Psychological Sciences at the University of Connecticut, USA. Her research concerns intergroup relations and power dynamics, touching on multilevel substate and international relations, structural balance theory, norm theory, prospect theory, stereotyping, generalized prejudice, and dehumanization. She employs methods including international surveys, social cognition experiments, and game experiments. Her work has appeared in *Political Psychology, Psychological Sciences, Journal of Personality and Social Psychology, Social Cognition*, and elsewhere. She is the coauthor of *Social Dominance Theory* and *Power Basis Theory*. She serves as Treasurer of the International Society for Political Psychology and on several editorial boards, and she is a fellow of American Psychological Association, Society for the Psychological Study of Social Issues, American Psychological Society, and the Society for Experimental Social Psychology.

Ellin K. Scholnick, PhD is Professor Emerita in Psychology and chair of the President's Commission on Women at the University of Maryland, USA. She has published chapters and articles on cognitive and linguistic development and served as book editor and president of the Jean Piaget Society. Additionally she has written chapters and coedited *Toward a Feminist Developmental Psychology* with Patricia Miller on feminist approaches to conceptualizing developmental psychology.

Amanda K. Sesko, PhD is Associate Professor of Psychology at the University of Alaska Southeast in Juneau, Alaska, USA. Her research focuses on stereotyping, prejudice, and social judgment with an emphasis on intersections of social categories. In her primary line of research she investigates the effects of prototypical standards of gender and race on social perceptions and judgments of individuals. Specifically, she is interested in understanding the processes and outcomes of invisibility as a unique form of discrimination that may be experienced by groups that do not fit gender and race prototypes—for example, Black women. Her work has appeared in academic journal such as the *Journal of Experimental Social Psychology*, the *Journal of Personality and Social Psychology*, and *Group Processes & Intergroup Relations*.

Stephanie A. Shields, PhD is Professor of Psychology and Women's Studies, Penn State University, USA. Her research is at the intersection of emotion, gender, and feminist psychology. In emotion she focuses on how emotion representation (e.g., emotion language) is used to assert or challenge status and power. *Speaking From the Heart: Gender and the Social Meaning of Emotion* (Cambridge, 2002) received the Association for Women in Psychology's Distinguished Publication Award, as did her special issue of *Sex Roles* on intersectionality of social identities (2008). She also writes on the history of the psychology of women and gender. Her experiential learning tool, WAGES (http://wages.la.psu.edu/), illustrates cumulative effects of unconscious bias in the academic workplace. She is a recipient of the Society for the Psychology of Women's Carolyn W. Sherif Award.

Leah R. Warner, PhD is Associate Professor of Psychology at Ramapo College of New Jersey, USA. Her work integrates feminist, critical race, and queer theories with social psychological research on emotion perception. Her work on applying intersectionality theory to psychology has appeared in journals such as *Sex Roles* and *Psychology of Women Quarterly*, and in edited volumes, such as *APA Handbook of the Psychology of Women*. She is on the editorial boards for *Sex Roles* and *Psychology of Women Quarterly*.

INDEX

Page numbers followed by *f* or *t* indicate figures or tables, respectively.

Printed in the USA/Agawam, MA
January 20, 2020

748512.017